Experience and Spirit

PETER LANG
New York • Washington, D.C./Baltimore • Bern
Frankfurt am Main • Berlin • Brussels • Vienna • Oxford

Dale M. Schlitt

Experience and Spirit

A Post-Hegelian Philosophical Theology

PETER LANG

New York • Washington, D.C./Baltimore • Bern
Frankfurt am Main • Berlin • Brussels • Vienna • Oxford

Library of Congress Cataloging-in-Publication Data

Schlitt, Dale M.
Experience and spirit: a post-Hegelian philosophical theology / Dale M. Schlitt.
p. cm.
Includes bibliographical references and index.
1. Hegel, Georg Wilhelm Friedrich, 1770–1831—Religion. 2. Philosophical theology.
3. Religion—Philosophy. I. Title.
B2949.R3S276 210.92—dc22 2006101479
ISBN 978-0-8204-9719-8

Bibliographic information published by **Die Deutsche Bibliothek**.
Die Deutsche Bibliothek lists this publication in the "Deutsche
Nationalbibliografie"; detailed bibliographic data is available
on the Internet at http://dnb.ddb.de/.

Author photo © D. Brunet, 2007

Cover design by Joni Holst

The paper in this book meets the guidelines for permanence and durability
of the Committee on Production Guidelines for Book Longevity
of the Council of Library Resources.

Printed in Germany

To the memory of my father and mother,
Martin and Adele, models of generosity

CONTENTS

ACKNOWLEDGMENTS

Chapter One is a revised and refocused version of my text, "Hegel, Georg Wilhelm Friedrich (1770–1831)," previously published in *Dictionary of Fundamental Theology*, ed. René Latourelle (New York: Crossroads, 1994) 407–414. Chapters Two and Three include materials from the following publications of mine: "Trinity and Spirit," *American Catholic Philosophical Quarterly* 64 (1990) 457–489; "Hegel's Reconceptualization of Trinity. Further Reflections," in *Sein—Erkennen—Handeln. Interkulturelle, ontologische und ethische Perspektiven. Festschrift für Heinrich Beck zum 65. Geburtstag*, ed. Erwin Schadel and Uwe Voigt (Frankfurt am Main: Peter Lang, Europäischer Verlag der Wissenschaften, 1994) 559–565; "A Post-Hegelian Christian Philosophical Theology," in Donald A. Crosby and W. Creighton Peden, eds., *American Liberal Religious Thought*, vol. 3: *Religious Experience and Ecological Responsibility*, ed. Donald A. Crosby and Charley D. Hardwick (New York: Peter Lang, 1996) 505–526. Chapters Four and Five draw in part upon my article, "John E. Smith on Experience," *Philosophy and Theology* 2 (1987) 105–123 and Chapter One of my volume, *Theology and the Experience of God* (New York: Peter Lang, 2001) 23–70. Chapters Six and Seven include excerpts from Chapters One, Five and Six of *Theology and the Experience of God*. The Appendix is an excerpt from my *Hegel's Trinitarian Claim. A Critical Reflection* (Leiden: E. J. Brill, 1984) 252–265. The materials incorporated here are reprinted with the kind permission of the publishers. All rights reserved.

I am particularly grateful to Bro. Réjean Gadouas, O.M.I., for his kind hospitality at the Oblate summer cottage outside Maniwaki, Québec, Canada, while I worked on the last chapters of this study, and to the St. Henry's Oblate Residence Community in Belleville, Illinois, USA, for encouragement and support during my stays in Belleville.

INTRODUCTION

During the 19th and 20th centuries, various philosophers worked hard to give expression to an internally coherent notion of God adequate to the reality to which they wished to refer. These efforts, continuing now in the 21st century, are rooted in the very nature of philosophy as a critical and constructive reflection open to, and on, the whole of reality. Western philosophers in particular have often carried out their reflections in relation to Christianity as an admittedly historically conditioned religion arising in part at least out of the fact that Jesus of Nazareth called God "Abba" and that he proclaimed the Kingdom of God to be at hand. Philosophers, often reflecting on various more specific Christian traditions, have taken into consideration in a special way at least four historical concerns and challenges. These are: first, the Enlightenment disdain for "positive" or revealed religion; second, a relativizing attitude engendered earlier by historical studies and more recently by the increasing awareness of religious pluralism; third, the overwhelming appearance of evil in the twentieth century; and, fourth, the renewed attraction of spirituality.

Many philosophers have responded to these and other concerns and challenges by trying to formulate a more adequate and internally coherent notion of God as well as by proposing a more satisfying understanding of the relationship between God and world. These efforts, but especially those in which philosophers are open to a more explicitly metaphysical approach, can with some justification and to some extent at least be identified as falling into one or another of three main philosophical streams, namely, ways of thinking along more Thomistic, more Whiteheadian or more Hegelian lines. With the present volume, I propose to take part in this ongoing effort at responding to these and other challenges by making a fundamental but not exclusive philosophical option for the Hegelian stream, given its particular significance for the philosophy of religion and philosophical theology. From the beginning I would note that I will do this by working toward the critical reconstruction of Hegel's notion of spirit. This critical reconstruction will involve identifying, and then elaborating further on, "experience" as a basic conceptuality with which to express certain Hegelian insights in a critically transformed and more contemporary fashion.

Indeed, today we need to work toward a renewed philosophical theology that will help us come to grips with the perduring importance of what is often referred to as revealed or positive religion, with religious pluralism and with the massive reality of evil, and that will allow us to speak to the resurgent interest in spirituality. So far the Thomistic stream has, with its theory of analogy, continued to remind us of the humility required of any effort to speak appropriately of an infinite God. It has as well, in calling upon Aquinas's complex theory of grace, urged a certain respect for, and need to maintain the relative integrity of, finitude while affirming the transcendent, active presence of God. The Whiteheadian stream has provided increased access to the contemporary scientific world by means of a complex but fruitful ontological generalization from finite and temporal human experience to a pan-experiential cosmology. However, I am convinced that it is Hegel who, despite serious hesitations on the part of many thinkers coming after him, has provided us with the basic, and indeed very important, understanding of a "true infinite" inclusive of and not merely over against finite reality. Furthermore, Hegel is so omnipresent in his direct or indirect influence on contemporary philosophy and theology that he almost inevitably comes to serve either as a positive or negative touchstone and point of reference for current reflection in the various areas of philosophical theology and even of philosophy in general.

In the present study I would like, then, to make a contribution to the renewal of philosophical theology by proposing a critical reappropriation of Hegel's notion of the "true infinite," while likewise maintaining an openness to the many insights found throughout Hegel's writings and lectures. Such a project cannot of course ultimately be carried out by any one thinker alone. We might simply note, for instance, that it would no longer seem possible for one person to come to an adequate grasp of Hegel's thought in general, or even more specifically his philosophy of religion, considered in conjunction with the relevant secondary literature interpreting that thought and with further developments in philosophy since his time. Furthermore, Hegel's own example of working, though perhaps in his case a bit too self-confidently, with previous historical and then for him contemporary alternative positions, serves to remind us that such a proposal must necessarily include discussion with, openness to and acceptance of the richness of thought found in other, and here I would again say especially Thomistic and Whiteheadian, philosophical schools and approaches. The present proposal, namely, to participate in the overall renewal of philosophical theology especially by reworking Hegel's notion of the true infinite, is to be seen as a thinking with, but also going beyond, Hegel in dialogue at least in a general way with that Thomistic and Whiteheadian thought.

Such a critical appropriation of Hegel's "true infinite" through interfecundating dialogue is philosophical theology because it is concerned, from a reasoned perspective, with God and the relationship between God and the world. It is, furthermore, reflection on contemporary reality with an explicit commitment to, and a willingness to call upon, the resources of a series of specific religious traditions and, in the present case, especially Christian religious traditions. Again, it is philosophical theology in that it intends to be responsible to the public canons of consciousness and thought. Such a philosophical theology will be contemporary especially in that it can only be carried out in at least implicit dialogue with other world religions, with the acknowledgment of the undeniable presence of massive evil and with an openness to present-day spiritual interests. These varying characteristics and concerns are given a certain unity in that they all form aspects of the concrete situation in and out of which philosophers in such a project must work. At the end of this study, there will surely remain the challenge to continue participating in the ongoing renewal of philosophical theology. However, with this vlume we will have taken a first step, hopefully a serious and solid first step, in response to that challenge by working out a basic, more adequate contemporary understanding of Hegel's "true infinite" inclusive of finitude. Hegel himself had, in a post-Kantian mode, tried to give full expression to the "true infinite" as a momentary totality in the movement of pure, conceptual or logical thought. On the level of religious representation and symbolism he had tried to give the notions of God, in its specifically Christian formulation as Trinity, and of Kingdom of God a philosophically interpreted presentation. Then, finally, on the level of philosophy he had worked to give these religious representations of the "true infinite" their true and adequate form as the very self-development of philosophical thought. But all these attempts to give such expression to the "true infinite" in, and as a movement of, conceptual or reflexive thought were ultimately, in my opinion, unsuccessful. Furthermore, I think Hegel did not give sufficient attention to what, especially since Freud and Nietzsche, has come to be called the "unconscious irrational" or, in a more polite and positive vein, in an Augustinian or more especially Rahnerian formulation, the "pre-reflexive." Here I am proposing that working with a wider, clarified and inclusive philosophical notion of "experience" will allow us to be more successful in giving expression to what Hegel considered the "true infinite." Rethinking the notions, for example, of God, Trinity and Kingdom of God in terms of "experience" amounts to continuing, though in a more modest fashion, Hegel's own efforts in this regard.

My intention, then, is to learn especially but not exclusively from Hegel while going beyond him in proposing a renewed philosophical theology in which we recuperate his notion of the true infinite now as a more flexibly and openly structured infinite inclusive of finitude and in which we continue to present God, that true infinite, as a movement of inclusive divine subjectivity.

This proposal will be developed in three overall steps, corresponding to the three major parts of the present study. In the first part, we will review various aspects of Hegel's philosophy of religion. In Chapter One we will survey Hegel's work in the area of the philosophy of religion. In Chapter Two we will spell out further his idea of spirit as movement of conceptual thought and the linkage he makes between that understanding of spirit and the notion of God as Trinity. And in Chapter Three we will further sketch out several of Hegel's basic moves and summarize a number of what we consider strengths and weaknesses of Hegel's philosophy of religion before setting out a preliminary statement of our own revised understanding of spirit.

In the second part of the study we will work toward the fuller elaboration of a notion of experience more adequate to the reality referred to by that word, whether it be used as a noun or as a verb. Chapter Four will present certain ideas of selected, important thinkers on the notion of experience. Chapter Five will provide us with a modest grammar of experience by working out the declension, so to speak, of various types, phases and forms of experience. Chapter Six will propose a further phenomenological look at experience that will then permit us to recognize the overall structure and movement constituting a moment of experience, and especially human experience.

In the third part of this study we will work with the newly established notion of experience to develop a philosophical theology in which we will envision God as an inclusive movement of enriching experience and spirit. Chapter Seven will contain phenomenological and further philosophical reflections on the Christian experience of God. Chapter Eight will contribute to our understanding of the bases upon which we can legitimately and appropriately speak of God. Chapter Nine will contain a series of reflections on evil, freedom and mystery that will open the way to a further understanding of fundamental philosophical ethics.

These three overall parts of the present study constitute three major steps in our argument toward a renewed post-Hegelian philosophical theology, with the first step then being a presentation on Hegel, the second the elaboration of a fuller notion of experience, and the third a constructive reflection on a number of questions in philosophical theology in light of this fuller understanding of experience. In the Conclusion, we will return to several themes treated throughout the study and propose that what our philosophical theology in fact amounts to is a philosophy of generosity, human and divine.

PART I

Thought and Spirit

HEGEL'S PHILOSOPHICAL THEOLOGY

In this first chapter we will take a more general look at what Hegel produced when he worked out his philosophy of religion before we go on to present, in Chapter Two, what I will call his problematic understanding of spirit and, in Chapter Three, my proposal to reformulate his project. To appreciate better what Hegel proposed and his unique position in the history of the philosophy of religion, we will, in the present chapter, first of all briefly review his publications in the area of religion, then present an overview of his philosophy of religion and, finally, specify in what sense we can justifiably consider it a philosophical theology.

Works on Religion

In early adulthood Hegel briefly studied theology before turning to philosophy. Then, throughout his philosophical career he maintained a deep and abiding interest in religion in general, in the various religions of the world in particular, and especially in Christianity.

His own writings and lectures bear witness to the earnest and effort with which he approached the philosophy of religion. At the beginning of the twentieth century, Hermann Nohl gathered Hegel's earlier philosophical reflections on religion and on Christianity into a volume entitled *Early Theological Writings*.[1] The *Phenomenology of Spirit*,[2] published by Hegel in 1807, is generally considered as having marked the beginning of his more "mature" or systematic philosophical reflection. In this fascinating but complex volume, Hegel treated religion as the penultimate step in the phenomenological movement from consciousness to self-consciousness on to what he called "absolute knowledge." He published his three-part *Science of Logic* [3] during the years from 1812 to 1816. He described his proposed movement of logical or pure thought in religious terms when he referred to it as "the presentation of God as God is in God's eternal essence before the creation of nature and a finite spirit."[4] Hegel published three successively augmented editions, in 1817, 1827 and 1830, of his summary of his philosophical system, *The Encyclopedia of the Philosophical Sciences in Outline*.[5] Here again, in these three editions, he placed religion as penultimate sphere in the movement or self-development of philosophical thought. In 1821, at least partially in response to Friedrich Schleiermacher's approach to religion in the first volume of *The Christian Faith*,[6] he gave the first of his four series of Berlin lectures on the philosophy of religion. Hegel himself never published these 1821, 1824, 1827, and 1831 religion lectures, which were in effect varied elaborations of the overall *Encyclopedia* outline of the philosophy of religion. However, their quick publication, along with a text of his on the proofs for the existence of God in a first edition[7] shortly after his death and then again in a much revised edition[8] several years later, gave rise to considerable controversy concerning just how seriously he took religion and, especially, Christianity. In the latter part of the twentieth century, the publication, based on work by Walter Jaeschke with Ricardo Ferrara and Peter C. Hodgson, of a critical edition of his 1821 philosophy of religion manuscript and of various auditors' transcripts of the later philosophy of religion lectures made these lectures truly available for the first time.[9] Their publication rounds out a century of renewed, indeed continually growing, interest in Hegel's philosophy and especially in his thought on religion in general and Christianity in particular.

Philosophy of Religion

In Hegel's "mature" view, religion was the elevation of human consciousness or finite spirit to God or to the infinite. Hegel proposed that this elevation took place in and as a movement of reflexive, conceptual thought. In fact, he insisted that spirit as such, including finite spirit, was a movement of thought. He literally defined both divine and human in terms of thought. And since religion was that which was most characteristic of the human being both as an individual and in community, it was also a movement of thought. Hegel had several reasons for proposing to develop his overall system, understood as the inclusive movement of spirit, and his constructive philosophical reading of religion in terms of a dynamic movement of unifying or encompassing thought.[10] One of these reasons, which is of particular present interest and importance, was his intention to philosophize in the public realm. He was convinced that reflexive thought was publically available and open to critical examination. Therefore he chose to work with reflexive thought rather than, for example, with something like intuition or feeling.

Hegel not only described religion as the elevation of finite religious consciousness to God or the infinite, but also consistently maintained that this elevation presupposed a more inclusive movement of spirit. From 1824 on, and especially in 1827, he more clearly and more systematically organized his lectures to reflect the structure of this inclusive movement. He insisted that the elevation of finite to infinite was really the continuation, so to speak, of a logically prior movement from an initial, unitary infinite to differentiation or finitude. With such an affirmation Hegel was able to develop his philosophy of religion as a dynamic, and of course dialectical, self-positing movement of spirit. Religion or, more specifically, the philosophy of religion was for Hegel the dialectical movement of spirit othering itself, through a first moment of negation, into finitude and, by means of a second moment of negation, namely, a negation of this finitude, returning in an enriched way to itself. Put more concretely, and in terms made explicit in the lectures of 1827, the philosophy of religion was the development of God as absolute spirit. True to his overall view of mediating dialectical development, Hegel presented the philosophy of religion as a movement from the concept of God to the various particular or determinate religions other than Christianity. He concluded his philosophy of religion with the presentation of the consummate religion as the negation of the limitation and the particularity of these finite or determinate religions. He identified this consummate religion, in its historical realization, with Christianity, and especially with his own Lutheran Christian tradition.

Hegel worked out his philosophy of religion, as a movement of thought, in the form of this internally self-developing movement of spirit. Since he identified this movement with the development of God as divine subject, he interpreted religion as a movement of divine subjectivity. It was a movement from God as substance to God as internally differentiated, and therefore true, divine subject or person. It was, indeed, a movement of inclusive divine subjectivity since God came to be seen as inclusive of finitude or the world. Thus religion was, for Hegel, a movement of reconciliation between human and divine, with this reconciliation occurring in the form of a self-positing inclusive divine subjectivity.

Throughout the Berlin lectures Hegel consistently developed his philosophy of religion in three parts. He called Part One "The Concept of Religion" and identified it as the realm of potentiality.[11] He used the logical term "universality" to describe this first moment in the philosophy of religion.[12] This first moment was as yet a more formally structured one. It remained on the level of the implicit. It was, he said, the divine idea as yet "in itself" (*an sich*). Though it took him some years to work out what would from a systematic perspective be an adequate structure for this first part of the philosophy of religion, he always began its presentation by insisting that religion was neither a question of the human nor of the divine alone, but of the two together. He always started the presentation of the concept of religion with the affirmation of an original unity, namely, with religion as the relationship between human and divine. He would then go on to posit, as arising immediately out of this initial unity, the distinction between God and finite religious consciousness. He spoke of this second step, namely, the arising of distinction, in terms of otherness. He came to see it as a moment of what he called theoretical or, in this case, distinguishing reason. It is this arising of distinction or difference that, more properly speaking, constitutes the moment of religion since it is here with this second step that one can appropriately begin to speak of an elevation from finite to infinite. Hegel would, in a third step, affirm the negation of this distinction by means of the movement of what he called practical or, in this case, integrating reason. Especially in the later lectures this last step came more clearly to be seen as the moment of community and cultus or worship. Practical or integrating reason was, for Hegel, the movement of thought in the form of will. He insisted that these three, more formally developed steps or moments in the concept of religion were instantiated, in various ways, in each of the finite religions of the world. They were fully realized in the consummate religion.

Hegel named Part Two of his philosophy of religion "Determinate Religion."[13] He described it as the moment of particularity and in effect identified it as the realm of actuality. It was, he would say, the appearance of the concept of religion or the divine idea "for itself" (*für sich*) or as explicitly realized in finite otherness. "Determinate Religion" consisted in a series of dialectically juxtaposed, and typologically elaborated, presentations of the various religions of the world except for Christianity. Hegel's successive, and in certain ways significantly varying, elaborations of this Part Two witness to the fact that he continued to study these religions very seriously. Throughout the years of his Berlin lectures he regularly incorporated considerable amounts of new material into his presentations of these religions. Some would say that, with regard to these religions, he was the best informed European of his day.

From one lecture series to the next, Hegel made significant changes in the internal organization and the order of presentation of some of the finite or determinate religions. Nevertheless, he always began this Part Two with what might today be called "primal religions," notably, those of Africa and North America. In these for Hegel phenomenologically earlier religions God was present more in the form of substance. Though Hegel placed these religions at an earlier stage in the phenomenological progression of determinate religions, he would not simply reject or abandon their views of God. He insisted that, while God was in these religions as yet understood and worshiped in some form of internally undifferentiated substance, such conceptions of God were still to be valued as more immediate instantiations of God. God as substance was subject, person and spirit—but still only implicitly so. Hegel continued his presentation of the various finite religions, which he ranged, generally speaking, according to their increasingly more explicitly developed and complex conceptions of God and of the relationship between human and divine. He grouped the finite religions geographically, treating of the religions of China, of India, of the Middle East, of Greece and of Rome. It seems he also rather boldly proposed that his phenomenological ranking and geographical grouping reflected the overall historical development of the various religions.[14]

Hegel's dialectical dynamic of the realization of spirit in and through a series of finite forms of religion is extremely complex, yet fascinating. He tried at one and the same time to present this second moment, "Determinate Religion," both as one in which the concept of God gained in complexity and as one in which there occurred, finally, a total alienation. He saw this total alienation realized in Roman religion, which he always placed last within the series of determinate religions. In its degradation and debauchery, Roman religion marked the low point, thus, the turning point in the phenomenology and in the history of religion. Here the previously more complexly developed notions of God seemed to collapse in a religion of ever greater negativity. For

Hegel, Christianity arose dialectically as the negation of that negativity.

Hegel entitled Part Three of his philosophy of religion lectures "The Consummate Religion."[15] In a way generally consistent throughout the four lecture series, he gave to Christianity and its basic doctrines a constructive philosophical interpretation in line with his overall understanding of spirit as dialectical movement of self-positing thought. As he had done with his presentations of the various determinate religions, again here he constructed a sort of typological presentation of Christianity. He called his philosophical reading of Christianity the consummate religion because it consummated, or fully realized, the structure of what he had earlier, in Part One, established as the more formal structure and movement of religion. The consummate religion was able to serve as this fulfilment of the structure of the concept of religion because it incorporated the reality which that concept had attained in and through the various finite religions. He presented this third moment, the consummate religion, as the moment of individuality and of freedom as he understood it. What was initially present to thought or religious consciousness "in itself" (*an sich*) and what was then realized "for itself" (*für sich*) in the otherness of the various finite religions came, in the consummate religion, to be integrated in a moment Hegel referred to as the appearance of the divine idea "in and for itself" (*an und für sich*). Thus the consummate religion is the religion of spirit. It is the religion in which God is known explicitly as spirit and in which God exists as spirit for finite spirit. In the consummate religion God is a movement of inclusive divine subjectivity.

From 1824 on Hegel more clearly develops his presentation of the consummate religion in three parts. The first element or sphere of the consummate religion is the one in which he returns to the originary unity of God and religious consciousness. But now this unity has become a more developed and internally differentiated sphere. In the 1831 lectures he will speak of it as the kingdom of the Father. In this sphere the concept of God, the divine idea, is present to thought in the form of Trinity, namely, of what would today be called "immanent" Trinity. According to Hegel, in Christianity God is the doubled dialectical movement of divine self-othering and of return spoken of figuratively as Father, Son and Holy Spirit. This is a movement of the momentary arising of differentiation as a dialectical moment of negation. The Son, or second moment, is not the immediacy of the first moment. Rather, this second moment is one of distinction or difference that immediately disappears. The Holy Spirit is this disappearance of difference, the overcoming of otherness. Hegel characterizes this overall movement of spirit, namely, one of differentiation and return, as a movement of life and love.

In the first sphere of the consummate religion, otherness is only apparent or implicit. It becomes real and explicit and phenomenologically available in and as the second sphere. The second sphere is that of God or the divine idea positing itself as a finite world of nature and finite spirit. This second sphere is, at least from the 1824 lectures on, the doubled sphere of differentiation and immediate reconciliation. In 1831 Hegel calls it the kingdom of the Son. In his various lecture presentations he carries out a long and impressive analysis of the Christian notions of creation, original innocence and original sin. He gives them a philosophical and existential reading as he works out a dialectical interpretation of the relationship between good and evil. He pursues his analysis of the alienation, which arises with the distinction between God and finite spirit, on to the point where he can say that alienation constitutes the very core of what it means to be human. The human person is trapped in a sort of self-enslavement. And yet, to be human is to be a thinking being and, consequently, to be spirit. The human person is not only internal self-alienation but, as thinking being, also and equally in principle the very overcoming of such alienation.

Hegel sets up the human person as finite spirit and, essentially, as thinking being. By so casting his understanding of what it means to be human in terms of internal alienation and the possibility of overcoming that alienation, he can establish what might be called the transcendental context in which revelation and incarnation can and do occur. He often speaks of divine self-revelation and, with the incarnation, he affirms a total divine self-revelation in the form of a single human being, the Christ. He in various ways insists that this divine self-revelation must occur in one individual if it is to be available to humankind as a whole. God reveals God self in a form of self-othering to the uttermost depths of finitude, to the death of Christ on the cross. The resurrection is the transition to a spiritual presence to and in the believing community.

The third sphere of the consummate religion is that of community or cultus. In the second sphere Hegel had, at least from 1824 on, presented the doubled moment of differentiation and immediate reconciliation in one divine-human self as the fulfilment of the second moment of the concept of religion, namely, that of theoretical knowledge. Now he presents the third sphere as the fulfilment of the movement of practical knowing. This is the moment of inclusive individuality. It is the moment in which immediate reconciliation is made available to, and realized in, the community of finite spirits. Here, by means of a philosophical reading of faith, doctrine, sacrament and sacrifice, Hegel presents the progressive realization, in the members of the spiritual community, of that reconciliation between human and divine which had already been achieved in Christ. He speaks freely of the Holy Spirit as divine presence within the members of the spiritual community. Throughout the various lectures he calls this sphere the kingdom of the Spirit. In this kingdom, namely, in and through finite spirit, God has become spirit for spirit. This consciousness of being at one with God, what Hegel calls the peace of God, is itself to be expressed in ethical living. Yet for Hegel the reconciliation between human and divine, a reconciliation really achieved here in this third sphere, remains burdened with religious representational form. That is to say, the overcoming of alienation occurs as yet in the form of an otherness still identified as God the Holy Spirit. For Hegel the reconciliation and peace achieved in the spiritual community, and in ethical living, find their final and appropriate expression in the renewed immediacy of pure philosophical thought. In such thought mediation is self-mediation without remainder of externally presented otherness.

Though Hegel insisted that it was for philosophy to make explicit the internal coherence of religious thought, he equally, and especially from the 1824 lectures on, argued that religion, as the penultimate form of absolute spirit, was the perduring vehicle of truth and the valid representation of reconciliation for the general population.[16] He consistently presented religion, and especially the Christian religion, as a dynamic phenomenological realization of the movement of spirit. Religion was the sphere or level on which spirit manifested itself as a dialectical movement of differentiation and enriched return. It was here in this sphere of religion that Hegel reformulated the more general religious notion of God into a movement of inclusive divine subjectivity, a movement of absolute spirit. To put it somewhat more crudely, Hegel argued that God was absolute spirit because God included the world.

To put it more philosophically, the true infinite was the infinite inclusive of the finite, and not merely a pseudo-infinite set over against the finite. By working with this reformulation of the notion of God, he was able to create a unique philosophy of religion in the form of a movement of self-positing inclusive divine subjectivity. He would then affirm that this movement was one of divine and human freedom. It was a movement of human freedom because the human person was freed from both external alienation and self-enslaving internal alienation. It was a movement of divine freedom because it was a movement of divine self-determination. God was spirit, that is, God was at home with God self in the other.

Hegel's Philosophical Theology

It would not be wrong to say that Hegel's whole philosophy is an effort to reformulate the notion of God in terms of a movement of absolute or inclusive divine subjectivity. He begins his encyclopedic presentation of his philosophy with a reference to God and ends the same presentation by citing Aristotle's famous definition of God as self-thinking thought, thus providing an interpretation of his whole system.[17] Furthermore, he speaks of logic, the first part of his mature philosophical system, as "metaphysical theology" (*die metaphysische Theologie*).[18]

Important as these interpretations by Hegel of his own thought are, it is even more important to note exactly what his philosophy, and in particular his philosophy of religion, is as such and what he did in developing that philosophy. In Part Two above in this chapter, we noted repeatedly that Hegel develops his philosophy of religion, and indeed his philosophy as a whole when it is considered from the perspective of his encyclopedic system, as a movement of inclusive or absolute subjectivity that he identifies with God. In a wide sense, then, Hegel's philosophy as a whole is a philosophical theology, for it is a movement of absolute or inclusive subjectivity developing from logic through nature to spirit. And in a more particular sense his philosophy of religion takes the form of an explicitly formulated philosophical theology. His is no extrinsic study of or reflection on religion as something "out there." In his philosophy of religion he is not satisfied merely to carry out a so-called scientific or analytic reflection on the phenomenal appearance of religions or on religious experiences. Rather, he develops his philosophy of religion as a movement of inclusive divine subjectivity. Hegel's philosophy of religion is, then, in the very strictest sense of the words, a fundamental philosophical theology. It takes the form of a philosophy of God and is a reasoned presentation of the development of God.[19]

In order further to develop our understanding of Hegel's philosophy of religion as a fundamental philosophical theology, we would do well to refer to the three classic functions or tasks that Christian fundamental theology in general has at various times fulfilled. Reference to these three functions will provide us with a sort of grid helping us, by applying them in an analogous way to what Hegel has done, better to understand his philosophical interpretation of religion as an inclusive philosophical theology.

These three functions are: first, the apologetic task of laying out the Christian tradition's basic justification and inner coherence; second, the foundational task of establishing the basis on and out of which Christian theology goes about its further analytic, systematic, and constructive tasks; and, third, the task of shedding light on basic themes in Christianity from the perspective chosen in working out the previous apologetic and foundational tasks.[20] We will now consider Hegel's philosophy of religion, or as we have come to call it, his inclusive philosophical theology,[21] from the point of view of each of these functions or tasks.

We could in fact say that Hegel's entire systematic philosophical project was apologetic in the sense that he constantly strove to set out the basic justification and inner coherence of his philosophy of absolute spirit. He seemingly entered into critical dialogue with any and every religious or philosophical position he came across. Of particular present interest are the critical attitudes he took toward the Christian theologians of his day, toward Christian theology itself, and toward religion in general or specific religions in particular.

He was strongly critical of Christian theologians, whom he accused of having abandoned their fundamental task of examining the inner rational content and coherence of the major Christian dogmas. He argued that they took refuge either in reflections or merely subjective feelings or, again, in less serious forms of historical studies. He felt that philosophy had to take up the tasks fundamental and systematic theology had left undone.

Hegel insisted that religion, including the Christian religion in its reflected form as Christian theology, does indeed make available the truth of reconciliation to humankind in general. But he always conditioned this positive valuation of religion with a further qualification. He argued that it is philosophy's task ever to identify the inner logical and rational coherence of religious beliefs. He found that even Christian theological reflection often remained too closely tied to "childish" or insufficiently critiqued, and therefore seemingly disparate, images. Still, even when he accorded to philosophy this all-important task of discerning the inner logical structure of religious reconciliation, he continued to maintain that religion as such, and Christianity with its theological reflection in particular, have a perduring value and importance. In their own way, religion and Christian theology make an ongoing contribution not simply replaceable by philosophical thought. From different perspectives, Hegel gave a certain continuing dialectical priority at one moment to religion and at another to philosophy. Though from the perspective of his systematic and speculative presentation he placed religion in a penultimate position just before the final moment of spirit as movement of philosophical thought, he did not simply subordinate religion to philosophy. Religion remained the necessary historical embodiment of the truth expressed in philosophy. However, even when these qualifications concerning the respective roles of religion and philosophy are kept in mind, it would seem that Hegel gives a mediating and interpretational function to philosophy vis-à-vis religion that many religious thinkers find unacceptable.

An interesting critical stance of Hegel's that many religious thinkers find considerably more attractive is his de facto criterion for the evaluation of any religion or religious world view. For Hegel this criterion is the question of whether or not, and to what extent, a particular religious tradition gives expression to freedom. For him it was then a question of whether a religion adequately represents divine freedom and, consequently, frees both the individual human person and the community from slavery to dehumanizing and one-sidedly objectifying tendencies. The theme of freedom constitutes the *leitmotiv* running through his philosophy of religion that we now describe as an inclusive philosophical theology. The way in which Hegel works with this theme of freedom still merits considerable further study.[22] It is a theme that has also come back time and again in post-Hegelian religious reflection. Often various modern religious references to freedom as constitutive characteristic of true religion, and even some more specific twentieth-century formulations of this theme, can be traced directly back to Hegel.

Hegel's apologetic stance involved a constant concern for exposition in the public realm, for inner coherence and for the internal purification of religion. He in fact carried out this more apologetic task by concentrating on what could be called the foundational task. That is, he worked out a basic understanding of spirit as movement of inclusive subjectivity. He proposed a dialectical movement of thought that, in its most fundamental movement, was a positing of the other and an overcoming of the estrangement involved in the arising of such otherness. He identified this doubled movement of spirit with a creative reinterpretation of the various classic proofs for the existence of God. He saw in the ontological proof an expression of what he called the movement from concept to reality, namely, the self-differentiation of God as absolute spirit. He intriguingly reformulated the more cosmological and teleological proofs for the existence of God as the dialectical return of spirit, namely, as the elevation of finite spirit to the infinite. His fundamental understanding of the dynamic of spirit as differentiation and dialectical return, religiously and theologically expressed in terms of the various proofs for the existence of God, provided the paradigm on the basis of which he worked out his overall philosophical system. He carried out his further analytic, systematic and constructive reflections on the basis of this understanding of spirit. It will be of particular interest to philosophical theology, and especially to any effort to work out a post-Hegelian philosophical theology, to recall that for Hegel this movement of spirit found appropriate religious expression in the Christian doctrine of Trinity.

Hegel used his fundamental understanding of spirit as movement of inclusive thought to elucidate basic themes in the various religions he examined. His efforts bore particularly rich fruit in his constructive philosophical interpretations of Christianity. Long before the Second Vatican Council he had spoken forcefully of divine self-revelation. It could even be argued that he introduced the notion into modern western philosophical and theological discussion.[23] His dialectical reconceptualization of God, and of the relationship between God and the world, allowed him to propose a moment of negativity in God. This he identified as the second moment in the "immanent"

Trinity. When Hegel referred to this moment in terms of negation, he was in fact introducing the structure of crucifixion and death into the divine itself. Strikingly, with the affirmation of differentiation in God, namely, of an identity inclusive of difference, he was confirming the infinite value and importance of the realm of history, which is by definition the realm of difference and change.

A more detailed list of Hegel's philosophical insights that have made their way into Christian confessional theology and into the various attempts to establish a contemporary fundamental philosophical theology would prove quite long. Perhaps one way to allude to these would be simply to indicate that Hegel brought together many seemingly less internally related Christian religious doctrines and theological themes. He integrated, for example, the themes of Trinity, revelation, grace, the kingdom of God, salvation history as the history of God, alienation, sin, reconciliation, Christology, church and spiritual community, the Eucharist, presence of the Holy Spirit, and responsible ethical living all into one overall sequential movement of thought. He was able to interrelate these religious themes because he presented them as aspects of the dialectical development of God as movement of inclusive divine subjectivity and, finally, absolute spirit.

Hegel's impressive philosophy of religion, understood as an inclusive philosophical theology, continues to pose constant challenges. From an apologetic perspective, it challenges us to work creatively in the public realm and to be self-critical in whatever we do. From a foundational perspective, it challenges us to reflect on the most basic religious questions, including that of the structure of the experience of God as dynamic movement of spirit. Hegel will not allow the philosophical theologian to remain content with merely external forms of argumentation. Rather, he forces such a theologian to go to the heart of the matter, namely, to the question of the articulation of the dynamic inner relationship between finite and infinite, human and divine. From an elucidational perspective, he provides a great many insights into, and concrete observations on, Christian theological themes. In a sense his philosophy is a goldmine. However, there are two approaches to his philosophy which, it would seem, should be avoided. One approach is that of simply picking up a philosophical insight here or there in merely eclectic fashion. The result would surely be an eclectic philosophical theology. Another approach is that of taking over Hegel's system without further critical reflection on the problematic concerning its inner coherence. This second approach would result in too easily carrying over into a reformulated philosophical theology weaknesses internal to Hegel's own philosophy.

It is really not possible for the philosophical theologian to remain neutral before Hegel's philosophy of religion or, better, his inclusive philosophical theology and the challenges it poses. Either Hegel has basically succeeded in giving expression to the inner logical structure, in particular, of Christianity or he has not. If the former is the case, then the philosophical theologian working in relation to various Christian traditions has to follow Hegel quite closely. If Hegel has not succeeded, then it falls upon such a philosophical theologian to come up with a rigorously formulated and more satisfying alternative position. In the past many philosophical theologians and, indeed, more confessionally rooted Christian theologians, have profited from the impressive scope and richness of Hegel's insight. Many of them have, however, resisted his overall philosophical position, and this for various reasons. As we will see in more detail in later chapters, such reasons would include hesitations as to whether Hegel has in fact preserved divine freedom with regard to the necessity to create a finite world, whether he has adequately expressed either the radical character of evil or the perduring of otherness or, more fundamentally still, whether he has been able to argue convincingly his own philosophical position. But when confronted with Hegel's unique and most impressive philosophical theology, perhaps the most concrete challenge facing the fundamental philosophical theologian is to be able to acknowledge his or her immense debt to Hegel without, then, letting that debt become a burden.

NOTES

1. *Hegels theologische Jugendschriften*, ed. Hermann Nohl (Tübingen: Mohr, 1907)/*Early Theological Writings*, trans. T. M. Knox (Chicago: University of Chicago Press, 1948).

2. *Gesammelte Werke*, vol. 9: *Phänomenologie des Geistes*, ed. Wolfgang Bonsiepen and Reinhard Heede (Hamburg: Felix Meiner, 1980)/*Phenomenology of Spirit*, trans. A. V. Miller (New York: Oxford, 1977).

3. *Gesammelte Werke*, vol. 11: *Wissenschaft der Logik. Erster Band: Die objektive Logik (1812–1813)* (hereafter abbreviated GW 11 and cited by page and text line), vol. 12: *Wissenschaft der Logik. Zweiter Band: Die subjektive Logik (1816)*, vol. 21: *Wissenschaft der Logik. Erster Band: Die objektive Logik (1832)* (hereafter abbreviated GW 21 and cited by page and text line), ed. Friedrich Hogemann and Walter Jaeschke (Hamburg: Felix Meiner, 1978, 1981, 1985)/*Hegel's Science of Logic*, trans. A. V. Miller (New York: Humanities, 1969) (hereafter abbreviated GL).

4. "die Darstellung Gottes ist, wie er in seinem ewigen Wesen, vor der Erschaffung der Natur und eines endlichen Geistes ist," quoted from the first edition, GW 11: 21.16–21/GL 50 (trans. amended).

5. *Gesammelte Werke*, vol. 13: *Enzyklopädie der philosophischen Wissenschaften im Grundrisse*, first original edition 1817, ed. Wolfgang Bonsiepen and Klaus Grotsch, with collaboration from Hans-Christian Lucas and Udo Rameil (Hamburg: Felix Meiner, 2000); *Gesammelte Werke*, vol. 19: *Enzyklopädie der philosophischen Wissenschaften im Grundrisse*, second original edition 1827, ed. Wolfgang Bonsiepen and Hans-Christian Lucas (Hamburg: Felix Meiner, 1989); *Gesammelte Werke*, vol. 20: *Enzyklopädie der philosophischen Wissenschaften im Grundrisse*, third original edition 1830, ed. Wolfgang Bonsiepen and Hans-Christian Lucas (Hamburg: Felix Meiner, 1992)/*The Encyclopaedic Logic*, trans. of Part One of the 1830 edition by T. F. Geraets, W. A. Suchting and H. S. Harris; *Hegel's Philosophy of Nature*, 3 vol., trans. of Part Two of the 1830 edition by M. J. Petry (New York: Humanities, 1970); *Hegel's Philosophy of Mind*, trans. of Part Three of the 1830 edition by William Wallace (Oxford: Clarendon, 1975).

6. Friedrich D. E. Schleiermacher, *Der christliche Glaube nach den Grundsätzen der evangelischen Kirche im Zusammenhange dargestellt*, vol. 1 (Berlin: G. Reimer, 1821).

7. *Werke. Vollständige Ausgabe durch einen Verein von Freunden des Verewigten*, vol. 11–12: *Vorlesungen über die Philosophie der Religion. Nebst einer Schrift über die Beweise vom Daseyn Gottes*, ed. Philipp Marheineke (Berlin: Duncker und Humblot, 1832).

8. *Werke. Vollständige Ausgabe durch einen Verein von Freunden des Verewigten*, vol. 11–12: *Vorlesungen über die Philosophie der Religion. Nebst einer Schrift über die Beweise vom Daseyn Gottes*, ed. Philipp Marheineke [and Bruno Bauer] (Berlin: Duncker und Humblot, 1840, 2nd ed.).

9. The text of Hegel's 1821 manuscript can be found in *Gesammelte Werke*, vol. 17: *Vorlesungsmanuskripte I (1816–1831)*, ed. Walter Jaeschke (Hamburg: Felix Meiner, 1987). The four lectures are published in *Vorlesungen. Ausgewählte Nachschriften und Manuskripte*, vol. 3: *Vorlesungen über die Philosophie der Religion, Teil 1: Einleitung. Der Begriff der Religion*, vol. 4: *Vorlesungen über die Philosophie der Religion. Teil 2: Die bestimmte Religion. A: Text. B: Anhang*, vol. 5: *Vorlesungen über die Philosophie*

der Religion. Teil 3: Die vollendete Religion, ed. Walter Jaeschke (Hamburg: Felix Meiner, 1983, 1985, 1984)/*Lectures on the Philosophy of Religion*, vol. 1: *Introduction and The Concept of Religion*, vol. 2: *Determinate Religion*, vol. 3: *The Consummate Religion*, ed. Peter C. Hodgson, trans. R. F. Brown, P. C. Hodgson, and J. M. Stewart with the assistance of J. P. Fitzer (vol. 1) and H. S. Harris (Berkeley: University of California Press, 1984, 1987, 1985).

10. Concerning Hegel on religion and thought, see, for example, Dale M. Schlitt, *Divine Subjectivity. Understanding Hegel's Philosophy of Religion* (Scranton, PA: University of Scranton Press, [1990]) 34–40.

11. For references and a more detailed presentation of "The Concept of Religion," see *Divine Subjectivity* 31–66, 151–155, 166–168.

12. "We can more loosely paraphrase what Hegel means by these three terms [universality, particularity, individuality]. Universality is the concept as simple relationship to itself, unposited negation. Particularity is the concept as differentiation, that is, as relation to its other (universality) and equally as being inclusive of that other. It is posited or expressed negation of universality. Individuality is the concept as self-related determinateness. It is the negation of the previous negation. In the movement of logic or pure thought, the thinking of individuality is the establishment of further determination. It is a concretizing advance which is, for Hegel, equally an enriched return to the unity previously identified as universality." *Divine Subjectivity* 48–49, with further remarks on p. 63 n. 62.

13. For references and a more detailed presentation of "Determinate Religion," see *Divine Subjectivity* 67–98.

14. See the extended remarks in Walter Jaeschke, *Die Vernunft in der Religion. Studien zur Grundlegung der Religionsphilosophie Hegels* (Stuttgart-Bad Cannstatt: Frommann-Holzboog, 1986) 288–295/*Reason in Religion. The Foundations of Hegel's Philosophy of Religion*, trans. J. Michael Stewart and Peter C. Hodgson (Berkeley: University of California Press, 1990) 277–284.

15. For references and a more detailed presentation of "The Consummate Religion," see *Divine Subjectivity* 99–129 and *passim* through Chapters Five to Eight of that volume. More specifically concerning the 1827 lectures, see Dale M. Schlitt, *Hegel's Trinitarian Claim. A Critical Reflection* (Leiden: Brill, 1984) 202–227.

16. Stephen Rocker presents an excellent argument in favor of an interpretation of Hegel that stresses the perduring value of religion in Hegel's philosophy. See *Hegel's Rational Religion* (London: Associated University Presses, 1995).

17. *Enzyklopädie der philosophischen Wissenschaften im Grundrisse* (1830) §§ 1 and 577/ *The Encyclopaedia Logic* § 1 and *Hegel's Philosophy of Mind* § 577. Hegel adds to the second edition of the first part of his *Science of Logic*, "und das unbestrittenste Recht hätte *Gott*, daß mit ihm der Anfang gemacht werde" GW 21:65.12–13/"and *God* has the absolutely undisputed right that the beginning be made with him" GL 78.

18. *Vorlesungen über die Beweise vom Dasein Gottes*, Philosophische Bibliothek, vol. 64, ed. Georg Lasson (Hamburg: Meiner, 1973) 86 and also see 85/*Lectures on the Philosophy of Religion*, vol. 3, trans. E. B. Speirs and J. Burdon Sanderson (New York: Humanities, 1962) 235–236.

19. With regard to Hegel's transformation of philosophy of religion into philosophical theology, I have taken inspiration from Walter Jaeschke, who places Hegel's philosophy of religion, what Jaeschke calls a "speculative philosophy of religion" (*spekulative Religionsphilosophie*), within its historical and philosophical context when he presents

it in the Introduction to his study, *Die Vernunft in der Religion* 9–17/*Reason in Religion* 1–9. He provides an excellent overview of the historical movement from "natural theology," namely, a special form of metaphysics, to philosophy of religion as worked out by Kant and presupposing its notion of God, to Hegel's own philosophy of religion that provides its own concept of God, on to the post-Hegelian critiques of Hegel's philosophy of religion. See also Walter Jaeschke, "Philosophical Theology and Philosophy of Religion," in David Kolb, ed., *New Perspectives on Hegel's Philosophy of Religion* (Albany: State University of New York Press, 1992) 7–18, esp. 8. While referring to Jaeschke, Peter C. Hodgson himself identifies with this reading of Hegel's philosophy of religion as a philosophical theology. See his article, "Hegel: Theologian of Freedom," *The Owl of Minerva* 37/1 (2005-2006) 73. And see Peter C. Hodgson, *Hegel and Christian Theology. A Reading of the Lectures on the Philosophy of Religion* (Oxford: Oxford University Press, 2005) vi with Chapters One and Two.

20. For further remarks on these three functions, see Dale M. Schlitt, *Theology and the Experience of God* (New York: Peter Lang, 2001) 23–70.
21. "Philosophical theology" here no longer refers to a form of metaphysics that does not include explicit reference to the finite knowing subject or self. Rather, it describes Hegel's philosophy of religion considered as a movement of absolute divine subjectivity inclusive of that finite self.
22. For a more recent sympathetic reading of Hegel's understanding of freedom, see, for example, Will Dudley, *Hegel, Nietzsche, and Philosophy. Thinking Freedom* (Cambridge: Cambridge University Press, 202) 15–119.
23. See Wolfhart Pannenberg, *Revelation as History* (London: Macmillan, 1968) 4–5.

2

HEGEL ON SPIRIT AND TRINITY

In the previous chapter we presented Hegel's philosophy of religion as a philosophical theology and, more precisely, as an inclusive movement of absolute divine subjectivity. Here we will first put in a wider historical and philosophical context Hegel's understanding of spirit, as he himself presented that context, in order to help us arrive at a clearer understanding of Hegel's problematic formulation of the concept of God as movement of spirit and Trinity. Then, in the next chapter, we will lay out our overall proposal to work with Hegel, while going beyond him, in elaborating a post-Hegelian philosophical theology.

Initial Remarks

Hegel was a philosopher's philosopher. He spent much of his life critically reflecting on previous philosophies and creatively constructing his own position in which he proposed to include and, better, comprehend all that had been given philosophical expression before him. With regard to religion, and his philosophical reflection on it in particular, this passion for inclusiveness assured not only that he would treat of it but that he would assign it a crucial role in his philosophy. Indeed, this passion helped him see a rich dialectical potential in the Christian doctrine of the Trinity. He complained that the theologians of his day had abandoned that doctrine. So he felt it was up to him, a philosopher, to revitalize trinitarian thought. As a result of his efforts, he left to posterity a brilliant, philosophically informed trinitarian proposal and argument in which he explicitly wedded the doctrine of Trinity to the modern concern for subjectivity.

Already fifteen hundred years before Hegel, the Christian doctrine of the Trinity had reached a full classic formulation arising out of and resulting from the fourth-century Cappadocian Church Fathers' critical and creative reconstruction of the Neoplatonic emanationist explanation of the overall structure of reality. In doing so they assured a place for the functioning of divine and

human freedom in the relationship between God and humanity.[1] The Cappadocian Fathers insisted that the Son and the Holy Spirit were not fatalistically
ordered descending emanations from the One. Rather, Son and Spirit were of
the same divine order as the Father. In this way the Father could enter freely
into relation with creation through the sending of the Son and the Spirit. This
free divine offer of Son and Spirit, in turn, allowed and called for a free
response on the part of humankind.

Like the Cappadocians, in developing his dialectical interpretation of Trinity Hegel himself worked critically and creatively with the philosophies of his
own time.[2] Indeed, he did more than merely participate in a reconstruction
of modern understandings of subjectivity. His dialectical interpretation of
Trinity as structured movement of spirit constituted, in itself, a significant
creative advance in the very development of those modern understandings of
subjectivity. His overall interpretation of true subjectivity or spirit and of
Trinity as movement of inclusive and, therefore, absolute divine subjectivity
were so powerful that his concept of spirit and his dialectical understanding
of Trinity as movement of spirit remain crucial points of reference in any post-
Hegelian attempt either to understand subjectivity or to elaborate a trinitarian
philosophical theology.

These rather direct statements concerning Hegel on spirit and on Trinity
call for further explication. We need to understand more exactly what he did
with the doctrine of the Trinity if we in turn wish to go beyond him in our
own working out of a trinitarian philosophical theology. So I propose that in
the present chapter we take a look at the way in which Hegel has come to
develop the notion of Trinity as a movement of spirit or true subjectivity and,
then, in Chapter Three we review certain problematic aspects of that development. Below, in overall Part Two of the present study, we will first examine
aspects of the thought of several philosophers who have reflected at greater
length on the notion of experience. Then we will work out a brief grammar
of experience and take a phenomenological look at experience before we, in
Part Three, propose a more explicit formulation of a post-Hegelian philosophical theology. There we will look with Hegel, that is, among other points from
an overall "Hegelian" perspective of concern to interpret God as a movement
of inclusive divine subjectivity, toward a trinitarian philosophical theology
that lies beyond, but also remains in a certain continuity with, his position.

Over the course of the present essay, our argument, at once historical and constructive, proceeds, in Part One, from an initial overview, in the previous chapter, of Hegel's philosophical theology to a consideration of Hegel on thought and spirit in the present chapter and the following one as well. Then that argument continues in Part Two below, where we will clarify what we mean by experience and, finally, in Part Three, where we will give expression to various basic elements of a post-Hegelian philosophical theology.

More immediately, in the present chapter we will, first of all, carry out a review of certain aspects of the way in which Hegel sees the notion of spirit developing from the philosophy of Descartes through the philosophies of Kant and Fichte on to his own philosophical concept of spirit. This will provide us with a more contextualized working understanding of what Hegel means by spirit. Then, second, we will look more directly at his dialectical interpretation of Trinity as movement of spirit.

With Hegel from Descartes on

We will concentrate on several aspects of Hegel's interpretations of the philosophies of Descartes, Kant, and Fichte as found in his 1825–1826 Berlin lectures on the history of philosophy.[3] Though one could examine at greater length Hegel's discussions of these and other philosophies found elsewhere in his lectures and published works, this more focused approach also has a certain value. First of all, Hegel in fact set up the history of philosophy from the perspective of his own philosophy and his own concept of spirit. So, when we read his history of philosophy we often learn as much about his thought as we do about the various philosophies he studied. Second, staying with his history of philosophy has the added advantage of helping us come to a more contextualized working understanding of his concept of spirit. Third, following along with Hegel makes it easier for us to enter into the spirit of his thought and concerns. It allows us to think along with him in order that we might, later on, attempt to go beyond his particular interpretation of spirit. Since he proposes to develop a movement of spirit occurring in and through the thinking, philosophizing subject, his philosophy should not be studied merely objectively or from a distance. Trying to think along with Hegel as he reviews and criticizes various philosophies is indeed a way of testing whether his philosophy can be actualized in oneself.

Before reviewing Hegel on the philosophies of Descartes, Kant and Fichte, we need to recall several characteristics of his overall understanding of the history of philosophy. He viewed this history as the history of thought. Since for him, and this is said by way of anticipation, spirit was the movement of dynamic inclusive conceptual thought,[4] the history of philosophy was equally the history of the development of spirit.[5] Hegel's history of philosophy was essentially the history of Western thought conceived as a dialectically structured monophylic movement toward the truth, namely, toward the necessary rational affirmation of the unity of subjectivity and objectivity, of subject and object, of concept and reality.[6] His history of philosophy was, essentially, the history of the discovery of thoughts about the absolute[7] that, as the unity of thought and reality, formed the object of this history. For Hegel the truth toward which the history of philosophy moves was, at least in his day, expressed in his own philosophical understanding of spirit as movement of inclusive and absolute subjectivity.[8]

Hegel interwove a number of elements or considerations as he constructed his history of philosophy. He would contextualize a specific philosophy by placing that philosophy in relation to what had come before it and summarize what he considered its particularly relevant aspects. He would applaud what he saw as its strengths and underscore what he saw as its inner contradictions. Reference to these contradictions served as a springboard for his consideration of the next philosophy. The transitions making up this dialectically progressing monophylic movement of thought were to be movements of sublation. Hegel would negate what had come before, take it up again, and move ahead toward a fuller and more explicit notion of truth.[9] By the time he got to modern philosophy, beginning for present purposes with the philosophy of Descartes,[10] he asserted that "thinking begins to plumb its own depths."[11] With the appearance of the Cartesian philosophy Hegel saw epistemological and ontological considerations beginning to converge toward and into what he considered the proper logical formulation of the movement of spirit. He found the questions of truth and of God coming into their own. Furthermore, from his presentation of Descartes' philosophy on, he regularly interwove his concept of spirit with the notions of God and then, especially in relation to Christianity, of Trinity. For Hegel, God as truth was the very content of philosophy.[12]

As we turn now to Hegel's lectures, we will focus especially on his views of the true nature of thought and of the development of the relation of thought to reality. Hegel quickly reformulates this relation into one of subjectivity to objectivity as he traces the development of the concept of spirit in modern philosophy.

Descartes' Philosophy

Hegel works out his overall evaluation of Descartes' philosophy[13] against the background of his own contrast between rationalism and empiricism. He says rationalism or idealism proceeds from thought, and empiricism or mere realism proposes to proceed by abstraction from experience.[14] He of course sides with rationalism or idealism and insists that Descartes is in principle such a rationalist. Hegel basically rejects the fundamental principle of empiricism, namely, that all knowledge comes from experience. He finds such philosophical empiricism exemplified primarily in Locke.[15] According to Hegel, Descartes is the first modern philosopher to begin with and from thought.[16] Thought, so to speak, begins to come into its own with Descartes' *cogito, ergo sum* ("I think, therefore I am"). Hegel sees in this phrase the first modern affirmation of the identity of thought and being or of thought and reality.[17] This identity remains of course merely immediate and initial. Being is not a syllgistically argued or mediated quality of thought but is here simply, and correctly for Hegel, identified with thought.[18] Descartes' beginning with the indubitability of *cogito, ergo sum* opens the way to an idealist philosophy that can begin without presuppositions.[19] Hegel goes on to interpret Descartes' working with the notion of God as an affirmation that there is in God a perfect identity of thought and being. God is the identity of thought and being.[20]

Hegel of course qualifies his enthusiasm for the Cartesian philosophy. First of all, with Descartes the thought in question is still that of a single individual. Second, Descartes falls into a philosophically unacceptable empiricism when it comes to establishing any particulars beyond the initial universal that thought is.[21] In Descartes' philosophy, thought is not yet fully free in its immanent production of that which is the object of such thought.[22] Descartes' distinction between those realities that are characterized by thinking and those realities that are characterized by extension is then not adequately philosophically deduced. Third, Descartes has in principle affirmed that God is the mediating link between the thinking subject and either the external world or one's body.[23] He resolves the epistemological question by an appeal to the veracity of God. However, this appeal is not philosophically argued.[24] The bridge between thought and being or extension, between subjective and objective, remains without adequate philosophical foundation. The linkage between them remains extrinsic. According to Hegel, Descartes makes a good beginning. He appropriately locates an initial unity between thought and being (or reality) in the thinking self. But Descartes does not see that his own starting point offers great potential for resolving the epistemological and ontological questions arising from the way in which he has formulated that very starting point. In his philosophy, thought remains abstract in the Hegelian sense of the word, namely, in that it remains implicit, unposited and undeveloped.[25] Descartes has not as yet been able to give expression to spirit as free thought going out of itself. He has not as yet recognized and worked out the objective movement of thought that gives rise to what is thought and then includes within itself that which is thought.

Kant's Philosophy

Hegel has already shown his overall idealist hand in presenting Descartes. So we can now focus, though necessarily at somewhat greater length, on certain selected aspects of his presentation of Kant's philosophy.[26]

In his critical discussion of Kant, Hegel more or less follows the sequence of Kant's three *Critiques*. With regard, first, to the *Critique of Pure Reason*, he initially organizes his remarks around three notions: sense; understanding; and, reason.[27] He is happy to note the important step taken by Kant when the latter focuses on the thinking subject as source of determinations such as universality and necessity. In this way, according to Hegel, Kant has in principle rightly proposed to examine knowing.[28] In his discussion of Kant on sense, Hegel does not always seem to take into consideration the transcendental character of Kant's concerns. He claims that for Kant such thought determinations as universality and necessity are found only in self-consciousness and belong to subjective thinking. He notes that for Kant unity comes from the side of synthesizing thought, and differences from the side of experience.[29]

After further discussion of the *a priori*, and yet still subjective, character of space and time, Hegel turns to Kant's notion of understanding. Among the many remarks Hegel makes, we should note two points in particular. These are, first, the spontaneity he sees as characteristic of Kant's notion of understanding and, second, the conception of experience with which he sees Kant working. When he looks at Kant's notion of understanding he finds a presentation of thought as spontaneous synthesizing or uniting activity. He discovers in Kant's proposal of the I as the unity of the pure apperception of self-consciousness what can only be described as an activist and productive Cartesian ego.[30] This unifying initial moment of thought brings determinate or particular categories, taken from ordinary logic, to bear on the manifold that is made available by the integrating action of the categories of space and time in the functioning of sensation. And, as if coming upon a foreshadowing of his own notion of spirit, Hegel stresses the fact that Kant sets up his four basic lists of thought categories in threes with the third in each of these groupings being the unity of the previous two.[31]

Experience, the second point we need to note, is for Kant the bringing together of these categories of the understanding with what sensation produces.[32] It consists of two moments: the empirical, or what comes from sensation, and the application of the synthesizing categories of understanding to the manifold that sensation provides. But sensation provides merely appearances; the thing in itself remains forever unknown. Hegel stresses that for Kant experience then has two aspects to it: sensation, which Kant calls the subjective or receptive aspect, and the unifying categories of understanding, which he calls the objective or active aspect. The subjective is merely in my sensation. Yet, for Hegel even Kant's objective aspect to experience is itself subjective in that the categories of understanding pertain to the pure I of my self-consciousness. We know and determine only appearances.[33]

After his remarks on Fichte, to which we will turn shortly, Hegel returns to consider reason as that form of thinking which, in Kant's philosophy, makes the infinite its object. He stresses the Kantian distinction between understanding, which works with the finite, and reason, which treats of the infinite. Reason needs to know and determine the infinite.[34] However, reason cannot do this for two reasons: first, the infinite is not given in external or internal experience and, second, the categories of thought are themselves only formal and empty. If we attempt to know the infinite we end in contradictions (antinomies).[35] From the perspective of his own philosophy and its stress on the importance of contradiction, Hegel naturally rejoices to see Kant's acknowledgment of the necessary presence of contradictions in thought. Toward the end of this treatment of Kant on the uses of theoretical reason, Hegel touches on the question of our knowing God. He points out that Kant rejects the deduction of God's being from the concept or idea of God as the most real of beings.[36]

When we turn to Hegel's first and briefer presentation of Kant on practical knowing,[37] we immediately notice his at least initially appreciative reading of Kant on freedom.[38] True will "is to be free, to determine itself; it is independent, absolute spontaneity, autonomous."[39] The true will's object is its own freedom, its being at home with itself and not being bound from without. Hegel considers the recognition of self-determination as the principle of freedom, which Kant's notion of the autonomous will brings to the fore, to be the turning point in human history and the highpoint in understanding what it means to be human.[40]

Hegel continues to remark on Kant's first two *Critiques*, namely, on Kant's understanding of theoretical and especially of practical reason, as he looks at the teleological principle Kant proposes in his *Critique of Judgement*. In line with our interest in Hegel's concept of spirit, we will, in this last section of our presentation of Hegel's more positive remarks concerning Kant, concentrate on two points arising in his discussion of Kant's teleological principle. These points make up two of the reasons Hegel gives for saying that in Kant's thought there is an unrequited need to "produce" the concrete.[41]

First, Hegel refers to Kant's treatment of that which is living (*das Lebendige*) in order to focus on inner teleology. For living beings have their own end within them. Hegel sees in this view of a living being the affirmation of the need for the concept, the universal, to be determined as the particular.[42] Second, he refers to Kant's postulation of God in order to resolve the antinomy arising out of the need to realize the good in the world. Here he works primarily with Kant's presentation of the postulate of God as it is found in the third *Critique*. The good is the absolute end, which gives determination to reality in human living as well as in the external world. Reason finds itself demanding a certain harmony between the good and reality.[43] But this harmony is evidently not realizable by subjective reason in everyday life. So in order to resolve this contradiction between, on the one hand, the demand that the good be realized and, on the other hand, the world in which such is not the case, practical reason calls for and needs to postulate God in whom one is to believe.[44] God is the third element in relation to the good and to the world. The postulated and believed existence of God assures an ultimate harmony between the good and the world, between the realms of free human action and causally necessary movement, between freedom and necessity.[45]

Hegel claims to have recognized many of the elements of the concept of spirit, understood as movement of thought, in Kant's critical philosophy. He sees thought acknowledged there as active and as the source of unity in relation to the manifold of experience. He finds in Kant the notion of freedom as autonomous will. Indeed, Hegel discovers many of the basic elements of his own notion of spirit, namely, as movement of self-positing thought when he looks at these aspects of Kant's philosophy along with others such as the distinction between understanding and reason, the teleological interpreted as need for concretization, and even certain aspects of Kant's understanding of God as unavailable to theoretical reason but immediately to be believed. However, as was the case with Descartes, here too he detects much that is still contradictory, and thus undeveloped, in Kant.

This longer review of some of what Hegel considers the more positive aspects of Kant's philosophy will let us list in more summary fashion what he thinks remains as yet contradictory and unresolved in that philosophy.

Hegel regularly insists that Kant works with the subjective and so, at least by implication, remains one-sided in his philosophical reflection. However, there seems to be a certain subtle shifting, if not slippage, in Hegel's use of "subjective" here. He tends to identify rather too easily the Kantian transcendental, which comes from the side of the thinking subject, with what would occur merely in the individual. Hegel is caught in a bind. On the one hand, when he considers the role of thought in Kant he seems to recognize that Kant is working on the transcendental level.[46] This recognition allows him to read Kant more approvingly. On the other hand, he seems to feel the need regularly to underscore that for Kant the thinking in question is merely subjective and, at times, only individual knowing.[47] This criticism of Kant as a subjective idealist opens the way for Hegel's further critique of Kant. It helps Hegel describe Kant's philosophy as dualist.[48] Though, according to Hegel, Kant made a tremendous breakthrough when he discovered the active character of thinking, he remains empiricist to the extent that in his philosophy thought still depends on sensation for the material that it unifies.[49] Kant's subjectivity is still merely subjective and not the source of objectivity.

Furthermore, Hegel detects in Kant other unresolved contradictions such as, first, a theoretically unknowable but practically postulated God and, second, the always frustrated drive for the worldly realization of the good. He sees in Kant's variously sketched dualism the philosophical expression of human alienation. His overall stress on Kant's philosophy as merely subjective and his strong underscoring of that philosophy's self-contradictory character set the stage for Hegel himself to go beyond Kant's more one-sided and self-contradictory position with his own more inclusive concept of spirit as movement of subjectivity inclusive of objectivity.

Fichte's Philosophy

Before gathering together the basic elements of Hegel's concept of spirit, we still need to consider briefly one or two aspects of Hegel's reading of Fichte's philosophy.[50] According to Hegel, Fichte follows in the tradition of Descartes and Kant when he identifies the I as an initial unity and now, along with Kant, the source of the categories of thought. The I is the certainty of my relation with myself, a pure abstract knowing.[51] But, whereas Kant merely took over the categories from formal logic, Fichte took the next, and indeed tremendous, step in the development of the concept of spirit. He attempted to show how the categories of thought arise in necessary fashion out of the initial I itself. Still, for Hegel, Fichte was only partially successful in this attempt to construct the activity of thought as the necessary elaboration of the categories of thought.[52]

A brief review of Hegel's presentation of the three basic principles of Fichte's idealism will help us place Fichte between Kant and Hegel along the way of the dialectically progressing development of the concept of spirit. According to Hegel, Fichte's first principle (*Satz*) is that of the identity of the I (I is I).[53] With the affirmation of this first principle, Fichte is attempting to work out philosophy as a scientific knowing of knowing, a doctrine of knowledge based in one principle.[54] The second principle is that the I sets for itself a non-I as object over against itself and as negative of itself. The I posits itself as limited by the non-I, which is an other over against the I itself.[55] The third principle is that each of these first two principles determines the other. To put it briefly, I posit the non-I as limiting myself and I limit the non-I. The I, as limited by the non-I, is passively posited. The I, as knowing it limits the non-I or object, is active. Fichte is trying with this third principle to account for the reciprocal interaction between self and other.[56]

Hegel claims that this ever-recurrent presence of the non-I over against the I, which latter should itself be absolute and inclusive in its own right, is the fundamental contradiction in Fichte's philosophy. He even calls this ever-recurrent presence an absolute contradiction[57] and labels Fichte's infinite the "spurious infinite." It is merely the infinite of infinite progression in which limit constantly recurs.[58] As is the case with Kant's philosophy, Fichte's too remains infected by an unresolved opposition.[59] The I, which should be absolute and "by itself," is always burdened with an accompanying other. It is never really free.[60] Still, for Hegel Fichte has in principle established the idea that thought is the self-positing of objectivity by subjectivity. The whole way in which Hegel presents Fichte's philosophy indicates that, in comparison with Kant's subjective idealism, he considers it to be an objective idealism. With Fichte, thought as such is creative. The epistemological has become ontological. The movement of thought and being are identified. Fichte has indeed gone beyond Kant's subjective idealism. But, as Hegel also observes in his critique of Schelling,[61] here in Fichte's thought the ontological has not yet received its appropriate logical formulation as the necessary progression of thought categories. Finally, Fichte has not been able to reintegrate subjectivity and objectivity in a true concept of spirit as movement of inclusive subjectivity. He has not worked out a philosophically argued movement of inclusive subjectivity as self-positing and self-sublating thought.

Hegel's Philosophy of Spirit

As we look back over Hegel's interpretations of the philosophies of Descartes, Kant, and Fichte in order to consolidate our understanding of Hegel's own concept of spirit, we can do no better than let ourselves be guided by the remarks with which Hegel is recorded as having ended his 1825–1826 lectures on the history of philosophy. In a very few words,[62] he proposes that bringing forth the concrete idea of logic as necessary progression of a series of dialectically developed thought determinations has been the work of spirit over a period of 3,000 years. To continue to paraphrase, and perhaps to expand slightly on, Hegel's own remarks, we can say that the task of modern philosophy has been to grasp this necessary development of thought as movement of spirit. Hegel calls this movement of spirit the self-thinking idea. He wants us to recognize that modern philosophy began in pure thinking with Descartes. It moved forward to the consequent opposition of the subjective and the objective. When Hegel speaks of this opposition, he is surely referring particularly to the philosophies of Kant and Fichte, though he does not mention them by name. The true reconciliation of this opposition occurs as we realize that the very thinking through of this opposition to its farthest extreme results in the resolution of the opposition. This resolution comes about for Hegel not only as Schelling thought, namely, in a first or implicit (*an sich*) fashion. Schelling had proposed that the absolute or God be considered initially as an intuited identity of, or indifference toward, the subjective and the objective.[63] But, according to Hegel, "eternal life itself" is the very production of the opposition and the positing of it in its own identity. For him, spirit is this structured movement of thought as the positing of opposition and the overcoming of this opposition. Descartes' *cogito, ergo sum*, Kant's notion of the active thinking subject, and Fichte's efforts to deduce thought categories from an initial "I" have become for Hegel necessary moments in the historical development of the concept of spirit.

This review of selected moments in Hegel's history of modern philosophy has allowed us to see how these moments lead, for Hegel, to the speculative formulation of the movement of spirit in his own philosophy. Hegel himself sees spirit as the development of thought in which truth is the end result inclusive of the process. Spirit is the movement of conceptual thought from an initial and as yet implicit or unposited unity of thought and being through dialectical self-differentiation to the realization of the identity of this self-differentiation with the initial, implicit unity. Hegel characterizes this dialectical moment of self-differentiation as negation. It is equally, then, negation of the initial unity or the positive. The dialectical moment is internally self-contradictory since it is explicitly negation and yet, as negation of the initial positive, contains the positive within it. The thinking through of this internal self-contradiction to its farthest extreme is the motor force driving thought on to the overcoming of this contradiction in a renewed and enriched moment of unity or identity. This renewed identity is identity of difference. So spirit is the structured movement of conceptual thought as the explicitation of particularity and differentiation, which are only implicitly present in initial identity, and then the consequent renewed and enriched integration of that differentiation with initial identity in renewed identity.

With his speculative formulation of spirit as the structured movement of integrating reason, Hegel has made a subtle but clear and radical shift from the way in which modern philosophy started with an already constituted I. The encyclopedic formulation of Hegel's philosophical system now begins not with such an already constituted I, but with the thought category of pure being as first moment in the movement of pure thought or logic.[64] The I is now the result of the necessary progression of logical thought determinations. For Hegel, the I is no longer the point of departure for philosophical reflection but the result of such reflection.

Hegel meant his philosophy ever to be the process of movement toward and resultant realization of truth. It was to express, for his own day, the true correspondence between thought and reality, subjectivity and objectivity. Spirit was this realization of truth in that it included thought and being, subjectivity and objectivity, in a fuller and more inclusive notion of reason conceived as movement of subjectivity.

Hegel's philosophy as a whole, in its encyclopedic presentation, is constructed as a movement of spirit from the first moment of logical thought through the self-diremption of that logic into a philosophy of nature and the mediation of logic and nature in the philosophy of spirit. His whole philosophical system is a movement of spirit as an inclusive movement of what he calls self-positing thought. This concept of spirit is then realized in various ways throughout his philosophy. The formal structure and movement of spirit can be seen with particular clarity in Hegel's conception of logic. He constructs his logic as an internally coherent and consistent necessary progression of thought categories. For Hegel, there is now no longer an independent subject thinking various logical thought categories. Rather, the very occurrence of the thinking through of these thought categories in and through finite thinking or spirit is itself the movement of subjectivity. Hegel in fact rather colorfully described this movement of pure thought as the presentation of God before the creation of the world.[65] After logic there follows the philosophy of nature, in itself merely renewed immediacy and devoid of spirit, and then the philosophy of spirit, in which Hegel treats of finite and absolute spirit. Absolute spirit consists in the philosophies of art and religion and in the final moment of philosophical thought as such. At the beginning of his *Encyclopedia*, Hegel had written that God, conceived as truth, is the content both of religion and of philosophy.[66] Then, in order to round out his understanding of spirit as the true reformulation and reconceptualization of the religious notion of God, he ends the 1827 and 1830 editions of the *Encyclopaedia* with his famous quote from Aristotle's *Metaphysics*: "for it is this, what God is" (τοῦτο γὰρ ὁ θεός/ *Toũto gàr ho theós*).[67]

In Hegel's philosophy God is no longer, as Hegel said was the case with Descartes, the external guarantee of the veracity of our faculties of knowing. Nor is God the unknowable noumenal reality that Kant postulated, nor again the initial absolute of Fichte (or Schelling). Rather, God is the very truth itself, namely, the self-positing unity of thought and being. God is spirit, the movement of conceptual thought inclusive of what is known. God is the very correspondence of subjectivity and objectivity in a resultant and more inclusive movement of absolute subjectivity.

Hegel's Dialectical Interpretation of Trinity

So far we have established a contextualized working understanding of Hegel's concept of spirit and, briefly, of God as spirit. Now we need to see how Hegel actually interprets Trinity as movement of spirit.[68] To do this, we will concentrate on his dialectical reconceptualization of Trinity as movement of spirit or inclusive conceptual thought in the third part of his philosophy of religion. This third part is his philosophy of the consummate religion, which, as was mentioned in the previous chapter, he identifies historically with Christianity. We will stay with his philosophical construction of the consummate religion both because it is here that he explicitly interprets the Christian doctrine of

Trinity as movement of absolute spirit and because he effectively[69] structures his overall presentation of the consummate religion itself as a movement of "immanent" and "economic" Trinity.[70]

Toward the very beginning of his presentations of the first sphere of the consummate religion Hegel speaks of God in traditional terms as "life" and "love." He sees in these terms expressions of what he understands the dynamic movement of spirit to be. He gives clear expression to his philosophical reading of God as life and love when, in his 1821 manuscript, he identifies his dialectical and developmental interpretation of God as spirit with the traditional Christian doctrine of Trinity:

> God is *spirit*—that which we call the *triune God*, (...) God is spirit, absolute activity, *actus purus*, i.e., subjectivity, infinite personality, infinite distinction of oneself from oneself, [as the term] "begetting" [suggests]. However, this that is distinguished (...) is contained within the eternal concept of universality as absolute subjectivity.[71]

It is especially in his 1827 lectures on the philosophy of religion that Hegel uses considerable terminology from his *Science of Logic* to describe this first element of the consummate religion as the overall appearance of the divine idea or the realized unity of concept and reality. Indeed, he will use what he calls the three moments of the concept, namely, universality, particularity, and individuality, to describe in that order the three elements of the consummate religion. His use of logical terms, and especially of the three moments of the concept, is particularly appropriate with regard to this first element since it is the appearance of the divine idea in the realm of thought. In and as this first element, God appears as what Hegel calls universality or the immediacy of the "in itself."[72] This self-enclosed movement of "immanent" Trinity is for Hegel the concrete universal because it contains otherness within itself. It is the moment of initial unity or identity. It contains otherness within itself as negation or moment of judgment and separation. With otherness so understood here as moment of negation, Hegel sets up a dialectical moment at the very core of God's being. He has built the formal structure of the crucifixion and death of Christ into the very movement of "immanent" Trinity. With otherness as moment of negation, he wants one to think together, dialectically, initial identity (God the Father) with the other (God the Son) of that initial identity in their momentary contradiction (positive and negative, universal and particular). But, here in the first element of the consummate religion, for Hegel this otherness arises as yet only as a sort of play. Still the distinguishing is itself, as difference, momentarily the entire idea. In line with Hegelian dialectical thinking, when the contradiction of universal and its negation or its other is thought through they are seen to have become a new identity (Holy Spirit). For the other is the other of this initial identity, which it thus includes. This inner dynamic of otherness, or particularity, functioning as mediating totality inclusive of the moments of universality and of resultant identity as individuality, presents the triadic structure of inclusive subjectivity. Here, this dynamic reveals the structured movement of initial, but in its own way already absolute, divine subjectivity.

The second element in the development of the consummate religion as movement of spirit is the appearance of the divine idea in the doubled movement of diremption and reconciliation.[73] It is the sphere of particularity, difference, and objectivity. It appears as the movement of judgment in which the divine idea comes into existence "for itself." In this element, characterized by contradiction, the divine idea others itself as an independent world in and out of which there arises finite spirit. Within this world, finite spirit in turn distinguishes itself from nature and from its own nature. This distinguishing, which goes on within finite spirit, gives rise to the contradictory reality of finite spirit as both good and evil. It is both one with its nature, namely, with what it should be, and is not what it should be. So, finite spirit is then self-estrangement. The very establishment of this contradictory character of finite spirit is itself the indication of a need for reconciliation. According to Hegel, such a reconciliation has to occur in an exclusive individuality. It has to take place in an individual divine-human self, in the mediating death of Christ. Continuing on, Hegel presents reconciliation in the particularity of the community's consciousness of an immediate existence spiritually interpreted as the risen Christ. As this historical appearance of the divine idea, the second element of the consummate religion is the moment of objectivity in the overall development of God as spirit. This historical appearance of the divine idea has taken place as an again overall triadically structured movement. The movement occurs from God, as presupposed universality, to the particularity of the community's spiritual consciousness of the risen Christ by means of mediating individuality (the doubled individuality of nature and finite spirit). Mediating individuality culminates or reaches its climactic depths in the death of Christ.

The objective reconciliation achieved in Christ has, in the third element of the consummate religion, namely, in spiritual community,[74] become for Hegel the subjective relationship of the individual subject to this objective reconciliation with the truth. The previous two elements of the consummate religion, and now this third element, are for Hegel the very progression of the idea of God and, indeed, of God as spirit.[75] They are the absolute eternal idea in itself, for itself, and now "in and for itself." These elements are the very life and activity of God consummated in the third element as the community or unity of the individual empirical subjects who are filled by the Spirit of God.[76] These subjects are individuals who live in the Spirit of God and with whom the Spirit of God is dialectically identified. God existing in and as the community of finite subjects is the very realization of God as spirit, the Holy Spirit or reconciling return of the divine idea out of the self-othering of judgment. The third element of the consummate religion is the movement of inclusive, and now absolute, divine subjectivity.

This third element develops as the reconciliation of the individual believer with the life, death and resurrection of Christ in three stages: the origin of the community in the outpouring of the Holy Spirit; the realization or actualization of the community through faith, doctrine, church, and Eucharist; and, the realization of the spirituality of the community in universal actuality as philosophy. In the first stage, the community originates in the particularity of a shared religious consciousness. In the second stage, Hegel sees the various *theologoumena* there discussed as the reconciling active presence of the spirit, of the objectively presented universality of truth mediating the objective reconciliation (already obtained in Christ) to the individual subjects. In the third stage, he presents the movement from the shared conscious inner enjoyment of the presence of God (which was achieved in the second stage) to an adequate mediation in self-knowledge, in philosophical thought. The knowledge of being at peace with God has become a knowledge of being at peace with oneself. Here in philosophical thought, knowledge or subjectivity is recognized as developing out of itself and as reconciling itself with itself. For Hegel, this rationality is true freedom. Philosophy is the conceptual or comprehending thought that, as essentially concrete, determines itself to its totality, the idea. It is absolute spirit, the very peace of God, true individuality.[77]

In this third element of the consummate religion, the mediation of particularity with inclusive individuality occurs by means of objective universality. This religious reconciliation in community results, as dynamic movement of spirit, both in a grounding return to the immediacy or identity of "immanent" Trinity and in the advance to philosophical thinking.

This realization of trinitarian divine self-determination is for Hegel movement of spirit in the form of a dialectical development of absolute divine subjectivity. The first element or moment in this movement of spirit presents itself as moment of initial divine subjectivity or "immanent" Trinity. The second element or moment of spirit is that of objectivity. As we have seen, in this second element Hegel treats of such religious themes as creation, original sin, incarnation, redemption, and reconciliation. The third element or moment of spirit is that of renewed and, now, inclusive divine subjectivity. As we have noted, in this third element Hegel speaks of the origin of the community in the outpouring of the Holy Spirit, actualization of the community through faith, doctrine, church and Eucharist, and the realization of the spirituality of the community as philosophy. However, the reconciliation here achieved between an initial subjectivity and objectivity remains one achieved "in God" who remains Other to finite consciousness. According to Hegel this true content of reconciliation must sublate itself into the true form of the self-thinking idea as absolute spirit. In the final or true form of absolute spirit, namely, in philosophical thought, form coincides with content and self with concept. As Hegel would say, concept and reality are united in the idea. In fact he has always interpreted the religious name or term "God" and the Christian doctrine of the Trinity from the perspective of the concept, understood as thought inclusive of reality, and from the perspective of the idea, understood as realization of that inclusiveness constitutive of the concept. But, from a speculative systematic perspective and from the point of view of his system as a whole, it is in the sublation of trinitarian divine subjectivity in philosophical, self-identical thought that Hegel formally and explicitly reconceptualizes Trinity. Furthermore, it is with this move from the philosophy of religion, understood as a philosophical theology, to philosophical thought as such that he retroactively grounds his dialectical interpretation of God as truth and of Trinity as the appropriate religious representation of God as movement of spirit.

The results of Hegel's effort to interpret Trinity as movement of spirit are quite impressive. When we consider his philosophy from our present perspective, we find that Hegel treats of "immanent" and of "economic" Trinity twice. He in effect presents "immanent" Trinity first of all as movement of self-determining inclusive subjectivity in the form of pure thought or logic and then again as first element or moment of universality in the philosophy of the consummate religion. He treats "economic" Trinity first when he presents the consummate religion, where he includes "immanent" Trinity within the "economic" trinitarian movement. He again treats of "economic" Trinity in philosophical thought. Philosophical thought is to be seen as grounding return both to the immediacy of "immanent" Trinity on the level of philosophy of religion and to the immediacy of logic on the level of spirit as a whole. Hegel's encyclopedic system is, in its totality, his philosophically reinterpreted presentation of "economic" Trinity inclusive of "immanent" Trinity. Since Hegel's philosophy is of a piece, his whole philosophy becomes a reconceptualization of the triune God—with God understood as movement of spirit or inclusive conceptual thought in the form of an absolute subjectivity.

Final Remarks

Hegel in a More Theological Context

In working out his philosophical reconceptualization of Trinity, Hegel himself did not seem to have been as aware of the intricacies of the Greek and Western trinitarian traditions as he was of modern Western philosophical developments. However, he did claim that his reconceptualization of Trinity gave philosophical expression to this Christian doctrine's rational content and inner dialectical movement. Indeed, he seems almost intuitively to have come upon, and perhaps even further developed, several fundamental insights progressively attained during the development of various classic Christian trinitarian theologies. His interpretation of Trinity shows certain affinities both with aspects of earlier, more philosophically oriented theological reflection on Trinity and with certain Reformation and post-Reformation insights. Insofar as his reconceptualization of Trinity takes the form of a dynamic, triply structured movement of divine subjectivity from the one (God) to the many (world) to an inclusion of the many in the one, we can see it as representing the culmination of a number of tendencies in Greek and Western Christian trinitarian speculation.

As with Christian trinitarian theologies in general, Hegel's reconceptualized movement of Trinity finds its ultimate beginning in the "one." Hegel gives this "one" a post-Kantian formulation as the first moment in the self-development of logical or pure thought, namely, pure being. Having pointed this out, we can now go on to indicate several important breakthroughs in the history of Christian trinitarian thought and to mention how Hegel's reconceptualization seems to manifest certain affinities with these breakthroughs or insights. For present purposes it will be sufficient to refer briefly to four classic authors, namely, Tertullian, Origen, Gregory of Nyssa, and Thomas Aquinas,[78] and to Martin Luther as well as, more indirectly, to mystics like Marie of the Incarnation.

The first in this series of breakthroughs or insights to be considered is the tendency in various trinitarian traditions to stress either the oneness or the threeness of God. Tertullian (c. 155–c. 220) can be seen as giving initial expression to the Western tendency to stress the oneness of God. Origen (c. 185–c. 254) provides an early expression of the Eastern tendency to emphasize the threeness of God. Tertullian stresses the fact that the divine power is one and undivided in its triple exercise. In *Adversus Praxean*[79] he affirms and explains Trinity, but goes to great lengths to preserve the oneness of the divine monarchy. Origen, in turn, is so concerned to assert the distinction between God the Father and Christ that he tends in his *Dialogue with Heraclides*[80] to speak of two Gods. In his *De Principiis*,[81] he continues to emphasize distinction when he writes of the Father's action extending to all beings, the Son's to all rational beings, and the Spirit's to the saints or those who are holy.

We can sense already here in Tertullian's stress on the divine monarchy and Origen's emphasis on distinction among the actions of Father, Son and Spirit the tension between two possible approaches to Trinity. In his reconceptualization of Trinity Hegel seems to have been at least implicitly aware of such a tension. As we have seen, and here very generally stated, he constructs a post-Kantian dialectical movement of Trinity that, from the perspective of his encyclopedic system, occurs initially in a more monosubjectival formulation as the first moment or element of Trinity, the kingdom of the Father. He works out a second element, the kingdom of the Son, as creation, estrangement and initial reconciliation of the world with God. He likewise develops a third element of Trinity, the kingdom of the Spirit. In this third element the movement of spirit is realized in a more intersubjectival manner as the presence of the Holy Spirit within the members of the spiritual community. With the transition from this third element, and from the philosophy of religion in general, to the final moment of philosophical thought where the otherness of religious representation is overcome, Hegel reintroduces a more monosubjectival formulation of the movement of spirit. It is as if he is struggling to go beyond the question of the tension between the one and the three, a question that, in a post-Kantian mode, has been transformed into the relationship between monosubjectival and intersubjectival constructions of the movement of spirit. It is as if Hegel is trying to get beyond these distinctions of monosubjectival and intersubjectival or singular and plural to achieve a more inclusive formulation of the movement of spirit as such. Ultimately, however, he does this in a formulation expressing the movement of spirit in the singular to recognize that there can only be one structured movement of true or inclusive infinite.[82]

Furthermore, as was mentioned above, Origen in particular worked out three differing ways for the three members of the Trinity to function in relation to created reality and, at least implicitly, three differing relationships of created reality to the three members of the Trinity. Over the centuries this approach, which stressed diversity of relationship, was generally overshadowed by the ever-stronger theological stress on the principle that the Trinity acted as one with regard to created reality. Hegel, however, seems to have sensed something of the diversity of ways in which the triune God might be related to created reality when he spoke of finite spirit as being related in the mode of thought to the initial moment of Trinity or the kingdom of the Father, in the mode of representation to the second moment of Trinity, that of externalization or self-othering as the kingdom of the Son, and in the mode of subjectivity to the third or inclusive moment of Trinity, the kingdom of the Spirit. Hegel seems to have captured something of what post-Reformation mystics such as Marie of the Incarnation would stress when they spoke of a distinct experiential relationship with each of the three divine Persons of the

Trinity.[83] A final point in this regard. Hegel seems effectively to have let go of, if not perhaps even gone beyond, the theological distinction of an "immanent" Trinity considered only in itself and an "economic" Trinity seen as the Trinity active in the world.[84]

After Tertullian and Origen, Gregory of Nyssa (c. 335–c. 395) provides a further important clarification in the history of the development of Christian trinitarian traditions. In a letter often attributed to his brother, Basil of Caesarea (Letter n. 38),[85] but which appears more and more to have been written by Gregory, he works out the distinction between *ousia* and *hypostasis*. He accepts a more Aristotelian or concrete notion of *ousia* than had Origen, who seemed to think of *ousia* in more generic terms. However, Gregory also calls upon a more Platonic, modified emanationist thought pattern in order to work out, at least in a general way, the relationships among the three *hypostases*. This integration of a more concrete understanding of *ousia* and a dynamic understanding of the relationships among the *hypostases* allows Gregory to go beyond Aristotle to affirm a triply realized concrete essence. It is this brilliant move on Gregory's part that allows trinitarian thinkers to remain with the concreteness of the three divine *hypostases* without needing to make further reference to either an abstract essence or a hidden Godhead behind the movement of the three divine *hypostases*. It is important to note that for the Christian this move by Gregory assures to history and otherness a perduring value by anchoring distinction within the absolute itself.

Before speaking more explicitly of Hegel in relation to this breakthrough on the part of Gregory of Nyssa, we need to look at one last classic thinker, Thomas Aquinas. In his own way Aquinas continues the direction taken by Gregory when he insists in his *Summa theologiae*[86] that there is only a distinction of reason between the divine essence and the three divine persons. In addition, his reworking of Boethius's well-known substantialist definition of person is of equal immediate interest. Aquinas comes to understand the divine persons as subsisting relations.[87] The identification of divine essence and divine persons, and the definition of person as subsisting relation, de facto further refine and purify Gregory of Nyssa's integration of Aristotelian concreteness with Platonic dynamic.

With Gregory's and Aquinas's insights in mind, we can turn to Hegel's conception of spirit as a dialectical movement structured in three moments.

We can see Hegel's concept of spirit as continuing the trajectory established by Gregory and Aquinas. It is just their sort of triple instantiation without substratum or further underlying subject that Hegel affirms when he speaks of spirit as a structured dialectic of self-othering and enriched return. For Hegel there is neither substance nor subject underlying this dialectic, which is itself the movement of inclusive divine subjectivity. Without necessarily being aware of it, Hegel in fact prolongs the trajectory set up by Gregory and Aquinas when he further purifies their conceptions in two ways. He does this first of all by means of his notion of dialectic when he introduces a more explicitly dynamic movement, a form of becoming, within his reconceptualized notion of Trinity. Second, in defining the three divine "persons" as moments of Trinity he overcomes any unnecessary residue of incommunicability possibly traceable to the Boethian definition of person. For Hegel there is simply the dialectical movement of spirit, a movement of divine subjectivity in its three moments. With this internally distinguished movement of divine subjectivity Hegel of course follows a strategy similar to that of Gregory. He too anchors the value of history and at least a certain form of otherness within the absolute itself.

Finally, we need to refer briefly to Martin Luther. It has recently been pointed out that Luther presented an at least implicitly dialectical understanding of Trinity in his *Small Catechism,* particularly when he spoke of the work of the Holy Spirit.[88] Luther's idea that we believe that we cannot believe without divine assistance provides a paradoxical juxtaposition of "believe" and "cannot believe" that seems to be one of the sources for Hegel's insight into what he saw as the dialectical character of the trinitarian God. This idea that Luther's implicitly dialectical understanding of Trinity and of the work of the Holy Spirit might be a source of Hegel's trinitarian insight would need to be explored at greater length, but the suggestion does help us see a bit more clearly the religious rootage of Hegel's brilliant philosophical reconstruction of Trinity as a dialectical movement of divine subjectivity whose middle term was negation and contradiction or, religiously stated, crucifixion and death.

Trinity as Movement of Spirit

Hegel claimed that God could not be conceived of as subject and personal unless God were conceived as Trinity. For him, a non-trinitarian conception of God left God as mere substance and without content, something about which one could not speak. Also, a non-trinitarian conception of God simply juxtaposed God and world, thus finitizing God. Hegel tried to argue this claim by interpreting the trinitarian God as a dialectical movement of spirit. For him the triune God was ultimately a movement of self-othering as nature and finite spirit, including the divine-human mediator, and of enriched return inclusive of the process in and through the spiritual community.

It is especially in his 1827 Berlin lectures on the philosophy of religion that Hegel succeeded in explicitly widening this trinitarian conception of God as spirit to cover the whole movement of his three-part philosophy of religion: The Concept of Religion; Determinate Religion; The Consummate Religion. We saw in Chapter One above that he had in fact transformed philosophy of religion into a philosophical theology. As Hegel himself noted, philosophy of religion was often seen as consisting in a more straightforward philosophical reflection on religion as the conscious relationship of human to divine. But in his own philosophy of religion lectures he reconstructs the philosophy of religion as a dynamic movement of divine subjectivity that develops as inclusive or absolute spirit in and through the various finite religions and culminates in the consummate religion, this last being identified historically with Christianity and especially with Lutheran Protestantism.

Hegel's constructive interpretation of Trinity as a movement of spirit and his reformulation of the philosophy of religion as a movement of divine subjectivity, i.e., as a philosophical theology, allowed him to place religion as penultimate moment in his overall encyclopedic movement of spirit. However, brilliant as these moves were, they also raise a particularly difficult question with regard to the relationship between religion and philosophy or the last moment in the encyclopedic formulation of his overall philosophy. This question revolves around the interpretation to be given to the transition from religion to philosophy especially, from the perspective of our present concerns, as it occurs in the Berlin lectures on the philosophy of religion and in his *Encyclopedia*. Hegel argues that the movement of spirit continues as a transition from a religious representation of the truth to a philosophical and conceptual realization of that truth. He says that religion's representation of the truth as the correspondence of concept and reality remains laden with the otherness characteristic of religion. The reconciliation that occurs in religion takes place in another, namely, in God. With the transition to philosophical thought, where self and concept are the same, that otherness is overcome. Mediation is self-mediation and is no longer burdened, one might say, with the awareness that reconciliation occurs in the other.

The question this transition from religion to philosophy raises is whether or not Hegel's system is ultimately atheistic. Perhaps once one attains the clarity of conceptual thought in philosophy one sees that the otherness characteristic of religious representation is to be left behind. In such a case it is hard to see how Hegel's philosophy does not lead to some form of atheism. On the other hand, if the final moment of philosophical thought is the identity *of* difference such that it always requires reference back to religion or that out of which it arises, then one might argue that Hegel's philosophy is not necessarily atheistic. For philosophy's conceptual thought simply expresses the structure and movement of what is going on in religion. This apparent ambiguity in the transition from religion to philosophy seems to be rooted in the complex character of the transition understood by Hegel as *Aufhebung*, which includes negation of what came before, preservation of the same, and advance or movement ahead. If one stresses negation, Hegel's system tends to lead to atheism. One no longer needs the point of view that acknowledges reconciliation with and in an other. If one stresses preservation, one need not necessarily interpret the move from religion to philosophy as leading toward atheism for one stresses the perduring significance of otherness.

It is very difficult to resolve this question and one can see arguments on both sides. However, if one conceives of the third aspect to *Aufhebung*, namely, "advance or movement ahead" as an advance that is an enriched return, then it would seem that philosophy's conceptual thought must for Hegel also necessarily remain rooted in and return to religion[89] as well as to logic and to the beginning of Hegel's encyclopedic formulation of the movement of thought. To the extent that philosophy would necessarily return to religion it could not be susceptible of any straightforwardly atheistic interpretation. But perhaps the ambiguity in Hegel's formulation of the transition from religion to philosophy cannot be fully resolved. It is not easy at this point in Hegel's system to maintain "advance" as "return" in a balanced conceptually expressed formulation, or "advance" and "return" in a clear and conceptually expressed equilibrium. Perhaps, then, the ambiguity implied in the transition from religion to philosophy is one of those points in Hegel's overall philosophy that will force anyone, who in today's world wants to remain faithful to Hegel's interests and concerns, to go beyond Hegel's formulation of the movement of spirit to a philosophical interpretation of Trinity based on a reconstructed post-Hegelian notion of spirit.

NOTES

1. I am grateful to Prof. Dr. Ekkehard Mühlenberg for this insight.
2. For a fascinating reading of Hegel on Trinity, see Cyril O'Regan, *The Heterodox Hegel* (Albany, NY: State University of New York Press, 1994), with abundant bibliography.
3. *Vorlesungen: Ausgewählte Nachschriften und Manuskripte*, vol. 9: *Vorlesungen über die Geschichte der Philosophie, Teil 4: Philosophie des Mittelalters und der neueren Zeit*, ed. Pierre Garniron and Walter Jaeschke (Hamburg: Meiner, 1986) (hereafter V 9 and cited by page and text line)/*Lectures on the History of Philosophy. The Lectures of 1825–1826*, vol. 3: *Medieval and Modern Philosophy*, ed. Robert F. Brown, trans. Robert F. Brown and J. M. Stewart with the assistance of H. S. Harris (Berkeley: University of California Press, 1990) (the pages of the German edition are helpfully provided in the outer margins of the English translation).
4. E.g., *Gesammelte Werke*, vol. 20: *Enzyklopädie der philosophischen Wissenschaften im Grundrisse*, third original edition 1830, ed. Wolfgang Bonsiepen and Hans-Christian Lucas (Hamburg: Felix Meiner, 1992) § 577 (hereafter E and usually cited by numbered paragraph)/*Philosophy of Mind*, trans. (of the third part of the *Encyclopedia*) W. Wallace (Oxford: Clarendon, 1975) § 577 (hereafter PM and cited only if quoted). Spirit is "the self-knowing idea" (*die sich wissende Idee*), V 9:188.532–533. See also G. W. F. Hegel, *System und Geschichte der Philosophie, Philosophische Bibliothek*, vol. 166, ed. Johannes Hoffmeister (Leipzig: Meiner, 1940) 242 (hereafter SGP)/*Introduction to the Lectures on the History of Philosophy*, trans. T. M. Knox and A. V. Miller (Oxford: Clarendon, 1985) 177 (hereafter ILHP).
5. V 9:188.529–533 with 545–552.
6. See, e.g., Hegel's own evaluation of the history of philosophy, V 9:188.527–544.
7. E p. 12/G. W. F. Hegel, *The Encyclopaedia Logic*. Part I of the *Encyclopaedia of Philosophical Sciences* with the *Zusätze*, a new translation with Introduction and notes by T. F. Geraets, W. A. Suchting, and H. S. Harris (Indianapolis: Hackett, 1991) p. 10 (hereafter EL and cited only if quoted or if a citation does not refer to a numbered paragraph).
8. When Hegel uses the word "absolute" to qualify spirit or subjectivity he is always implying an, in some way, already either "made explicit" or realized unity of thought and being or of concept and reality.
9. On sublation, see Hegel's remarks in *Gesammelte Werke*, vol. 21: *Wissenschaft der Logik, Erster Band: Die objektive Logik (1832)*, ed. Friedrich Hogemann and Walter Jaeschke (Hamburg: Meiner, 1985), p. 94 line 11 to p. 95 line 23 (hereafter GW 21 and cited by page and text line)/*Science of Logic*, trans. A. V. Miller (New York: Humanities, 1969) 106–108 (hereafter GL).
10. E.g., V 9:72.45–47.
11. "hat das Denken angefangen, in sich zu gehen." SGP 252/ILHP 183.
12. E § 1.
13. V 9:90.619–102.997 with endnotes V 9:289–307.
14. V 9:89.581–601.
15. E.g., the brief overview of Locke in V 9:117.440–118.456 and Hegel's critical remarks in V 9:122.579–595.
16. V 9:88.543–551 and 92.669–670.
17. V 9:93.719–731.

18. V 9:94.738–745.
19. V 9:92.682–685, 93.702–706.
20. V 9:98.888–893.
21. V 9:101.959–960.
22. V 9:93.711–713.
23. V 9:97.860–98.863 with 101.988–102.996.
24. V 9:96.831–97.833.
25. V 9:72.45–47.
26. V 9:149.360–156.575, 162.742–164.829, 167.914–179.266 with endnotes V 9: 384–392, 396–398, 400–407. In these 1825–1826 lectures Hegel interweaves his treatments of Kant, Fichte, and Jacobi.
27. V 9:150.395–156.575 and 162.742–164.829.
28. V 9:149.361–374.
29. V 9:150.398–409.
30. V 9:152.469–153.490 with 156.183–185.
31. V 9:153.495–154.503.
32. V 9:154.529–530.
33. V 9:155.545–156.575.
34. V 9:162.744–760.
35. V 9:163.768–787.
36. V 9:164.802–816.
37. V 9:167.914–169.974.
38. V 9:168.918–947.
39. "frei zu sein, sich selbst zu bestimmen, er ist selbständig, absolute Spontaneität, autonomisch." V 9:168.928–930 (my translation).
40. V 9:168.935–947.
41. V 9:169.975–976. See comments by Garniron and Jaeschke, in V 9:402 note to V 9: 169.976–977.
42. V 9:170.982–988.
43. V 9:171.25–28.
44. Hegel spends some time discussing Jacobi's and Kant's, for him, effectively common understanding of belief in God as a form of immediate knowledge of God. He rejects a direct and unmediated knowledge of God. See V 9:174.127–177.217.
45. Hegel repeats this point in several ways in V 9:171.30–172.64. And see V 9: 173.86–88.
46. E.g., V 9:153.485–488.
47. E.g., V 9:155.559–560.
48. V 9:172.57.
49. E.g., V 9:151.435–438.
50. V 9:156.576–162.741 with endnotes V 9:392–396.
51. V 9:156.580–157.588.
52. V 9:157.591–595, 160.684–686.
53. V 9:158.634–159.642.
54. V 9:158.627–631.
55. V 9:159.643–645 and 650–657.
56. V 9:159.658–160.674.
57. V 9:161.727–728.
58. V 9:162.733–736.

59. V 9:160.689–691.
60. V 9:161.729–732.
61. V 9:188.527–529.
62. V 9:188.527–552.
63. E.g., V 9:180.274–280.
64. E § 86.
65. GW 21:34.6–11/GL 50.
66. E § 1.
67. E § 577/PM § 577. The English translation is taken from Walter Jaeschke, "Philosophical Theology and Philosophy of Religion," in *New Perspectives on Hegel's Philosophy of Religion*, ed. David Kolb (Albany: State University of New York Press, 1992) 7.
68. For a longer overview, see Dale M. Schlitt, *Divine Subjectivity. Understanding Hegel's Philosophy of Religion* (Scranton, PA: University of Scranton Press, 1990) 171–198. See also Dale M. Schlitt, "Hegel's Reconceptualization of Trinity. Further Reflections," in *Sein—Erkennen—Handeln. Interkulturelle, ontologische und ethische Perspektiven. Festschrift für Heinrich Beck zum 65. Geburtstag*, ed. Erwin Schadel and Uwe Voigt (Frankfurt am Main: Peter Lang, Europäischer Verlag der Wissenschaften, 1994) 559–565.
69. Hegel's presentations of the first element or sphere of the consummate religion remain constant and consistent throughout his 1821, 1824, 1827, and 1831 lectures on the philosophy of religion. However, he varies the distribution of christological *theologoumena*. We will work somewhat with his 1821 manuscript but more so with the 1827 lecture transcripts when discussing the first element or sphere of the consummate religion, and with the 1827 lectures alone when speaking of the second and third elements.
70. "Immanent" Trinity traditionally refers to God considered in God self and "economic" Trinity to God considered in relation to creation. With reference to Hegel, "immanent" Trinity refers directly to the first element in the presentation of the consummate religion. However, even here for Hegel God is already considered as being in relation to thought and not as totally independent of finitude. Without qualification "Trinity" here generally refers to both "immanent" and "economic" Trinity.
71. "Gott ist *Geist*, d. i. das was wir *dreieinigen* Gott heißen. (…) Gott ist Geist, die *absolute Tätigkeit*, actus purus, d. I. *Subjektivität, unendliche Persönlichkeit*, unendliche Unterscheidung *seiner von sich selbst*, Erzeugung; aber dieses Unterschiedene (…) ist *im evigen begriff* der *Algemeinheit* als *absoluter Subjektivität* gehalten." *Vorlesungen: Ausgewählte Nachrifften und Manuskripte*, vol. 5: *Vorlesungen über die Philosophie der Religion, Teil 3: Die vollendete Religion*, ed. Walter Jaeschke (Hamburg: Felix Meiner, 1984), p. 16 lines 419–425 (italics in the original) (hereafter V 5 and cited by page and text line)/*Lectures on the Philosophy of Religion*, vol. 3: *The Consummate Religion*, ed. Peter C. Hodgson (Berkeley: University of California Press, 1985) 78 (the pages of the German edition are helpfully provided in the outer margins of the English translation).
72. V 5:199.690–215.73 with the overviews in 197.608–617 and 198.669–670.
73. V 5:215.74–251.24 with the overviews in 197.618–198.645 and 198.671–199.678.
74. V 5:251.25–270.520 with the overviews in 198.646–651 and 199.679–681.
75. V 5:196.601–197.607 with 198.646–651.

76. "Spirit" (*Geist*) will be capitalized when used by Hegel to refer more explicitly to the religious notion of "Holy Spirit."
77. Hegel sketches further forms of the realization of this communitarian religious consciousness which need not be discussed here.
78. Though the responsibility for remarks concerning these thinkers is my own, I have profited from the insightful work of Prof. Dr. Ekkehard Mühlenberg. See, for example, his *Epochen der Kirchengeschichte* (Heidelberg: Quelle und Meyer, 1980) esp. 71–74.
79. *Adversus Praxean Liber. Treatise Against Praxeas*, ed. (With Introduction, Translation, and Commentary) Ernest Evans (London: S.P.C.K., 1948) ch. 1–8, Latin pp. 89–97, English pp. 130–140.
80. *Dialogus cum Haraclite, Entretien d'Origène avec Héraclide, Sources chrétiennes*, vol. 67 (Paris, Cerf, 1960) 52–67 but especially 52–61/in *The Library of Christian Classics*, vol. 2: *Alexandrian Christianity*, Introduction and Notes by John Ernest Leonard Oulton and Henry Chadwick (Philadelphia: Westminster, 1954) 437–440, but especially 437–439.
81. E.g., *Traité des principes, Sources chrétiennes*, vol. 252 (Paris: Cerf, 1978) first treatise, ch. 3 paragraphs 7–8 pp. 156–165/[*Origen*] *On First Principles*, trans. G. W. Butterworth (London: Society for Promoting Christian Knowledge, 1936) first treatise, ch. 3 paragraphs 7–8 pp. 36–39.
82. However, in his important and carefully worked out study, *Recognition. Fichte and Hegel on the Other* (Albany, NY: State University of New York Press, 1992), Robert R. Williams seems to argue more straightforwardly for the intersubjective-social character of spirit in Hegel's thought (see, e.g., p. 2 with p. 16) and for an intersubjective interpretation of Trinity (see, e.g., at least implicitly on p. 283 n. 88).
83. One might profitably consult Marie of the Incarnation's recounting of her first (1625) and third (1631) revelations. See her *Écrits spirituels et historiques*, vol. 2 (Paris, Desclée, 1930), 233–236 and 285–287/*Marie of the Incarnation*, Selected Writings, ed. Irene Mahoney (New York: Paulist Press, 1989) 74–76 and 99–100. I am grateful to Dr. Robert Michel, O.M.I., for help and guidance regarding the writings of Marie of the Incarnation.
84. This point is suggested by Cyril O'Regan in his review of Dale M. Schlitt, *Divine Subjectivity. Understanding Hegel's Philosophy of religion*, in *American Catholic Philosophical Quarterly* 64 (1991) 520. O'Regan makes the point more from the fact that for Hegel the first element of Trinity is included within the third or final element.
85. Saint Basil, *The Letters*, vol. 1, with an English translation by Roy J. Deferrari (Cambridge, MA: Harvard University Press, 1961) 196–227 (Greek and English texts).
86. The *Summa Theologiae* is hereafter abbreviated *S.Th.* References to and citations from it are according to the Leonine text and follow the standard form identifying "part" (I, I-II, etc.) and "question" (q.), "article" (a.), " location in the body of the article" c.), and "particular response to the introductory objections" (ad 1, ad 2, etc.). The Latin Leonine text of the *S.Th.* with which I have, for convenience' sake, worked is Sancti Thomae Aquinatis, Doctoris Angelici Ordinis Praedicatorum, *Summa Theologiae*, cura Fratrum ejusdem Ordinis, 5 vols. (Matriti: Biblioteca de Autores Cristianos, 1961–1965, 3rd ed.). English translation: *Summa theologiae* (Cambridge?, England: Blackfriars in conjunction with Eyre and Spottlswoode, 1964–1981). The present reference is to *S.Th.* I q. 28 a. 2 c.

87. *S. Th.* I q. 29 a. 4 c.
88. Alan M. Olson, *Hegel and the Spirit. Philosophy as Pneumatology* (Princeton, NJ: Princeton University Press, 1992) e.g., 10, 15–16, 32.
89. This is one of the fundamental points argued by Stephen Rocker in *Hegel's Rational Religion* (London: Associated University Presses, 1995), who provides abundant bibliography on the question of Hegel's understanding of the relationship between religion and philosophy. See also Stephen Rocker, "The Integral Relation of Religion and Philosophy in Hegel's Philosophy," in *New Perspectives on Hegel's Philosophy of Religion* (Albany: State University of New York Press, 1992) 27–37.

3

WITH AND BEYOND HEGEL

Hegel's dialectical interpretation of Trinity as movement of spirit appears problematic today not so much because Hegel understood the underlying notion of spirit, with which he was working, as inclusive or absolute subjectivity, but because he insisted that this movement of subjectivity take, essentially, the form of a movement of self-positing conceptual thought. However, in the many years since his death in 1831, the Western world has become suspicious of thought's purportedly pristine and universal character as well as hesitant about the idea of a conceptually transparent absolute.

Nevertheless, Hegel's effort to work out a new philosophical theology by interpreting Trinity in terms of a movement of divine subjectivity surely remains the single most important attempt to reformulate the notion of Trinity in modern times. This fact alone would be reason enough to take him as an important point of historical reference in any contemporary philosophical project to reinterpret Trinity and, therewith, to propose a post-Hegelian philosophical theology. Beyond historical considerations, Hegel's idea of linking Trinity with an appropriately reformulated notion of subjectivity would in itself, given its own rich development, seem to continue to provide a particularly valuable way to reflect coherently and meaningfully on Trinity as we begin the third millennium in the common era after Christ and move more deeply into the twenty-first century. There are, furthermore, specific insights of his that remain important today and that need to be retrieved in a new and wider contemporary understanding of spirit as monosubjectivally and intersubjectivally formulated movement of subjectivity. These specific contributions and their perduring value constitute further reasons for working with Hegel as we attempt to go beyond his particular dialectical interpretation of Trinity toward a renewed philosophical understanding of Trinity that will take the form of a post-Hegelian philosophical theology.

After our review of the way in which Hegel saw the concept of spirit develop in modern philosophy and after a summary of his reconceptualization of Trinity as movement of spirit, I will now in the present chapter sketch out in preliminary fashion my overall proposal to develop a renewed philosophical formulation of Trinity. We will proceed in four steps by: first, reviewing some of the major concerns and moves on Hegel's part in his elaboration of a philosophical theology that will help us set the stage for a presentation of my own proposal; second, establishing a brief list of several of the many important philosophical contributions Hegel has made; third, giving an indication of the problematic character of his philosophical theology; and, fourth, making an initial presentation of the direction I propose that we take in working with Hegel while going beyond him. Then, in Part Two below, more precisely in Chapter Four, we will, in a further step in our argument examine various philosophical resources. In Chapter Five we will propose a grammar, and then in Chapter Six a phenomenology, of experience. These three chapters will permit us to develop the basic notion of experience with which we will work when we return to my proposal to elaborate, in Part Three below, a post-Hegelian philosophical theology in the form of a renewed understanding of Trinity and spirit.

Hegel: Major Concerns and Moves

Hegel himself acknowledged the importance of religion by assigning to it a strategic place and a major role in his overall philosophical system. His philosophy of religion represents one of the great achievements in philosophical reflection on religion in general and on God in particular. There is so much in his thought on religion and on God to appreciate, profit from and rethink today. Among the many strengths of his approach to and philosophical reflection on these topics, we could in a sense plunge directly into his philosophy of religion by noting here in a special way his deep appreciation for the drive beyond alienation toward wholeness and integration characteristic of the human person and especially of religious communities. He brought together religion's concern for wholeness and integration with his concept of spirit as dynamic, dialectical and, finally, inclusive movement. He brought them together by working with what he called the movement of reflexively available conceptual thought. He made much of what has come to be his hallmark distinction between understanding (*Verstand*) as thought in its function of separating or distinguishing and reason (*Vernunft*) as thought in its function of unifying or integrating what had previously been separated.

Working with this rich and dynamic notion of thought as doubled movement, Hegel then made a philosophical generalization. He incorporated the doubled movement of thought both as distinguishing and as unifying or relating into a logically sequential movement of thought. For him this constituted the phenomenological movement from an initial moment of identity to a moment of distinction or differentiation on to a moment of realization of the unity of the two. He expanded this reading of the phenomenological movement of thought into what he called the dialectical movement of spirit, which in all its forms and manifestations was a movement of self-othering and return, a movement of thought proceeding from an initial unity to a differentiation on to a renewed and enriched unity of the two. For Hegel spirit is then the underlying structured movement of thought common to and undergirding, or occurring in and through, what today might be distinguished as either more monosubjectivally formulated movements of thought or intersubjectivally structured encounters resulting in a sense of wholeness and integration. He carried this philosophical generalization to the point where, in his philosophy of religion, he constructed the concept of God as a movement of inclusive divine subjectivity from an initial unity to a moment of self-differentiation on to an overcoming of this alienating self-differentiation in a renewed and enriched unity or advance as moment of integration. God was for Hegel this movement of spirit as a movement of differentiating and integrating conceptual thought.

What seems to have motivated Hegel in the elaboration of his philosophy of religion as, what we called in Chapter One above, a post-Kantian philosophical theology was his pervasive concern, expressed almost everywhere throughout his mature philosophy, both duly to recognize and then finally to overcome the various forms of alienation he saw present in his day or looming on the horizon. He felt it was important to recognize and accept the already existing, or at least potentially threatening, reality of alienating tension in the individual, political, social, cultural and religious spheres of life. Within his own philosophical context he saw such divisive tensions given paradigmatic formulation in Kant's dualist philosophy, which could not finally reconcile either the knowledge of phenomena with noumenal reality or the awareness of the self with the really available presence of the other. He acknowledged these tensions and immersed himself fully in them, but refused to allow either them or Kant's philosophy to be the final word. Learning particularly from Fichte's attempt to overcome the Kantian dichotomy, Hegel built upon what he saw as the earlier mentioned distinguishing function of thought to account for the necessary presence of alienation. Thinking through the moment of selfhood gave rise to the moment of otherness. He likewise built upon the previously mentioned integrative function of thought. Adequately thinking through otherness led to the realization that the other was the other of the self. Thus Hegel overcame any such alienating distinction and separation by stressing that the two were related and, finally, brought together in the moment of unifying thought. He proposed an absolute idealism or movement of self-positing thought that gave rise to the other and then recognized that this other was the other of the self. What he tried to do was to integrate the thinking of distinction and difference into his overall movement of spirit, which then became a threefold movement from initial unity to distinguishing or separation on to the overcoming of this difference and separation. He built upon the integrating function of thought to account for the drive toward wholeness and integration he recognized as characteristic of the human person and of religious communities.

Given Hegel's heavy thrust toward, and one could say privileging of the value of, wholeness and integration, it is finally impossible to distinguish completely among three questions that one might legitimately ask of Hegel: what did he say in his philosophical theology; how did he work out that philosophical theology; and, why did he find it necessary in effect to transform philosophy of religion into such a philosophical theology, indeed, a philosophy of God. Ultimately the answer to all three of these questions is his realization that the true infinite must include the finite, otherwise the infinite is reduced to another finite alongside finitude. To conceive of God as infinite, Hegel had to think God and the human or, more widely, the finite, together.

He did indeed recognize the omnipresent reality of alienation, and especially internal human self-alienation as well as the alienation characteristic of the relationship between human and divine. He wanted to overcome these and all other forms of alienation. This he did by making it a necessary moment in the movement of spirit as movement of distinguishing and reconciling

or mediating thought. This distinguishing and reconciling or mediating movement of spirit found its religious expression in a philosophically reinterpreted
concept of Trinity, as we saw in Chapter Two above. Hegel interpreted the
second "person" of the Trinity as the paradigmatic, necessary moment of
alienation or crucifixion and death within the wider movement of divine
subjectivity as one of self-othering and enriched, advancing return. This
movement of spirit found its overall philosophical expression in the totality
of Hegel's mature or encyclopedic philosophy. As we noted in Chapter One
above, Hegel's whole philosophy was indeed a unique philosophical theology
beginning and ending in his reinterpreted concept of God because it, namely,
his philosophy as a whole, was formulated as the very movement and indeed
the development of God. In and through the development of human conceptual thought God moves toward, and is then the accomplishment of, that
wholeness and integration that is the overcoming of the alienation between
world and God.

In addition to this overall richness and complexity of Hegel's philosophy
of religion, there are many reasons why that philosophy of religion remains
of great interest today. One of these reasons is certainly Hegel's claim to have
developed an inclusive philosophy. Philosophy and theology continue to be
fascinated by, and often to resist, Hegel's claim to have developed a philosophy in principle open to and able to account for the totality of reality. Hegel
insists that his formulation of the dynamic movement of spirit underlies all of
reality and contains a place for all within it. In fact, given Hegel's claim to
inclusiveness, it would be hard for anyone attempting to work out a contemporary philosophical theology to do an end-run around his philosophy. His
claim to inclusiveness cannot simply be set aside. It remains and must be dealt
with more directly.

We should return to the question of Hegel's fascination with alienation
and with reconciliation or mediation. These are surely themes as important
and fundamental today as they were in his own. Indeed, because of him they
are perhaps more important and more fundamental now than they were close
to two centuries ago. We should also note his conviction concerning the
continuing importance of the notion of subjectivity, not of course any one-
sided and inadequate notion but, rather, his proposal that otherness itself in
its ultimate and inclusive formulation will take the form of a movement of

inclusive subjectivity. In an initial way we can refer to some of the strengths of Hegel's position by saying that he has wedded the notion of subjectivity with that of the true infinite which is, by definition, inclusive of the finite. It is surely this post-Kantian version of the infinite as infinite or inclusive subjectivity that will prove, when appropriately modified, the key to a proposed post-Hegelian renewal of the philosophy of religion as a philosophical theology.

Hegel's own formulation of the true infinite as movement of absolute or inclusive subjectivity has, however, been the subject of much debate and critique. This ongoing discussion has contributed to surfacing a number of what could be called weaknesses in Hegel's thought. Briefly stated, as we will see in somewhat more detail below, these weaknesses can be divided into those arising more from philosophically based and argued objections to Hegel's formulation of the movement of spirit and those arising, even if often argued philosophically, more directly out of concerns for religious adequacy.

Among the more philosophically based hesitations concerning Hegel's concept of spirit there are concerns for adequacy and for internal coherence. With regard to adequacy, time and again philosophers, and theologians working philosophically, have tried to indicate various aspects of reality (with "reality" used here in a very loose sense) that do not seem to find a place in Hegel's philosophical system. However, often such arguments do not in themselves seem convincing. Hegel has so constructed his formal concept of spirit that it is possible for him to integrate almost anything into his system. There are, though, several more specific philosophical objections concerning the adequacy of his philosophy of religion or, rather, its inadequacy, to the phenomenon of religion as such and of the plurality of religions that would seem to prove more convincing. These inadequacies would indicate certain possible weaknesses in his thought. Among such inadequacies I would simply mention here, with others to be treated shortly below, the fact that, without further nuance, it does not seem possible, as Hegel tries to do, to define religion solely or even primarily as a movement of thought. Furthermore, despite great flexibility in the working out of his various lecture presentations on the non-Christian religions, he insists time and again that the history of religions follows in a certain chronological order according to the logical development of thought determinations such as being, nothing, becoming, and so forth, as they are developed in his *Science of Logic*. Put rather bluntly, this aspect of Hegel's philosophy of religion does not seem to interpret the history of religions correctly.

Among the more religiously based, though often philosophically as well as religiously expressed, hesitations concerning Hegel's concept of spirit are concerns for the ways in which Hegel deals with the questions of evil, freedom, and mystery. These concerns are directly rooted in and arise out of his insistence that spirit is a movement of conceptual thought available to and occurring in human thought. While, on the one hand Hegel was, within his post-Kantian philosophical context, pretty well cornered into conceiving of God as a movement of thought, on the other hand he seems to think he had to accept, and indeed revels in, the concept of a God whose development is fully transparent to the human mind. Consequently, God's development had to proceed along logically necessary lines. Within such a movement, evil becomes a necessary moment in this process of divine self-development. It is in fact the perceived loss of the sense of mystery, the redefinition of divine freedom as logically necessary movement of thought, and the relativizing of evil by setting it within a wider dialectical development that constitute the essence of the religious objection, at least from a Christian perspective, to Hegel's particular concept of God as spirit.

Important Contributions by Hegel

One could distill many important philosophical insights from Hegel's constructive history of the development of spirit. Indicating a number of them in order then to profit from them will further justify speaking of working *with* Hegel on an understanding of spirit and Trinity while also wanting to go *beyond* his own position to formulate a post-Hegelian philosophical theology. I would, in effect, like to prolong, while also giving a course correction to, the trajectory he sketched from Descartes to his own philosophy. Here and in the rest of the present chapter as well as in the chapters that follow, we will be working, perhaps in a more initial way, toward doing for our day something of what he attempted for his own. In light especially of remarks made in Chapter Two above, we need now simply recall several of Hegel's many important philosophical insights.

Among these many insights we can highlight four notions or, perhaps better, clusters of notions which are of particular present importance. There is, first of all, Hegel's insistence that one begin with an initial unity of thought and being. Though his location of this initial unity as first moment of a dynamic movement of pure thought proves problematic, it should be possible to recoup his insight into the importance of an initial unity by relocating that unity. The second point to be underscored is the importance of continuing to work with an appropriately formulated notion of subjectivity. Hegel has taught that the movement of subjectivity must be dynamic and developmental. He has likewise pointed out the central role of otherness in any adequate understanding of subjectivity. He has, furthermore, stressed the importance of both spontaneity and receptivity in the relationship between self and other. It should be possible for us to give further prominence to the notion of otherness and, consequently, to restructure the relationship between self and other in a wider and more flexible notion of subjectivity. The third point is Hegel's development of the true infinite, which as we have mentioned is the infinite inclusive of finitude. Hegel has gone a long way toward showing that finitude is self-contradictory when considered in itself and not in relation to an inclusive infinite.[1] He has indicated the importance of working not only with an initial unity but also with a final or inclusive unity. The problem remains one of formulating our understanding of that inclusive unity in such a way as not to diminish the otherness of the other. The fourth insight on which we need to focus is Hegel's identification of the epistemological and the ontological. Bringing up the question of this identification is, to some extent, to recapitulate Hegel's three previously mentioned contributions: initial unity; dynamic movement of subjectivity; the true infinite. Hegel wanted to argue these three notions, and indeed his whole philosophy, in the public realm. But his way of going about the identification of epistemological and ontological in the logical remains problematic. Though in itself brilliant and creative, the way in which he identifies thought and being appears somewhat narrow and restrictive to many now in the first years of the 21st century. There should be other ways to continue some form of identification of these two, namely, thought and being or epistemological and ontological in a more widely conceived movement of spirit.

The Problematic Character of Hegel's Philosophical Theology

Though the immense sweep of Hegel's thought on God as spirit continues to fascinate and even, at times, to convince, there has emerged over the past century and a half a certain consensus with regard to possible weaknesses in his conception of philosophical theology. Brilliant and inclusive as his dialectical interpretation of Trinity and his overall proposal of a philosophical theology are, they nevertheless prove problematic to many.

After having briefly noted in more preliminary fashion one or the other of Hegel's possible weaknesses and then reviewed some of the strengths of Hegel's position, now in a further reflection we need to note more explicitly several difficulties that can be raised in relation to Hegel's interpretation of Trinity as dialectical movement of spirit. We can group these difficulties in two areas, following our previously mentioned distinction among various difficulties or hesitations. First, those more generally relating to his resultant interpretation of Trinity and constituting more religiously based hesitations, raised of course as well by philosophers, concerning his overall philosophical theology and his concept of God as spirit. Second, some more philosophically based difficulties or hesitations relating more directly to the underlying concept of spirit or absolute subjectivity with which he is working.

A number of critiques have been offered concerning Hegel's dialectical interpretation of Trinity. These generally take as their point of reference and comparison mainstream Christian trinitarian theological traditions. It has, for example, been suggested that Hegel works with a merely monosubjectival and reverse subordinationist formulation of Trinity. Father and Son are not fully free and equal moments in the movement of spirit. Only the last or inclusive moment is fully personal. Or again, that he has confused and falsely integrated Trinity and creation. Others have strongly opposed the notion of sin he proposes in conjunction with his interpretation of Trinity as dialectical movement of differentiation and enriched return. They argue that dialectical separation cannot be considered the essence of sin and evil. However, from the perspective of our present concerns perhaps the most fundamental objections raised against Hegel's interpretation of Trinity revolve around the notions of divine freedom and of God as mystery.

As I indicated at the beginning of the previous chapter, those responsible for the classical Christian formulations of Trinity made great efforts to preserve divine and human freedom. And Hegel himself laid extremely strong emphasis on the importance of freedom, which he defined essentially as self-determination. However, the way in which he worked out his concept of freedom in relation to Trinity remains questionable. We can see the problematic nature of his understanding of divine freedom with particular clarity when we consider that understanding in relation to the way in which he interprets creation as appearance of the divine idea as nature and finite spirit. We can succinctly summarize his stance regarding creation, and thus concerning the initial relationship between God and world, by referring to the last paragraph of his *Science of Logic*, where he describes the transition from logic to the philosophy of nature.[2] There he writes quite eloquently of the "free self-release" of the concept into nature. Traditionally, and surely due at least partially to a certain Neoplatonic influence, Christian theologies tended to explain creation as an act flowing out of the divine fullness. And in one sense Hegel also uses this reasoning to explain the transition from logic to nature or, we could say with certain qualifications, from God to world. For Hegel does see the absolute idea at the end of the *Logic* as the culmination of the process of self-positing thought. Within the realm of logical thought, the absolute idea is moment of fullness as end result inclusive of the process. However, what is for Hegel the motor force bringing on the transition to nature or the philosophy of nature is not this fullness and richness of the absolute idea as such. Rather, it is the logically formulated absolute idea's renewed immediacy, namely, its own lacking in relation to that reality which can be realized only through differentiation into the realms of nature and finite spirit. So, in Hegel's philosophy the transition from logic to nature and finite spirit, which is paradigmatic of the transition from "immanent" Trinity to created world, is not directly rooted in overflowing abundance but in need. Furthermore, the transition becomes a necessary one since thought cannot remain with the immediacy of logic.

Another problematic aspect of Hegel's overall dialectical interpretation of Trinity to which we should call attention is the question of divine mystery. This question is intimately linked with the previous consideration of the reason Hegel gives for there being a world and finite spirit. The triune God conceived as spirit is, in Hegel's philosophy, the movement of self-positing conceptual thought. God is God self this movement of thought occurring in and through finite spirit as thinking being. And it is true that Hegel understands finite spirit to be taken up into the movement of absolute spirit. But if God is reconceptualized as this movement of conceptual thought occurring in and through finite thought, God becomes conceptually transparent to that finite thought. It then seems difficult to speak of divine mystery when the movement of God as conceptual thought is made available in such a transparent way. At this point the problematic character of divine freedom and of divine mystery in Hegel's philosophy meld into one overall question of the necessitarian character of the movement of logical thought. Hegel insists that thought moves forward or progresses in necessary fashion,[3] with the end result that divine freedom and mystery become for Hegel the transparency of the necessary self-determination of conceptual thought.

To bring together these remarks concerning more religiously based hesitations concerning Hegel's philosophical theology, we can say that they involve concerns for the way in which Hegel deals with the questions of evil, freedom and mystery. For Hegel, God's development had to occur along logically necessary lines. The consequent relativizing of evil as necessary moment within a wider dialectical development, the redefinition of divine freedom as logically necessary movement of thought and the perceived loss of the sense of mystery constitute the essence of the religious objection, at least from a more traditional Christian perspective, to Hegel's particular concept of God as spirit.[4]

A number of more philosophically formulated critiques have likewise been levelled directly against various aspects of Hegel's underlying concept of spirit or absolute subjectivity. Some of these concerns parallel in various ways the previously indicated more theological hesitations concerning Hegel's interpretation of Trinity. One of these more philosophically formulated concerns that seems to come back quite often is the hesitation to accept negation as the single essential characteristic of otherness. Identifying otherness with negation has indeed allowed Hegel to respond to a number of difficult issues before him. One of these issues was the twofold problem, first, of the Kantian subject that alone actively bestows unity on the object in virtue of the object's being thought and, second, of the contradictory Kantian notion of knowledge of an unknowable "thing in itself." Hegel's identification of otherness with negation enabled him to eliminate, we could say, the thing in itself. It likewise allowed him to acknowledge that the subject or self is not just a unifying or imposing moment. Rather, the subject or self is also, and most importantly, the result of the object's having been thought.[5] Hegel could assert this since the moment of otherness as negation is to be thought through first as negation of the original affirmation and then negation of its own negation or resultant positive. According to Hegel, the movement of spirit is one from initial subjectivity (affirmation) through objectivity or otherness (negation) resulting in inclusive subjectivity (negation of negation).

This formulation of a generalized and dialectically structured phenomenological movement is indeed impressive. Nevertheless, since Hegel's day many have continued to express serious hesitations concerning the very heart of this dialectic, namely, concerning his identification of otherness and negation. They ask if this identification is adequate to the various dimensions of otherness as such. Hegel had defined otherness in terms of negation in order to integrate it into his ultimately inclusive movement of spirit. But otherness as such and in its widest sense is surely equally primordially, and not sequentially, both "not myself" and possible source of enrichment. It has a doubled, that is, negative and positive, character and cannot thus be defined, even initially, in terms of negation alone.

Perhaps Hegel himself sensed this difficulty, for he immediately recalls that negation is negation *of* an initial identity. On the basis of this renewed attention to a negative in tension with a prior positive, he then moves on to a renewed positive. However, the focus on negation as essential characteristic of otherness might be more culturally and temporally conditioned than Hegel suspected, or at least let on. As was just mentioned, otherness or difference certainly bears within itself a note of negation as "difference from." But, depending on the context, it would often if not always seem to bear an at least equally primordial and essential characteristic as positive. Otherness would seem not only to be, to use one of Hegel's phrases, the moment of diremption or going over into but equally, and not dialectically subsequently, that from which one can receive.

Again with regard to adequacy, Hegel's interpretation of religion as movement of conceptual thought does not seem to have taken sufficiently into account the many levels at which an individual or a community is religious. Also, for the sake of completeness, we could mention again that such an interpretation does not seem to correspond to the actual history of religions when it presents that history as progressing in a certain chronological order in one way or another linked to the logical development of thought determinations as presented in Hegel's *Science of Logic*.[6]

Finally, there are hesitations concerning the internal coherence of Hegel's philosophical theology in its widest formulation. I have previously argued that there are at least three points where Hegel cannot convincingly present his philosophy, and particularly his philosophy of religion, as a philosophical theology.[7]

These are, first of all, his philosophy's beginning in the initial logical thought determination of pure being (*reines Sein*). There is great difficulty surrounding the thought determination of pure being as first moment of pure thought in Hegel's encyclopedic system.

Hegel argues that the movement of logical or pure thought begins with pure being as its initial moment.[8] It is the initial and unexplicated unity of thought and being and is likewise beyond the distinctions of subjectivity and objectivity or form and content. It is simply the beginning of and initial moment in the movement of logical or pure thought. The logic of Hegel's overall philosophical position forces him to assert both that pure being is a totally empty and initial thought determination and yet that it is the first thought determination in the movement of pure thought itself. Pure being is both empty beginning and initial moment of conceptual thought. But to affirm that such an initial moment of conceptual thought is available in some way to finite thinking is quite problematic. On the one hand, Hegel cannot appeal to direct intuition, since this would throw his thought into the realm of the subjective, understood here as "merely" subjective. And he wishes at all costs to argue in the public realm of reflexively available conceptual thought. On the other hand, to affirm that one can think through a totally empty thought determination on the level of conceptual thought does not seem possible. In fact Hegel uses this very difficulty to move immediately to the next thought determination, namely, that of "nothing." But simply proposing the transition to the next thought category does not resolve the difficulty of thinking a totally empty thought determination on the level of conceptual thought. Such a completely indeterminate and contentless initial moment in the movement of pure thought cannot be thought by finite thought or spirit and is thus not available to human thinking.

Second, and much more briefly now, we can note that Hegel tries especially in his *Phenomenology of Spirit* to argue to the immediate religious perception of the divine-human unity which is the historical Christ.[9] I would propose that any such affirmation of an immediate perception is a reading back into a specific historical situation of a dogmatic position taken centuries after the appearance of what Hegel refers to as the divine-human unity.

Third, he structures his understanding of the Christian or spiritual community according to a syllogistic form of divine self-mediation that cannot be justified by recourse to the syllogistic form in question.[10] In that syllogistic form the proposed logical movement from universal to particular to individual is in fact a movement from universal to individuals. The syllogistically structured form of self-mediation that was to have taken place between divine and human in the Christian community cannot be argued on the basis of an analysis of the structure of the syllogistic movement proposed by Hegel as structuring the communitarian reconciliation of divine and human just before the final mediation of the two in philosophical thought.

These hesitations regarding adequacy and coherence, which identify what I would call weaknesses in the structure and movement of the overall philosophical theology Hegel proposed, force us, while learning from his strengths and overall insight into the nature of inclusive divine subjectivity as the "true infinite," to try to go beyond him.

Indeed, Hegel does give reasons for the overall position he takes in working out his philosophy as the culmination of the history of thought up to his own day. He reasons out every move that he makes. At each step along the way, either in the development of his encyclopedic system or in his reading of the history of philosophy, he tries to argue his concept of spirit as structured movement of self-positing conceptual thought in the form of an inclusive and absolute subjectivity. But questions concerning the final success of his proposal still arise both from within the context of his own formulations and due to concerns raised by and insights offered in the history of philosophy since Hegel's day. Along with more general theological hesitations concerning his dialectical interpretation of Trinity, these questions, which point out several problematic aspects of his philosophy, provide the springboard for a contemporary reformulation of his notion of spirit. In so doing, these more internal questions as well as various post-Hegelian concerns and insights push toward a reconceptualization of Trinity and spirit that will take the form of a post-Hegelian philosophical theology.

Going Beyond Hegel

Hegel then rightly appreciated the overall drive beyond alienation toward wholeness and integration characteristic of the human person and particularly of religious communities. He interpreted this drive as the dynamic movement of spirit understood both as process and as result inclusive of that process. He realized that this dynamic movement was more than merely the human hunger for fulfilment. It was a manifestation of the more fundamental dynamic development of the very source and object of that hunger. In light of this realization, he constructed a philosophical theology that included necessary reference both to the divine and to the human, with the latter considered individually and in community.

This bringing together of a concern for wholeness and integration with a dynamic, inclusive concept of spirit enabled Hegel to work out a philosophy of religion that remains unique within the history of philosophy and theology. As was indicated in Chapter One above, his philosophy of religion, indeed his overall philosophical system, was in fact a philosophical theology, that is, a philosophically argued presentation of the development of God as movement of trinitarian divine subjectivity occurring in and through human thought. God was, then, for Hegel the movement of conceptually expressed divine subjectivity inclusive of the world as necessary moment within that movement. God was a movement of spirit understood as a dialectical movement of conceptual thought, a dynamic variant on Aristotle's notion of God as self-thinking thought.[11]

Taking a Cue from Gadamer

After reviewing the problematic character, problematic from both philosophical and more explicitly religious perspectives, of Hegel's own philosophical theology and, thus, noting why it is necessary to go beyond Hegel, we turn to the question of how to do so.

Over the years I began to think over the possibility of reworking Hegel's concept of inclusive divine subjectivity as true infinite in terms of a movement of experience rather than of thought. Structuring the true infinite as a movement of experience seemed to make it possible to correct a number of perceived weaknesses in Hegel's concept of spirit. It would allow for a greater sense of mystery, a more independent status to otherness, a less restrictive reading of the nature of religion now in terms of experience rather than in terms of thought, and so forth.

Then a few years ago I came upon Hans-Georg Gadamer who, in his *Truth and Method*,[12] proposed to rehabilitate what Hegel had called the bad infinite or infinite progression, and this by means of appeal to a notion of experience defined in terms of language. Needless to say, Gadamer's proposal immediately caught my attention. I was quite aware that Hegel had worked with at least three understandings of the infinite. He had refused to accept as finally adequate the notion of an abstract infinite set over against finitude since such an infinite simply became another finite. He also, and quite vehemently, had refused to acknowledge as adequate on its own the notion of an infinite progression that for him, rather, when appropriately thought through would finally resolve itself into the true infinite inclusive of finitude. Gadamer wanted to get away from this idea of a true infinite or an absolute knowledge as final, totalizing moment. As mentioned, he proposed to remain with an infinite progression that took the form of an open-ended series of linguistically constituted experiences.

Gadamer's proposal represented a major step in the direction I wanted to follow. It did not, however, seem to take adequately into consideration what Hegel had appreciated, namely, the religious striving for, and in a religious experience one's at least momentary realization of, a sense of wholeness and integration. To take this striving for and experience of fulfilment adequately into account, and in fact to take into account the reality of spirit as both dynamic movement and result, it seemed to me important to rehabilitate not only Hegel's bad or false infinite but also his true or inclusive infinite. Furthermore, after some reflection and after reading a critique by Benoît Garceau,[13] I could no longer accept Gadamer's effectively identifying experience and language, a point to which I would like to return in Chapter Four below. It became clear that if one wished to work out a post-Hegelian philosophical theology, it would be necessary to go beyond both Hegel's working with thought and Gadamer's working with language to a more pragmatist under-standing of experience, taken in its own right, and to a more open notion of the true or inclusive infinite.

Ironically it is with something like this more pragmatist understanding of experience that we are left, structurally speaking, when we make a critique of Hegel's proposal to begin the movement of spirit in the unity of pure thought. What we end up with is no longer the concept of spirit essentially as a self-othering and enriched advancing return. We do keep the affirmation of an initial unity, but now that unity is the givenness of the relationship be-tween selfhood and otherness.[14] This is certainly the point of departure for any more pragmatically oriented consideration of the structure and movement of experience as a movement from initial selfhood and otherness, in relation-ship, on to resultant enriched or impoverished selfhood. We should note in a preliminary way that enrichment here means "qualitative increment or more" and impoverishment refers to "qualitative reduction or loss." With Gadamer we are able to acknowledge that this movement of experience is a form of growth or becoming, indeed a becoming ever ongoing in its finite and open-ended tetradic formulation as a movement from initial selfhood and other-ness, in relationship, to either enriched or impoverished selfhood again renewedly serving as initial selfhood in relationship with otherness, what Hegel would have called the "bad" infinite. The challenge then remains, in a post-Hegelian move that has truly learnt from Hegel, to develop a more open, true infinite inclusive of this tetradically structured movement of finite experi-ence.

Contours of a Post-Hegelian Christian Philosophical Theology

First Remarks on the Movement of Spirit. The direct response to the ques-tion we have been examining, namely, of how to proceed in going beyond Hegel is: replace his concept of spirit as a movement of dialectically develop-ing inclusive thought with a notion of spirit as movement of enriching experi-ence. So the concern for how to proceed in going beyond Hegel develops into a consideration of what would be the contours of a post-Hegelian philosophical theology built on the basis of a notion of spirit as such a movement of enriching experience.

Briefly stated, in contrast to Hegel's proposal to move, from the point of view of his system, from an initial or abstract form of the infinite to the finite to a renewed and inclusive infinite, a post-Hegelian philosophical theology will move, in a wide sense, from finite to infinite which latter respectfully includes that finite. In its logical formulation, such a move will occur as a multiform analysis of the movement of finite enriching experience leading to the conclusion, through further reflection on the structure and movement of that experience, that such a finite movement requires the wider context of an infinite or inclusive movement of enriching experience within which it occurs. As we will see in Part Three below, in its more religious formulation such a move will occur first of all as a phenomenological analysis of the basic structure and movement, occurring in a Christian context, of a human experience of God, whether that experience occur as the experience of a community, as the shared experience of a couple or of friends, or as the experience of an individual person. This analysis will be followed by a further philosophical reflection on the move from finite to infinite. This finite point of departure, the overall Christian experience of God, will then allow us to reflect as well in a further phenomenological analysis on the experience of God taken in a more subjective sense as the true infinite, with this true infinite understood as God's experience of our finite reality. To rehabilitate both Hegel's bad infinite, here in its form as infinite progression, and his true or inclusive infinite, it will be necessary to speak of the genitive in the phrase "experience of God" as both objective and subjective.

The brief reference made earlier in the present chapter to some of Hegel's important philosophical contributions and to hesitations concerning the viability of his conception of spirit and of Trinity have already enabled us to shed light on the contours of a more widely conceived notion of spirit. Moreover, they themselves become stepping stones toward a revision of Hegel's reading of the relation between subjectivity and objectivity or, better, between self and other. For example, if we see the placing of initial unity as first moment in a movement of self-positing thought as problematic, it is because "initial unity" has been misplaced. Hegel's thought determination of pure being, as pure implicitness, is an unwarranted speculative generalization from the phenomenological reading of the movement of finite thought. Initial unity is in fact both psychologically and philosophically rather to be located between self and other. Initial unity is not to be located logically or phenomenologically prior to the distinction between self and other, and then seen as giving rise to them, but is simply the initial given relationship between them. Initial unity is the initial givenness of the relation between self and other, whether that relation be one between communities, communities and individual selves, between couples or groups of friends, between couples or friends, on one hand, and individual selves, on the other, between individual selves, or (with certain caveats) within the thinking self.

When one begins an analysis with this initially given relationship between self and other as point of departure, otherness is no longer seen at first only as "momentary" negation of initial unity. Otherness is equally primordial constitutive pole in the relationship between self and other. Hegel had of course rightly seen that the relation between self and other is dynamic and developmental. But now spontaneity and receptivity become, in principle at least, ways of functioning characteristic both of self and of other. In a sense, then, every experience in a more formal sense involves "enrichment" or, perhaps better, "development" insofar as it involves a form of progression beyond a starting point. Nevertheless, contrary to Hegel's reading, the result of the relationship can, while formally speaking indeed constituting a development, be either negative or positive. The relationship can be either impoverishing or enriching. The result of the relationship between self and other can be one either of disintegration or of integration. The result is either an impoverished or an enriched self. As we will note in more detail in Chapter Six below, impoverishment can come from the side either of self or of other, or from both. Indeed, enrichment comes primarily from the presence of the other to the self. For enriched selfhood is respectfully included otherness that, as we will see, occurs paradoxically through self-gift.

This dynamic movement from the initial givenness of a relationship between self and other to an enriched or impoverished self, whether that self be communal, shared or individual, is a form of becoming. It is no longer Hegel's concept of becoming as movement essentially from implicit to explicit. Rather, it is a movement of becoming either as qualitative loss or again as qualitative increment, as disintegration or integration, as impoverishment or enrichment. The shifting of the location of initial unity from a first moment, which would be prior to differentiation, to being the givenness of a relationship between self and other allows for the introduction of real newness into the dynamic movement of becoming that true selfhood is. It allows otherness to be not only negatively related, as non-self, to initial selfhood, but also, and at least equally, positively related to selfhood as possible source of enrichment.

In order to simplify the discussion, it will be necessary for the present moment to leave to one side consideration of impoverishment in order to concentrate on qualitative increment or enrichment. Given this simplification, we can say that what has been described so far in our initial sketching out of the contours of a post-Hegelian notion of spirit and, by extension, a philosophical interpretation of Trinity is a movement of becoming from initial selfhood in relation to otherness on to resultant enriched selfhood. However, in order to recognize the reality of this movement in its finite manifestation as enriching growth, it is important to recall that in such manifestation resultant enriched selfhood is equally initial selfhood again in relationship with recurrent otherness. This process of enriching becoming is itself ongoing. And, when it occurs, the enrichment through respectfully included otherness is, in everyday experience, always only partial and temporary.

In this proposal, finite spirit is no longer considered primarily a movement of conceptual thought. Nor is it simply a product of language. It is wider than a movement either of thought or of language and, as movement, includes them both. Thought (*Denken*) would seem to be the fundamental category with which much German philosophy has been more at home, and language (*langage*) a fundamental philosophical category in French-speaking milieus. But in the English-speaking world, and increasingly in the German and French as well as other language contexts, it is only the notion of experience, with what we might call its at least implicit North American pragmatist conditioning, that is coming to be seen as wide enough to express this encompassing or inclusive movement of becoming here considered, for the moment, as qualitative increment. It is only this notion of experience, taken as relationship, process and result, that can express adequately for today the movement of spirit as one of qualitative increment or enrichment. For it is only this notion of experience that can cover enrichment both in its finite and in its infinite realizations without subordinating either of them to an unacceptable overarching paradigm of the type that would infringe on the infinite and on the difference of the true infinite from the finite.

As I will argue more fully in Parts Two and Three below, experience, as movement of enrichment or qualitative increment, is in its finite realization a movement of becoming or enriching growth as initial selfhood and otherness in relationship resulting in enriched selfhood that is equally renewedly initial selfhood in relationship with recurrent otherness. In its infinite realization experience is a movement whose formal structure is a movement of becoming or enrichment as initial selfhood and otherness in relationship resulting in enriched selfhood.

This initial contemporary reformulation of spirit no longer presents the inclusive movement of spirit as a movement of dynamic self-positing conceptual thought. Thought and language remain of course ways in which the here proposed reconstructed movement of finite spirit takes place. And spirit remains the development of selfhood. But finite spirit is now seen as tetradically structured movement of experience as qualitative increment or enriching growth. Infinite or absolute spirit becomes triadically structured movement of experience, pure qualitative increment or enrichment without the external limitation of recurrent otherness. Concerns that have arisen after and in reaction to Hegel, and even the so-called post-modern concerns, have necessitated a shift in the location of initial unity and a consequent reemphasis on the role of otherness as possible source of enrichment. In this new formulation of the notion of spirit, experience itself, whether in its finite or in its infinite realization, is relation, process, and result. It is no longer simply that from which thought abstracts or that in which thought expresses itself. Rather, these here proposed fundamental adaptations of Hegel's concept of spirit now allow for the resituating of thought within the context of this widened notion of spirit, with the latter understood as movement of enriching experience. Reflexive conceptual thought takes on the possibility of functioning in a variety of forms as privileged monosubjectival formulation of the structure and movement of finite experience. Thought's reflexive character allows it to provide a series of never-ending perspectival looks at, and conditioning expressions of, the wider movement of experience. When compared with this more specific understanding of thought as reflexive, monosubjectival and perspectival, finite experience itself and as such comes to be seen as manifesting more the character of an intersubjectival encounter—as long as the word encounter is not taken here to imply a merely psychologizing reading of fully formed and perduring selves entering into various relationships. The here proposed more North American and quasi-pragmatist reformulation of Hegel's concept of spirit as movement of experience acknowledges more effectively the ongoing reality of finite becoming. Finite becoming is no longer negative "moment" in the movement that Hegel called the true or inclusive infinite. It is ongoing point of departure for reference to, and reflection on, the true infinite. This reformulation of Hegel's concept of spirit also implies that there is a dialectical aspect to the dialogically structured relationship between finite becoming as such and the movement of infinite becoming.[15] The movement of infinite becoming forms the inclusive context within which finite becoming can perdure as movement both of qualitative increment and of limitation. The arising of the "more" that constitutes real but limited qualitative increment or enriching growth ultimately points to and calls for the affirmation of an inclusive movement of experience in which otherness occurs not as a recurrent principle or source both of enrichment and of limitation but as source of overall enrichment.

First Remarks on Trinity. After highlighting several of Hegel's important philosophical insights, then noting hesitations concerning the viability of his philosophical theology as he formulated it, and thereafter proposing an initial, general reformulation of his concept of spirit that we will followed up on and further develop in Chapters Six and Seven below, we can now continue in an equally initial way with a more explicit, yet still programmatic, philosophical reflection on Trinity. We will do this by trying to look with Hegel toward a philosophical formulation of Trinity lying beyond, but also in a certain continuity with, his own position. Hegel had interpreted Trinity as a movement of inclusive or absolute divine subjectivity in the form of self-positing conceptual thought. Here we propose to maintain his identification of Trinity with a movement of spirit as inclusive divine subjectivity. However, in line with our effort to work toward a reformulation of his concept of spirit, we will in Part Three below, and especially in Chapter Seven, present an interpretation of Trinity as movement of spirit with spirit now understood in terms of, and as movement of, enriching experience. It is no longer a question of interpreting divine life and love as the self-development of a conceptually transparent absolute. Rather, divine life is to be understood as the less directly conceptually available self-development of Trinity as movement of experience in its highest realization: the mystery of love or ongoing free self-offer.

Finite spirit[16] does not experience itself as movement simply of enrichment in its highest realization, namely, pure love, but as tetradically structured movement. Even as movement of enriching experience, finite spirit is, as I will propose in Chapter Seven below, contradictorily both enrichment or qualitative increment and limitation. The relationship between self and other results in an enriched self that finds itself, in the very moment of its enrichment, renewedly in relationship with recurrent otherness. Even in its resultant enrichment finite spirit is equally renewedly limited by the recurrent presence of the again possibly enriching other. There are then at least two approaches through which finite spirit can become aware of and reflect on that triadic context in which it can perdure as both enrichment and limitation. In a first approach, which remains in its own way in the public realm, we enter upon a more direct interpretation of the Christian doctrine of Trinity in terms of the understanding of infinite spirit as triadic movement of enriching experience. However, we can also focus more directly on a second approach to finite spirit's becoming aware of its own triadic context. That second approach remains more directly in the public realm and more available to public scrutiny. In it finite spirit can by self-reflection and analysis come to see that the very structure of enriching experience as qualitative increment, that "more" which is seen in life, should occur in principle simply as a triadic movement. The experience of enrichment is essentially a movement from initial selfhood and otherness in relationship giving rise to resultant enriched selfhood. This triadic movement is spirit as the true or inclusive infinite since there is no recurrence of otherness.[17] In line with the first approach, we will in Chapter Seven below pursue further this interpretation by means of a sort of general phenomenological presentation of a number of elements present in various ways in communal, shared or individual affirmations by Christians of an experience of Trinity. Working within specifically Christian traditions while still remaining within the public realm of discourse will allow us to elaborate a post-Hegelian philosophical theology by giving Trinity a philosophical interpretation as the loving context within which finite spirit lives and moves and has its being. In line with the second approach, we will, in a sort of reformulation of a number of the traditional proofs for the existence of God, in that same chapter argue at a more reflexive level to the need for an inclusive context to the tetradically structured movement of experience that we are.

Concluding Remarks. With our initial, more programmatic remarks on spirit and on Trinity we have gotten ahead of ourselves. However, before moving on, recapitulating why we need to go beyond Hegel's philosophical theology while profiting from it will help us recall and further specify, in a more positive fashion, several goals for the present project.

From a more religious perspective, or at least from a point of view rooted in Christian theological traditions, we can recall the importance of working toward a philosophical theology that permits an insight into evil more respectful of its obdurate character, proposes a surer sense of divine freedom and provides room for a greater sense of mystery than does Hegel's philosophical theology.[18]

From a more philosophical perspective, we will have to work out a philosophical theology that will give otherness its due, namely, one that recognizes its obdurate reality and its doubled primordial character as both positive and negative. We will want to propose a philosophical theology that can more easily consider religion in its totality as involving thought, symbol, action, feeling, and so forth without necessarily defining all such aspects of religion in terms of thought.

Again, from a more philosophical perspective, we should recall that the crucial question with regard to internal coherence was Hegel's inability, judged according to his own criteria, to establish a first moment of pure thought available to conceptually expressed human thought. It was with and from this initial unity that Hegel proposed to launch his dialectical development of spirit as a movement of thought from identity to difference to renewed and enriched identity. A post-Hegelian philosophical theology will need to establish a new starting point for a renewed understanding of God as inclusive movement of spirit.

We are now ready and indeed need, in the following Part Two, to spell out a fuller understanding of experience. In Chapter Four we will review several understandings of experience then, in Chapter Five, work out in more detail a grammar of experience and, in Chapter Six, develop a phenomenology of experience in order to establish an appropriate understanding of enriching and impoverishing experience before going on, in Part Three, to propose a post-Hegelian philosophical theology in the form of a movement of inclusive divine subjectivity as enriching experience or spirit.

NOTES

1. On Hegel's notions of finitude, false infinite and true infinite, see the Appendix, "Hegel's Finite and Infinite," to the present volume.
2. *Gesammelte Werke*, vol. 12: *Wissenschaft der Logik, Zweiter Band: Die subjektive Logik 1816)*, ed. Friedrich Hogemann and Walter Jaeschke (Hamburg: Meiner, 1981) 253 lines 11–34/*Hegel's Science of Logic*, trans. A. V. Miller (New York: Humanities, 1969) 843–844.
3. *Gesammelte Werke*, vol. 21: *Wissenschaft der Logik, Erster Band: Die objektive Logik 1832)*, ed. Friedrich Hogemann and Walter Jaeschke (Hamburg: Meiner, 1985) 48 lines 18–21/*Hegel's Science of Logic* 63; *Vorlesungen: Ausgewählte Nachschriften und Manuskripte*, vol. 9: *Vorlesungen über die Geschichte der Philosophie, Teil 4: Philosophie des Mittelalters und der neueren Zeit*, ed. Pierre Garniron and Walter Jaeschke (Hamburg: Meiner, 1986) 188 lines 528–529 and 546–548/*Lectures on the History of Philosophy. The Lectures of 1825–1826*, vol. 3: *Medieval and Modern Philosophy*, ed. Robert F. Brown, trans. Robert F. Brown and J. M. Stewart with the assistance of H. S. Harris (Berkeley: University of California Press, 1990) (the pages of the German edition are helpfully provided in the outer margins of the English translation).
4. Without necessarily attributing these specific concerns to him, regarding various points of critique of Hegel's philosophy, one could do well to consult, for example, Franz Anton Staudenmaier, *Darstellung und Kritik des Hegelschen Systems. Aus dem Standpunkte der christlichen Philosophie* (Mainz: Kupferberg, 1844; reprint ed. Frankfurt am Main: Minerva, 1966).
5. Hegel's concern to give more recognition to the role of the object or other would at first seem ironic since he stresses the full constitution of the "object" by the positing subject. But it should be recalled that this "self-positing" by the subject is a "going over into" or a movement of loss of self. Hegel posits initial subjectivity as "self-sacrificial" rather than as "dominating." Regarding his desire to give more recognition than Kant did to the role of the "object" in the establishment of the self, see John E. Smith, "Hegel's Critique of Kant," in *Hegel and the History of Philosophy*, ed. J. J. O'Malley, K. W. Algozin, and F. G. Weiss (The Hague: Nijhoff, 1974) 119.
6. On the various difficulties surrounding Hegel's apparent claim that his logical ordering of determinate religions, namely, the religions of the world other than Christianity, also follows a historical ordering, see Walter Jaeschke, *Die Vernunft in der Religion. Studien zur Grundlegung der Religionsphilosophie Hegels* (Stuttgart-Bad Cannstatt: Frommann-Holzboog, 1986) 288–295/*Reason in Religion. The Foundations of Hegel's Philosophy of Religion*, trans. J. Michael Stewart and Peter C. Hodgson (Berkeley: University of California Press, 1990) 277–284, where on p. 290 of the German text and p. 280 of the English translation, he notes, as previously mentioned in Chapter One above, that Hegel's presentation of determinate religion resembles more a geography of religions than a history of religions.
7. For a fuller argument of these points with appropriate citations in Hegel's texts, see Dale M. Schlitt, *Hegel's Trinitarian Claim. A Critical Reflection* (Leiden: Brill, 1984) 74–85, 158–184 and 227–238.

    In a study that I came upon late in the writing of the present text and that is presented as a sort of *adieu* to Hegel (p. ix), Walter Desmond, in *Hegel's God. A*

Counterfeit Double (Aldershot, Hants, England: Ashgate, 2003), argues that attention must be paid to the reality itself under consideration. He writes: "Also one cannot judge Hegel just in terms of the immanent coherence of his claims. (…) rather, one must have dwelled in the ambiguous plurivocity of being religious, enacted philosophical reflection about the ultimate astonishments and perplexities there occasioned, strained one's soul to the utmost to remain true to the God that is God and that may be shown, or not shown, ambiguously or not, in this milieu of finite being. While internal instabilities and even incoherences in Hegel are not unimportant, there is something more important—fidelity to the 'matter itself' (*die Sache selbst*); fidelity that is enacted in thought that seeks to be true to the fullness of what the 'matter itself' shows" (10–11). I myself would give somewhat more importance to the effort to carry out an internal critique of Hegel's thought, which critique once worked out provides, I would think, a surer insight, along of course with a full consideration of the "matter itself," into how to go beyond Hegel. Desmond's prolonged expression of dissatisfaction with Hegel's philosophy of religion reflects and exemplifies, in many ways, a number of the hesitations indicated here in the text of the present chapter. Desmond rigorously objects to Hegel's understanding of transcendence and speaks of Hegel's movement of dialectical thought as erotic rather than agapeic. Though in his objection, I would suggest Desmond may not fully acknowledge certain aspects of Hegel's complex thought, and perhaps none of us will ever be able to do this satisfactorily, in my own estimation he does correctly point to a number of important areas of Hegel's thought, including Hegel's understanding of evil, where one would well want to hesitate, correct and go beyond by paying particular attention to the matter itself. See also Desmond's important work, *Beyond Hegel and Dialectic. Speculation, Cult, and Comedy* (Albany: State University of New York Press, 1992). For a discussion of Desmond's *Hegel's God. A Counterfeit Double*, see the issue of *The Owl of Minerva* 36/2 (2005) that is devoted to a critical reading of it. In this issue one might well note Desmond's own remarks in "Hegel's God, Transcendence, and the Counterfeit Double. A Figure of dialectical Equivocity?" 91–110. For a very impressive, more appreciative and positively apologetic reading of Hegel's philosophy of religion, see Peter C. Hodgson's masterful study, *Hegel and Christian Theology* (Oxford: Oxford University Press, 2005). Hodgson responds to Desmond explicitly on pp. 248–259. For a critical discussion of Hodgson's volume, along with helpful remarks by Hodgson himself, see *The Owl of Minerva* 37/1 (2005-2006), where the issue is devoted to a review of Hodgson's volume.

8. See Schlitt, *Hegel's Trinitarian Claim* 55–58 and 74–83.
9. See Schlitt, *Hegel's Trinitarian Claim* 146–168.
10. See Schlitt, *Hegel's Trinitarian Claim* 202–230.
11. It would seem that Hegel's rather more dynamic reading of Aristotle was due, in part at least, to the fact that his reading of Aristotle seems to have been influenced by his reading of Neoplatonic philosophers. I am grateful to Dr. Mark Nyvalt for initially drawing my attention to this possible influence.
12. *Wahrheit und Methode*, 2nd ed. (Tübingen: J. C. B. Mohr, 1965) 329–344 and 52–66, 449–452/*Truth and Method*, 2nd revised ed., trans. revised by Joel Weinsheimer and Donald G. Marshall (New York: Crossroad, 1990) 346–362 and 55–70, 474–477.
13. "L'herméneutique philosophique de H.-G. Gadamer et la recherche de la vérité," *Église et Théologie* 10 (1979) 275–288.

14. This is a conclusion I had come to with my publication, in 1984, of *Hegel's Trinitarian Claim* e.g. 243, 268, though there, in light of concerns for selfhood and subjectivity guiding that study, I had tended more to speak of initial selfhood as beginning. It has then been encouraging to note that John Russon, for example, has in the context of a discussion of his study, *Human Experience. Philosophy, Neurosis, and the Elements of Everyday Life* (Albany: State University of New York Press, 2003), stressed from the perspective of his interests that what one begins with in experience is the given relationship. In "The Virtue of Stoicism: On First Principles in Philosophy and Life," *Dialogue* 44 (2006) 347–348, he writes: "Most simply, I am arguing for the need to replace the notion of 'substance' or 'thing' as the basic element of reality with the notion of 'relation.' (…) Our reality is, I argue, 'situated,' which, again, says we exist as a network of relationships."

15. The ways in which dialectical and dialogical are being used here will be further spelled out in following chapters.

16. Finite spirit here indicates that we are focusing more explicitly on finite movements of enriching experience and not referring directly to moments of impoverishing experience.

17. See Schlitt, *Hegel's Trinitarian Claim* 267–273 as well as Chapters Seven and Eight below.

18. Within the framework of the present chapter, it will not be possible to reflect extensively on the questions of evil, freedom, and divine mystery. We will come back to these questions more indirectly over the course of the following chapters and more explicitly in Chapter Nine below. For now we can simply say that working with a wider notion of experience rather than with Hegel's concept of reflexive conceptual thought will allow for a less transparent and less necessitarian affirmation of God who is now understood as a movement of experience. With regard to evil, focusing on experience will allow for understanding evil, at least one form of it, as impoverishing human experience in comparison with the good understood, at least in one sense, as enriching experience. In general, working with a notion of God as movement of experience allows for a greater sense of mystery and gives more independent status to otherness as such than would working with Hegel's notion of God as movement of conceptual thought. And we will want to come to terms at least in principle with the wide variety of religions, though without needing to integrate them into a uniserial chronological order of development and complexification.

PART II

Experience

4

GADAMER, ROYCE, DEWEY, SMITH

In Part One, we reviewed various aspects of Hegel's philosophical theology. There we saw that he developed a concept of inclusive divine subjectivity that took the form of a dialectical movement of thought. We noted some of that philosophical theology's strengths and weaknesses. It is especially the former that provide the occasion and the impetus for working with Hegel, while the latter serve as reasons urging us to go beyond him by presenting a movement of inclusive divine subjectivity understood as a movement of experience. Now, in Part Two, I propose that, in a further step in our overall argument, we examine in more detail the notion and reality of experience before going on, in Part Three below, to sketch out a post-Hegelian philosophical theology.

Initial Remarks

"Experience" is a slippery, elusive notion.[1] Attitudes toward and understandings of it vary from culture to culture and from philosophy to philosophy. In the western world thinkers have generally evaluated it either positively or negatively as an avenue or opening to objective reality. They have characterized it both as passive receptivity and as active, creative thrust outward from the self. Several American pragmatists have seen experience more inclusively in somewhat Hegelian fashion, though without the phenomenologically based structure of "self-positing," as containing the self experiencing and the other experienced within it, namely, within experience considered as an overall process. More generally stated, however, in the English-speaking world the variously interpreted notion of experience serves as one of the most significant and fundamental of philosophical categories. We can illustrate this fact by referring to a remark attributed to Paul Tillich, who arrived on the North American scene at a more mature age. He found himself faced with the task of adapting both to the English language and to its various forms of conceptualization. After some time he is reported to have concluded that experience as a notion and term is the English-language equivalent of the continental terms for "being." The fact that experience, like "being," or even "thought" and "love," is both a very general and a fundamental notion not easily explicable in terms of other conceptualities goes far toward explaining why there is such overall ambiguity surrounding the notion and its use as well as why there are such varying attitudes toward and understandings of its nature, functions and revelatory value.

Despite and perhaps even because of this ambiguity, experience has been able to serve as such a significant, and often the most fundamental though not necessarily always so explicitly reflected upon, philosophical notion across the relatively pragmatic and efficiency oriented English-speaking world and, increasingly, in other language contexts as well.[2]

In the present chapter we will highlight certain aspects of the thought of a continental European philosopher, Hans-Georg Gadamer, and of three American philosophers, namely, Josiah Royce, John Dewey and John E. Smith on the notion, reality and functions of experience. As we noted in the previous chapter, Gadamer had himself proposed a shift from Hegel's notion of thought to that of experience, with the latter then considered as basically linguistic in character. Gadamer and the three other philosophers whose thought especially on experience is to be reviewed in the present chapter have proven very helpful in my own efforts to try to go beyond Hegel while working with him. All four have themselves, in various ways, known of, or made efforts to correct, modify or even reject, Hegel's philosophy. They will help us move from Hegel's working with thought as preferred point of reference and basic category to our using experience as point of reference and more inclusive basic category.

Gadamer's Proposal

In an important section on experience (*Erfahrung*) in his volume, *Truth and Method*,[3] Hans-Georg Gadamer enters into discussion especially with Aristotle, Hegel and Heidegger. He uses this approach in order to sketch out his own distinctive view of experience, which he interprets as an ongoing dialogue in the direction of truth. Though we can appreciate his philosophical generalization of hermeneutics when we see it more directly in relation to Heidegger's thought, we can best understand what Gadamer would consider his fundamental breakthrough with regard to the notion of experience by looking at his reaction against, and yet learning from, Hegel's own way of approaching experience. He rejects the Hegelian sublation of experience into a movement of thought that results in an absolute or inclusive knowing. Indeed, Gadamer himself states that his own elaboration of a more hermeneutical interpretation of experience as ongoing dialogue is an attempt to rehabilitate what Hegel had so colorfully called the bad or spurious infinite (*das Schlecht-Unendliche*).[4] For Hegel this spurious infinite was infinite progression, an inadequate form of infinity that, in its self-contradiction, had to resolve itself into a true or inclusive infinite. In contrast to Hegel's view, for Gadamer experience is an unending progression of experiences that render the experienced individual ever more open to new experiences. Gadamer had already appropriated from Aristotle the view that experience bore the character of an event and was, as such, unrepeatable. He combined this insight with what he retained from Hegel, namely, that experience is always negative. So, for Gadamer the newness involved in experience always contradicts, in one way or another, what we have previously known. In each experience, in each move beyond what was previously experienced and known, we suffer as we experience our own finitude and historicity. And yet each experience, as "a having gone beyond," also opens a new horizon in which the "objects of experience" situate themselves and out of which we anticipate the future. Experience is indeed dialectical.

Gadamer then appeals to the phenomenon of language in order to argue that both the objects of experience and experience itself are linguistic in nature.[5] In fact, in more or less typical hermeneutic fashion he goes so far as to state that all he is interested in when he speaks of real experience is the linguistic, with "linguistic" to be taken here in a very sophisticated and broad sense. For Gadamer, this linguistic and dialectical process takes on the nature of an ongoing dialogue. In a nutshell, with this appeal to language Gadamer has recovered from Hegel a particularly creative interpretation of experience as being negative, dialectical and dialogical, as having the character of an event and, most fundamentally, as being a linguistic process.

Gadamer's admittedly fascinating continental European recovery of the notion and nature of human experience remains, however, limited by its reductionist linguistic turn in which Gadamer understands experience in terms of something else, namely, language. While noting that this is indeed a limitation, we need also to underscore that it is especially through proposing this particular interpretation of experience and of the experienced other that Gadamer has de facto raised at least two important questions. First of all, and more implicitly, he points out that there is for the adult human person ordinarily no such thing as a pure experience totally without some influence of language and, I would think one should add, thought, gender conditioning, genetic substrate, tradition, religion and, especially, culture. In later chapters we will come back at least in a general way to the specific question of the relation between language and experience. Yet already now it is important to recall that when we speak of the linguistic nature of all human experience we are speaking from a Western perspective since, for example, the Buddhist experience of *Nirvana* is surely beyond the linguistic. But secondly, and more directly germane to the present reflection, Gadamer has, in a way that goes against his own position, raised the question of the experience we have—in, with and through language, thought, gender conditioning, genetic substrate, tradition, religion and culture—of surely knowing more than the language used and more than the linguistic signs perceived. What we experience is an otherness, in fact an other who or which is not simply reducible either to language or to other factors that we might see as conditioning the experience. There is, in and through these various signs and conditioning factors, an other available as a momentary whole. It would seem that this other is not merely known in self-contradictory fashion as a more or less "unknowable" Kantian "thing-in-itself." Rather, in somewhat more Hegelian fashion it is experienced as revealing and expressing itself in one way or another, honestly or dishonestly, with and through such language. Of course, as mentioned, this availability of an other is surely a revelation conditioned not only by language but also by a whole host of other factors and influences.

Now, with specific reference to language and, indeed, to its primary form, spoken language, there are surely experiences in which language straightforwardly mediates an other revealing itself through that language. But there are also occasions in which certain nonlinguistic forms of communication such as, for example, facial expressions or gestures may qualify, or even reverse, the meaning of the oral language being used. Also, recent psychological studies tend more and more to assert either the pre-linguistic or even non-linguistic character of various forms of intentional human activity. We need merely think of a baby nursing at the breast. The mother's experience is surely thoroughly linguistically conditioned. But the very young baby's truly intentional activity would seem only in the loosest of senses to be linguistic. While recognizing the extreme importance of language, we must acknowledge that the "more" we experience as unified other is present to us, and admittedly even often "absent," in ways too complex and involving far too many factors to be reduced to the linguistic alone.[6]

Further Philosophical Resources

A number of years ago, long before reading either Hegel or Gadamer, I wanted to do doctoral work on the notion of Trinity and on the Christian affirmation of the trinitarian experience of God. I was looking around for help in understanding better the notion of experience and came upon several American philosophers who reflected at great length on this notion. The first of these was Josiah Royce, whose integration of pragmatist and idealist themes gave birth to a fascinating philosophy of religion in his well-known later study, *The Problem of Christianity*,[7] on which I would now like to focus.[8]

Josiah Royce: Experience as Triadic Process of Interpretation

Within Royce studies the question of continuity in development versus shift in position seems to me to remain inadequately resolved despite Royce's own observation in this later work, *The Problem of Christianity*, published in 1913: "In spirit I consider my present book to be in essential harmony with the bases of the philosophical idealism set forth in various earlier volumes of my own, and especially in the work entitled 'The World and the Individual' [published in 1899–1901]" (1:x). And more specifically concerning community: "I strongly feel that my deepest motives and problems have centered about the idea of the Community, although this idea has only come gradually to my clear consciousness."[9] Certainly Royce's later notion of loyalty as love for the community finds roots in his earlier concern for the relationship of individual to whole.[10] With regard especially to the conceptualization of God, John E. Smith picks up on these observations of Royce's when he appreciates, and apparently agrees with, Gabriel Marcel's stress on continuity. Smith writes, "He [Marcel] sees clearly the extent to which the Absolute Knower of Royce's earlier thought develops into the Interpreter of the later community doctrine."[11] Finally, even a cursory review of Royce's transitional 1911 Bross lectures, published as *The Sources of Religious Insight*,[12] would appear to confirm Marcel's insistence that "Royce did not alter the foundation of his ontology."[13]

Granted such perceived continuities in Royce's thought, I would suggest it is both fair and important to focus upon the later Royce of *The Problem of Christianity*. It is especially in this work that he proposes, in a way quite reminiscent of Hegel's intention almost a century earlier, to reconceptualize basic Christian doctrines such as Kingdom of God (e.g., 1:34–38 with 349–354) and, implicitly, Trinity (e.g., 1:200–201, n.1), which two doctrines he in effect appears to identify. For present purposes, it is particularly important to concentrate on this work since it is here that Royce, after reading Charles Sanders Peirce, first clearly and explicitly develops his notion of the triadic structure of the cognitive process of interpretation and equates this process with experience (see, e.g., 1:xi along with 2:281–291). Yet, with reference to *The Problem of Christianity*, Royce does say, "The present work contains no mere repetition" (1:x–xi). He speaks of "the novelty of some of my metaphysical theses in my second volume" (1:xiv). He likewise acknowledges his growing debt to William James regarding the nature of an idea (e.g., 2:180– 181, 186). While continuing to criticize James's individualistically conceived notion of the self (1:xiv–xvi, 2:314–319), Royce, probably at least to some degree due to badgering by James, more clearly distinguishes the selves constituting a community of interpretation (2:103). In so doing he effectively escapes the criticism made of his earlier thought, namely, that it was monistic.[14] By so elaborating a social theory of individual selves constituting an ongoing community of interpretation, Royce, in *The Problem of Christianity*, corrects the seeming one-sidedness of William James's more individualistic conception of experience[15] and clearly foreshadows George Herbert Mead[16] on the socially constructed self. This community of interpretation, in its many aspects, was meant to be a contemporary reconceptualization of the biblical metaphor "Kingdom of God" or, as Royce phrased it, "Kingdom of Heaven," and this in terms of three leading ideas in Saint Paul, namely, community, the moral burden of the individual, and atonement (1:xxxvii–xxxix, 38–45). Royce's specific understanding of the relationship between the Beloved Community and its Founder appears somewhat dated in view of almost a century of further research.[17] There are as well some rather disconcerting inconsistencies between his original outline and actual presentations in the later lectures, or at least some overall loose ends. Nevertheless, the net result of Royce's reconceptualization of Pauline ideas is an impressive, seminal study of the structure of reality conceived in terms of a communal and individual movement of interpretation.

Though with *The Problem of Christianity* Royce clearly reflects a socio-pragmatic orientation, when it comes right down to the heart of the matter in Lecture 11 (2:109–163), he develops his central notion, namely, interpretation, in reference to, comparison with and opposition to what he sketches as the other two, merely dyadically structured cognitive processes of perception and conception. Every interpretation is "an expression of mental activity" (2:160) and is a mental act (2:149). It is a mental process and a type of knowledge (2:114). Royce's understanding and structuring of interpretation is thus grounded in the mental; this comparative point of origin carries through and conditions all of his further elaboration and widening of the notion of interpretation. This mental rootage gives Royce's later thought a continuing idealistic cast.[18]

In developing his understanding of the cognitive process of interpretation, Royce goes to some length to distinguish it logically and functionally (2:158–160) from the previously mentioned cognitive processes of perception and conception. He envisions the history of philosophy as a shifting of emphasis upon either perception (e.g., Bergson, Pragmatists, etc.) or conception (e.g., Plato). He generalizes: "The contrast between the cognitive processes called, respectively, perception and conception, dominates a great part of the history of philosophy. This contrast is usually so defined as to involve a dual classification of our cognitive processes" (2:117).

Royce claims that in real life pure perception and pure conception appear to be abstractions. "In recent discussion it has become almost a commonplace to recognize this union (i.e., of perception and conception) as constantly exemplified in human experience" (2:121). He insists that such an "experiential" synthesis of the two does not as yet yield "a genuinely triadic classification of the types of knowing processes" (2:124). Rather, he refers to Peirce's triadic theory of interpretation and sign, and then proposes that human cognitive processes are not exhaustively described in terms of dyadically structured perception and conception (see also 2:187–188). He argues that these two are not truly unitable without a third cognitive process, namely, interpretation. According to Royce, in philosophy there is often an unfortunate and unsuccessful attempt merely to relate them antithetically as cash (perception) to bank-note (conception) (2:124). But

> neither perception nor conception, nor any combination of the two, nor yet their synthesis in our practical activities, constitutes the whole of any interpretation. Interpretation, however, is what we seek in all our social and spiritual relations; and without some process of interpretation, we obtain no fulness of life. (2:136)

Despite his overly modest claims to the contrary (2:115–116), Royce goes into some detail in a magisterial presentation of Peirce's thought on interpretation and points out not only that there are three types of cognitive processes, but that the third of them, namely, interpretation, is itself triadic in structure. "Interpretation always involves a relation of three terms. In the technical phrase, interpretation is a triadic relation" (2:140). "Thus an interpretation is a relation that not only involves three terms, but brings them into a determinate order. One of the three terms is the interpreter; a second term is the object—the person or the meaning or the text—which is interpreted; the third is the person to whom the interpretation is addressed" (2:142).

This fundamentally triadic structure distinguishes interpretation from perception and conception. It elucidates and explicates what Royce focuses on as interpretation and what he repeatedly calls a third type of knowledge (e.g., 2:188) in which we know minds or signs of minds.[19] There is for Royce, in addition to that which is interpreted and that to whom it is interpreted, an essential element or, better, idea, by which the two are related, compared, understood. This can be labelled "the interpreter" and holds primacy of place in the process's determinate order: interpreter; interpreted; interpretee. Interpretation differs from perception and conception in three respects: first, interpretation is a conversation; second, "the interpreted object is itself something which has the nature of a mental expression (sign)" (2:148); third, as a cognitive or mental act the interpretation is itself a sign and calls for further interpretation (2:148–149). "And so,—at least in ideal,—the social process involved is endless" (2:149). The social process of interpretation creates what Royce calls the community of interpretation, an actual, concrete infinite that John E. Smith in turn refers to as Royce's social infinite.[20]

In Lecture 12 Royce further develops his notion of interpretation as "a fundamental cognitive process" (2:167), "an essentially social cognitive process" (2:168). Without detailing a summary, we can say that according to Royce the three elements verified in interpretation structure the interaction between individuals, the relationship of an individual within her or himself (2:244ff) and the relationships constituting the community as a whole (2: 204–221). In each of these instances, the three elements of interpretation must remain distinct from one another or there is a reversion back to the dyadic and, consequently, to an inadequate explanation of the phenomenon taking place. "Interpretation (...) involves relations which are essentially triadic" (2:159).

This triadically structured notion of interpretation becomes for Royce, by means of a metaphysical generalization (2:145), the basic conception by which he explains reality, God and, of particular interest here, experience (2:289–291). In regard to this generalization, at one point Royce highlights the philosophical lineage, to which we have already referred, of his triadically structured notion of interpretation when he praises and prefers Peirce's mathematically and socially based triadic over what is for Royce the more restricted and problematic understanding of triadic found in Hegel. Royce makes the perhaps somewhat daring statements that Peirce's theory "is, historically speaking, a theory not derived from Hegel (...) [and that] Peirce's theory (...) promises new light upon matters which Hegel left profoundly problematic" (2:186). Royce in fact claims that all reality is to be conceived in terms of experience that bears the triadic structure of the cognitive process of interpretation: "Our experience, as it comes to us, is a realm of Signs" (2:289). And a sign is an expression of mind (2:283). "Now our doctrine of the world of interpretation extends to all reality the presuppositions which we use in all our dealings with past and future time" (2:290).

Royce's view of experience as interpretation establishes a world basically cognitive or mental and for Royce, therefore, essentially communal (2:288).[21] It is especially Royce's continuing understanding of reality as intelligible manifestation of mind that has enabled him to elaborate a triadically structured understanding of experience as interpretation, namely, a form of knowledge. As long as Royce stays with this notion of reality as intelligible manifestation of mind, his thought remains quite clear. This is witnessed to by the remarkable clarity with which he can elaborate the necessarily triadic structure of interpretation as a process involving mental signs. However, as soon as he proposes a metaphysical generalization from interpretation to experience as process of interpretation and to universe as community of interpretation, his thought becomes more ambiguous.[22]

There are several causes for this resultant lack of clarity. One of these is surely the relatively uncritical and unreflective way in which Royce would seem to me more to state than to argue what would seem to be his metaphysical generalization of the cognitive process or mental act of interpretation. The lack of critical awareness manifested in this metaphysical generalization can be exemplified, for instance, already early on in his rather unreflected juxtaposing of interpretation and comparison.[23] Significantly, the notion of comparison plays less and less of an important role as Royce develops his thought throughout *The Problem of Christianity*.

A second and more fundamental cause of ambiguity would seem to arise out of Royce's admittedly fruitful but nevertheless somewhat uncritical blending of pragmatism and idealism. In *The Problem of Christianity* Royce has attempted an ontological hybridization as he modifies his own previously more overtly idealist stance, while yet developing what we might, with certain qualifications, call the idealist side of Peirce, embracing James' understanding of the volitional character of ideas (2:186, 292–293), and yet elaborating his own social understanding of interpretation within the context of an analysis of cognitive or mental processes that retain for him a strongly intellectualist cast. We can exemplify this intellectualist cast to the later Royce's thought, while acknowledging its Peircian and Jamesian backgrounds, by recalling his constant reference to "ideals," "mind," "idea," "Christian ideas," "signs." In view of this overall intellectualist cast to Royce's ontological hybridization, it is difficult to decide whether Royce be an "idealist pragmatist" or "pragmatic idealist."[24]

The ambiguity arising out of the tension between pragmatic and idealist elements that is found at the heart of Royce's thought shows up as well in the very structure of *The Problem of Christianity*. On the one hand, a more critical reading of Royce would lead to the conclusion that a principle of selectivity entered in whereby his homing in on the essentials of Christianity in the first volume of *The Problem of Christianity* was conditioned by his pre-established epistemological and metaphysical concerns of the second volume. But such a conditioning would itself appear to violate his "idealistic" theory of interpretation since the theory itself not only allows for but presupposes a mental "given" not determined by, but only interpreted by, the interpreter. On the other hand, a more benevolent reading of Royce's work would claim that the structure of his two volumes indicates a greater openness to the given, to a type of phenomenological or, in a widened sense, "empirical" basis for his thought than his analysis of interpretation would at first sight allow. Such a reading would stress that Royce's vision of the essential elements of Christianity, as laid out in the first volume, is what determines and conditions his philosophical reconceptualizations in the second volume. This approach would, then, despite the designation of the essential elements of Christianity as "the Christian ideas," tend to underscore the pragmatic side of Royce's thought.

The fundamental tension between "idealist" and "pragmatist" in Royce has perhaps caused ambiguity, but it has also resulted in a great richness of thought. His attempt to integrate the rational and the volitional allowed him to work out a fascinating theory of community. His blending of both in a wider notion of the mental, namely, in the cognitive process of interpretation, represents an enriched transformation of Peirce's thought and, at least in Royce's mind, of Hegel's thought as well. Royce himself had logically, though not necessarily in terms of historical dependence, viewed the transition from Hegel's dialectic to Peirce's theory of signs and interpretation to his own communitarian/individual theory as a process of widening of conception and of application (2:185–186). Royce himself, then, understood experience as a triadically structured process of interpretation. However, since he evolved his theory of interpretation out of an analysis of cognitive or mental processes and since his understanding of interpretation always retained an intellectualist cast, there arises an important question concerning his metaphysical generalization of the notion of the cognitive act of interpretation.[25] Though Royce's notion of interpretation may well have been a widening of Peirce's own thought, or at least a widening of the application of that thought, his description of experience as interpretation and the consequent equation of experience with the cognitive process of interpretation would, in the final analysis, still seem to restrict the understanding of the notion of experience itself. It would seem to leave a residual mentalist coloring to his understanding of experience. Royce would of course be correct in affirming that experience is reflexively available only in terms of mental activity, but that would neither equate the two nor reduce experience to the cognitive process of interpretation. Indeed, the very ambiguity and yet the fruitfulness of Royce's attempt to blend rational and volitional encourages us to push beyond his own residually mentalist formulation of experience as interpretation to suggest the need to focus more directly on a wider notion of experience, taken in its own right and on its own terms, that could incorporate the rational and the volitional as exemplifications of it. These exemplifications would then serve as reflexive gateway to elaborating the appropriate structures of that wider, more inclusive notion.

John Dewey: Three Forms of Experience

After reflecting at some length on Josiah Royce's pragmatist/idealist interpretation of experience, I continued my search for a more radically developed notion of experience, one that treats experience in its own right, on its own terms and not in terms of another notion that could easily restrict its meaning and coverage. In my search I came upon the thought of John Dewey, who remains in many ways the most characteristic American philosopher.[26] I read the second edition of his *Experience and Nature*,[27] a work described as "philosophically the most fundamental of Dewey's books."[28] He included in this edition a new, clearer and more helpful introductory or first chapter entitled "Experience and Philosophic Method" (text 10–41, remarks by Dewey 3–5). Upon reading the book, and especially its revised first chapter, I immediately became impressed with his effort to work out an understanding of experience as instrumental and consummatory that would allow him to overcome so many distinctions which, over the centuries, philosophers had transformed into dichotomies. Among them, for instance, he lists body and soul (191–192), experience and nature, science and art (268–269).[29]

The background against which Dewey developed his own philosophy of experience in *Experience and Nature* was at least twofold: more immediately, the Empiricist tradition; more remotely, Greek philosophy. For him, the Empiricist understanding had relegated "experience" to the personal, subjective, unverifiable and consequently unreliable (137). In addition to reacting against this understanding, Dewey developed his philosophical position on experience as a conceptualizing of what he called the "modern attitude" toward experience in contradistinction to and against the background of Greek philosophy in which

> experience (...) signified a store of practical wisdom, a fund of insights useful in conducting the affairs of life. (...) Modern theory has quite properly extended the application of the term to cover many things that the Greeks would hardly have called 'experience,' the bare having of aches and pains, or a play of colors before the eyes. (266)

Over the course of *Experience and Nature* Dewey develops a holistic, continuous view of reality in which experience provides insight into nature (e.g., 5) of which it is, so to speak, a part and in which art is "the culminating event of nature as well as the climax of experience" (8).

More particularly regarding experience, Dewey describes it as an inclusive whole and not just the act of an experiencing subject (18–19). It is the interaction between an organism and its environment (e.g., 159),[30] an event (13), stable and unstable in a vital mix (47), marked by needs (59), wider than what is known (27), characterized by tendencies not teleology (279–280), social (157, 307–308) and to be shared (157, 159).[31] And experience is future-oriented.[32] In this overall understanding Dewey is dependent, to a certain extent, on Charles Sanders Peirce but he references especially William James (see, for example, 18–19). Stephen David Ross sums up Dewey's thought: " 'Experience' for Dewey represents a fundamental metaphysical category, through which he attempts to criticize various historical dualisms. It represents the human process which is seen to be a union of various factors—organism and environment, subject and object, what is experienced and how it is experienced."[33]

Dewey's understanding and use of experience arise from his psychological background[34] and positive impression of the value of the empirical, scientific method which latter arises out of experience and returns thereto in search of verification (10–41). This pattern, beginning with the understanding of experience as an "integrated unity" (19) prior to our usual philosophical distinctions and returning to it, flowered in Dewey's description of the types or forms, I would even say phases, of experience. Francis E. George has summarized them as "primary, non-reflective experience, (...) secondary reflective experience and finally (...) reflectively enriched consummatory experience."[35] Dewey's denotative method (8) of immediate or naturalistic empiricism (1) operates entirely within experience so structured. We might go so far as to see that method operating through these three functionally distinguished types of experience and thus moving from primary non-reflective experience to secondary reflective experience and, finally, to reflectively enriched consummatory experience.[36]

With this threefold structuring of experience Dewey wished to indicate a "constancy of means, of things used for consequences, not of things taken by themselves or absolutely" (64–65). As he uses the word, structure does not then imply an idealistic, selective view but, rather, the "functional character" of experience (indirectly stated, 66). In another context he even speaks of the logic of experience, namely, of a sequence and interaction of various typical functions of experience.[37]

Needless to say, given my interests, these three types of experience immediately caught my attention. Dewey describes the first of these functionally structured types of experience, namely, primary, non-reflective experience, as "gross" (e.g., 32), as that from which we start and which occurs "chiefly in modes of action and undergoing" (29) that form the context for knowing (29). "Human experience in the large, in its coarse and conspicuous features, has for one of its most striking features preoccupation with direct enjoyment" (69). We might argue that here Dewey is speaking of experience *per se* rather than primary experience. However, I would propose that he means both but especially, given the context, gross or primary experience. Dewey is often not clear with regard to distinguishing between experience as such and primary experience. Functionally, gross or primary experience, parallel to its function in science, is the origin, problem-setter and furnisher of first data for reflection as well as the point to which secondary or reflective experience returns for verification in, or better in Dewey's widened form of denotative method, enrichment of, the primary experience (15–16). Primary or gross experience is in fact an "unanalyzed totality" (18).

Secondary, reflective experience, what we usually call thought, involves selectivity (31), has its own basis in choice (34–35), and is conscious experience characterized by an abstractive tendency to unity (60–62, 269). Its functions are regulation (96), criticism, which is "the control of the course of events so that it may yield, as ends or termini, objects that are stable and that tend toward creation of other values." Such experience "introduces the topic of value-judgements or valuations" (9). Reflective experience's function is therefore creative, controlling and critical—in a word, enriching. It is, in a real sense, a prolongation of gross or primary experience, which is its context.[38]

Dewey saw experience as an event or activity definitely including the object experienced. He distinguished this activity functionally as consummatory, as the end of the process of experiencing when that end is understood as fulfilment, "consummatory, of means" (275). He even speaks of "ends, or consummatory consequences" (9).

In fact, Dewey so ties together experience and the object experienced that often when he refers to the object he is in fact speaking of the overall experience that is a relationship between the one experiencing and that which is experienced.[39] He can then, in opposition to Aristotle, speak of consummatory objects:

> Actually, consummatory objects instead of being a graded series of numerous and unalterable species or kinds of existence ranked under still fewer genera, are infinitely numerous, variable and individualized affairs. (…) The contingent, uncertain and incomplete give depth and scope to consummatory objects while things not directly had, things approachable only through reflective imagination and rational constructions are the conditions of such regulation of their occurrence as is feasible. (96)

In speaking of consummatory experience,[40] Dewey goes on to see essence as but a "pronounced instance of meaning" (144) so that "the very essence of a thing is identified with those consummatory consequences which the thing has when conditions are felicitous" (144). Consummatory experience therefore validates, consummates reflective experience that itself had, in turn, arisen out of gross experience as context. It is a return to experienced things in which they now have a significance beyond what they originally had. Qualities had ceased, as Dewey says, "to be isolated details; they get the meaning contained in a whole system of related objects; they are rendered continuous with the rest of nature " (16).

This consummatory experience remains somewhat vague in Dewey's thought, but can be exemplified in discourse, namely, communication seen as an "exchange which procures something wanted" and "an immediate enhancement of life, enjoyed for its own sake" (144). "Discourse itself is both instrumental and consummatory" (144). That experience is consummatory, in the sense of fulfilment of ends, anchors and justifies Dewey's understanding that experience is really future-oriented.[41]

For Dewey, these three types of experience are, as has been mentioned, functionally distinct. To further distinguish them, or to attempt to consider reflective experience independently of primary experience is to lose the all-important context. To try to stop with reflective experience is the sin of the idealist and is to misunderstand the fundamentally instrumental nature of thought.[42] Reflected experience and consummatory experience are then, each in its own way, prolongations and developments of gross or primary experience.

It was only later on, after reading in Hegel, that I noticed the Hegelian coloring Dewey seems, perhaps intentionally, to have given to this threefold description of experience. Though he explicitly identifies empirical method as the model upon which he draws, it seems to me that he has as well transformed the three moments of "in itself" (*an sich*), "for itself " (*für sich*) and "in and for itself" (*an und für sich*) constituting Hegel's dialectical movement of spirit into these three modes or types of experience. Dewey's insistence that we begin with a unity is surely reminiscent of Hegel's own systematic position and Dewey's insistence that experience is a totality inclusive of experiencing self and experienced other certainly reminds us of the forms (*Gestalt*) of consciousness Hegel has presented in his *Phenomenology of Spirit*.[43]

That which I would identify as Dewey's transformation of Hegel's movement of spirit, and indeed Dewey's thought in general on experience, prove quite attractive. His non-dualist, non-monadist pluralism and general openness, his over-all evaluation of and the role he gives to experience prove quite congenial to both modern and post-modern minds. We might even say that, despite certain limitations, they are, in a general sense, convincing. His overall openness, less so however with regard to religion, the sheer scope of his interests, his ability to conceptualize various themes and interests found in the American experience all undergird his philosophical insights. He has indeed mirrored many aspects of that experience: the pragmatic, the social, the experiential, the generally optimistic, the pluralistic and the psychological. This he has done without an appeal to mind and will as cosmic or psychologically independent entities and likewise without drifting into the other extreme of psychological subjectivism.[44]

Dewey developed especially well the aspects of experience rooted in the psychology of the individual though he admits, if I recall rightly, that he never fully spelled out that psychology. More importantly, his view of experience as not only consistent with and contiguous to nature but rather a part and development of nature, indeed a way of insight into nature, provides the category of experience with greater metaphysical density, perhaps to the point of allowing it to be consistently invoked as the most appropriate universal category of philosophical reflection.

Very distinctive of Dewey's thought is his understanding of ideas and thinking itself as instrumental. Not only did Dewey take over from science its empirical method, but, in the process, he transformed it so that verification becomes enrichment with the end-result being enriched experience. This is important since, just as with Royce the notion of interpretation loses much of its verve if removed from his understanding of the world as ultimately mental, with Dewey the notions of primary, reflective, and consummatory tend toward the banal when considered without reference to the instrumental.

There remains, however, in Dewey's understanding of experience, at least as found in *Experience and Nature,* much that is ambiguous. We can see this, for example, in the question of the relationship between the notions of gross or primary experience and of experience *per se.* We can also see it in the difficulty we run up against when we try to work out in more detail the relationship between the various types of experience that Dewey proposes.[45] We might ask him just how necessary it would be for each experience, to be a true experience, to come to be reflective, and also consummatory as well? Significantly, Dewey has to a great extent left it to George Herbert Mead and others to work out in more explicit fashion the social side of experience, so that, though he does refer to this side and does seem to presume that individual and social experience share common characteristics,[46] the communitarian aspect of his presentation of the notion of experience needs further development.[47] Again, if I recall rightly, John E. Smith has noted that Dewey focuses less on "inner experience."[48]

Surprisingly, there would seem to be a need to widen somewhat the notion of experience as we find it presented in Dewey's thought. We get the impression that, despite his best intentions, Dewey still restricted it unnecessarily. Perhaps his naturalism is more open than he suspected. Francis E. George has, for example, examined Dewey's aversion to dialectic and concluded that the notion and reality of limit situations, seen as a type of experience that is negative but without development, lead to the use of dialectic as a form of discourse attempting to deal with paradoxical modes of consciousness. George concludes "that the philosopher of experience should be prepared to use as many methods as experience itself demands and that dialectic can be useful in locating and clarifying experiences of negation."[49]

As we saw in the section immediately above in the present chapter, the later Royce's more or less idealistic interpretation of reality seems to make the world and experience more ordered, systematic, meaningful, rational and so forth than it in fact actually appears experientially to be.[50] Fascinating though Royce's thought, and indeed Hegel's, may be, their more idealistic approaches seem to bring with them the danger of having to take over lock-stock-and-barrel a particular thought pattern that tends to downplay change, contingency and chance. Due to its openness, Dewey's world view appeals to many people, more so perhaps than does Royce's or Hegel's, despite the latter's apparently greater internal consistency. Perhaps Royce and Hegel offered too much.

Nevertheless, any number of times Dewey's remarks in *Experience and Nature* remind us, at least negatively, of Royce and, positively but more indirectly, of Hegel in the sense that Dewey seems to take exception to whatever would have a more directly Roycean ring to it.

Given my overall present interest in developing a philosophical theology in the form of a philosophical interpretation of Trinity, perhaps I could close these remarks on Dewey's notion of experience with a few questions. First, is it not possible that in Dewey's notion of primary non-reflective experience there are resources for understanding God as Holy Spirit? Or, at least, could we not see the Spirit of God at work somewhat more directly in this form of more immediate experience? In turn, could Dewey's presentation not be improved by developing further his understanding of the inexhaustability of primary experience? Second, could we not further work out his understanding of reflexive, secondary experience and its instrumental role that might, then, in turn further contribute to an understanding of the role of the divine *Logos* in the world. Perhaps redemption is not a notion totally removed from Dewey's understanding of reflexive experience's critical role. Third, in Dewey's thought consummatory experience is rather ambiguous and presents more difficulties. Perhaps Dewey could have given greater emphasis to the engaging, involving quality of a consummatory experience that is really "mine." Could not consummatory experience be widened to include this engaging quality by considering it as a form of experience that includes more explicit reference both to myself and to the other within it? Could consummatory experience then not shed light on our understanding of God as goal or purpose of our lives? Experience as such, and especially consummatory experience, is, for Dewey, future-oriented and seems to hint at realized possibility or potential.

We might best consider such questions as these, and the projections they imply, in a discussion concerning the realm of analogy where there is posited a similarity between the finite and the infinite. Or, more radically, we might come to see these types of experience as corresponding more directly to realities in the divine, so that, in turn, experience ultimately finds its unity there, with primary, secondary and consummatory as functional but real distinctions. For the moment, it will perhaps suffice to paraphrase a pious remark by a famous theologian,[51] the Dewey who wrote *Experience and Nature* might not appreciate these last thoughts, but perhaps the Dewey who is in heaven will.

John E. Smith: Experience as Revelatory Encounter

Again, before reading Hegel but after Dewey, I had also turned to John E. Smith, who has written extensively on Dewey and especially on Royce. I found his notion of experience as revelatory encounter and funded result most helpful. I discovered that, in a very real sense, Smith encapsulates, clarifies and makes more easily available, through his own writing, much of what various thinkers we have reviewed, as well as those we have not directly touched upon, have in a pragmatist vein said about experience.

Indeed, in the contemporary field of English language philosophical and, more precisely, philosophy of religion studies it is especially John E. Smith[52] who has consistently and insistently called for a renewed and more explicitly formulated understanding of the nature and role of experience. He has done this by means of an appeal to actual philosophizing along the lines set out by the classical American philosophical tradition rather than settling for a merely empiricist view of experience or restricting attention to more narrowly linguistic studies. In this classical American tradition Smith discerns at least four common concerns or themes which in fact likewise represent his own ongoing philosophical interests: purpose; community; religion; and in view of present interests, most fundamentally, experience.[53]

There is vaguely discernible beneath the surface of much of Smith's own thought, and in particular of his developing understanding of experience, a current of moderated and modified later Roycean thought as well as a deep appreciation of the thought of Peirce, James and Dewey. In fact, with more particular reference to Royce, Smith is himself the best known contemporary interpreter of Royce's thought. He has given new life to the later Royce's more pragmatic idealism by highlighting and developing Royce's rich experiential and social sides.

Smith, who is professor emeritus at Yale University, opened his impressive philosophical career with his highly respected study, *Royce's Social Infinite,*[54] first published in 1950. From this point on he has been concerned with the question of experience as the interrelationship between self and world, self and God, and self with itself. He has consistently argued that these interrelationships are, to put it very succinctly, reliably revelatory of reality. In his lecturing and writing on the nature and role of experience, Smith has constantly returned to this essentially pragmatist theme: the revelatory value of experience.

Perhaps even more so than Dewey, Smith quickly manifested a perduring, even obstinate interest in rehabilitating the notion of experience in the Anglo-Saxon or, perhaps better, Anglo-American philosophical world. Over the years he rejected as reductionist any interpretation of experience that refused to recognize the full epistemological and even ontological significance of experience.[55]

Without intending to survey in more complete fashion Smith's overall thought on experience, we can now rather more selectively refer to several of his writings on experience in order to bring together certain aspects of his creative, open-ended understanding of it.[56]

By 1957 Smith had already published an Italian article (reprinted in English)[57] in which he sketched three basic attitudes toward experience. First there is "The Ancient or Aristotelian Type" of empiricism in which "experience must be taken as basically historical or funded information over a period of time" (TAP 45) and in which there is no "reductive appeal to sense perception or experience as the final arbiter of all knowledge claims" (TAP 45 n. 3). Second, the "Classical or Enlightenment Type" of empiricism (TAP 46), that Smith holds responsible for the separation of experience and reason (TAP 48). And, third, "The Inclusive or Reconstructive Type" of empiricism in which "experience is taken as an affair related to the self in <u>all</u> of its aspects" (TAP 49). Smith opts for this third or inclusive understanding of experience. He insists that knowledge is a part of experience; it is in essential continuity with experience (TAP 50-51). He spends most of the rest of the article showing that, in opposition to the inclusive or reconstructive attitude toward experience, classical empiricism and especially that of Locke and Hume, opposes experience and thought to one another.

Though classical empiricism will remain his mortal enemy for many years, at this point in his struggle Smith clearly conceives of his task more in terms of a reintegration of thought into a wider conception of experience. In doing this, he speaks very briefly of encounter (TAP 49), a term he will use more often especially later on in the development of his thought on experience. But even here the idea contained in the notion of encounter, namely, that of revelatory interrelationship, is already present, though assuredly in the framework of and in a formulation conditioned by his concern for cognitional functioning, when he speaks of "the intercourse of a many-sided self with a complex world" (TAP 50). Here, in the overall context of his concern to validate a notion of experience more inclusive than that of classical empiricism, Smith terms a digression his seeing the need to develop a wider notion of experience adequate for morality, religion and political life as well as science (TAP 50). What he at this point called a digression can, in the light of his later studies, be seen as his proposal to construct a more inclusive and complete notion of experience.

In a short but important article, "The Experiential Foundations of Religion,"[58] Smith in 1958 continues his struggle with classical empiricism as he develops themes and points of view which come back time and again in his writings: 1) again, the distinction between the classical or British type of empiricism and the inclusive or reconstructive approach found in but not limited to American pragmatism; 2) his option for the reconstructive understanding of experience as reliable and revelatory; 3) the possibility of experiencing God. Though our attention here must center primarily on the second point, where Smith puts forward his own interpretation of experience, we should keep in mind that much of the motivating force behind his study of the notion of experience, and particularly concerning this 1958 article, is to begin constructing a model with which he can affirm the direct but mediated experience of God. He continues to speak of the classical empiricist understanding of experience as that of sense, of the subjective, of a set of contents opposable to reason (see esp. RG 174–175) and he quickly, and quite rightly, sees that such a view of experience not only complicates but, finally, eliminates any question of God within experience. It is for this reason, among others, that he prefers the second understanding of experience, which he claims is shared by such philosophers as Hegel, Bradley, Peirce, James, Dewey, Whitehead and, surely, Royce (RG 174, 179). In summary fashion, then, Smith at this point sees experience as a reciprocal affair involving

> an organic togetherness of the experiencing self and the experienced world; *second*, and as a direct consequence, experience is impossible without interpretation from the side of the self and cannot be taken as the passive reception of 'bare' data ready and waiting to impress themselves upon us; *third*, experience cannot be limited to 'sense' (...) *Fourth*, in addition to bringing relation back into experience, the broader conception focussed attention as well upon what might be called the 'intensive quality' of experience for the concrete self. (RG 179–180)

After adopting this second view of experience, Smith continues, in the course of his discussion on the experience of God as direct but not immediate, briefly to widen the application of this distinction to all experience. "There is no inconsistency in holding that a given item of experience can be *present* to a concrete individual and thus *directly experienced* by that self without that experience being immediate or exclusive of a reflective medium through which its meaning comes to the self. And although the distinction needs to be maintained throughout the whole of experience, it is especially important for the experience of God" (RG 182). All experience is understood to demand some interpretation or remain forever impossible to articulate.

When we see this seminal article, "The Experiential Foundations of Religion," within the context of the other articles gathered into *Reason and God* and in relation both to the title of the book and to the introductory appeal for actually doing philosophy (esp. RG xi–xii), we recognize that Smith is taking important steps here in the development of his own more constructive interpretation of experience.

A particularly helpful expression of Smith's efforts to affirm the general epistemological or revelatory value of experience and to defend that value can be distilled from his *Religion and Empiricism*,[59] published in 1967, and from "The Recovery of Experience," the first of his studies in his volume, *Experience and God*,[60] published in 1968.

First, to sift out essential features of the notion of experience in *Religion and Empiricism*, the 1967 Aquinas lecture, where, as is often the case, Smith's overall concern is with religion and possible experience of God. In this volume Smith's fuller development of the notion of experience against the immediate background of a renewed critique of classical empiricism and linguistic empiricism was significantly influenced by studies like those he published between 1957 and 1967 on American philosophical issues and conveniently gathered in *Themes in American Philosophy*. In discussing classical or British empiricism, Smith insists that, despite their attempts, neither Locke nor Hume were able consistently to confine experience to the limits of sensation (RE 14, 18–19). He then views linguistic empiricism, especially that of A. J. Ayer and the earlier Wittgenstein, with particular disdain, but sees a possibly more fruitful interrelationship between theology and linguistic empiricism opened up in the writings of the later Wittgenstein (RE 31). However, it is in the third section of this Aquinas Lecture, namely, in "Religion and Pragmatic Empiricism" (RE 42–66) that Smith sketches what he considers the more adequate notion of experience. He distills from Peirce, James and Dewey his "richer view of experience" (RE 43). He then presents experience as a valid medium of disclosure, as the "record and result of complex interactions and transactions between the human organism or language-using animal and the environment" (RE 44). Experience is, therefore, not primarily a private, mental content and not identifiable with sense alone (RE 45). It is not only singular, sensible, and immediately present, but includes context and tendency (RE 47). He goes on to talk not only in terms of content but also of dimensions of experience as he turns to experience of the transcendent (RE 50ff). It is important to note that Smith continues to emphasize the quality and reliability of experience as source of contact with oneself, with another self and with all of reality.

In the essay, "The Recovery of Experience," published in the collection entitled *Experience and God,* Smith continues to take the same general stance toward classical empiricism (EG 26ff) and linguistic empiricism (EG 41–45) and to work with experience as reliably revelatory. However, here he goes on to develop several points he had not stressed in *Religion and Empiricism* but which are easily discernable in his thought as far back as his early studies on Royce.[61] He uses and further elaborates on the notion of encounter far beyond what he had previously done and focuses attention more explicitly on the interrelational character of experience.

Before looking at the further delineation of the contours of his interpretation of experience, we should underscore that Smith does insist on the inevitability of an at least implicit theory of experience for any philosophical approach toward experience. He speaks of the need to make this theory explicit, and then to discover "by critical comparison and reflection whether it [a theory] is more or less adequate than other theories" (EG 22). In a way reminiscent of Dewey, he sees that the ultimate criterion of adequacy will not be a naive but rather an enlightened return to experience itself. While Smith speaks as if naive experience is not enough, he does recognize that adequacy to what we actually undergo and encounter is still the first step in giving an account of experience (EG 22–23). Furthermore, no one characteristic or predicate should be singled out as normative (EG 27). He lists several obstacles to an adequate theory of experience: seeing experience as merely mental and subjective; assuming a medium of expression is essential for an experience; assuming it is good enough to concentrate on one type of language to analyze experience (EG 23). In the context of this discussion on the need for a theory, Smith raises, even if only briefly, the question of structure. "A theory of experience does, of course, involve specifying a structure that is general; (…) but the generality involved will take the form of an attempt to express the nature of experience as an activity and a way of approaching reality" (EG 27).

We can sum up Smith's development of the notion of experience, and in fact the whole essay of his that we are here reviewing, by citing the following:

> In the most basic sense, experience is the many-sided product of complex en-
> counters between what there is and a being capable of undergoing, enduring,
> taking note of, responding to, and expressing it. As a product, experience is a
> result of an ongoing process that takes time and has a temporal structure. (EG
> 23)

Indeed, Smith's whole article can be seen as the unpacking of what is said in this citation.

For Smith, then, experience is an encounter with "an ongoing stream that is temporal in character" (EG 24), an encounter that involves an asymmetrical relationship between experiencer and that which is experienced (EG 24). The experiencer is no *tabula rasa* and, like experience itself, manifests a certain structure. The experiencer refracts and reflects, within different contexts of meaning, what is really there (EG 25). The term "experience" can be applied to a single encounter, but such can never be considered alone, for experience is also funded result and cumulative (EG 27). In speaking here of experience, Smith seems vaguely to have harkened back to ways in which Royce spoke of interpretation. He continues, in a manner again reminiscent of Royce, and indeed to some extent of Dewey, to emphasize the social nature of experience. He bases that social character in experience's being seen as repeated encoun-ter (EG 30) in which the stress is to be placed on continuity and identity. Then he acknowledges differences between the continuing experience of a single self and the relations between two different selves.

Smith touches briefly on what appeared earlier in Royce as purposive will and self constituted by relationship to community when he writes of the self as arising out of reflection on the experience of a public world and the self's selective interest (EG 34). Experience is then constructive, with both experi-enced and experiencer taking part in the construction, though for Smith the experiencer refracts and does not add. To overcome any dualistic conception of subject and object, he insists that experience is at all stages "encounter" and, as involving always experiencer and what is experienced, "is at the very least a dyadic affair and it is even possible that it is irreducibly triadic in character" (EG 35). He does not elaborate further on this triadic character upon which Royce had so insisted.

It will be sufficient for present purposes to underscore Smith's interpretation of experience as "the many-sided product of complex encounters" by referring again to Smith's assertions in reaction to his mortal enemies, the two previously seen reductive views of experience. First, in rejecting the classical theory's seeing experience as a mere succession of data received by an individual mind (EG 36), Smith asserts that there are dimensions of experience such as the historical, the scientific and the religious that are not merely dimensions of the interpreting mind (EG 37). That there are such dimensions of experience itself is for Smith based on two factors, neither of which are to be given priority: the multiple character of the items of experience and the purposes of the self (EG 37–38). Second, he reacts to linguistic empiricism's own doubled reduction of experience insofar as linguistic empiricism insists that experience is only available through the normative function of expression and that one form of language, that of formal logic, can serve as model for expressing experience. Against these reductionist views found in classical, and especially linguistic, empiricism, Smith points to a distinction between, and yet equally a wider linguistic movement within experience from, "what is *encountered* to *what* is encountered, from the reality presented to its naming and description" (italics in the original, EG 42). For Smith, experience as encounter should not be subordinated to the expression of that experience. Language or expression conditions encounter but never exhausts it (see EG 41–45).

In this study, "The Recovery of Experience," Smith has come to speak of experience as repeated encounter. But experience is equally "the ensuing product of encounter (...) a unique synthesis, derived from the two intersecting terms [the reality encountered, the experiencing self]" (EG 38). He asserts that experience is revelatory precisely because it is constitutive encounter. He rejects as inadequate to what we undergo and encounter (RG 22–23) both the reduction of experience to what he calls classical empiricism's viewing of experience as a question of sense data presented to an individual mind (RG

26ff) and linguistic empiricism's restriction of experience to one or more forms of linguistic expression (RG 41–45). On the basis of the inadequacy of merely subjective or, again, either linguistic or individualistic interpretations of experience, he argues to a more comprehensive view of experience as re-velatory constitutive encounter and funded result. In fact, besides using more direct arguments concerning adequacy to what one undergoes and what one encounters, he builds explicitly upon the insights and positions of a variety of American pragmatist thinkers, and especially Dewey. He is also at least im-plicitly working against the background of, and profiting from the fundamen-tal and extremely important role played by, the notion of experience in the English-speaking thought world when he proposes to see experience as multi-dimensional encounter and product of that encounter.

In his 1970 Warfield Lectures, subsequently published in 1973 as *The Analogy of Experience*,[62] Smith lays out his proposal for a constructive analogi-cal use of experience as a new way of understanding religious truth. For present purposes it will not be necessary to treat of the general content of this seminal study. It will suffice to highlight his overall intentions, indicate cer-tain aspects of his proposal of an analogy of experience and refer briefly to his more concrete experiential referents in order to continue to surface character-istics of experience as he presents it.

Smith's primary twofold intention is, reminiscent of Royce's project, to propose a new type of religious understanding (AE 31) that had nevertheless already arisen out of the Reformation (AE 25) and, then, on the basis of this new understanding, to sketch a more contemporary theological interpretation of several fundamental Christian conceptions or ideas (e.g., AE 29–30). Smith proposes an analogy of experience as a new approach to understanding and, more specifically, to grasping religious truths (AE Chapter Two, esp. 29–31). He intends to reinterpret "faith seeking understanding" as understanding through asymmetrical analogous references (AE 49, 51) always beginning from and with finite experiences (e.g., AE 29–32) so as to come to some valid and reliable understanding of God and selected central Christian conceptions (AE 43). After his discussion on analogous understanding as a legitimate alternative to univocal and equivocal ways of understanding (on analogy, esp. AE 44–52), Smith reflects, but in a very real sense goes beyond, his long-standing and ongoing concern to affirm the reliability and revelatory value of experience when he indicates that he wishes to present the objective character of experience as the ontological basis for his proposed reformulation of "faith seeking understanding" (AE 53). But, in line with his decision not to work out a general ontology (AE 53) and parallel with the overall Augustinian and Anselmian starting points in faith as already incipient understanding (AE 21–22), he says he does not intend to prove (AE 57) the appropriateness of an analogous affirmation of the understanding gained from specific finite experiences either to an understanding of God as transcendent reality or to an understanding of other Christian conceptions. Rather, in a somewhat more "theological" mode he wishes to begin with the givenness of these Christian conceptions and, again in harmony especially with Royce's intention, to make them understandable to the contemporary person (AE xvi–xx, 52). He intends to do this in a more pragmatist vein by means of appeal to concrete experiential referents (AE 43).

Smith argues that any form of grasping meaning, and particularly meaning in the religious sphere (e.g., AE 48), must ultimately be verified by reference to and reverberation with one's own experiences. For him these experiences, or more generally stated, experience itself provides a more complex form of understanding than is possible on the basis of reflective reason alone (AE 24). Then, after sketching his theory of an analogy of experience (AE 29–32 but also 52–57), he proceeds to reflect on and comes to an understanding of "man, of God, of Christ and of the church or community of love founded by the One who first brought it into being" (AE 43).

We can distill the more theoretical understanding of experience lying behind Smith's elaboration of these Christian conceptions from Chapter Two, "A New Approach to Understanding: *Analogia Experientiae*," and from Chapter Three, "Analogy and Experience," along with further remarks garnered from throughout the other chapters. In the second half of Chapter Two (AE 32–42), Smith lists in succinct but now definitive fashion, and in continuity with his earlier sketches, the contrast between the notion of experience in classical empiricism and the reconstructed conception of experience which he makes his own:

> There is the contrast between experience as the domain of sense (...) and sharply distinguished from reason or thought, and experience understood as the

funded and meaningful result of a multidimensional encounter between a concrete person and whatever there is to be encountered. Second, there is the contrast between experience as a body of data present to a theoretical observer who regards the *knowing* of those data as the primary concern, and experience in its variety embracing the moral, aesthetic, scientific and religious dimensions which give point and purpose to the life of an individual person. Third, there is the contrast between experience seen as a private mental content (...) and experience as an objective disclosure of what is there to be encountered. (AE 33)

He then reflects on these three characteristics of experience as funded result of encounter, as having a variety of dimensions and as serving as objective disclosure of what is to be encountered. For him understanding experience as encounter means that one experiences not just sense data but "a center of intention or purposive unity which constitutes that person as one self" (AE 35). Experience has such a variety of dimensions because the meaningful life of the experiencing self is constituted by experience that manifests itself in many modes (AE 37). It is objective in that it discloses reality (AE 38). It becomes, for Smith, "an intersubjective way of meeting reality which issues in the funded result of many encounters whereby it [reality] is disclosed" (AE 40). Experience is objective, secondly, in that it has a shared character and objective form as custom, tradition and habitual life (AE 41). Such experience is an "uninterrupted flow of events with contemporaneous fields of content" (AE 41). Yet it is equally punctuated, since it is realized as experiences, some of which have decisive import in human life (AE 41–42). Here, as ever, Smith is careful to understand experience widely enough to allow for and justify speaking of really experiencing a transcendent reality (AE 39).

In the second half of Chapter Three (see AE 52–61, esp. 52–53 and 57–59), Smith is principally concerned with backing up his ontological claim concerning the nature, status and function of experience in reality so as to provide a basis for his analogy of experience between that which is finite and finitude's ultimate ground. Though in elaborating this analogy of experience he is quick to emphasize that we should appeal to specific experiences, Smith here concentrates on his theory of experience as objective reality (AE 52). In listing several lines of argument that are to give indirect support for attributing to experience a definite ontological status in reality, and thus for using experience as a quite legitimate medium for analogy (AE 57), he is in fact highlighting several aspects of his understanding of experience. "First, experience is an identifiable emergent in the evolutionary history of man and human consciousness and thus possesses a legitimate status in the scheme of things" (AE 57–58, see 53). As this evolutionary result of the emergence of a sign-using animal and a world exhibiting some recurrent patterns, experience itself is an objective constituent of reality (AE 58). Therefore, Smith argues, it is not reducible to a merely subjective and internal phenomenon but is, again reminiscent of Hegel on thought or Royce on interpretation and Dewey on experience, effectively an encounter inclusive of experiencer and that which is to be experienced (AE 58). Though here as elsewhere Smith generally focuses on human experience, his reference to experience as an identifiable emergent (AE 53, 57) hints at a possible wider understanding of the objective ontological status of experience. For experience could be understood as an emergent in some way in continuity with that out of which it has emerged. We could in fact consider it, beyond the realm of human interaction, as a cosmologically significant reality analogous to the general approach taken, for example, by Alfred North Whitehead. As such a cosmologically significant identifiable emergent, experience may then point to more continuity between the formal structures of experience in the human sphere and the structures of other spheres of reality as well as of reality as a whole than Smith has explicitly indicated. Furthermore, he has often spoken of experience as funded result (e.g., AE 33, 40). Seeing experience as funded result would point out yet another sense, more internal to the movement of experience itself, in which experience, in Smith's understanding as inclusive encounter, is an identifiable emergent, namely, a result of an encounter or interrelationship.

While concentrating on properly human experience, Smith sketches further characteristics of that experience. First, it is pervasive and capable of assuming intersubjective form (AE 58 also 40). Second, it is in fact intersubjective and again, therefore, objective because it is subject to experimental intervention, control and reaffirmation (AE 58). Third, though he does not elaborate, Smith in clearly Roycean fashion affirms that there is structural recurrence in experience (AE 60, also 33), that it is temporally conditioned (AE 59 with 126) and, in line with his understanding of the self as center of intention or purpose, that it is essentially social (e.g., AE 23, 40, 59, 82). Underlying these affirmations that experience is characterized by recurrence, the quality of being shared in the present and through time and the possibility of critical comparison is Smith's more radically stated interpretation of life itself as constituted by experience. "One who experiences is a person who lives in his experience and whose experience constitutes his life (...) Experience is meaningful life" (AE 37 see 25). Finally, Smith asks if there are not some fundamental experiences, we could say, funded resultant encounters that transcend the boundaries of religion, culture and race and that are then deeper than the languages used to give expression to them (AE 60).

With *The Analogy of Experience*, in what could practically be called a hymn to a pragmatist understanding of experience, Smith espouses a position honoring experience as signifying "being in the world," involving "interacting with the world" and embracing "all that is ingredient in human community and history." Experience is a "many-sided interaction between man (...) and all that is to be encountered," furnishing "a richer and more complex form of *understanding* than is possible on the basis of reflective reason alone." Yet "experience without interpretation is dumb." So experience "transcends reason in concreteness and is therefore the matrix within which all understanding takes its rise." And culminantly, "Religion (...) is at the center of experience and vice versa" (AE 23–24). This "hymn to experience" gives evidence that Smith has continued to maintained a career-long concern with the themes of purpose, community, religion and experience. These concerns have characterized his philosophical project from as early on as his *Royce's Social Infinite*.

We can see and appreciate Smith's very important philosophical contribution in offering a general understanding of experience that, in a way reminiscent of what was Dewey's position as well, opens the way to conceiving of thought as a reflective form of experience. Thought itself can now come to be seen as that form of experience which provides reflexive access to human experience in its many forms and dimensions. Smith's interpretation of experience helps open the way to a non-dualist view of reality accessible to phenomenological analysis and reflexive argumentation.

Smith himself does allude to a possibly triadic structure to experience, a structure so important in various ways to Hegel, Peirce and Royce. He has indeed made available to us the more pragmatist notion of experience as fundamental philosophical category. However, while we are now able, with the notion of experience, to underscore the important pluralist character of concrete reality, as it stands Smith's thought remains, I would say, especially an opening toward, or even a crying out for, the recouping of a more explicitly developed sense of experience as structured movement. In addition, his writings leave open the question of the more general ontological implications of his interpretation of experience as revelatory constitutive encounter and funded result. But his argument that experience has an ontological status in reality, his recourse to analogy's reference from finite to infinite and his claim that experience constitutes life all call for and push inexorably forward toward a more explicitly generalized, even metaphysical, structuring of the notion of experience. His own insistence that experience is characterized by structural recurrence, is temporal and social in character, and is both revelatory encounter and funded result set up the general parameters for a philosophy of experience at once religious, metaphysical, psychological, cosmological and social.

In such a philosophy, when we surface what is implicit in Smith's own work and push beyond it, we come to see experience as a movement of becoming. As we will propose in the next chapters, it is in fact a tetradically structured movement. That movement is the relationship between initial selfhood and otherness, each of which exists in this relationship for the other, a relationship resulting in a newly constituted impoverished or enriched selfhood that, in turn, is equally initial selfhood in relationship with renewed otherness. Such an understanding of experience as tetradically structured finite becoming will, as we will propose in Chapter Seven below by means of an analysis reflecting the religious dimension of experience, point to the possibility of affirming a supportive context within which it occurs, namely, a triadically structured movement of becoming as selfhood and otherness in relationship resulting in enriched selfhood. We will come to see experience, which appears so slippery and elusive in its English-language usage, in its finite formulation as tetradically structured movement of enriching or impoverishing becoming. And, we will come to affirm it, in its paradigmatic formulation as supportive context, as triadically structured movement of enriching becoming, internally structured inclusive totality. Though we have here gotten way beyond the present step in our overall argumentation, I would already now suggest that these respectively tetradically and triadically structured movements of becoming are, each in its own way, that of which Hegel, Gadamer, Royce, and Dewey are really speaking and that to which Smith is in fact referring when he describes experience as constitutive revelatory encounter and funded result.[63]

NOTES

1. John Dewey referred to experience as a "weasel word" in the version of his first chapter that appeared in the first edition of *Experience and Nature*. This version is available in "Appendix 2: I. Experience and Philosophic Method," in *The Later Works, 1925–1953*, vol. I: *1925*, ed. Jo Ann Boydston with associate textual editors, Patricia Baysinger and Barbara Levine (Carbondale, IL: Southern Illinois University Press, 1981) 365–392. For the expression "weasel word," whose earlier usage regarding experience Dewey attributed to Ralph Perry, see 365.
2. For remarks on the notion of "experience" in several other language contexts, see Dale M. Schlitt, *Theology and the Experience of God* (New York: Peter Lang, 2001) 270 n. 23.
3. *Wahrheit und Methode*, 2nd ed. (Tübingen: J. C. B. Mohr, 1965) 329–344, and also of interest 52–66, 449–452/*Truth and Method*, 2nd revised ed., trans. revised by Joel Weinsheimer and Donald G. Marshall (New York: Crossroad, 1990) 346–362, and also of interest 55–70, 474–477. This revised translation is based on *Gesammelte Werke*, vol. 1: *Hermeneutik I. Wahrheit und Methode* (Tübingen: J. C. B. Mohr [Paul Siebeck], 1986). The German text will be cited according to the 1965 publication. For an excellent exposition and critique of Gadamer's hermeneutical interpretation of experience, see Benoît Garceau, O.M.I., "L'herméneutique philosophique de H.-G. Gadamer et la recherche de la vérité," *Église et Théologie* 10 (1979) 275–288. I am especially grateful to Prof. Garceau for drawing my attention to this aspect of Gadamer's work and am following his lead in this reading of Gadamer. However, responsibility for this summary presentation remains my own.

    For a very helpful, brief presentation of Gadamer's distinction between a more negative interpretation of experience as *Erlebnis* or "something you have" and a more positive interpretation of experience as *Erfahrung* or "ongoing integrative process in which what we encounter widens our horizon, but only by overturning an existing perspective, which we can then perceive was erroneous or at least narrow," see Joel Weinsheimer and Donald G. Marshall, "Translators' Preface," in *Truth and Method* xiii–xiv.
4. In *Wahrheit und Methode* xxii–xxiii/*Truth and Method* xxxvi–xxxvii, Gadamer states this position more indirectly. Later on in *Wahrheit und Methode* 451/*Truth and Method* 476, he explicitly mentions that he developed his universal hermeneutics on the basis of language in order, along with his wanting to resist the objectivising tendency of science, to avoid Hegel's "true" infinite. Our present project involves rehabilitating not only Hegel's bad infinite that, as was mentioned, Gadamer has tried to do, but Hegel's true infinite as well. On Hegel's concept of finite and infinite, see the Appendix, "The Contours of Hegel's Finite 'and' Infinite," at the end of this volume.
5. E.g., Gadamer, *Wahrheit und Methode*, more concerning that which is experienced: "Die hermeneutische Erfahrung hat es mit der *Überlieferung* zu tun. Sie ist es, die zur Erfahrung kommen soll. Überlieferung ist aber nicht einfach ein Geschehen, das man durch Erfahrung erkennt und beherrschen lernt, sondern sie ist *Sprache*, d.h. sie spricht von sich aus so wie ein Du" (340)/*Truth and Method*: "Hermeneutical experience is concerned with *tradition*. This is what is to be experienced. But tradition is not simply a process that experience teaches us to know and govern; it is *language—*

i.e., it expresses itself like a Thou" (358), More concerning the process of experience: "Die Sprachlichkeit der menschlichen Welterfahrung gibt unsere Analyse der herme- neutischen Erfahrung einen erweiterten Horizont" (423);/"The fact that human experience of the world is verbal in nature broadens the horizon of our analysis of hermeneutical experience" (447). See Garceau, "L'herméneutique philosophique" 279–281.

6. With regard to the question of language, see Garceau, "L'herméneutique philo- sophique" 286–288. In addition, I am grateful to Prof. Lawrence Sullivan for having pointed out the qualifying function of human bodily activity vis-à-vis oral language.

As a first response to possible deconstructionist criticisms, we should note that the present study intends neither to presume nor to work with a substantialist notion either of the self or of the other. For a brief discussion of the wholeness we experi- ence and the "more" involved in relation to deconstructionist positions, see William Desmond, "Hegel, Dialectic and Deconstruction," *Philosophy and Rhetoric* 18 (1985) 244–263; A. T. Nuyen, "Derrida's Deconstruction: Wholeness and *Différance*," *The Journal of Speculative Philosophy* 3 (1989) 26–38.

7. Josiah Royce, *The Problem of Christianity. Lectures Delivered at the Lowell Institute in Boston, and at Manchester College, Oxford*, 2 vols. (New York: Macmillan, 1913; reprinted 2 vols. in one, Hamdon, CN: Archon, 1967) vol. 1 p. x (cited hereafter according to the Archon reprinting with volume and page references indicated in the following notes and in the body of the present chapter's text on Royce). *The Problem of Christianity* has been republished with a new Introduction by John E. Smith, (Chicago: The University of Chicago Press, 1968). For further information on *The Problem of Christianity*, see Ignas K. Skrupskelis, "Annotated Bibliography of the Published Works of Josiah Royce, in: Josiah Royce, *The Basic Writings of Josiah Royce*, ed. John J. McDermott, vol. 2 (Chicago: The University of Chicago Press, 1969) 1216.

8. Though here and below I will be using more autobiographical references as a means of ordering my presentation of the three American philosophers treated in the present chapter, there are of course further reasons for selecting these authors. Among these reasons, they have all contributed significantly to the development of a philosophy of experience and they reflect, among themselves, a certain overall movement toward an ever more explicit focus on experience as basic philosophical category. In treating of them, we are able as well to treat, at least indirectly, of other important pragmatist thinkers, usingt the word in a rather general sense, not in- cluded in the present review. Indeed, if one will pardon the redundant phrasing, my reading in these authors constituted part of my experience leading to further reflec- tion on experience, its nature and roles.

9. Remark by Royce at a dinner in his honor. Cited by John E. Smith, *Royce's Social Infinite* (New York: Liberal Arts, 1950; 2nd ed. with new preface, Hamdon, CN: Archon, 1969) 3, cited here and hereafter according to the Archon edition.

10. It is in *The Problem of Christianity* itself that Royce speaks of loyalty as love for the community, 2:103. See also, e.g., 1:vii–ix, 206–210.

11. *Royce's Social Infinite* xiv. On whether God is the interpreter or the community of interpretation, or both, note *The Problem of Christianity* 2:219, and see Smith, *Royce's Social Infinite* 83 n. 36 and Edward A. Jarvis, *The Conception of God in the Later Royce* (The Hague: Martinus Nijhoff, 1975) 162–169. On the wider question of continuity and discontinuity in Royce's conception of God, see Jarvis 169–186.

12. (New York: Charles Scribner's Sons, 1912).

13. Gabriel Marcel, *La metaphysique de Royce* (Paris: Aubier, 1945) 213/*Royce's Metaphysics* (Chicago: Henry Regnery, 1956) 147. However, Marcel here goes on to claim that the shift from "God" to "Absolute Community" is no more than a terminological modification. This is surely not valid without further nuance. Marcel continues, rightly pointing out that "même la doctrine exposée dans la *Conception de Dieu* et dans *le Monde et l'Individu* n'était intelligible qu'à condition que Dieu fut conçu comme une Communauté"/"the doctrine expounded in [Royce's] The Conception of God and in [his] The World and the Individual is only intelligible when God is conceived as a community." Nevertheless, as Jarvis, *The Conception of God* 173–186, points out, Royce does seem to have shifted away from a position more easily interpretable as monist. See further in John E. Smith, "Royce: The Absolute and the Beloved Community Revisited," in *Meaning, Truth and God*, ed. Leroy S. Rouner (Notre Dame: University of Notre Dame Press, 1982) 135–153.
14. Jarvis, *The Conception of God* 173–186.
15. Frank M. Oppenheim, *Royce's Mature Philosophy of Religion* (Notre Dame, IN: University of Notre Dame Press, 1987) 310, makes this point more specifically regarding religious experience.
16. *Mind, Self and Society* (Chicago: The University of Chicago Press, 1934). Royce speaks of the socially constituted self without giving attention to the question of a possible ego/self relationship. Mead goes a step further in discussing the self as socially constituted but preserves the ego or more accurately the "I," as opposed to the "me," from social construction. E.g., *Mind, Self and Society* 214. For more precise remarks on Royce, see James Harry Cotton, *Royce on the Human Self* (Cambridge, MA: Harvard, 1954) and John E. Smith, "The Contemporary Significance of Royce's Theory of the Self," in *Themes in American Philosophy* (New York: Harper, 1970) 109–121. See further on Mead and on the distinction between ego and self in Wolfhart Pannenberg, *Anthropologie in theologischer Perspektive* (Göttingen: Vandenhoeck & Ruprecht, 1983) 179–235/*Anthropology in Theological Perspective* (Philadelphia: Westminster, 1985) 185–242; _____, "Person und Subjekt: zur Uberwindung des Subjektivismus in Menschenbild und im Gottesverständnis," *Neue Zeitschrift für Systematische Theologie und Religionsphilosophie* 18 (1976) 133–148.
17. John E. Smith sympathetically contextualizes Royce's position. See "Introduction," *The Problem of Christianity* 19–21, where he situates Royce's position within the historical struggle between liberal and orthodox Christianity. For Royce's own comments, see *The Problem of Christianity* 1:xxiv–xxix.
18. Robert Cummings Neville, "American Philosophy's Way around Modernism (and Post-Modernism)," in *The Recovery of Philosophy in America. Essays in Honor of John Edwin Smith*, ed. Thomas P. Kasulis and Robert Cummings Neville (Albany: State University of New York Press, 1997) 266–267, clarifies that "both the later Royce and the 'early [John E.] Smith' were well acquainted with the writings of Charles Peirce in which interpretation is explained as action, the action of employing and modifying habits. Interpretation is thus not 'mental' in any sense that contrasts with the real world but is more like the form of the human side of the interaction that constitutes experience." I would agree that the later Royce did not wish to contrast "mental" with the real world. But I would want to note that he did describe interpretation as a cognitive act or mental process and I would suggest that one of the reasons why he would not contrast such an act with the real world is that even for the later Royce the real world remained an expression of mind(s). This last point would seem to me to be the conclusion to be drawn from the fact that Royce saw a basic continuity

between his previous thought and what he said in *The Problem of Christianity*. We should also note, on the one hand, the later Royce's metaphysical generalisation of Peirce's theories of sign and interpretation and, on the other hand, that same Royce's explicit statements concerning interpretation as a cognitive and mental process as well as concerning his understanding of sign as the sign of a mind.

19. Royce notes that an interpreter works with two minds other than his own. So the interpretation is a "third" or mediating idea, with idea understood in a Jamesian sense as a "leading" (2:180–181). Signs coming from the mind interpreted give rise to this third in the mind of the interpreter, who "addresses this 'third' to the mind to which he interprets the first" (2:204).

20. See his *Royce's Social Infinite* 11, 86 and throughout the volume. On the temporal character of the process of interpretation and on the relationship between the three elements in the process of interpretation, on the one hand, and the three dimensions of time, namely, past, present and future, on the other, see 83–87. Also, briefly, Oppenheim, *Royce's Mature Philosophy of Religion* 31–32.

21. See John K. Roth, "Introduction," *The Philosophy of Josiah Royce* (New York: Crowell, 1971) 27.

22. In addition to the more formal areas of ambiguity indicated here following in the body of the present chapter, it might be helpful to note again the ambiguity concerning the location of the divine in Royce's later thought. Had Royce more consistently recalled the triadic structure of interpretation in its fullest realization and in which the three "elements" must always remain distinct if they are to explicate what the dyadics cannot, he might have been able to present in a clearer way Absolute, Beloved Community, Spirit, Founder, Interpreter and so forth in a more explicitly trinitarian formulation. For helpful background information, see Michael William Calligan, "Royce on God and Experience: A Study of The World and the Individual" (Ph.D. dissertation, Tulane University, 1973).

23. See Smith's remarks on the confusion in Royce's treatment of comparison and interpretation, "Introduction," *The Problem of Christianity* 29.

24. Mary Briody Mahowald refers to "idealist pragmatism" in *An Idealist Pragmatism. The Development of the Pragmatic Element in the Philosophy of Josiah Royce* (The Hague: Martinus Nijhoff, 1972). John E. Smith speaks of Royce's theory of reality as a "voluntarism" and an "ethical idealism," in "Creativity in Royce's Philosophical Idealism," in *Contemporary Studies in Philosophical Idealism*, ed. John Howie and Thomas Buford (Cape Cod, MA: Claude Stark, 1975) 197. See also Smith, "Introduction," *The Problem of Christianity* 1. In his *Royce's Social Infinite* 46 n. 96, Smith notes that Dewey objected to calling Royce a pragmatist but then Smith himself refers to Royce's "absolute pragmatism." *Purpose and Thought. The Meaning of Pragmatism* (London: Hutchinson, 1978) 26.

25. In his *Royce's Social Infinite* 90, Smith calls Royce's interpretation "living reason."

26. Due to the length of Dewey's career, the breath of his interests and the depth of his philosophical insight, many have come to see, as Gérard Deledalle put it, "C'est donc toute l'histoire de la pensée américaine qui apparait en filigrane dans l'œuvre de Dewey." *L'idée d'expérience dans la philosophie de John Dewey* (Paris: Presses Universitaires de France, 1967) unnumbered introductory page/"The whole history of American thought appears in filigree in Dewey's work," my trans. Jo Ann Boydston, ed., *Guide to the Works of John Dewey* (Carbondale: Southern Illinois University Press, 1970) provides an invaluable introduction to Dewey's life and thought. I am grateful to Dr. Colin O'Connell for research concerning Dewey on experience.

27. *The Later Works, 1925–1953*, vol. I: *1925*, ed. Jo Ann Boydston with associate textual editors, Patricia Baysinger and Barbara Levine (Carbondale, IL: Southern Illinois University Press, 1981, 1st ed. originally published 1925, 2nd ed. 1929) (Hereafter page references in the text of this section on Dewey as well as in the relevant notes refer to the 1981 version of the second edition.) Already now we could note that Dewey felt quite frustrated by the fact that he did not seem to be able to bring others to understand what he meant by "experience." This frustration was such that he later proposed to speak not of "experience" but of "culture" and to rename his book, "Nature and Culture." He said that he found the historical obstacles to his use of the word insurmountable. But he continued to insist that "if 'experience' is to designate the inclusive subject-matter it must designate both what is experienced and the ways of experiencing it." John Dewey, "Appendix I. The Unfinished Introduction. Experience and Nature: A Re-Introduction," in *The Later Works* 361. Though there are great ambiguities in his presentation of experience, I think we should be grateful that he never really got around to changing the word either in the text or in the title of his book. Interestingly, Tina Manferdini, *L'io e l'esperienza religiosa in John Dewey* (Bologna: Zanichelli, 1963) 3, uses the term "culture" as a way of helping to explain what Dewey means by experience.

28. Francis E. George, O.M.I., "Dewey and Dialectic," in Robert C. Whittemore, ed., *Dewey and his Influence. Essays in Honor of George Estes Barton, Tulane Studies in Philosophy* 22 (New Orleans: Tulane University, 1973) 22.

29. Among many relevant studies on Dewey's understanding of experience, the following have proven particularly helpful: Yu-Shan Han, "The Meaning of Experience in the Thought of John Dewey," Ph.D. diss., Boston University, 1929; approaching Dewey on experience from the perspective of Dewey's *Art as Experience* (New York: Minton, Balch & Co., 1934): Jack Kaminsky, "Dewey's Concept of *An* Experience," *Philosophy and Phenomenological Research* 17 (1957) 316–330; Carmela Metelli di Lallo, *La dinamica dell'esperienza nel pensiero di J. Dewey* (Padova: Liviana Editrice, 1958); Stephen D. Ross, "The Philosophy of Experience: an Analysis of the Concept of Experience in the Philosophy of John Dewey," Ph.D. diss., Columbia University, 1961, a study quite critical of the ambiguities in Dewey's thought on experience; Dinesh Chandra Mathur, *Naturalistic Philosophies of Experience. Studies in James, Dewey and Farber against the Background of Husserl's Phenomenology* (St. Louis: Warren H. Green, 1971) 67–111; Manferdini, *L'io et l'esperienza*; Deledalle, *L'idée d'expérience*; George, "Dewey and Dialectic" (1973); Francesco Coppola, *Esperienza e valore nel pensiero di John Dewey* (Naples: Morano, 1978); John E. Smith, *Purpose and Thought. The Meaning of Pragmatism* (London: Hutchinson, 1978) 78–95, esp. 78–89 and 142–147. These works contain additional bibliography concerning Dewey on experience.

30. See Ross, *The Philosophy of Experience* 28.

31. Manferdini, *L'io e l'esperienza* 22–23, insists that for Dewey experience is, in a wide sense, primordially social in that the "I" is located within the experience.

32. Metelli di Lallo, *La dinamica dell'esperienza* 41, speaks of experience, according to Dewey, as a "processo o progetto di anticipazione e di rinnovamento incessante delle situazioni, proteso verso il futuro"/"process or project of incessant anticipation and renewal of situations, stretched out toward the future," my trans. See also Smith, *Purpose and Thought* 86.

33. "Abstract," in "The Philosophy of Experience," 1. After noting some difficulties in Dewey's thought, Ross goes on, on p. 2, to say: "Dewey's conception of experience offers the possibility of a systematic philosophy of the human process in which all features of experience are unified through a central philosophic category (…) [representing] the human process as propulsive, cumulative, active and yet random, trivial, inconsequential. As this category is developed, as theories of art, knowledge and morals are interpreted in its perspective, it becomes clearer and more sharply defined, then a systematic philosophy emerges. This is Dewey's philosophic method."

34. Herbert Schneider, "Dewey's Psychology," in Jo Ann Boydston, ed., *Guide to the Works of John Dewey* (Carbondale: Southern Illinois University Press, 1970) 1–14. Furthermore, Manferdini, *L'io et l'esperienza* 6, speaks of Dewey's notion of experience as the resulting synthesis of two sets of interests, namely, the biological-evolutionary and the historical-sociological.

35. "Dewey and Dialectic" 22. It must be admitted, however, that it is not easy to sort out, in clear detail, just what Dewey means by the various types, forms or even phases of experience. For example, Metelli di Lallo, *La dinamica dell'esperienza*, speaks of two types of experience that Dewey distinguishes in one of his writings (49), then a page later (50), regarding another of Dewey's writings, writes of at least two grades (*gradi*) of experience. On the following page (51), she notes the existence of first and second phases (*fase*) of experience and a page later (52) refers to experience itself as the first stage (*stadio*) followed by a second step, experience-in-becoming (*l'esperienza-in-sviluppo*), which is what we call thought. She then, on the same page, goes on to speak of three stages. Manferdini, *L'io et l'esperienza* 11, speaks more traditionally of two forms of experience, namely, primary experience (*esperienza primaria*) and secondary experience (*esperienza secondaria*) and their interrelationship.

36. In this regard, one might consult Dewey's *Experience and Nature* 5–6, 9, 15–17, 28–29, 30–31, 34, 59–62, 67–68, 96–97, 143–145, 275. As Manferdini, *L'io et l'esperienza* 28, writes, "Dewey abitualmente definisce il metodo empirico come il metodo denotativo, cioè descrittivo. La caratteristica di tale metodo non risiede soltanto nel prendere le mosse dall'esperienza primaria, ma anche e soprattutto nell'usare I prodotti secondari della riflessione (idee, ipotesi, teorie, ecc.) come vie di ritorno a qualche situazione problematica dell'esperienza primaria"/"Dewey habitually defines the empirical method as the denotative method, that is, a descriptive one. That which is characteristic of this method is not to be found only in taking [into consideration] the movements of primary experience, but also and especially in using the secondary products of reflection (ideas, hypotheses, theories, etc.) as ways to return to a particular, problematic situation of primary experience," my trans. On Dewey's view of experience, considered from the perspective of Dewey's denotative method and without mentioning the notion of consummatory experience, as moving from primary experience through reflective experience to a return to primary experience, see, for example, Smith, *Purpose and Thought* 144–147.

37. See Ross, "The Philosophy of Experience" 72.

38. Coppola, *Esperienza e valore* 21, speaks of reflective experience as carrying primary experience to its fulfilment (*compimento*). He then notes that this reflexive experience becomes, in turn, the content of a new situation. We might, however, want to add that reflective experience does this especially in as it returns to gross or primary

experience. If it were to do this on its own alone and not as a return, we would fall into the trap of what Dewey would identify as an idealist position. It would seem that this content of a new situation may well be, for Dewey, consummatory experience becoming again a new primary experience or at least an element in a new primary experience.

39. "Things interacting in certain ways *are* experience; they are what is experienced." Dewey, *Experience and Nature* 12.

40. Dewey himself uses the term "consummatory experience" in *Experience and Nature* 258 when he refers to "past consummatory experiences." He also speaks of a "consummatory union of environment and organism" (159).

41. In contrast with my tendency to identify consummatory experience as a third phase or form of experience, Manferdini, *L'io et l'esperienza* 36, 45, 46, 50, within the context of her distinction between consummatory and instrumental in Dewey, has in effect identified the consummatory aspect of experience with primary experience in that she identifies consummatory with immediate. She identifies instrumental with reflective experience in that she identifies it with mediation. However, my reading of Dewey, *Experience and Nature* 113, where, within a discussion of rational knowledge and science, he says, "These emergent immediate events remain the beginning and the end of knowledge," leads me to think that if consummatory were linked with immediate, it would have to apply as characteristic at least to both primary experience and what I am calling consummatory experience. It may well be, then, that according to Dewey it to some extent applies to both, but can be seen as specifically characteristic of the here-proposed third type or phase of experience.

42. In a letter to Max Otto, dated January 25, 1929, Dewey clarifies the three functional forms of experience: "What I meant—only didn't know it—was that *reflective analysis* & its products form a *method* for leading back to the *subjectmatter* of direct or 'gross' experience; so that the *former* designates or denotes a path & projects a goal to be found in the latter—which being illuminated, clarified & directed by reflective findings as method, *also* tests and checks the latter." Cited in "Textual Commentary," in John Dewey, *The Later Works, 1925–1953*, vol. I: *1925* ed. Jo Ann Boydston with associate textual editors, Patricia Baysinger and Barbara Levine (Carbondale, IL: Southern Illinois University Press, 1981) 408. Ultimately, the fact that for Dewey there need to be three forms of experience, namely, gross or primary experience, reflected experience and consummatory experience, rather than the more traditionally spoken of two functional forms, that is, gross or primary experience and reflected experience, is rooted in Dewey's very conception of empirical method with its required return to the subject matter under investigation.

43. See Schlitt, *Hegel's Trinitarian Claim* 121–139, esp. 129–131. In "The Philosophy of Experience," 5–6, Ross briefly discusses one "Hegelian" characteristic of Dewey's, namely, the tendency, while stressing individual experience, to consider individual and cultural or societal experience more or less together rather than separating them out. In his "Introduction," in John Dewey, *The Later Works, 1925–1953*, vol. 1: *1925*, ed. Jo Ann Boydston with associate textual editors, Patricia Baysinger and Barbara Levine (Carbondale, IL: Southern Illinois University Press, 1981) xvii, Sidney Hook, speaks of "echoes of Hegel and Peirce (…) in this [Dewey's] analysis." For Dewey's own remarks on Hegel's influence on him, see "From Abstraction to Experimentalism," in Dewey, *The Later Works, 1925–1953*, vol. 5: *1929–1930*, ed. Jo Ann Boydston, textual editor Kathleen F. Poulos (Carbondale, IL: Southern Illinois University Press, 1984) 147–160 and specifically concerning Hegel 152–155.

44. Schneider, "Dewey's Psychology" 10–11.
45. See Ross, "The Philosophy of Experience" e.g. 261.
46. Ross, "The Philosophy of Experience" 4–5.
47. Schneider, "Dewey's Psychology" 7.
48. Regrettable, I have not been able to retrace the exact reference.
49. "Dewey and Dialectic" 36–37.
50. A point raised in question form by Prof. John K. Roth many years ago.
51. I thought it was Karl Barth but have subsequently been unable to document the reference.
52. E.g., *Reason and God* (New Haven, CN: Yale, 1961) xii; *The Spirit of American Philosophy* (New York: Oxford, 1963) 204–206; *Experience and God* (New York: Oxford, 1968) 5–6; *The Analogy of Experience* (New York: Harper, 1973) 33; *Purpose and Thought* 10, 78–79.
53. *Themes in American Philosophy* (New York: Harper, 1970) 1–6. For an earlier, three-fold formulation see *The Spirit of American Philosophy* 188.
54. (New York: Liberal Arts, 1950; 2nd ed. with new preface, Hamdon, CT: Archon, 1969).
55. On Smith's thought on experience in general and on what I have elsewhere suggested could be called three phases in the development of that thought, see Dale M. Schlitt, "John E. Smith on Experience," *Philosophy and Theology* 2 (1987) 105–123, with a selected bibliography of Smith's works up to and including his 1973 *The Analogy of Experience* on 122–123.

   In "American Philosophy's Way around Modernism (and Postmodernism)," in Thomas P. Kasulis and Robert Cummings Neville, eds., *The Recovery of Philosophy in America. Essays in Honor of John Edwin Smith* (Albany: State University of New York Press, 1997) 251–268, Robert Cummings Neville has indicated some serious reservations (266–267) about my study of Smith on experience. For further remarks and my response, in which I try both to recognize the weaknesses in my previous study and to clarify certain points I had made there, see my *Theology and the Experience of God* 62–63 n. 16.
56. Further on John E. Smith on experience: Douglas R. Anderson, "John E. Smith and the Heart of Experience," in Thomas P. Kasulis and Robert Cummings Neville, eds., *The Recovery of Philosophy in America. Essays in Honor of John Edwin Smith* (Albany: State University of New York Press, 1997) 115–130 with Smith's response, "Philosophy in America: Recovery and Future Development," in Kasulis and Cummings, eds., *The Recovery of Philosophy in America* 281–283; Robert Cummings Neville, "American Philosophy's Way around Modernism (and Postmodernism)," in Kasulis and Cummings, eds., *The Recovery of Philosophy in America* 251–268 esp. 253–255 with Smith's response, "Philosophy in America: Recovery and Future Development," in Kasulis and Cummings, eds., *The Recovery of Philosophy in America* 299–307.

   It will be important to stress that my concern here is with Smith's presentation of his own thought on experience more than with his presentations of and commentaries on other philosophers, though of course in such presentations and commentaries Smith does bring forth elements of his own thought on experience. In the remarks in the present chapter, I have continued to rely on Smith's studies that I find most helpful for getting directly at his own thought on experience. However, it should be noted that both Neville, "American Philosophy's Way around Modernism (and Postmodernism)" 266 n. 8, and Smith himself, "Philosophy in America: Recovery and

Future Development" 302, have said that one should deal more explicitly with Smith's study, *Purpose and Thought. The Meaning of Pragmatism* (London: Hutchinson, 1978). Having read this excellent volume, I still prefer, for present purposes, to remain with Smith's works being reviewed, in the present chapter, in my survey of his thought on experience.

57. "Tre tipi e due dogmi dell'empirismo," *Revista di Filosofia* 48 (1957) 257–273; Eng. version: "Three Types and Two Dogmas of Empiricism," *The Christian Scholar* 43 (1960) 199–212, reprinted in John E. Smith, *Themes in American Philosophy* (New York: Harper, 1970) 42–60. Hereafter cited in the text of the present chapter according to the pagination of the English version in *Themes in American Philosophy* and abbreviated TAP.

58. *The Journal of Philosophy* 55 (1958) 538–546, reprinted in *Reason and God* (New Haven, CN: Yale, 1961) 173–183, hereafter abbreviated RG and cited, according to this reprinting, in the text of the present chapter.

59. (Milwaukee: Marquette University Press, 1967) see 42–66, hereafter cited in the text as RE.

60. (New York: Oxford, 1968) 21–45, hereafter abbreviated EG and cited in the text.

61. E.g.: Self as refracting (through purpose) and partially constituted by experience; the social character of experience.

62. (New York: Harper, 1973), hereafter abbreviated AE and cited in the text.

63. This is of course not to conclude that Smith himself or any of the others here mentioned would necessarily be interested in or willing to follow this path.

A GRAMMAR OF EXPERIENCE

Being as experience is so simple and yet so complex, so familiar and yet so elusive, I suggest that, after our review of several philosophers on experience, we now, as a further step in our overall argument, continue our effort at greater understanding of what we mean when we speak of experience by approaching it from two complementary methodological perspectives. The first of these perspectives will be grammatical. In our consideration of experience from this first perspective, we will describe the characteristics of experience and conjugate its forms. This grammatical sketch will set the stage for a further analysis of experience from a second perspective, namely, that of the phenomenologist who "looks" at experience as structured movement of self and other in their relationship with one another. Both our grammatical and our phenomenological considerations will focus more explicitly on human experience. However, we should note from the outset that what we say here concerning human experience could, with appropriate adjustment, likewise be predicated of experience considered on wider, more cosmological and even metaphysical levels.

In a very modest way, then, we will in the present chapter work out a grammar and, in the next chapter, a phenomenology of experience. In our grammar of experience, the description of the characteristics of experience and the conjugation of its forms will proceed in three major steps. First of all, we will recall and further develop some of the insights we have gathered from various philosophers of experience. Then, in a second step we will note several characteristics of experience as such before, in a third step, sketching out a number of varieties of experience by establishing five different listings of forms of experience. Within this third step, in working out these lists we will, first of all, identify three overall types or phases of experience, second, describe the forms of experience distinguishable on the basis of the types of self involved and, third, note the possible forms of experience we can differentiate on the basis of the "location" from which or the "place" in which the other presents itself to the self. Fourth, we will examine the other as present or "absent," and, fifth, refer to the forms of experience distinguishable on the basis of the possible types of resultant self.[1] As is usually the case in any attempt to distinguish and differentiate that which relates or refers to the human, such distinctions and differences will of course overlap and reappear in ways that will surpass our necessary but always insufficient attempts to categorize and classify them. The human self is, or at least strives to be, an integrated whole. While that self is of course the sum of its experiences, it is, in its striving, more than these varied experiences.

Appropriating Insights from Others in the Past

In many ways, my own reflection over a number of years on the question of a post-Hegelian philosophical theology, in which the notion of experience would play a central role, proceeded backwards. As was mentioned in the last chapter, instead of following what would have been a more logical and chronological order, namely, starting with Hegel and then reading later philosophers, I first read Royce, Dewey and Smith on experience and only later on turned for several years to a study of Hegel. After extensive reading in Hegel, I noticed striking similarities as well as profound differences between his idealist construction of experience and Royce's, Dewey's and Smith's varyingly pragmatist readings of it. Among many points of possible comparison, I noted that Hegel's essentially triadically structured inclusive infinite seemed to find echoes, though perhaps only echoes, in Royce's triadically structured notions of experience understood as a process of interpretation, and of the Beloved Community seen as community of interpretation. Dewey, in turn, seemed to have transformed the Hegelian dialectic into a triply structured movement of experience. However, as we mentioned in Chapter Four above, he himself spoke rather more explicitly of his denotative method and of his understanding of the forms of experience as having been modeled on empirical methodology. And while Smith was at home with many philosophers, especially Peirce, James and Dewey, he showed what appeared to me to be an affinity between, on the one hand, his notion of experience as encounter and result and, on the other hand, Hegel's concept of spirit as process and result inclusive of this process. Only then did I discover that Hans-Georg Gadamer had already attempted to rehabilitate what Hegel had called the "bad infinite" (*schlechte Unendlichkeit*), namely, infinite progression, by developing an understanding of experience as an ongoing process that was linguistic in nature.

Smith, in particular, has effectively transformed Royce's somewhat more mentally imaged, cognitively functioning understanding of experience as a process of interpretation into a wider understanding of the process of experience, taken on its own terms, that does not need to be explained through recourse to some other mental or linguistic process or activity. Experience is not this or that. It is experience.

In fact, I would see Smith's development as continuing the movement along an historically much longer trajectory that is, in hindsight, traceable from as far back as Hegel's move beyond Kant's dualism on through Charles Sanders Peirce to Royce's reworking of Peirce's triadic into a theory of the beloved community, in which theory experience is understood as a movement of interpretation, on to Dewey's understanding of experience as an inclusive whole occurring in three forms. I would then suggest that a look back over the modern and contemporary history of philosophy will reveal a certain trajectory of common concern traceable from Hegel's attempt to move beyond the dualism of Kant, to Peirce and Royce, with their triadically structured understandings of interpretation, to Dewey's reaction against dualisms, and on to Smith's insistence on experience as constitutive revelatory encounter. They are surely all trying to overcome a perceived dichotomy between self and other that would appear to find its modern philosophical roots in Hume and Kant and, before them, in Descartes.

Smith himself worked to widen further Dewey's presentation of experience in order to show that "as trajectory of self-realization" experience needs to be understood in a way that goes beyond Dewey's more reductionist instrumental reading to include, in a more forceful and explicit way, a religious dimension.[2] Smith's position at the contemporary end of the trajectory that I have proposed indicates something of the importance of his efforts to rethink the notion of experience. He has set the English-speaking world's philosophical stage for further development of a renewed and constructive philosophy of experience.

The richness of these post-Hegelian philosophies of experience allows for seemingly endless points of further comparison among them. For example, for

Smith, experience is pervasive and capable of assuming intersubjective form. It is in fact intersubjective and therefore, in at least partial contrast to Gadamer's insistence on the originality and uniqueness of each experience, then objective because it is subject to experimental intervention, control and reaffirmation. For Smith, again, experience is of course characterized by structural recurrence, is temporally conditioned and essentially social. His more radically stated interpretation of life itself as a reality constituted by experience complements and undergirds these affirmations that experience is characterized by recurrence, by the quality of being shared in the present and through time, and by the possibility of critical comparison. For Smith, experience is revelatory constitutive encounter and funded result.

In complementary and mutually corrective fashion, Gadamer's more linguistic and existentialist interpretation and Dewey's and Smith's more pragmatist readings of experience provide important access to the at least implicit understanding of experience operative in much of the contemporary Euro-North American cultural and intellectual community.[3] On the one hand, Gadamer alerts us to the conditioning and constructive functions of language in human experience. He also rightly recalls the experience both of negation and of newness. He speaks of negation and, consequently, of a sense of personal finitude as inherent characteristics of any moment of human experience. He likewise refers to the essential uniqueness and the aspect of newness characteristic of a truly human experience. In any moment of experience we, to some extent at least and in one way or another, both suffer and rejoice. On the other hand, from the perspective of our present concerns, I would argue that Smith helps correct Gadamer when Smith insists that even properly human experience is wider and more inclusive than linguistic experience.[4] He complements Gadamer's description of experience as event and as being unique when he points out a certain recurrence characteristic of human experience. Yet Gadamer's insistence on the more existential characteristics of experience does lend emotive depth and resonance to Royce's interpretation of experience and to Dewey's three forms of experience as well as to Smith's analyses of multidimensional experience as revelatory constitutive encounter and funded result.

Already at this point in our effort to learn from the past, I would suggest that a critical appropriation of insights, taken especially from the philosophies of Gadamer, Royce, Dewey and Smith, into the nature and function of human experience provides us with an understanding of experience that is more adequate to the reality in question and can at least in principle be shared by people of very different intellectual persuasions and interests.

As we continue our recall of past insights, we should point out that Smith himself does allude to a possibly triadic structure to experience, a structure so important in various ways to Hegel, Royce, and Dewey. Especially Dewey and Smith have made available to us the more pragmatist notion of experience as fundamental philosophical category. This notion seems inherently more flexible than the basic concept with which Hegel worked, namely, that of thought (*Denken*). Working with experience should help us remain more open to the important pluralist character of concrete reality, while also allowing us at the same time, with Hegel, to account for the sense of wholeness and integration that occurs in any moment of enriching experience in which we participate and of which we become aware at least from time to time.

Toward the end of Chapter Three above, I noted that a critique of Hegel's thought, and especially of his affirmation of a beginning in the initial unity that is pure being, leaves us with a different initial unity, namely, the relationship between self and other that, in turn, gives rise to an enriched or impoverished resultant self. It is striking to notice that Gadamer, Royce, Dewey and Smith, each in his own way, also open the door to an understanding of human experience as the multidimensional relationship between self and other that results in a self which is, globally speaking, either enriched or impoverished. This enriched or impoverished self has, from the perspective of the negative side to the experience, left something behind, and thus experiences its own finitude. From the perspective of the positive side to the experience, it has found itself at a new vantage point. This resultant self equally finds itself immediately and ever renewedly in relationship with an other. Thus, we can say that we have, in a preliminary way, rehabilitated Hegel's notion of the bad infinite without having to make a Gadamerian reduction of experience to language. We have then arrived at an understanding of human experience as a finite movement of becoming. It is a tetradically structured movement of either overall enrichment or impoverishment, a movement from initial selfhood and otherness in relationship on to resultant enriched or impoverished selfhood. And this resultant selfhood is itself ever renewedly initial selfhood and otherness in relationship.

Working now with "relationship" rather than Dewey's notion of "interaction" or Smith's use of "encounter" allows for a wider understanding of experience and its various forms.[5] Among these forms we might think, for example, of a more monosubjectival or internal movement of becoming such as the movement of thought within a given person, or of a relationship between a self or personal center of intention and a nonpersonal other, or, again, of a more intersubjectival relationship, hence an interrelationship, between a self or personal center of intention and another self.[6] Whatever form the movement of experience may take, I would again propose that it is the tetradic structure of that movement or becoming which underlies Gadamer's understanding of human experience as infinite progression, Royce's notion of experience as interpretation, Dewey's stress on a philosophy of experience's ability to overcome dualisms, and Smith's insistence that experience, as a process or encounter, exhibits a certain recurrence. This same structured movement also undergirds, but rather more implicitly, Dewey's speaking of enriched experience and Smith's assertion that experience is funded result. Of course, though this enriched experience or funded result is to some degree always an admixture of enrichment and impoverishment, it can, as we have already indicated, be characterized overall as resulting either in an enriched or an impoverished self. *Mutatis mutandis*, this enriched or impoverished self (and of course the initial self) can, as we will note further below, be the shared awareness of a community or of two persons (a couple or friends) or, again, the individualized awareness of a single person.

As we come slowly to the end of these remarks concerning several insights culled from selected philosophers writing on experience, we would do well to recall the overall goal of the present study by noting that our understanding of experience as structured movement, equally relation, process and result, will provide a particularly helpful point of reference and an insight commonly available to those who would like to do further work, from various perspectives, in the area of a post-Hegelian philosophical theology.

After bringing together a number of these insights and recalling again that Hegel remains ever in the background of our discussion, I would like, in proposing to go along with but especially beyond Hegel and these philosophers, to sketch out further characteristics of experience as such before listing, in somewhat greater detail, various forms that experience takes.

Characteristics of Experience

As we begin these remarks on various characteristics of experience, it might be helpful to recall briefly the approach being used in these considerations in general, and in the present chapter in particular. From one perspective, namely, when considered in itself, what we are doing here, whether it be myself writing or another person reading what I write, is, to use for the moment Dewey's term, a primary or gross experience with all that term implies for Dewey. From another perspective, namely, when considered as a reflection by myself as writer or an aid to reflection by someone as reader, again to use Dewey's term, what we are doing is a reflected experience. Thus, from both perspectives the present activities of writing and reading presuppose, in a rather more ordinary sense, reference to my own experience and to that of the reader. From the second perspective, these activities of critical and constructive reflection and analysis presuppose what Dewey had called primary or gross experience. These two forms of reference to experience will be present, though only occasionally explicitly noted, throughout the present analysis of and reflection first on several characteristics and then on various forms of experience. They will as well, of course, be present in the subsequent phenomenology of experience that will follow in the next chapter below and on throughout the rest of this study. Now, however, we turn more specifically to the question of experience and its characteristics.

In his day, Dewey felt it necessary to speak of experience and nature, which is of course the title he gave to one of his major works.[7] I would propose that Dewey has in fact opened the door to a view in which experience and nature will no longer need to be juxtaposed and with which, if we push his understanding of experience far enough, we can in fact go beyond his explicit concern to locate human experience *within* nature. In so locating experience, Dewey succeeded in affirming the ontological density of experience as a given reality and Smith, in turn, has significantly reinforced this affirmation of the solid ontological status of experience as event, encounter and result of that encounter. We can indeed go further, even to affirming the generalized ontological and cosmological significance of experience as that which constitutes reality as such. Everything that occurs is, in one way or another, a moment of experience. So we no longer need to speak of experience and nature but can, rather, speak more simply of the nature of experience.

As mentioned at the beginning of this chapter, in the present analysis and reflection we are not in a position to carry out a more explicit discussion of this ontological and cosmological significance being attributed to experience as it occurs in the non-human world, and so we will continue to focus here primarily on human experience.[8] These experiences are, then, events and relationships that make us what we are. We are indeed the sum of "our" experiences, namely, the ones in which we have already participated and due to which we experience a sense of loss vis-à-vis what we were in the past and a sense either of momentary wholeness or some form of disintegration, or perhaps something of both. And yet we are more than that sum of the specific experience in which we participate at any given moment, since we retain the potential for further experiences, and strive to surpass any given experience.

These experiences are both objective and subjective in character. They are objective primarily in that they are given relationships between self and other. They are there. They can of course be described as objective in other senses as well, several of which we have already discussed in the previous chapter. For example, experience in general bears a certain recurrent structure, and experiences in particular can, in a certain sense and to a certain degree, be repeated. Experience is conditioned by many factors that, one would ordinarily think, render them subjective, and this in the sense that the subject or self resulting from the experience may, as again initial self, have itself brought them into play in the moment of experience or have been influenced by these factors in expected or unexpected ways. These factors may include language, established thought patterns, cultural and social influences, gender, temperament, genetic predispositions, and the like. However, these very conditioning factors also underscore the objective character of experience in the sense that they themselves are givens and their very "givenness" militates against the idea that experience is merely subjective, at least in the sense of being in some way capricious. These factors themselves can be taken into consideration. They can be studied, analyzed and reflected upon.

But experience, as selfhood and otherness in relationship giving rise to resultant selfhood that is renewedly initial selfhood in relationship with otherness, can equally be considered subjective, and this in several more specific senses of the word. Indeed, I would propose that experience can be "capricious" in the sense that the experiencing self involved can take a decision, with this word understood in a very wide sense, that is both unforeseen and not reducible to the factors impinging upon that decision. More fundamentally, experience is essentially subjective in that it necessarily includes reference to a self as subject and, often enough, also to an other who is equally a self or subject in a given relationship. Furthermore, experience necessarily involves reference to the self that results from the relationship between initial self and other. The "subjectivism" characteristic of experience is itself an objective fact. Working carefully with the notion and reality of experience leads us to see that experience is both objective and subjective in character and cannot be reduced either to the objective or to the subjective alone. It is objective, subjective and even goes beyond this distinction. Surely we can rejoice in the fact that experience is, at the same time, though from different perspectives, wholly objective and wholly subjective.

A further basic characteristic of experience that is equally objective and subjective, and which even to some extent underlies both of these characteristics, is the fact that experience always involves some sense of immediacy. Of course, this immediacy takes on different forms according to the types of experience in question, whether that experience involve, for example, more direct contact with a given other or more reflexively mediated presence when one is, for example, thinking over a problem or a riddle. The form this immediacy takes can also vary according to the type of other with which the self finds itself in relationship. The beauty of a sunset would be immediately present to the self in a more direct fashion than would another person who, as a self, is present, as Smith has noted, in a more mediated way through words, signs and the like. In such a situation, when we say that we know or experience another person , we are speaking of a direct encounter as mediated immediacy.[9]

It will come as no surprise that an ontologically dense, equally objective and subjective experience characterized by a form of immediacy will involve emotion. Often in the past we have tended to relegate the more specifically emotional character of experience to the realm of the "merely" subjective, meaning that emotion refers only to the state of the experiencing self within the relationship between self and other. While it is true that the self is a primary *locus* of emotion, we need to recall that both self and other may, in a given experience, be selves, so that emotion can be attributed to both of them. However, whether emotion be attributed to the experiencing self or to the experiencing and experienced self as well as to the experienced and experiencing other, the fact is that emotion remains an integral element in the relationship between selfhood and otherness giving rise to resultant enriched or impoverished selfhood. Emotion, understood for present purposes in a very general way as affective engagement in favor of or against the relationship between self and other, colors and essentially qualifies the experience as such. At times emotion becomes so strong that we focus more directly on it and speak of an emotional experience or even of an experience of one or more specific emotions. A particular emotion can even become so forceful that it takes on the air of a personal being that encourages, rejoices, stalks or threatens us. It would be hard to overemphasize the fact that experience is essentially emotional in character.

While we are speaking of the emotional character of experience, we would do well to recall Gadamer's rather existentialist remark that experiences superceding one another leave us, in a new experience, both, on the one hand, with a certain sense of loss regarding what we were and what we had experienced previously and, on the other hand, with a certain sense of newness in a given, unique experience. I would add that there is of course also, very importantly, a sense of gain if we are talking about an overall enriching experience or, again, of loss if we are talking about a primarily impoverishing experience. The emotional tenor of an experience can, then, result from an experience or be rooted in any one or more of the elements, moments and aspects of an ongoing movement of experience.[10]

Varieties of Experience

So far we have spoken more generally of the characteristics of human experience as such. Along with insights gained from several philosophers, we stressed the point that experience has ontological status in as and because it is real relation, process and result. It is both objective and subjective, brings with it a sense of immediacy or direct involvement and, consequently, bears an emotional coloring.

If we now wish to consider such experience in its various forms, we will do well to distinguish experiences as such, among many possible approaches, in the following five ways: first, according to overall type and phase; second, according to the nature of the initial self, and of course consequently the resultant self, that as renewedly initial self finds itself in relation with an other; third, according to the way and *locus* or "location" in and from which the other involved is present to the self; fourth, according to whether, more specifically, the other may be "absent" to the initial and/or resultant self; and, fifth, according to the qualitative change that occurs in the resultant self precisely as result.

Overall Types and Phases of Experience.

While keeping Hegel in mind or at least in the background, in line with Dewey's thought we would do well to recognize three overall types of experience. There is, first of all, that initial experience Dewey called primary or gross experience. I would prefer to call it, more formally speaking, first experience, in order to stress, perhaps more than Dewey did, that the types of experience we are examining are, ideally, phases of a much wider and more inclusive process of human experience. Of course this first phase, this first experience, stands as well on, and can be considered on, its own. For it is an ontologically dense relationship of self and other resulting in an enriched or impoverished self. It is, as has been mentioned, both objective and subjective, and yet transcends such labels in its very "givenness." A sense of immediacy marks in a particular way this first phase of experience. Again, the presence of the experienced other to the experiencing self is, in human experience, always a presence to varying degrees conditioned by all those factors that make up the human reality, factors such as, for example, language, thought, culture, religion, gender, genetic heritage and conditioning, past experiences. It is in this first type or phase of experience that emotion is surely the most spontaneous and usually, but not always, the sharpest. To appreciate this more immediate and often especially emotion-laden phase of experience, all we need to do is recall, in a more positive vein, a moment when we have admired a peaceful mountain lake, had an insight, or met another person whom we love and have not seen for some time.

We humans are, however, such that we cannot normally remain at this level of first experience. When it occurs, we participate in and equally are this first experience while of course surpassing it in the sense that we are also a striving beyond any given experience. Unless we try more superficially to flutter from one first experience to another, which is surely an undesirable form of escapism and a refusal to become the reflective, thinking being that nature has destined us to become, we must needs move on to the second type and phase of experience. Dewey refers to this second type as reflective experience, what I would identify as or name second experience. We usually call it, in a general way, thought. As thought, it occurs internally and is borne and given expression to by one or more mentally expressed languages. It is often externally formulated in spoken or written language. As Dewey had done, we too should note that this second experience involves selectivity, has a certain basis in choice and is not only conscious but even, to a more or less extent, self-reflexively conscious. This second type and phase of experience is characterized by an abstractive tendency to distinguish and to unite, something Hegel had noted and around which he so brilliantly built his whole philosophy over a century and a half ago. Again, as with first experience, this second experience is characterized by its reality, its "givenness," its being both objective and subjective in character. The immediacy here in question takes on a special character as our personal relationship with our thoughts and what we express in language, conditioned as thought and language may be by so many factors. In this second type of experience, emotion normally subsides somewhat to permit critical, creative and constructive reflection on the first experience with, then, subsequent modification or intensification of the emotion or emotions that colored the first experience. Seen in this way as a critical, creative and constructive reflection on first experience, second experience becomes indeed a prolongation of that first experience. The non-substantialist human self that is participant in, and constituted by, the first experience participates in, and is constituted by, the second type and phase of experience.[11]

Neither Dewey nor Hegel could be happy with the idea of remaining at this second experience. For Dewey, it would amount to resting in idealism, and all the subsequent dualisms, he found unacceptable. For Hegel it would in effect mean staying at the level of thought that does not finally reconcile. From our present perspective, to remain with this second experience would imply a certain phenomenological schizophrenia in which we would not be able to reconcile within ourselves the fact that the initial self participating in the first experience is the progenitor of the initial self now participating in the second experience, and that the latter initial self is both the result and the inheritor of the former. More fundamentally and radically stated, the resultant self of the first experience is the initial self of the second experience. And the resultant self of the second experience becomes, in turn, the initial self in a third type or, equally here, phase of experience.

This third form, type or phase of experience, better referred to in the present context as third experience, is what Dewey called consummatory experience and of which Hegel, in his own way, would have spoken as the enriching return to the initial moment in the movement of thought constituting for him a movement of spirit. I would identify this third experience, again initial selfhood and otherness in relationship giving rise to enriched or impoverished selfhood, as the type of experience that leads normally to engaged action, whether that action be deeper understanding and appreciation of first experience lived now in a new way or a decision to follow through and do something in particular. In either case, it is an enriched or impoverished advancing return to first experience. It is of course ontologically dense in that it constitutes the reality of the given moment. It is both objective and subjective, is characterized by a renewed sense of immediacy and, one would hope, by a balanced and appreciative, more integrated emotional stance on the part of the initial self as well as of the other if it is itself a self in the sense in which we are using it here, namely, as an active, self-aware participant in the experience, and most especially on the part of the resultant self.

These three types and phases of experience, namely, first experience, second experience and third experience, are each in its own way relation, process and result. Each is a structured movement of becoming, namely, initial selfhood and otherness in relationship giving rise to resultant selfhood that is equally renewedly initial selfhood in relationship with otherness. First experience is, however, that which launches the overall movement of human experience. Second experience arises out of and prolongs first experience as the critical, creative and constructive examination of first experience. Third experience is a return in a new way to first experience that validates and consummates the second experience. It is, in fact, a synthesizing prolongation of first and second experiences. The three, as Dewey says, "functionally distinct" types of experience constitute three phases in a fully lived overall movement of experience. Indeed, third experience is itself the moment of experience that undergirds and, more forcefully stated, constitutes what Aristotle had called the experienced person.

Communal, Shared and Individual Self.

After presenting the three overall types or phases of experience, namely, first, second and third experience, we need to take another look at human experience in order to spell out and further differentiate the various forms that experience can and does take, whether it be first, second or third experience. This time we will not be speaking of types of experience that constitute a series of phases resulting in the experienced person but, rather, of the ways in which we can distinguish further forms of experience on the basis of the nature of the initial self that is in relationship with the other and, of course, later on, of the self or selves that result from this relationship.

Especially Hegel, Royce and Dewey seemed to say that experience could be social or individual or both. In fact, Hegel and Royce each explicitly proposed a structured movement, the former doing this in terms of thought and the latter in terms of interpretation, that were equally constitutive of the social and the individual self. In his book, *Experience and Nature*, Dewey tended to leave to others the fuller development of the idea of social experience. When primarily developing his own position on experience, Smith seemed to work with the notion of the experience of an individual self that is, of course, fully subject to social and other conditioning.

On the basis of my own experience, of reading and of discussion with others, I would propose that experience, considered from the perspective of the experiencing self, can be, at one and the same time, one or more of the following: communal; shared; individual. It is communal when the experiencing self is a number of people gathered physically or at least virtually in one area and sharing certain features and interests in common, people who together find themselves in relationship with a common other. This could be a scout troop, a parish community, a university community, a monastic group, a marginalized and threatened people, perhaps a web-site chat group or any other of the almost infinitely varied and variable gatherings of humans who have in common and share sufficient features and interests to permit them, together, to stand in relationship to a common other and to become an enriched or impoverished communal self as a result of the relationship.

An experience is shared, as "shared" is being used here, when two persons, perhaps good friends or a married couple, together find themselves in relationship with an other common to both of them. The two persons, so to speak, look out together in the same direction, recognize a common other and, we would hope, react together in harmonious, complementary fashion. Essentially, they share, and share in, a common experience.

The easiest form of experience to which especially we in the "western world" can refer is the individual experience. This is the one we in a more nominalist and even individualist cultural context spontaneously think of when we speak of experience. Here the initial self finds itself in relationship with an other and lives, often very personally and intensely, the experience in which it participates and by which it is ultimately reconstituted as resultant self. This form of experience, to which expression is given in such terms as "my experience," "a very personal experience" and the like, carries with it the profound capacity to convince the person or self, who participates in the experience, of the reliability of the experience. It carries with it as well a sense that the individual person involved can never fully express or explain the particular experience in question to another person. Other people of course come, to a certain extent at least, to appreciate and understand the experience on the basis of their own parallel experiences and of the efforts of the experiencing self to provide access to its personal experience by giving expression to that experience through signs, words, gestures and the like. Ironically, despite the real difficulty we may have in expressing our personal experiences, it is precisely such experiences that carry so much weight and convince other people when we who participate in the experience live in accord with the experience of which we were a part and in which we profess to have participated. Hence the strong witness value of an appeal to personal experience.

Communal, shared and individual forms of experience are, in a sense and using the word in a very general way, dialectically related in that, from various perspectives, each takes on a momentary priority. Individual experiences are fundamental in the sense that any communal or shared experience must of course likewise be, in some way, the experience of the individuals making up the community or sharing a common experience. With certain adjustments, we can posit a similar relationship between communal and shared experiences with the former at times dependent on the latter. And yet, from another perspective, communal experiences are the more basic since they constitute the wider, conditioning context within which shared and individual forms of experience occur. In essence, communal, shared and individual experiences all have a dialectically maintained concomitant priority, depending on the perspective from which they are considered.

The Other Within, Without and Up Ahead.

Just as there are three basic types of or phases to experience, and three basic forms of experience in light of the nature of the experiencing self, so there are at least three forms of experience distinguishable on the basis of various ways in which the other can be present in the initial relationship between self and other and, consequently, in the following process or concrescence, to borrow a word from Alfred North Whitehead, that is human experience.

As we begin to distinguish the various ways in which the other can be present, we need to recall that the other in question can manifest itself and be present[12] in any number of possible shapes and forms. It may present itself as a self-reflexively conscious communal, shared or individual self, a simply conscious self or, again, an other that gives no indication of consciousness. The other in the relationship between self and other could be a friend, someone out of history or in our contemporary world, a pet, the physical world around us or an aspect of it, a future possibility, a thought, word or feeling, and so forth.

So the initial self finds itself in relationship with one or more of these others that appear primarily either within or from outside of the experiencing self. If it is a question of the other being present in effect wholly within the self and its conscious awareness, then we commonly refer to the experience in question as an inner or interior experience. There are of course many gradings or shades of interiority involved here, ranging from the presence of the self's own barely objectified self within the innermost recesses of self-consciousness to the presence of thoughts, words and various sensations within the self's consciousness, taken in a rather wide understanding of the word, on to the almost intuited sense of another's presence within us. An other within, giving rise to an experience as interior, can indeed be our own self-image, our thoughts, emotions and even various inner states as well as a deep sense of someone or something within us, perhaps even present in a parapsychological way.

The self can likewise find itself in relationship with an other present from without, and this in three basic ways. In the first of these, the other can be present as a reality presenting itself as already existent either in the past or in the present. If the other is a past reality, it is then present through memory. If one's focus is specifically on the other as present precisely through *memory*, then we would of course consider this to be more of an interior experience. If, however, the focus is on the past other in *its own right* and as a reality presenting itself as existent in its own right, then its presence would engender a form of presence of the other that, while present within, is in fact a presence from without the self. When the other presents itself as actually present in the relationship between self and other, we are dealing with what we most commonly refer to as an experience, namely, a more straightforward relationship between self and other, whether that presence be more immediate or mediated through various signs or, again, mediatedly immediate through various signs as would be the case of the presence of another person who, as other characterized essentially by its interiority, is immediately present in a mediated way.

The other may also be present from without in a third way so significantly different from the way in which a past or present other, namely, an other present as past, or present as present, is present to the self that it gives rise to a third way or form of experience when experiences are distinguished on the basis of the *locus* or "location" in or from which the other is present to the self. In this case, the other is present as not-yet-being-present. It is an other that remains potential and future from the perspective of the initial self. In this way or form of experiencing, the experience is again one we would locate as "external," but external in the specific sense that the other's presence is now mediated more by imagination, by signs and at times by proleptic events than by memory. If the focus falls on the presence through *imagination*, then this experience could be considered an interior one, but if the stress is on the other as other that, though it is not yet fully present, presents itself through sign, symbol and event, then the other gives rise to what we could call an experience from without and located, more specifically, "up ahead."

In considering briefly, then, these experiences of the other as presenting itself within, without or up ahead, we come to delineate three forms of human experience based on where the other appears and how it "locates" itself in relation to the initial self and on throughout the consequent process of experience. However, as we have seen, these three forms tend to overlap and in fact always involve at least an element of interior experience if we are speaking of human experience. Furthermore, given the profound singular sense of interiority characteristic and even constitutive of the individual human self, the notion of an experience of an other presenting itself from within applies in a particularly appropriate way to the experience participated in by a single individual.

The Other as "Absent"

With reference to the other in the relationship between self and other that is experience, so far we have spoken of the other as present in some more straightforward way. Given philosophical currents such as the philosophies of suspicion that have been so important over much of the past two centuries or so of Western thought, given as well such recent philosophical approaches as, for example, deconstructionism and, most importantly, given the fragile, war-torn world in which we have lived for so long now and the personal anguish that so many people suffer, it is extremely important to come to terms, even if only briefly, with the experience of the absence of the other.

Surely one of the most emotionally charged experiences we can live through is this experience of absence. Though the question of absence would seem to arise especially in light of impoverishing and essentially negative experiences, it can of course also arise in relation to, even out of, more enriching and positive experiences. Indeed, we can experience great joy and peace if we are happy at the absence, for instance, of pain or someone who has threatened us and our well-being. However, far too often it is a question of an agonizing experience due to our longing for an other that is experienced as being absent. The experience may, for example, be one of the absence of someone we loved and continue to love, and from whom we are now separated. It can be an overwhelming sense of loss in life, perhaps the death of someone to whom we were very close. Perhaps even the experience of the absence of meaning in life or of goodness in general. Whatever the case may be, if we look more closely at the experience of absence, we find that it is not an experience of total absence, which would be a contradiction in terms. Rather, it is an experience of mediated absence.[13] Indeed, we can experience the other as absent, but we cannot simply experience the total absence of the other.

In an experience of the other as absent, the other remains present, in one way or another. The other may remain present through the reality of a past presence, the imagining of a possible presence, the realization that what was formerly perceived as present is no longer, or was not, or will no longer for now, or will never again be present. An experience of mediated absence is always an experience of some form of loss. Perhaps a loss that permits us to say, "Good riddance!" But so often, rather, it is a loss that plunges us into shorter- or longer-term anguish at being, in some way, alone.

Finally here, experiences in which the other is present within or without, to which we referred above, can and often are or become, themselves experiences of a *presence as absence* that, in turn, gives a particular emotional coloration to the experience in question and to the self resulting out of the relation between self and other.

The Enriched or Impoverished Resultant Self.

Ever since I made a number of critical remarks in Chapter Three above concerning Hegel's concept of spirit as self-relationality occurring in and as a dialectical movement of thought, I have been suggesting that we should, rather, consider spirit more adequately and more appropriately as a movement of enriching experience: initial selfhood and otherness in relationship giving rise to resultant, enriched selfhood. I have, furthermore, proposed that this triadically structured movement of enriching experience occurs, in its finite, human forms, as a tetradically structured movement of initial selfhood and otherness in relationship giving rise to resultant, enriched selfhood itself equally and simultaneously again initial selfhood in relationship with otherness.

As I have also previously noted, finite human experiences are, moreover, relationships, processes and results that, in one way or another, as movements of becoming not only follow upon, but also supercede and go beyond, previous experiences. The self resulting from any process or structured movement of human experience has, from the perspective of the negative side to the experience, left something behind, sensed its finitude and fragility, and, from the perspective of the positive side to the experience, found itself at a new vantage point. The self resulting from any process or structured movement of human experience lives a sense of loss rooted in the very nature and structure of experience as such. It is no longer what it was. Yet the same resultant self equally has a sense of gain and of newness, again rooted in the very nature and structure of experience. It is something that it was not before the process had taken place. From the perspective, then, of its nature and overall structure, human experience is always characterized by a sense, often only vaguely recognized, of both loss and gain.

However, there is another perspective from which human experience is a relationship and process resulting in either an enriched or an impoverished self. In this sense, the resultant self is, at least overall, enriched or impoverished, namely, is qualitatively more or qualitatively less than the initial self, not from the previously mentioned structural perspective of its being a resultant self as such, but more specifically on the basis of its participation in the process or interaction with the other with whom it is in relationship. Depending on the ways in which self and other comport themselves in the given and developing relationship, the resultant self is, overall, either enriched or impoverished and senses at least subtly a certain momentary wholeness or disintegration. Already now, then, we can, on the basis of the way in which the resultant self is enriched or impoverished, further distinguish movements of experience as ones that are enriching or impoverishing.

Thus, we can situate our understanding of spirit as the structured movement of experience and, more precisely in light of present concerns, human experience when such a movement results in an enriched self, with enrichment considered as qualitative increment occurring on the basis of a process or interaction with the other. In its more general formulation, spirit is a movement of becoming or concrescence: initial selfhood and otherness in relationship giving rise to resultant enriched selfhood.

Concluding Remarks

Indeed, then, the varieties or forms that experience takes and that we have sketched out are numerous. From the overall perspective of the self, experience is communal, shared and individual. When, from the perspective of a consideration of the other, we differentiate various forms of experience, an experience is inner or external, with this latter perceived as arising from the presence of an other from without or up ahead. Again, with reference to the other, experience can be an experience of "absence." From the particular perspective of the resultant self, experience can be enriching or impoverishing. And each of these many forms of experience develops, in its own way, according to the pattern of first, second and third experiences that we have previously laid out. The more mathematically inclined might wish to calculate the number of potentially distinguishable interrelated forms of experience. But of course human reality usually escapes any attempt to arrive at such mathematical precision.

Our grammar of experience, namely, our attempt to spell out what we mean by such experience and to conjugate it, namely, to distinguish varieties or forms of experience, does permit us to clarify somewhat, indeed to bring together into a certain coordinated unity, the complex effervescence we call human experience. Furthermore, the interweaving of the sets of types, phases and forms of experiences that we have worked out from different perspectives or points of reference helps us explain, always however inadequately, what underlies the amazing variety of cultures, societies and individuals that characterize the history of humankind. Nevertheless, this seemingly unending variety of human experiences, even in its unpredictability and its inability to be regimented, does also manifest a fundamental continuity and a certain rhythm. While ever acknowledging the irreducible multiplicity characteristic of reality, we, more appropriate to what we are doing here in our philosophical reflection as a sort of second experience, try to note and focus on patterns and rhythms and repetitions. One of these patterns to which we now need to pay particular attention in the next chapter is the structured movement of human or finite experience that, I would propose, both makes possible the incredible variety of, and explains the rhythm common to, all human experiences, whether they be first, second or third, whether they be communal, shared and/or individual, whether they be experiences of a presence within, without or up ahead, or experiences of "absence," and whether they be enriching or impoverishing experiences.

NOTES

1. In principle one could also attempt to distinguish experiences according to their overall emotional tone, but the possibilities and combinations are almost endless. Suffice it to note the fundamental importance of emotional and affective coloration in any moment and movement of experience.
2. Douglas R. Anderson, "John E. Smith and the Heart of Experience," in *The Recovery of Philosophy in America. Essays in Honor of John Edwin Smith*, ed. Thomas P. Kasulis and Robert Cummings Neville (Albany: State University of New York Press, 1997) 126–127, quotation on 127.
3. Though the more immediate context of this study is the Euro-North American community, I have been struck in various conversations by the ways in which a number of Latin Americans, sub-Saharan Africans and people from the South Pacific have also seemed to feel comfortable and at home with understandings of experience similar to what is being worked out in the present study. It would seem to be primarily in certain Asian religious and philosophical traditions that we find major hesitations concerning the ultimate significance of the self-other structure and dynamic of real experience.
4. Some time ago, George P. Schner, now deceased, pointed out that it is important to complement Smith's insistence on the fact that experience is wider than the linguistic with the fact that language conditions, and even can initiate, human experiences. I would add that, when language initiates a human experience, it is in fact functioning as an other in relation to the experiencing self.
5. Though Smith will speak of self-encounter in the sense of encountering questions and the like within ourselves, I think that "relationship" will allow us to establish an even more inclusive notion of experience that will not leave open the idea that there might be a more substantialist self that "encounters" the other. It can be used to refer both to "relationship" and to "interrelationship." "Relationship," then is used here in a very general way to indicate that the self and other refer, from the initial stage in the development we call experience on as long as the movement of experience continues, directly to one another and that they are not adequately thought one without the other. Self and other can be thought of as two poles in this relationship. Their existence is, as we would say in Latin, *esse ad* ("being toward").

    Concerning Smith on "self-encounter," see, for example, his *Religion and Empiricism* (Milwaukee: Marquette University Press, 1967) 44, cited by Anderson, "John E. Smith and the Heart of Experience" 126.
6. Here we are of course more interested in the forms of experience characteristic of a self that is aware and, indeed, often self-aware. It would be possible to widen this consideration of the forms of experience to include the relations among less aware, or even not self-aware, initial moments in the relationship between "self" and other. In this regard one would immediately think of Alfred North Whitehead's way of understanding experience as fundamental notion applicable at the level of cosmology.

    With regard to the more intersubjectively occurring relationship between self and other, each side of the relationship is indeed from one perspective "self" and from another perspective "other." The tetradically structured movement here proposed is the generalized formulation of the monosubjectively and intersubjectively occurring relationship somewhat more from the side of the phenomenologically self-aware moment in the given relationship between self and other. Depending on a variety of considerations, either the other as other or the self as aware and self-aware can be the predominant focus of attention within the movement of experience. Phenomenologically speaking, the "self" has a certain underlying priority within the given relationship between self and other. From the perspective of direct, focused awareness, the "other" may well exercise a certain priority within the given relationship between self and other.

7. *Experience and Nature*, in *The Later Works, 1925–1953*, vol. I: *1925*, ed. Jo Ann Boydston with associate textual editors, Patricia Baysinger and Barbara Levine (Carbondale, IL: Southern Illinois University Press, 1981, 1st ed. originally published 1925, 2nd ed. 1929).

8. The outstanding philosopher who has so masterfully constructed a cosmology of experience is of course Alfred North Whitehead, upon whose thought I am drawing from time to time in a more general way. See, for example, his *Process and Reality*, published in 1929, corrected edition, ed. David Ray Griffin and Donald W. Sherburne (New York: Free Press, 1978).

9. Smith has developed this point, at least in part, as a way of affirming a direct encounter with, as mediated experience of, God. He speaks of mediated immediacy. See Dale M. Schlitt, *Theology and the Experience of God* (New York: Peter Lang, 2001) 35–37, 64–65.

10. That is, the initial self in relation to the other, the way in which each participates in the movement of becoming that is the experience, the resultant self, and so forth.

11. Cataloging forms of human experience is always a difficult enterprise. While the notion here of a second experience would seem to be clear enough and to follow quite naturally from a first experience as that first experience's prolongation in the realm of reflection and thought, it could of course occur that what is here described as a second experience would, in a specific case, be in fact a more reflexive form of first experience. One might, by way of example, think of the working out of a mathematical problem that would not as such in any evident way presuppose a more direct relationship to a prior first experience.

12. "Manifest" and "be present" are used here in a very general way. The forms this manifestation and presence take will be further specified and spelled out in Chapter Six below.

13. The position taken here is somewhat parallel to that espoused by Hegel, who is famous for having denied the existence of Kant's "thing-in-itself" (*Ding-an-sich*). He claimed that it was self-contradictory to say that one could not think the "thing-in-itself" since, in referring to it, one is already thinking it, at least in some way.

6

A PHENOMENOLOGY OF EXPERIENCE

In the last chapter I proposed a grammar of experience in which we appropriated a number of insights from the past concerning the nature of human experience as such, then indicated several of its characteristics and distinguished some of its types (considered ideally as phases) and forms. Now, if we wish to account still more fully for the overall dynamic of human experience as well as the varied forms that experience can take, namely, for the reality that we live and that we are, we need to examine the structure and movement of that same experience, a structured movement[1] common, *mutatis mutandis*, to all types, phases and forms of human experience since all involve a developing relationship between self and other. We need to spell out in greater detail the various possible ways in which the structured movement of experience takes place. However, while wanting to enter into greater detail, we will still in effect carry this out in a minimalist way, which is to say that we will note explicitly only what would seem more important to a serious understanding of the structured movement of human experience and indeed, in a very general way, of experience as such. This second methodological perspective from which experience is to be considered will take the general form of a phenomenology of experience, namely, a look at, analysis of and reflection on the ways in which self and other relate to one another.

In fact, to be more precise, this overall phenomenological look at the ways in which self and other relate to one another includes moments of description, analysis and further reflection on experience as such or a given experience in particular, which then permits us to speak here of our phenomenological look, analysis and reflection as a critical reconstruction of the structured movement of experience or even a particular experience. Depending on the aspect of the phenomenological process one wishes to stress more in a given context, one could refer more globally to that process simply in terms of "look" or "analysis" or "reflection" while realizing that description, analysis and reflection are always involved in the process no matter which of the three terms might be used to refer to the process.

We will carry out the here proposed analysis in the shadow of, indeed while having learned from, Hegel's monumental effort to establish a science of logic and a phenomenology of experience, which latter Hegel finally came to call a phenomenology of spirit.[2] Our phenomenological analysis of the structured movement common to the varieties of human experience that have been sketched out in the previous chapter will in turn take the form of a self-reflexively elaborated critical reconstruction of that experience. Before proposing such a critical reconstruction, and in line with the appropriately more self-reflexive character of analyses carried out in philosophical theology, it will be helpful to underscore several points concerning the nature of a phenomenological look at, analysis of and reflection on human experience.

Initial Remarks

If we consider for a moment the general notion of a phenomenology, we see that today it carries with it the idea of a process in which some "given" in experience is to be looked at and described, analyzed and reflected upon.[3] And "experience" as used in such a case usually refers more directly to the experience of the experiencing self. But, the question of such a "given," and consequently of the notion of experience involved, quickly becomes quite complex. For there is, first of all, in any movement we refer to as "experience" the "givenness" of the initial, underlying relationship between self and whatever other is involved. Given this relationship, there is, second, the experiencing self and, third, what is then more traditionally considered as "given," namely, the other or, in some cases, at least a series of phenomena with which the self finds itself in relation. Fourth, there is the "givenness" of the result of the relationship between self and other. However, this quadruple "given" is never some pure relationship, presence and result unconditioned by language, thought, interest, gender, tradition, culture, religion and genetic substrate, as we have come to realize, for example, through prolonged reflection on the Enlightenment disdain for "positive" or revealed religion, through various historical studies, the increasing awareness of religious pluralism, and various scientific studies. Rather, in one way or another, there is always question of a relationship, a presence and a result as given in and to some level of human communal, societal, shared, or individual consciousness within the overall movement of experience. Therefore, since human consciousness develops in tandem with these "conditioning" factors, they play a constitutive role in the very awareness and analysis of as well as reflection upon the quadruple "given" or the relationship within which the self experiences and the other is present, and out of which the result occurs. This conditioning occurs from the side of the self. If the other that is involved in the relationship between self and other is itself also a finite, self-reflexively conscious self, then the conditioning also occurs from the side of the other insofar as both the intention of self-manifestation and the means of that self-manifestation arise out of a consciousness itself conditioned by these factors. In effect, language, thought, interest, gender, tradition, culture, religion and genetic influences all play a constitutive role in the whole process of the appearance of the triply given "phenomenon" itself, namely, relationship, other and re-sultant relationship within the overall fourfold given, that is, the previous three plus the initial self. They are part and parcel of, so to speak, the pack-age, namely, of the experience itself. They even condition the phenome-nological analysis of that experience, with experience now referring to the more inclusive overall movement of selfhood and otherness in relationship giving rise to enriched or impoverished resultant selfhood that is itself re-newed initial selfhood in relationship with otherness.

Indeed, the very existence of a specific language or languages, forms of thought, interests, gender conditioning, traditional, cultural and religious as well as genetic influences can be an essential condition making certain ex-periences possible. These influences are surely omnipresent, but are not the sum total of what is present. The self experiencing and the other that is experienced are, as we will see below in our phenomenological analysis, more than the sum of these conditioning factors and mediating signs.

With regard, then, to the question of a conditioned quadruple "given," we will have to keep in mind the qualifying character of this conditioning. If, for example, human experience is always conditioned and constitutively affected, even at times perhaps in some way initiated, by such factors as language, thought, interest, tradition, culture, religion, genetic influences and, to some extent at least, gender, we might easily conclude that all such experiences are then relativized and rendered fundamentally unreliable. However, rather than

take this route, we might alternatively propose a position that I would es-
pouse, namely, that such particularity does not necessarily relativize. Instead,
it provides the inescapably concrete point of departure for any more universalizing analysis. Differently conditioned concrete points of departure do not
necessarily force the conclusion either that human experience is inevitably
atomized or that human experiences are merely to be maintained in simple,
relativizing juxtaposition. These necessarily conditioned concrete points of
departure provide the essential basis for the type of analysis that we here
envisage. They are, in fact, that which is taken up into a more universalizing,
self-reflexively carried out phenomenological analysis. As so analyzed, they
are that which the philosopher then offers for consideration by those with
whom she or he proposes to communicate.

We have come full circle with this brief discussion of the conditioned
quality of the quadruple "given" to which we attend to in a phenomenological
analysis and have in fact returned to the question of experience. Or, rather,
we have never left that question, for the very carrying out of a specific phenomenological analysis with its constructive and generalizing effort is itself
a type of experience, indeed what we have earlier called a second experience.

In addition to the notion of a certain "given," a phenomenological analysis
of experience or, in a particular case, of an experience implies some sense of
underlying structure and movement in that experience. It is this underlying
structured movement that spells itself out in, and comes into focus through,
the phenomenological analysis. For example, in an Hegelian context a phenomenological analysis of a specific experience, a figure or *Gestalt* as Hegel
would call it in his *Phenomenology*, would manifest the structured movement
of that moment of experience in part, at least, by bringing to light the dynamic movement of a series of logical concepts that underlie and structure the
dialectically related arising and presence of what is "given" to human consciousness within that figure or shape. In the present reflection, the phenomenological analysis will be rooted somewhat more loosely in the notion
of experience developed so far in the present study. Thus, the analysis will
work with the notions of self and other in their variously realized relationship
constituting experience. Carrying it out will, at least in principle, amount in
large measure to paying attention to the ways in which self and other function
and relate to one another in this relationship.

Here, then, we have in effect reinserted the more subjective notion of the experience of an experiencing self or subject into the wider context of a figure or shape of experience conceived as relationship between selfhood and otherness giving rise to resultant selfhood. In a sense, then, we have left the relatively more recent view of a phenomenological analysis as an analysis of what is "given" or present to an individual consciousness or to consciousness as such and returned to something closer to what Hegel had proposed in writing his *Phenomenology of Spirit*. There the role of the reader of that work was that of a phenomenological observer who followed the progression from one phenomenological form or shape to another. However, whereas in Hegel's case the forms or shapes of consciousness were ultimately structured according to, and rooted in, logical concepts, in the present proposal the reader or phenomenological observer is one who remains more directly focused on the experiences themselves. The phenomenological observer "looks at" and sees the structured movement of human experience itself as it occurs in various experiences. Thus in the present case it is the role of the phenomenological observer to note simply and directly the differing ways in which the self and other relate to one another in a given movement of experience and, as elements in this "look," describe and analyse the structure and movement discovered as well as carry out some further reflection upon it.

In a phenomenological analysis such as the one here proposed, we, the phenomenological observer, need to look at the structured movement of enriching and impoverishing human experience with a focus upon the initial self, the other and the resultant self. First of all, we will look at the parallel developments of self and other, which as self and other are in relationship with one another in the overall movement of experience. Each of these parallel developments constitutes, in its own way and from its particular perspective, a view of the overall relationship between self and other and can in principle be read on its own. In a sense, each perspective presents the structured movement of the overall experience. However, a fuller phenomenological analysis of the relationship between self and other requires that the phenomenological observer or reader follow the development of the movement of experience from each of these two parallel perspectives, each of which retains a certain priority, within the overall relationship, that is rooted in the nature of self and other.[4] Following this presentation of the doubled parallel perspective on the dialectical development of self and other in this dialogically structured relationship,[5] in which we can consider self and other as two poles or points of reference in that relationship, we will look at the resultant self.

A Phenomenological Analysis

Self	Other

Faith and Indifference. From the perspective of the self, the first condition for any enriching experience or movement of spirit, namely, for participation in a relationship between selfhood and otherness resulting in enriched selfhood, is that the communal, shared or individual self be opened to, recognize and turn toward the other as at least possibly non-threatening source of enrichment. Perhaps more accurately stated, the initial self is what could be referred to as a "decisional" moment developing as three steps or sub-moments, namely, openedness to, recognition of and turning toward the other. The steps in this triply structured, dialectically developing stance vis-à-vis the other are but three distinguishable forms of an overall attitude of initially passive "openedness" and then active openness on the part of the self or, again better, an active openness that the self is. An infant's relation to a parent is a particularly direct example of this

Appearance and Non-Appearance. From the perspective of the other, the first condition for any enriching experience or movement of spirit, namely, for participation in a relationship between selfhood and otherness resulting in enriched selfhood, is that the other, infinitely varied as it may be, has to have entered into relationship with the self, even if the other is only present as absent, as was noted above in the previous chapter. The other enters this relationship initially by appearing to, and thus impinging upon, the self. This initial appearance to the self occurs directly and through signs which are themselves indeed simply a form of the other's overall initial appearance. In fact phenomenologically speaking, at this initial stage in the development of the movement of experience the other is simply the appearance which becomes call and invitation, then demand on the initial self to notice it and to enter further into relationship being opened to, recognizing and turning toward. One need simply think, for example, of an infant nursing at its mother's breast or resting safely in its father's arms. Beyond infancy throughout everyday human living this triply structured stance, which takes on many culturally and societally conditioned shapes and forms, is a type of faith stance vis-à-vis reality. Without such a basic "openedness" to, recognition of and trusting turn toward reality in general it would be impossible for societies, communities, friends, couples or individuals to function. With more specific regard to individuals, it has even become quite common in recent years to speak of the stages of development in this attitude of trusting, active openness to reality, that is, in what we commonly enough refer to as human faith.[6]

Against the background of this experience and affirmation of the necessity of some form of basic human faith, and in view of our present interests, we can now concentrate our attention on the self in its being opened to, recognizing and turning, perhaps only very briefly, toward others in general or toward an other in particular. In so concentrating our attention, we can identify three elements, namely, those of

with it. The other, as initial appearance, invitation and call as well as demand, disturbs, in a very general, even metaphorical, sense of the word, the initial self. As this initial appearance, call and invitation to, as well as demand on, the self, the other invites the self to recognize and turn toward it as at least possibly non-threatening source of enrichment. On the part of the other, the moments of initial appearance, call and invitation, then demand, are but three dialectically developing steps or what we could call sub-moments in the other's initial effort, within a more elaborate, longer overall process or structured movement of self-manifestation. Initial appearance is simply the condition of the possibility for the other to be in relationship with a self. Call and invitation, then demand, further specify, characterize and determine the initial appearance of the other seen from the perspective of the other's now initially established relationship with and impact on the self. Appearance, call and invitation, then demand constitute three dialectically developing steps or sub-moments constituting the essential first moment in the other's epiphany, or manifestation of itself, to the self.

We can continue describing this

content, outlook and comportment.

In our relationships with others we inevitably come, as unified human beings, to be opened to, recognize and identify the ones with whom we are in relationship and with whom we are dealing. There is always an element of content in our relationships. And we can assert this straightforwardly enough with regard to everyday experiences. There is, as well, the aspect or element of outlook or perspective, in line with which we function in relation to the other person or persons. Our most fundamental perspective or, literally speaking, "outlook" must be one of at least initial trust if we wish to be part of a potentially enriching experience. This trusting outlook can be recognized and even characterized by a whole host of emotions, with one such as, for example, joy predominating or several intermingled, what we so easily refer to as mixed emotions. Indeed, often the stance of the self before the other is one of both fascination and fear. This predominant emotion or this intermingling of emotions then contributes to giving a specific emotional coloring to the entire experience. When we bring together our outlook of trust considered on the more or less emotive level and our content as other at

initial effort on the part of the other to show itself to the self by focusing for a moment on the other as it appears to, makes a call to and invites, then demands that the self with whom it enters into relationship recognize its appearance as worthy of notice and at least potentially enriching. In so focusing, we can further describe appearance, call and invitation, and then demand in terms of what appears, how it appears, and why it appears to the self in the experience, with each of these phrases of course always taken in a very wide, even metaphorical, sense since they refer to all possible forms of otherness and, in principle, to all forms of experience.

Though the other appears initially as a single, qualified and conditioned "given" both to the phenomenological observer and to the experiencing self, in its initial appearance the other here remains basically undefined and nondescript. Thus, what initially appears in a way quite undefined slowly takes on, through call and invitation, then demand, further definition and gives further precision to that initial appearance. This appearance thus progresses, in turn, as call and invitation to, then demand on, the self, with which it enters in relationship, least in some way identifiable on the cognitive level, we see that our trusting outlook, and our recognition, come together as a way of comporting ourselves vis-à-vis this other, namely, as a turning toward that other with whom we find ourselves in relation.

Most generally stated, then, this human faith is that openedness, recognition, perspective of trust and way of comporting oneself characteristic of the communal, shared or individual self in its relationship with otherness as potential source of enrichment. The self is these three dialectically developing steps or sub-moments of being opened to, recognizing and turning toward the other. This human faith gives human existence its specific shape and character as convinced, trusting and engaged turning[7] from self to others. Human faith, in opposition to indifference, is an enthusiastic, in a deeper sense of the word, openedness to, recognition of and turning toward others as source of possible enrichment. It is the first moment in the self's ongoing act of conversion to the other that occurs in and with the hope of overcoming human impoverishment in its many forms.

This reference to indifference reminds us though that a movement

to recognize and acknowledge that appearance, to consider it worthy of notice and a possible source of enrichment.

More generally stated, this appearance by the other, this disturbing of and entry into the existential horizon of the initial self is that initial appearance which thereby opens the self to the other. It is, then, the establishment of itself, within the relationship between self and other, as a call upon the self to recognize it, an invitation to the self to turn trustingly toward it and an immediate demand upon it to regard the other as possible source of enrichment and, especially at the level of human experience, worthy of notice. The other's appearance at the beginning of and within the overall movement of experience co-creates, along with the initial self, that very experience. More precisely, the appearance of the other creates the possibility of an enriching experience by its having entered into relationship with the initial self and, together with the initial self, co-creating the overall moment and movement of experience as well as the first overall form or figure of experience in which appearance gives rise to faith. The overall appearance of the other then unfolds in and through three of experience can be impoverishing as well as enriching. In many situations, of course, indifference may simply be a way of coping with the appearance of otherness in its overwhelming variety. In this sense, indifference is simply the more or less neutral attitude of the self in relation to many others, a process of filtering out, so to speak, certain others. However, in the cases that are of more direct concern here, there arises a reasonable expectation or need on the part of the other to be recognized by the self. In parallel with these positive steps or sub-moments of faith, there are three forms of volitional or "decisional" act, so to speak, that stand as impoverishing and disintegrating moments along the phenomenologically sequential path of the communal, shared or individual self's being in relationship to the other. In an experience that is a movement of qualitative impoverishment due to the attitude of the self acting prematurely or out of fear in a situation where the other makes an appearance constituting a legitimate call upon the self, the volitional act, which the self in fact is in this phenomenological moment, takes, in opposition to faith, the form of the self's triply possible refusal to allow itself to be opened to

dialectically developing steps or sub-moments, namely, initial appearance, call and invitation, and demand. It is the first, triply developing moment in the other's ongoing act of manifestation of itself to the self as possible source of that self's enrichment that can occur in a seemingly unlimited number of ways and variety of forms.

This reference to enrichment provides us with the occasion here, in a phenomenological look at the movement of experience which focuses on the other, to recall that a movement of experience can also be one of more immediate impoverishment. Such impoverishment, as qualitative decrease, can of course take many forms. From the side, so to speak, of the other we here are more directly concerned with those forms of appearance of the other that will lead, in a movement of experience, to a qualitative decrease and to a certain disintegration within the self resulting from the experience. In an experience that is a movement of qualitative impoverishment due to the appearance of the other, the other can be fundamentally incompatible with the self to which it appears. That is to say, the other can be such that the self, and here we are of course referring more the other, to recognize the other or to turn in an initial way toward the other. In response to the fundamental human fascination with and yet malaise before otherness, the self can and often does lose courage. It can close in upon itself, or refuse to recognize the other or, again, refuse to turn toward the other in trust. It can lose courage on the everyday human level and become fearful, overly leary of, and even closed to, the possibility that the other is trustworthy and reliable source of enrichment. If faith is in a real sense the self's enthusiasm for the other, indeed, the self *as* enthusiasm for the other, then in these three senses the refusal here considered is the self's ignoring, and remaining indifferent toward, the other, a refusal to begin its conversion to the other. The self is, then, this impoverishing, ignoring and remaining indifferent toward the other.

So, from the perspective of the self, faith or indifference constitutes the first moment in that development. When as that moment the self is considered from the perspective of its relationship to the other, it is the first overall figure or form of relationship of self to other structuring that relationship as one of faith, or indeed indifference, in relation to

explicitly to the human self, is reduced or even crushed in its own reality. Natural disasters serve as easy examples of such an impoverishing experience. Or, and in its own way much more devastating, the other can, if it is itself what we traditionally refer to as a volitionally endowed communal, shared or individual self, falsify its appearance. It can initially and purposefully or intentionally appear as something that it is not, or at least is not fully. It's initial appearance can be a misrepresentation of itself, indeed a misleading call and invitation that leads to impoverishment. That appearance can make an unreasonable and inappropriate demand on the self. If we rightly expect the appearance of the other to be a generous offer of possible enrichment, we nevertheless find that it can also be a potentially false and impoverishing one for the self, for the other if it is itself a self, and for the overall experience as a whole.

Presence and Absence. If the first form that an other takes when it is in relationship with the self is one of appearance, namely, initial appearance, call and then invitation become demand, the phenomenologically and dialectically sequent way the appearance of the other. This first overall attitude on the part of the self is, in relation to the appearance of the other, both passive and active and of course finds further expression in the series of dialectically developing steps or sub-moments, which we can now call sub-forms, through, according to and as which this overall attitude occurs.

Hope and Despair. If the first attitude or stance of the communal, shared or individual self toward the other is one of human faith, then the second overall way in which the self comports itself in this relationship is human hope. This human hope is a moment phenomenologically and dialectically consequent upon the self's initial conversion to the other as possible source of enrichment. It is the self's perspective or outlook and comportment taking the form of a desire and longing for that other, indeed the self as that desire and longing.[8] One simply wishes to bridge the gap between oneself and that other which one has come to recognize, acknowledge and appreciate.

At this point we have used both "self" and "one" to refer to the self in its relationship with the other. In fact, in this phenomenological look

in which the other relates to the self as a possible source of enrichment takes the form of a presence, or an "absence as presence," as a further manifestation of the other to the self. The movement on the part of the other is one from appearance to presence, including absence as presence, as further self-manifestation. In this form of, and way of being in, the relationship between self and other, the other is present as more or less manifest or explicit, direct and indirect offer of itself to the self. Direct, in that experience is itself most fundamentally the relationship between self and other. Indirect, in that the presence of the other is often mediated by a series of signs that can represent the other in various ways within the context of the now ongoing, dialogically structured relationship between self and other and on various levels of sense, as well as emotion, knowing and willing within the self. Ultimately, whether direct or more indirect, the other's offer to be more manifestly present to the self in the relationship constituting a movement of experience is one and the same. A phenomenological look at self and other in relationship, which focuses more directly on the other, permits the phenomenological observer to see at, analysis of and reflection on the moment and movement of experience from the perspective of the self, namely, with a focus on the self but also recognizing that it is a self, namely, the phenomenological observer that is carrying out the look, "self," "one," "we," "community," "friends," "couple," "individual" and so forth are used, in one sense, interchangeably but, in another sense, chosen with a certain sensitivity to the immediate context in which the various terms are used. This multiple form of reference to the self, whether here in referring to the self as a moment of hope or elsewhere, is rooted in the multifaceted reality that the self and, more widely, experience are and in the varied forms of selfhood that can be in relationship with otherness.

Often the communal, shared or individual self's longing for the other has been considered an aspect of love, of *eros* taken in the widest sense of being a fundamental drive, often conceived as need-based, toward the other. But here, when we see it as a totalizing characteristic of selfhood in its relation to otherness, this longing takes on a consistency of its own and comes to denote properly the desire for that to which one has been opened, which one

that the other and the signs of its presence in the relationship between self and other can be distinguished but cannot finally be separated one from the other. For the other in the relationship between self and other is simply this more direct or more indirect presence.

However, the other now more explicitly present to the self is never fully transparent to the self, at least not within the confines of everyday human experience and history. After an appearance in which the other, along with the self, constitutes the relationship between self and other, the other continues its participation in that relationship as an offer of real but less than fully transparent presence as manifestation of itself to the self.

Whether the other be some natural reality or phenomenon, using the word "phenomenon" now in a very general sense to cover either a more direct or a more mediated presence, or, more properly, itself a communal, shared or individual self, its being manifest but not-yet-being-fully-present takes on two forms. The first of these forms is what we could call more specifically a phenomenological incompleteness. We could equally refer to this as a sort of horizontal opaqueness on the part recognizes and toward which one turns. However, that which is desired has not yet been fully attained and is perhaps not even fully attainable within the confines of everyday human experience and history. Hope then is, most generally stated, that longing for what is not yet fully present to oneself, and to which one is, in turn, oneself not yet fully present.

This not-yet-being-fully-present takes on two forms. The first of these forms of "not yet" is the phenomenologically identifiable awareness, on the finite level, that in any at least potentially enriching relationship we long for the other. Again, on the finite level, this active longing for the other is the ever-present reminder of the inevitably incompletely transparent presence, or indeed "absence as presence," to us of whatever we experience. We do experience another person in her or his wholeness as person. But whether we think, for example, of a mother loving her baby or of two good friends who get to know one another ever better, in any such experiences our initial and repeated longing for the other is itself preliminary evidence that we never come to grasp, or be grasped totally by, the other with whom we find ourselves

of the other in the given, potentially enriching relationship between self and other. The other's offer of more manifest presence to the self is such that it always remains mysterious in some way and in various degrees, depending on the nature of the other and the self involved. The offer of a more manifest presence can be renewed time and again without exhausting the reality of what the other is. So the second of these forms of inexhaustible offer of more manifest presence is really the temporally reflected, and historically expressed, phenomenon seen to be repeatable from one experience to another and through a series of experiences. The future offers the possibility of a qualitatively fuller and richer presence on the part of the other in question, or on the part of various others. It of course likewise offers an even less complete or less manifest presence of the other, and thus the possibility for impoverishment of the self in the relationship of the two selves if the other is itself also a self. This general, historically realized second form of "not yet" gives a temporal and sequential expression to the inevitably incomplete presence or, better here, transparence of whatever enters into relationship with a self. When we in relationship. So the second of these forms of "not yet" is really the temporally reflected, and historically expressed, awareness of the incompleteness of any single human experience or the accumulated series of such experiences. The future offers the possibility of a qualitative more, a further enrichment. It of course likewise offers an even less complete shared presence and, consequently, human impoverishment. This general, historically realized second form of "not yet" is the one usually stressed in philosophical and theological reflections on eschatology. This second form of "not yet" gives temporal and sequential expression to the inevitably incomplete presence or, better, transparence to us of what we experience. When we then take history as the accumulation of a series of communal, shared and individual experiences, we recognize that the first or more phenomenological form of "not yet" in any given human relationship expresses itself in its second or more historical and temporally experienced and sequenced form of "not yet" as a longing for that fullness the future may hold.

It is this longing for what is not yet either phenomenologically or temporally fully present, what we then take history as the consecutive and cumulative movement of a series of communal, shared and individual experiences, we recognize that the first or more phenomenological form of "not yet" in any given relationship between human self and any other expresses itself in its second or more historical and temporally experienced and sequenced form of "not yet" as the other's real but partial and incompletely manifest presence. This presence takes the form of a further manifestation of the other to the self, a presence whose fullness and transparency, or at least greater fullness and transparency, may come to be realized in the future.

It is this as yet phenomenologically, or phenomenologically and temporally, incomplete presence of the other, this further but not yet complete manifestation of the other to the self, that, from the perspective of a consideration of or focus on the other, forces us to confront rather directly the question of evil. The presence of otherness as possible source of enrichment can, if not carefully weighed and balanced, degenerate into a debilitating overvaluing of any and all difference, an overvaluing that leads the self to accept in rather simplistic fashion have called hope, that forces us to confront rather directly the question of evil and overcoming it. Yet it is the longing for what is not yet fully present that can, if not carefully understood, either degenerate into a form of escapism or take on the semblance of a naively positive, pollyanna reading of the world in which we live. In view of the twentieth-century experience, so marked by world wars, hunger, personal psychological disintegration, ecological disasters, discrimination and even genocide, and of the twenty-first century so far scarred by various forms of terrorism, it is essential that we be able to identify a concrete human community in which evil itself is truly experienced as hurt[9] and yet where hope arises. There must be some concrete moment in human experience where we can identify the presence of hope while fully acknowledging the reality of evil. It is only in and out of a gathering of individuals who share hurt and hope that we can, then, adequately counteract the tendency to slip into either presumption or despair. Such a sharing must surely be one of the reasons why basic human communities give enduring hope to their members.

In the light of our overall initial such forms of difference simply for the sake of that difference. In a world frenzied by the ever increasing search for the new and different, a world too easily convinced of the importance of even the most superficial change and seemingly ever less ready to take a sober second look at the true value and significance, in particular, of proposed more profound societal changes, it is essential that the multiform presence of a wider range of others be recognized and properly contextualized. The other or others that are in relationship with the self present themselves to the self as complementary or even competing sources of possible enrichment or impoverishment. It is, then, this contextualized presence of the other that will make it possible for the self appropriately to long for or, if necessary, to resist the presence of the other. This contextualized presence makes healthy comparison possible.

In light of our initial phenomenological reading of the presence of the other, and against the background of the arising of a wider context spontaneously and inevitably created by the presence of otherness as such, we can further reflect on the presence of the other in the structured movement of human, and understanding of hope, and against the background of this view of the human community as one simultaneously of hurt and of hope, we can briefly reflect on our everyday human hopes.

For the community, couple, friends or individual, the phenomenologically distinguishable moment of longing for the other, a longing that is constitutive and characteristic of every moment of enriching human experience or spirit, takes on a much deeper meaning. In its repeated recurrence, resulting in a human community's, a couple's or friends' or again a single human person's orientation toward the future, this immediate longing for the other as source of possible enrichment of life gives evidence of, and so comes to be seen as, a concrete instance and realization of the underlying, fundamental perspective and comportment of the self that we call hope.

More specifically, this longing for the other and for the enrichment that the presence, or even the "absence as presence," of the other can bring is itself the structure of our relationship to others and to otherness in general. In this relationship, the communal, shared or individual self comes to experience what we

in principle any, experience.

The moment of direct or indirect presence of the other to the self is itself a moment phenomenologically distinguishable from the previous one of the other's appearance. It is a moment characteristic and constitutive of every movement of truly enriching human experience or spirit and, as such, takes on a much deeper meaning. In its repeated occurrence making possible an ever-fuller presence of the other to an experiencing self in a structured movement of experience, this recurrence of otherness as possible source of enrichment gives evidence of, and comes to be seen as, a concrete instance and realization of the underlying, communal and dialogical structure of reality.

More specifically, this either direct or more indirect presence of the other to the self and the potential enrichment this presence of the other will offer in the experience is itself the structure of the relationship of otherness as such to a communal, shared or individual self. In this relationship the other is, or others are, according to the circumstances, a more fully complete either unique or renewable presence to the self.

The other continues then to be a

recognize as a temporally expressed, longer-term longing for final fulfilment.

The hope or looking forward that we are, that the self is, at this moment in the dialectically developing movement of conversion from self to other continues to be characterized by the structure of a longing for the other with whom we find ourselves in relationship. We have already been in relationship with many others who have been or continue to be sources of enrichment. However, the twentieth century's massive evil witnesses to, and our participation in a community both of hurt and of hope reflects, both our own present incompleteness and the present incompleteness of our participation as self in the relationship between self and other. This double incompleteness creates the space and time within which we long for more, for a fuller life and for the fullness of life. Hope, then, is the communal, shared or individual self's perspective or outlook and comportment of longing, realized through the self's longing directed immediately to specific others and through them to otherness in general.

Hope is the perspective or outlook and, indeed comportment of

single, multiple or repeated presence in the dialogically structured bipolar relationship of selfhood and otherness giving rise to resultant selfhood. So many "others" are sources of human enrichment. And so many "others" are, unfortunately and perhaps sometimes disastrously, sources of human impoverishment. This potentially double effect of the presence of otherness reflects both the incompleteness of the presence of the other to the self and the present incompleteness of the relationship between other and self. This double incompleteness creates the space and time within which the very presence of the other is an announcement of a possible further, more complete, more transparent form of presence of the other to the self. At least insofar as it is a possible source of enrichment, the presence of the other is the promise of a consummatory revelation. That presence is a promise realized at this point incompletely through the presence of an other or a multiplicity of others to the communal, shared or individual self.

The presence of the other to the self is in itself an admittedly inherently ambiguous proleptic sign of that form of further, or future, presence which can and hopefully will the believing self, whether that be the selfhood of a community, of a couple, of friends or of an individual, insofar as it longs for the final overcoming of evil in the full realization and final enrichment of human life beyond all possible impoverishment. Hope implies, and works from, the perspective of an awareness of and a certain dissatisfaction with the present societal or individual situation. It reflects a sense of present societal and individual incompleteness. The outlook of the self is one of or, better, the self is here a moment of steadfastness, confidence and even joy in the midst of tribulations. Such hope does not unnecessarily resign itself to any injustice or even to any merely given *status quo*. Rather, it expresses itself in attempts at better societal and personal enrichment especially in the form of a sense of wholeness, integration, well-being, and balance. But it refuses to rest in any of these admittedly all-important social and personal accomplishments or to see its final goal in any of them.

Most generally stated, then, that longing for the other which arises out of faith's openedness to, recognition of and initial trusting turning toward the other as source of enrichment is hope. This longing is

be the source of definitive human enrichment constituting the final overcoming of evil and offer of life beyond all possible impoverishment. By its very nature, this presence of the other hints at the possible overcoming of a societal or individual situation that, in the light of this ever new presence, shows itself to be unsatisfactory. This presence gives rise to a sense of present societal and individual incompleteness. The presence of such an other is the occasion and a cause for the self's outlook of steadfastness, confidence and even joy in the very midst of tribulations. In line with whether the other is itself a self or not, the presence of the other is more or less intentionally the reason for a refusal to accept an unjust social *status quo*. That presence is, in so many different ways, the source of hope for the success of attempts at better societal and personal enrichment that will give rise to a sense of wholeness, integration and well-being within the resultant self as well as balance with its ambient world. Yet this presence of its other, always incomplete at this moment in the structured movement of experience, pushes beyond these more immediate realizations and accomplishments.

characteristic of the self, and indeed the self is this longing. The self is opened trustingly to that other both in a given experience and to the future in a temporal series of such experiences. This longing gives to human existence its specific shape and character as communal, shared and individual, patient and persevering, joyful and confident longing for the final, enriching fulfilment of all human striving and longing. The perspective or outlook of hope is one of patience, perseverance, joy and confidence. Its comportment is one of expectant longing. And its content, or what is longed for, is the ever more fully transparent presence of the enriching other. The comportment of the self as this moment of hope is one of participation in the hoped for triumph of good over evil, with evil here understood as impoverishment in its many forms. Hope is, par excellence, the human attitude toward history in that it is a confident longing for what is not yet. It is a longing that renders human faith more concrete and engaged in the sense that, as a longing for otherness in its various enriching forms, it gives rise to a sense of impatience with, and as well responsible non-tolerance of, societal and personal evil. It distinguishes itself

Most generally stated, then, the more manifest presence of the other arises out of, is phenomenologically and dialectically, and often enough temporally, consequent upon, and continues the further development of the prior appearance of the other as initial appearance, call and invitation, then demand, to a conversion possibly leading to enrichment of the self. This direct or more indirect presence is always an incomplete manifestation susceptible of becoming fuller and more transparent. It gives rise to the communal, shared and individual self's patient and persevering, joyful and confident longing for the final, enriching fulfilment that the reasonably complete or ever fuller temporal presence of the other offers to the self. This very presence of the other announces the possibility of a participation in the hoped for triumph of good over evil, of enrichment over impoverishment. The multiform presence of the other or of others, indeed of otherness in general, is the way reality, whether internal or external to the self, stands in relationship to that self. The presence of otherness in the form of one or more others prolongs and further concretizes the apearance of the other. It makes that appearance more concrete, attractive from any simplistic understanding of seemingly inevitable or necessary and uninterrupted growth, since it arises in and out of a community of hurt and hope. The attitude of hope continues that conversion to the other which is human faith and guides or gives that faith further direction into love.

However, just as with the first attitude or stance, namely, that of faith considered as first moment in the overall dialectically developing movement of conversion, there can be a refusal rooted in unjustified indifference, so too here in regard to the "longing for" which we have called human hope, the self can take on a self-impoverishing stance in relation to the other. Even if one were to be opened, and actively open, to the other, it is still possible for a sort of malaise to set in and to find expression in the self's decision prematurely or out of fear not to continue along the movement of conversion to the other that presents itself appropriately to the self. Phenomenologically and dialectically consequent upon either a more enriching openness to the other, or a refusal seen as indifference when considered in opposition to faith, is a refusal considered in opposition to hope, namely, a second overall way

and engaging in that its more manifest availability to the self creates within the self a longing for it and for the possibility of overcoming any presently or previously existing societal and personal evil. In its best form, the multiple presence of the other offers the self a concrete opportunity to become enriched, namely, to grow, develop and flourish in a realistic way. The presence of the other continues and intensifies the self-manifestation of the other that began with its appearance. It constitutes the second overall moment in the dialectically developing trajectory according to which and in line with which the other can manifest itself to the self.

However, just as with the first form of the offer of the other to the self as a triply developing structured appearance there can be a form of appearance that leads to the impoverishment of the self, so too here the presence of the other can be such tht it is the occasion of the impoverishment of the self to which it is present. Even if the other has appeared to the self in an initially enriching way, it is still possible for the other to cease to be present in a way that continues to be enriching. Phenomenologically and dialectically consequent upon a more enriching or in which the self can decline to comport itself positively in relation to otherness considered as potentially enriching. In this instance the blockage takes the form of the self's refusal to go beyond an initial turning toward the other. The self despairs by refusing to hope, that is, by not longing for the other. Indeed, in this moment the self is this despairing. This despair, or refusal to long for the other, can occur first of all as refusal to long for the other already present to us but always, and inevitably, incompletely transparent in this presence. In addition to this refusal to long for what is phenomenologically not yet fully present, the self can resist longing for that which is not yet temporally fully present. That is, it can refuse to long for that other which is not yet fully present to it. The ultimate case of such refusal to long for the other not yet fully present would be the refusal to long for the final overcoming of evil or human impoverishment. The self can then indeed despair of any such final overcoming.

The malaise before the decision to hope, namely, to long for the other as source of enrichment, the dread leading to despair, seems rooted today especially in the twentieth century experience of massive more impoverishing appearance of the other, with the latter considered as the opposite of the former, is a form of presence that is impoverishing when seen in comparison with the potentially enriching form the other's presence could take in relation to the self. This overall second form of the way in which the other can function as source of impoverishment of the self takes the form either of withdrawal after an initial appearance, call and invitation, then demand, to the self to enter into a relationship with the other or the continued initially impoverishing appearance now as a menacing presence. In the first instance, the other pulls back and does not continue its potentially enriching further manifest presence to the self in the relationship that is the movement of experience. The other does not continue along the trajectory of further transparency and intensified presence to the self. In the second instance, the intensified impoverishing or menacing presence strengthens the potential for impoverishment already brought about. In either of these cases, whether it be one of withdrawal of an initially enriching appearance or the continuation of an impoverishing appearance, the presence of the other is such that it and recurrent evil and now in the early twenty-first century experience, in particular, of terrorism. The only realistic response to this temptation to refuse to long for the other would seem to be, as was mentioned, the decision to participate in a community that experiences both hurt and hope. Such a community can, even despite the hurt, continue to encourage its members to share not only in the hurt but also in the longing for the other as possible source of enrichment, a longing that in fact brings them together. In opposition to hope, then, this form of blockage is a despairing refusal to continue the conversion to the other, already initiated in faith. Here the other is understood in the widest possible sense as referring either to a present societal, shared or individual other, to an other present in the future or to an ideal other as the indication of what a society, a couple or friends or, again, an individual, might become. In any of these cases, the blockage is a refusal to be steadfast and even joyful in the midst of tribulation. Since both the self and the other here may be communal, shared or individual, the refusal is as well then the unnecessary resignation to societal injustice. It is equally the despairing acceptance of

is then phenomenologically, or both phenomenologically and temporally, not yet fully manifest in its presence.

In the world as we know it there is always the possibility that finite otherness, in whatever form, will extinguish human existence as such, so that human self-awareness itself will disappear from our known universe. In the cosmic scheme of things, this might not be the end of all self-awareness in our universe, but it certainly would by definition be, again from a finite perspective, the termination of any human hope of a final overcoming of evil as human impoverishment.

To return, then, to a more specifically historical perspective, during the twentieth century and into the twenty-first century humankind has witnessed almost unimaginable, massive hurt and evil brought about by political, economic, inter-ethnic, interreligious and other conflicts. The other, as a community of human selves, has been a cause of immense human suffering. In most of these cases, both sides in the conflict suffer, and each side is then effectively a source of impoverishment for the other. This functioning of each side as other reminds us that the relationship between self and other, in which the other is equally qualitative societal, shared and personal disintegration. So whether merely unintentional or, more importantly, explicitly intentional, this blockage is a refusal to give some expression to hope by means of attempts at better societal and personal integration, with this latter understood as enriching moments of wholeness and balance. It is the settling into a despairing acceptance of the *status quo*, whether societal, shared or personal, and, consequently, into impoverishing disintegration.

So far we have considered the relationship between communal, shared and individual self and other, from the perspective of the self, in terms of two overall perspectives or outlooks, stances and ways in which the self comports itself vis-à-vis otherness when otherness is considered as source of possible enrichment. First of all, we spoke of faith as fundamental openedness to, recognition of and turning toward the other and of its opposite, the refusal to be opened to, to recognize and to turn toward the other as possible source of enrichment. Then we looked at hope as the self's longing for the other and considered the blockage that can arise in opposition to hope and that transforms what should

a communal, shared or individual self, can be the highest form of either enriching or, of course, also impoverishing experience.

In opposition, then, to the other's continued offer of itself to the self as a more manifest direct and indirect potentially, and often already actually, enriching presence of the other to the self, the other's withdrawal as a previously appearing source of enrichment for the self becomes a particular form of presence as "absence," an appearance formerly recognized by the self and now hopelessly, despairingly longed for. If, in line with its impoverishing appearance, the other continues then to manifest itself in its ever more impoverishing presence to the self, it prolongs and worsens the previously begun qualitative decrease in the self. It causes a certain disintegration in the self which, if carried to an extreme, will result in the very destruction of that communal, shared or individual self.

So far we have considered the relationship between communal, share and individual other and self, from the perspective of the other, in terms of several ways in which the other participates in the relationship with the self. First of all, then, we spoke of the appearance of the other have been longing into a refusal to long for that possibly enriching other. In either form of refusal and blockage, whether in contrast to faith or to hope, the self manifests, and indeed is, a stance of malaise before the other, a dread that creates a situation in which the self fails by refusing to be converted to the other. These refusals are blockages, in a wider sense of the word, whenever they occur. They are such in the strictest sense of the word when the refusal is a direct, reflexive and reasonably free decision or volitional act.

From the perspective, then, of the self, the second overall figure or form of relationship between self and other structuring experience as dynamically, that is, dialectically developing, dialogically related trajectories of self and other is that of hope or despair in relation to the presence or "absence as presence" of the other. This second overall attitude or stance on the part of the self is primarily active and of course finds further expression and nuance in the innumerable concrete ways in which the self itself can react to the presence or "absence as presence" of the other. It develops out of, prolongs and further concretizes the phenomenologically prior stance of

as possible source of the other's enrichment. This appearance occurred in a threefold, phenomenologically and dialectically sequent way as initial appearance, call and invitation, then demand to the self to consider it as possible source of enrichment. We considered the fact that the other could equally appear in this threefold way as a source of impoverishment.

Then we looked at the other's direct and indirect presence to the self, a presence that develops out of, prolongs and further concretizes the phenomenologically prior appearance to the self. We saw that this presence of the other could be such that it engendered within the self a longing for the other that is not phenomenologically, or perhaps also not temporally, fully present and transparent to the self. The other's presence, or absence as presence, gave rise in the self either to a longing for the other as source of possible enrichment or despair at the sense that the other was unattainable or, worse yet, a source of impoverishment. The presence of the other continues, in this form or figure of experience in which the presence of the other gives rise to a longing on the part of the self, to create in the self a fascination or the self, namely, that of faith or in-difference.

Love and Violence. There now follows a third, and final, more positive stance or comportment of the self in its relation to possibly enriching otherness. That third stance is love, the radical phenomenological and dialectical completion of the prior two overall ways, namely, faith and hope, in which the self can comport itself in relation to the other in the overall movement of enriching experience.

Love, as we will see, is the final realization of these more positive movements, or better, moments in the conversion of self to other insofar as it is the self-giving of the self to the other.[10] The proposal to see love, here understood in terms of self-giving, as the final realization of these movements of turning toward and longing for contains a certain paradox within it. Indeed, there is a danger that the first two orientations of the self, if taken on their own without reference to love so defined, can easily be misunderstood in an egoistic and selfish fashion. Turning toward and longing for, if not completed and taken up into self-donation, never truly and respectfully attain the enriching other.

fear, and perhaps at times both, that began with the other's initial appearance.

Revelation and Concealment. There now follows a third, and final, more positive moment of epiphanic self-manifesation on the part of the other when it is being considered as possible source of enrichment for the self in the relationship between self and other. This third moment is one of self-revelation, the radical phenomenological and dialectical completion of the prior two moments of appearance and presence in the overall dialectically developing movement of self-manifestation on the part of the other within the overall movement of enriching experience.

Revelation is the final realization, on the part of the other, of these more positive moments in the relationship between other and self insofar as any revelation by the other, if the other is successfully present to the self and does not itself interrupt the relationship or find the relationship interrupted by the self, then involves at least some exposition of what it truly is not only externally but also, at least minimally, internally. All otherness, all others of course are characterized by some at

On their own, they do not sufficiently take into account the other's intrinsic value, in its own right, as other. To put it bluntly and without further nuance, there remains the paradox, expressed in a sort of ecological principle, that one achieves fullness of life only in giving, not in taking. True enrichment occurs only through one's giving over of oneself to the other as other, a real form of liberation from self-enslavement.

The initial conversion or turning toward, which human faith is, finds its further direction in and through hope and both find their purpose in love as self-giving. With this schematic understanding in mind, we can proceed to develop a fuller understanding of the truly dialogical relationship between self and other that we identify as love. As was the case less explicitly with faith and hope, here too but now more explicitly, we want to consider the phenomenon of self-giving to an other or to others.

As we begin what will be a triple consideration of generous self-giving, we come immediately up against not only the question of love of neighbor or other-love but the thorny and long-discussed question of self-love. The problem and reality of self-love was already at least im-least minimal interiority. Such interiority comes to be the dominant and defining characteristic of self-aware beings, whether they be considered individually, in various shared situations or, again, in communal contexts.

So the other is characterized by a certain exteriority and interiority. This proposal to see self-revelation as the final realization of the more positive moments of appearance, which becomes call and invitation, and then demand, and of presence, which can as well be "absence as presence," contains a certain paradox within it. For there is the danger that the first two moments of the other's self-manifestation to the self, if taken on their own without reference to the vulnerability involved in self-revelation, can easily be misunderstood in an imperialistic way. Appearance and presence, if not completed by being taken up into self-revelation, never truly and respectfully serve as a source of potential enrichment for the self. Appearance and presence easily transform themselves into tyranny if not further accompanied by the vulnerability that comes with self-revelation. The other becomes more fully present to the self in the relationship between self and other only plicitly present, as a sort of faith in oneself and hope in oneself, in our previous reflections on faith and hope. But the question cannot remain merely implicit when we speak of love, which is characterised by a more active stance than are faith and hope.

With regard to neighbor-love, it is of course easier to see that love presupposes some form of distinction and some form of overcoming of that distinction. There must be an other to which we can give ourselves. In love of neighbor or other-love we find this distinction verified and available on the affective, volitional and reasoning levels. And, in some way, we also find the overcoming of this distinction as an attraction of the self for the other that finds expression in and takes the form of self-giving. Love of neighbor becomes, within the ongoingness of everyday events and history, the paradigmatic and self-justifying expression of a real and either communal, shared or individual self-transcendence. It is much easier on such a dialogically intersubjectival level to envision love as paradoxical completion of faith and hope.

However, concerning self-love it is much harder to see how self-giving to the "other" realizes and fulfills

through, so to speak, letting its guard down, by letting what it is within come to the fore. The "within" must be externalized in some way so that it is manifest to the self without losing its "withinness" or character as that which is interior.

The appearance of the other to the self follows its ideal trajectory toward further manifestation by becoming present to the self, and both appearance and presence find their true purpose, goal and completion in revelation. With this schematic understanding in mind, we can now proceed to a more developed phenomenological view of the relationship between other and self that we identify as the other's revelation of itself to the self. As was the case with appearance and presence, here too we want to consider the phenomenon of the other's self-manifestation to the self.

Beings as such, and certainly human beings in particular, are torn between two needs, namely, that of self-revelation and that of self-protection through discretion, reticence and, unfortunately, false self-revelation or deception. Thus, as we begin this consideration of the further development of the relationship between other and self particularly from the perspective of the other, this paradoxical control over faith as turning toward and hope as longing for. As with self-knowledge, so too with self-love there surely occurs distinction and some form of union. Of course, this distinction and union take place on a more monosubjectival level. One does need to have faith in oneself. And a healthy person does hopefully wish him or herself well. But in the present way in which we have been considering self-love so far, the other is merely the projected self as other. Indeed, the structure of self and other in relationship is maintained on both this monosubjectival level and that of intersubjectivity. But within an analysis of love in the everyday realm of finite historical reality, love of neighbor surely takes on a certain inner consistency of its own and can more easily and clearly be justified. Without further reflection on what love is, namely, without going beyond this analysis of love in the everyday realm of finite reality, self-love remains problematic. We must come back shortly to this question.

Love of neighbor or other-love, as the giving of oneself to another, is the essential structure of all forms of love and is based, in part at least, on the felt awareness that otherness we come up immediately against the question of progressive, prudent and appropriate self-revelation as a form of self-giving on the part of the other to the self. The problem and reality of manifestation as truly appropriate self-giving, here understood more properly as revelation, was already at least implicitly present, as a sort of self-giving through appearance and through presence, in our previous look at these first two moments along the other's dialectically developing trajectory toward greater self-manifestation. But the question of self-gift cannot remain merely implicit where we speak of revelation.

If the other that reveals itself to the self can be characterized by "what you see is what you get," namely, by its exteriority with only the most minimal interiority, then the comportment and perspective of the other is quite direct and relatively unmediated. Its initial moment of self-revelation to the self is essentially a prolongation of its phenomenologically prior appearance and presence to the self in the relationship between other and self. In fact, for the most basic relationships between an other only minimally characterized by interiority and the self to which it reveals itself, this may be all the self-revelation that is *qua* otherness is in principle source of enrichment.

As was the case with our phenomenologically and dialectically sequent turning toward, and longing for, the other, the completion of this movement of conversion of the self from itself to the other through love is the continuation and further intensification of that process of conversion in which we find ourselves urged outward from ourselves.

The structure of our experience of the mystery of love, understood as self-giving made on the basis of a prior turning toward the other in faith and a longing for the other in hope, is realized in communal, shared and individual form. It gives expression to the sense of freedom of which we in a given moment or over time in life become aware and in which we rejoice. For the discovery that we already exist within the supportive embrace of someone who has loved us allows us to accept responsibility even for those weaknesses and faults we unconsciously commit.[11] We are loved, as the cliche goes, warts and all. More profoundly, this fact that we are somehow first loved helps rehabilitate the notion of self-love, which, as has already been mentioned, seems so problematic when we consider it on

reasonably possible and that can be expected. Only in the most minimal sense of the word could there even here be a question of deception. In this case, the other would be source of impoverishment of the self only if there were a fundamental incompatibility between the other and the self, as might occur, to pardon such a quite banal example, if a truck fell on someone.

If, on the other hand, the other is itself a reality more profoundly characterized by its own interiority, and especially if the other is itself a communal, shared or individual self characterized by self-awareness and volitional activity, then this initial moment of self-revelation takes on many of the characteristics of human faith, namely, of the first moment of the self's conversion to the other. The other recognizes and turns toward the self with which it is in relationship. It has appeared to, become present to, and now opens itself in an initial way to, the self with which it has entered into relationship. This opening occurs through various signs, language, gestures and the like. However, these are not merely external signs. They are, in a real sense, the very other as it reveals itself and its inner being to the self. They could be its own. Self-transcendence, with its ever-present danger of collapsing into mere selfishness,[12] is not only completed but, more importantly, corrected by the fact that we discover that we ourselves have always already been loved. If in self-love that other which we love, to which we give ourselves in such self-love, is our self objectified as other, then it is the reflection of the other that has been loved. Once we realize we are loved by someone, we can truly love ourselves in our wider and proper context. If, as much as possible, we love ourselves as we have been loved, then we will want what is truly best for ourselves. That is, we will freely want to give ourselves, namely, what others have loved, to others. In the light of our being loved, we find that true self-love is self-sacrifice. So this paradox of love reappears at the very heart of properly contextualized self-love.

The experience of love is not only the stance and comportment of one communal, shared or individual self toward another, but is ideally mutual. In this case the structure of self-giving so far described occurs from self to other in both directions. Indeed, one form of self-gift is the readiness to receive. Self-gift to the other includes both appreciation of considered distinct from the other only if they were considered, in some simplistic way, merely from a limited point of view on the part of the self. Thus, if the revelation is true and authentic, then the other is itself true and authentic and at least a potential source of enrichment for the self. If, however, the signs are not truly revelatory of what the other is within, then, paradoxically, the other becomes momentarily these signs and becomes itself a deceptive reality. The other is these signs which, in fact, however, it is not. Consequently, the other itself becomes impoverished with an internal incoherence between what it is and what it reveals itself as. In this way it is a potential source of impoverishment of the self.

If the first moment of self-revelation is either one of simple "what you see is what you get" in the case where an other's interiority is truly minimal, or one of an initial revelation, accurate or deceptive, of an other's greater level of interiority to the self in the relationship between other and self, then when self-revelation continues any further, the other, in a way analogous to the stance of human hope, continues in a phenomenologically consequent moment of self-revelation to reveal the other and a wanting the other to be its, her or his best self. And, furthermore, the structure of love as self-giving is realized beyond the mutual in the communal, where the experience of being loved urges various members of a given community, small or large, local or even global, to turn to one another, to long to be present to one another and to come to give themselves, in so many ways, to one another. On and within each of these levels, namely, the individual, mutual, communal and inter-communal, there must come a moment of truth if love is to be real. The distinctness of each person, of each group and of each community will be respected if self-giving is really self-giving to the other. There must be justice, but always within the context of spontaneous and generous sacrificial self-giving to the other.[13]

Most generally stated, then, love is self-giving. It remains in some ways a mystery and a paradox how we can truly find ourselves in losing ourselves, how we can become enriched through self-sacrifice. More clearly than with regard to faith and hope, here, where it is a question of love, content, outlook and comportment are one and the same. The other is effectively the content or what it is within to the self with which it is in relationship.

If there is no significant "within" or real level of interiority in the other, this continuing self-revelation merely prolongs, or perhaps interrupts, the previously established level of self-revelation.

If, however, the other is more deeply characterized by interiority, it can surely continue its self-revelation through further signs, gestures, acts and so forth. For if the "within" or the interiority of the other is strongly characteristic of the other, there will always be something further to appear, make present and reveal. So the other proceeds to give further external expression to what it is within. This external expression is indeed, at the moment of the expression, that which the other is. If this expression truly indicates what the other is within, then there is coherence, congruity and continuity within the other itself. If, however, this expression inappropriately presents the other otherwise than the way it is within, then the other falls into internal incoherence, incongruity and discontinuity. For then the other both is what it externally signifies itself to be and is not what it so signifies itself to be at the same time and from the same perspective, point of reference, whether that other be oneself in self-love or neighbors in this word's many senses. Outlook is the spontaneous and free, in its ideal form truly joyous, character with which we give ourselves to the other. And of course comportment is itself this self-giving. Love, then, is that perspective or outlook and way of comporting oneself in relation to others that gives to human existence its specific, truly effective self-transcending shape and character as the free giving of oneself both to oneself and to others. It is the completion of the conversion from self to other begun in faith and given direction by hope. Love is that way of balanced and appropriate selfless being in the world that undergirds the phenomena of human enrichment and of virtuous living as participation in the hoped for final overcoming of evil.

Throughout history there have been many efforts, some more secular and some more religious, to describe love and to highlight its various social, psychological, affective as well as emotional characteristics. Among them, one in particular has continued to inspire readers and to fire their imaginations for two millennia, the Pauline hymn to love: "Love is patient; love is kind; love is

namely, from the perspective of itself as other existing, in this relationship, for the self. The other presents itself either as a moment of internally coherent and thus true self-revelation or of internally incoherent and false self-revelation. Of course, a given moment of self-revelation can be a mixture of the two, and often is, but the formal elements of this second moment of self-revelation remain identifiable as true or as deceptive.

This phenomenologically and dialectically sequent, second moment of self-revelation prolongs and further presents the other's self-revealing stance in relation to the self. The other can, in this moment be either a source of enrichment or of impoverishment or, again, of both, with one of the two, namly, enrichment or impoverishment, finally determining the character of the relationship at this point in its development. This second and, we could note, penultimate form of self-revelation is, if enriching, a generous gesture in which the other in its interiority makes itself available through reliable self-externalization in signs, gestures and so many other forms of self-manifestation. It arises out of an initial moment of self-revelation and provides a springboard not envious or boastful or arrogant or rude. It does not insist on its own way; it is not irritable or resentful; it does not rejoice in wrongdoing but rejoices in the truth. It bears all things, believes all things, hopes all things, endures all things" (1 Co 13:4–7, New Revised Standard Version). Love is indeed the giving of oneself to the other, the ultimate act of generosity.

However, just as love is a third and final stance or comportment of the self in its relation to possibly enriching otherness, so there is a third moment in which the self can unjustifiably, and indeed selfishly, block its conversion to the other that legitimately presents itself as possible source of enrichment. This third moment is the refusal to love, namely, the refusal to reach the other by appropriate self-gift to the other, which is the only way for the self respectfully to include the other while respecting the other's own otherness. In malaise and fear before the other, the self mistakenly tries to preserve itself by refusing to let go, to give of itself and, thus, to rediscover itself anew in and through the other. The self keeps and takes, rather than appropriately giving of itself. And more specifically with regard to self-love, the other to

for a further and, from the perspective of this phenomenological analysis of the movement of experience, final moment of self-revelation by the other to the self with which it is in relationship.

To recapitulate, then, before our phenomenological look at manifestation as revelation, we had so far considered the relationship between other and self, from the perspective of the other, in terms of two ways in which the other relates to the self when otherness is considered a possible source of enrichment of the self. First of all, we spoke of the appearance of the other that occurs in three phenomenologically and dialectically sequential moments of initial appearance, call and invitation, as well as demand. The basically undefined and nondescript initial appearance takes on further determination as call and invitation and then demand on the self to consider the other as source of possible enrichment or impoverishment.

Next, we looked at the other in its subsequent move on beyond appearance to presence, including presence as absence or, better, "absence as presence." Appearance and presence constitute the first two epiphanic moments in the overall manifestation of the other to the which we refuse to give ourselves in an appropriate way is our self objectified as other. But this objectified other is not merely the projection of what we presently are. We refuse to give ourselves over to and to become, by letting go of our old selves, that self which others' love of us has called us to be. Refusing to become the self others have loved, namely, the self that gives itself appropriately to others, is the second form of blockage or refusal as seen in opposition to love. A third form that this refusal to give appropriately of oneself takes, whether that self be communal, shared or individual, is that of a refusal to enter into a relationship of mutual love and self-giving or, again, of interactive, multisided communal self-giving. A refusal to accept love from others is in fact again a refusal to give oneself appropriately to the other. The self is not open and receptive to the other's self-offer. This structure of a refusal to give of oneself is common to the various cases so far indicated and finds expression as the self's refusal to give itself appropriately and in various ways to otherness in its many forms.

Still, this description of the self's voluntary act of blockage as refusal to give oneself appropriately to the self. As we have now seen, there follows a third overall moment in this movement of manifestation, namely, the other's self-revelation to the self. If the other continues its manifestation beyond its appearance and being present to the self, this self-revelation takes the initial form of an effort to have the external indicate what the other is within itself. Presuming that the other continues to reveal itself further to the self, that revelation takes the form of a more explicit indication on the exterior of what the other is within. If congruent with what the other is within, this externalization is, for that moment, what the other itself is. If not, then there exists a paradoxical incoherence *within* the other itself. If the other is fundamentally congruent within itself, it can serve as a source of enrichment for the self. If it is fundamentally incongruent in its self-revelation, no matter what else it does, by that very fact it impoverishes the self and itself. It is true neither to itself nor to the self with which it is in relationship.

The third and final moment of the other's self-revelation to the self is, as a structured movement, essentially the same as the last moment in the movement of conversion on the part of the self in its relationship to other remains but one side of the coin, namely, one side of the reality being considered in opposition to love. The refusal to give oneself appropriately to the other implies the determination to relate oneself inappropriately to the other or at least opens out to that possibility. Any way of relating actively to the other that is not an appropriate form of self-gift to the other is, by definition, a form of violence since any such relating does not respect the otherness of the other. Such inappropriate relating may take the form of violence against oneself or against others. That which should be appropriate self-giving becomes, instead, in an active stance on the part of the self violent keeping, taking and dominating. In any of these cases, what should have been a moment of enriching experience or spirit as conversion to the other is deformed into possession and domination. A decision in favor of violence, or a volitional act of violence, transforms a potentially enriching experience or movement of spirit into a moment of impoverishing experience.

From the perspective, then, of the self, the third overall figure or form of relationship between self and other structuring experience as dynamically developing relationship

the other, a moment that has been identified as love. Here manifestation as self-revelation takes the form of and becomes itself conversion. Of course, where the other is only minimally characterized by interiority, this moment remains basically a simple prolongation of the previous two moments of self-revelation as external manifestation of what the other is within. The role of signs, gestures, appearances is then relatively minor. As was said, "What you see is what you get."

However, if the interiority characteristic of the other concerned is greater and provides the other with enhanced power of self-determination, then the movement to externalize and communicate what one is within takes on much greater importance and, in the case of self-reflexive beings, becomes a question of ultimate concern. Especially with self-reflexive others the movement of self-revelation, namely, the external expression of what one is within takes on the form of an act of love understood as self-giving to another, namely, to the self with which the other is in relationship. This is true of course only if the externalization that occurs is congruent and coherent with what the other is within itself. In making externally available between self and other is that of love or violence in relation to the self-revelation of the other. This third overall attitude or stance on the part of the self is both active and passive. The self actively gives of itself to the other or does violence to the otherness of the other. Especially in a relationship between two selves, it truly receives, or refuses to receive, the self-gift of the other to itself. Love finds further, unlimited nuance and expression in the innumerable concrete ways in which the self can react to the self-revelation of the other.

Love or violence, then, is the third and final phenomenologically identifiable stance on the part of the self toward the other or of two selves to one another. One or the other, namely, love or violence, is equally the third and final dialectically developing moment in the self's movement of conversion, or refusal to consummate that conversion, toward the other. One or the other of these stances is indeed the very being of the self in its dialogically structured relationship with the other. With love, or with violence, we see that the dialectically developing movement of the self from initial openedness, or again refusal to be so opened, to the other on through to

what it is within, the other makes itself ever more fully available to the self as source of enrichment. In effect, the other does really give itself to the self.

When, however, the other falsely exteriorizes and misrepresents what it is to the self, the other manipulates and deceives the self, usually as a power play of one sort or another. If the other falsely exteriorizes what it is within, and what it thinks, feels and knows, to a self that has turned to the other in trust, longed for the other and given itself to the other, then the other violates the self and commits an act of violence against the self.

Whether it be honest or self-contradictory, self-revelation is, from the perspective of the other, the third and final phenomenologically identifiable overall form or figure of experience. One or the other, namely, honest or self-contradictory self-revelation, is equally the third and final dialectically developing moment in the other's self-manifestation to the self with which it is in relationship. The other is itself at this moment honest or self-contradictory self-revelation (with the latter being a form of concealment) in its dialogically structured relationship with the communal, shared or self-gift to or violence toward the other, a movement ideally realized as conversion to the other, merges with that of the dialogically structured dynamic relationship between self and other that constitutes experience. Self-gift to or violence toward the other is the culmination of the dialectically developing movement of conversion, or refusal to convert, to the other in which the self is, successively, each of the stances of faith or indifference, hope or despair, love or violence. The self-gift of the self and the relationship of the self to the other merge into one.

individual self. Here the dialectically developing movement of self-manifestation finally, as self-revelation, converges with the overall dialogically structured relationship between other and self. This striking convergence of dialectical and dialogical brings to completion the very movement of experience as it gives rise to the resultant self.

Resultant Self. The relationship between communal, shared or individual initial self and other evolves, then, through the process we have so far observed in our phenomenological look at, analysis of and reflection on the structured movement of experience. This process started with the initial, given relationship between self and other and developed according to the series of sequent forms, figures and shapes of relationship between self and other that we have come to see in our phenomenological analysis of the dialectically developing movements constituting the conversional, or non-conversional, movement of the self and the manifestational, or non-manifestational, movement of the other, namely: faith and indifference / appearance and non-appearance; hope and despair / presence and absence; love and violence / revelation and concealment. The result of this dialogical relationship between self and other is the initial self now as resultant self.

Where the movement is one of appropriate generosity on the part of self and other, we see that the result is an enriched communal, shared or individual self. Where it is one of selfishness, using the word in a very wide sense to indicate some form of refusal by self and/or other to give appropriately of itself to the other participant or pole in the relationship, then we see that the result is an impoverished self. Often in a concrete situation we find that the development is one of a mixture of generosity and selfishness, so the result in that case is usually a self that is, to varying degrees, both enriched and impoverished while, overall, generally being identifiable either as one or the other.

If, on the one hand, the result is at least principally one of enrichment, the resultant self is concomitantly characterized by a new sense of integration within itself and of oneness with all that is around it. It senses at least minimally within itself a certain wellness and well-being as well as a certain balance with the world around it. It is qualitatively more than it was before the experience. It is, in a real sense, richer and more complex than it was before. If, on the other hand, the result is at least principally one of impoverishment, the resultant self is concomitantly characterized by a new sense of at least partial disintegration within and malaise in relation to all that is around it. It is qualitatively less than it was before the experience. It is poorer for the experience.

Given the nature of experience as in principle a structured movement of initial selfhood and otherness in relationship giving rise to resultant selfhood, there is, however, another sense in which the resultant self in a movement of finite experience inevitably suffers both loss and gain. Recalling what Gadamer has pointed out concerning the inevitable sense of loss in every moment of experience, we can note here that, from a structural perspective, in any moment of experience, whether as enriching, impoverishing or a mixture of both, the initial communal, shared or individual self, now become resultant self, has necessarily from the point of view of experience as such left something behind, namely, what it was before. This loss engenders a certain sense of anxiety that inevitably accompanies, or at least follows upon, even the previously mentioned resultant sense of wholeness, integration, well-being and balance with the ambient world. Indeed, the self is no longer what it was before. Yet, at the same time, it is something new that one would hope appropriately incorporates in a new way what it was before by reaching a new standpoint and way of being. Thus, the resultant self has suffered a gain as well. Every structured movement of experience is inevitably destabilizing and yet, ideally, in its result enriching. In any case, each experience establishes some form of new equilibrium that is the resultant self.[14]

In our finite experience, initial selfhood become resultant selfhood is of course, equally, renewedly initial selfhood in relationship with recurrent otherness. The sense of both loss and gain continues. The dialogical interplay between self and other occurs again and again as the self progresses in a dialectically structured dynamic development through or, better, as a series of potentially enriching or impoverishing moments as stances of the self vis-à-vis the other. The other likewise moves in a dialectically structured dynamic development through a series of potentially encouraging or menacing moments or ways of relating to the self. In the self's movement of conversion, or non-conversion, and in the other's movement of epiphanic self-manifestation, or non-manifestation, each moment is the dialectically developed successor of the previous moment or moments. Each is momentary totality of self or other. Self and other, each, in its own way, variously takes the initiative, responds or refuses to respond within the given situation or dialogically structured relationship. Furthermore, within a given relationship, each of these polar moments of self and other constitute, when considered together, figures or forms of relationship between self and other, as well as further sub-figures or subforms, succeeding one another dialectically, that is, by ceasing to be what they were and becoming something new.

Further Remarks

Our perspective as phenomenological observer is of course itself one of a self in relationship with an other, in this case two others, namely, an initial self and an other in a potentially enriching relationship in which both progress in various ways through that relationship which then gives rise to an enriched or impoverished resultant self. Our privileged position as phenomenological observer has permitted us to follow the dialogical interactions of self and other, in relationship, through each one's dialectical development in two parallel trajectories, namely, that of the self following a trajectory of possible conversion to the other and the other following a trajectory of possible self-manifestation to the self. In its ideal form, as movement of experience resulting in enriched selfhood, namely, a movement of spirit, experience or the dialectically developing dialogical relationship between self and other takes on the basic characteristic of a spousal relationship. It is then in effect the

generosity of self and other, or self and other as another self in the relationship between two selves, existing ontologically and ethically one for the other.
Within this overall dialogically structured relationship between self and other,
the parallel dialectical movements of conversion and manifestation, or in the
case where the other is itself a reflexively aware self, manifestation itself as
movement of conversion, give birth, so to speak, in a movement of spirit, to
enriched resultant selfhood.

In its dialectical development, the self takes on, or better, becomes itself
a series of attitudes and stances toward the potentially enriching other with
which it is in relationship. In parallel fashion, in its own dialectical development, the other manifests itself, and indeed is these manifestations, in a series
of ways of relating or moves whose ideal goal is self-revelation to the self in
the relationship between self and other. In each of these stances or ways of
relating, self and other are, momentarily, just that, namely, the stance or way
concerned. Each stance or way subsequent to the initial one arises sequentially out of the one prior to it and is, momentarily, the totality of that which
it is. Each stance or way is the momentary dialectical totality of what the self
or other is.

Thus, the self as a series of sequent attitudes of faith, hope and love or of
their opposites, and the other as a series of parallel sequent stances of appearance or non-appearance, presence and absence, and revelation or the lack
thereof, form a dialectically sequent series of dialogical relationships between
self and other that give structure to the movement we identify as experience
and here, more specifically, human experience. These overall forms of dialogical relationship, namely, faith/appearance, hope/presence, and love/revela-
tion, along with the further forms of such partnerships within each of these
dialogical relationships, give structure to what we have identified as dialectically progressing movements of conversion of the self to the other and of
manifestation by the other to the self that constitute all forms of experience
sketched out and conjugated in the grammar of experience elaborated in
Chapter Five above.[15] Experience can then, to shift somewhat from the earlier
spousal metaphor, be seen as a sort of conception, namely, the relationship
between initial self and other, then gestation in which the self and other
develop along parallel dialectical trajectories within a dialogically structured
relationship in a process that, in the convergence of dialectical and dialogical,

gives birth to a resultant self.

In this two-fold dialectically developing dialogical relationship between self and other, "dialectical" has been used to refer essentially to the development of a monophyletic series of attitudes or stances of the self and a similar series of ways of relating on the part of the other that are "momentary totalities" one following the other in respective trajectories of development of self and other. The motor force, so to speak, underlying and driving the self on is the phenomenologically observable inevitable urge of the self outward from itself, an urge that can of course be blocked at any given moment. The motor force underlying and driving the other on is the phenomenologically observable inevitable givenness of its initial self-manifestation. In each of these ideally generous dialectical developments, more literally understood in relation to a self-aware self and much more generally understood in relation to a self or other characterized by only minimal interiority, dialectical advance occurs through a decisional act. "Dialogical" refers here essentially to the bipolar structure of the relationship between self and other in which each retains throughout the movement of experience its own phenomenologically observable givenness and reality, the one parallel to the other while interacting with the other. This ontological givenness of self and other as dialectically developing parallel and, hopefully, appropriately converging movements is, especially but not only when both self and other are selves, equally and at the same time an ethical givenness. The other calls out to and then invites the self to consider it and demands that the self do so. Where self and other are selves, they call out to, and by this way of being invite, each one to consider the other and, thus, they make demands upon one another.

In this dialectically developing dialogically structured relationship, the initial self is that which is opened to and turns toward the other with which it finds itself in relationship. It either continues or blocks the further development of this conversional move toward the other. Ideally, the self is a movement outward from itself to the other, a sort of urge outwards. The other is that which in this relationship initially appears to and then impinges upon the self. It either continues or discontinues, appropriately or inappropriately, its trajectory of epiphanic self-manifestation to the self with which it is in relationship. Ideally, the other is a movement toward the self, and especially its appearance but also its presence or "absence as presence" and self-revelation constitute an invitation and call to the self to embrace it and an ontological and ethical demand to take it into consideration. The resultant self is the result of this dialogical relationship carried out as a series of two dialectically developing movements of possibly enriching convergence between self and other or of possibly impoverishing divergence between them. The resultant self is in fact the goal of the relation and process through which it, as initial self, and the other have developed. Ideally, over the course of this double trajectory the self has appropriately given itself to the other in love, which paradoxically results in an enriched self that thereby respectfully includes the other, on the basis of the other's self-revelation, in its new reality as renewed-ly initial self in relationship with the recurrence of otherness in the form of the initial appearance of an other. As finite movement of enriching experi-ence, this movement is one of inclusive subjectivity that is equally not inclu-sive.

To repeat what has already been stated in the previous chapter, with the notion of "repeat" here understood in a Kierkegaardian sense of repetition that involves novelty, newness and, indeed, a sense of movement forward,[16] our phenomenological look at experience as a spiral movement of becoming reveals it to be a tetradically structured movement. That movement is the relationship between initial selfhood and otherness, each of which exists in this relationship for the other, a relationship resulting in a newly constituted impoverished or enriched selfhood that, in turn, is equally initial selfhood in relationship with renewed otherness. In this sense, experience is a tetradically structured movement of finite becoming. The essential movement, however, which would fulfill the requirements of a movement of experience as such is simply a triadically structured one of initial selfhood and otherness in rela-tionship giving rise to resultant selfhood. As was mentioned at the end of Part One above and will be discussed in more detail in Part Three below, I propose that any movement of experience that results in an enriched self, whether structured tetradically or triadically, be recognized as and named a movement of spirit.

In Part One above, we reviewed Hegel's development of a philosophical theology, whose fundamental category was that of thought, and then pro-posed to continue in a general way his project, but now doing so by replacing that category with the notion of experience. I have strongly suggested that this "substitution" would allow for more flexibility, a recognition of the obduracy of evil, a greater respect for freedom and a deeper sense of mystery that an adequate philosophical theology would seem to require.

Here in Part Two, using several different approaches, namely, reviewing what selected philosophers have said about experience, sketching out a grammar of experience and carrying out a phenomenological analysis of experience, has permitted us to propose an understanding of experience as relation, process and result that reflects the richness of experience. We have come to discover in experience a notion and basic philosophical category that enables us to work with both the more universal and the more particular in such a way that we no longer need to consider them as mutually exclusive or even their relationship to one another as seriously problematic. Our notion of experience is that of a reality at one and the same time universally formulated and concretely realized.

To complement and further develop these various approaches, namely, reviewing something of what has previously been said concerning experience, sketching out a grammar of experience and doing a phenomenological analysis of experience, we needed in this last, namely, in the phenomenological analysis, to make an explicit appeal to the dialectical and the dialogical. Usually dialectical thinking is associated with more monophyletically formulated movements of thought and dialogical thinking is linked with more dipolar thinking. However, we needed to make this appeal to these two forms of thinking and to work with both of them if we wished to express more adequately in reflexive form the richness of experience.

Over the course of the present Part Two of our study we have, then, come to see that experience has at least three meanings. Experience is, first of all and in the most fundamental sense, the dynamic, dialectically developing dialogical relationship between self and other giving rise to resultant selfhood. It is, in a second and derivative but more commonly understood sense, that which the self undergoes in the course of its conversional trajectory, or blockage thereof, toward the other with which it is in relationship. In a third sense, experience is the accumulation of what the self has learned and integrated through a series of experiences, with this word "experience" taken in both the first and second of the three meanings here indicated.

Now, in Part Three we will explore and interpret a number of themes in philosophical theology. We will do this by working with our fundamental notion of experience understood, ideally, as the movement of inclusive subjectivity and spirit that had been proposed at the end of Part One.

NOTES

1. For several remarks on the history of this term "structured movement" in relation to Hegel's thought, see Dale M. Schlitt, *Hegel's Trinitarian Claim. A Critical Reflection* (Leiden: Brill, 1984) 21 n. 58.
2. Concerning Hegel's *Phenomenology of Spirit*, see Schlitt, *Hegel's Trinitarian Claim* 121–127.
3. I noted this earlier on in *Theology and the Experience of God* (New York: Peter Lang, 2001) 41–47.
4. Often one tends to speak of the "subjective" in relation to the self and of the "objective" in relation to the other. However, such a way of phrasing the distinction would certainly require considerably more nuance.
5. The relationship between self and other takes on a more obviously dialogical structure if one is considering a relationship that takes the form of an interrelationship between self and other, which latter is itself a self-aware self. However, I would suggest that even the more monologically formulated relationship that occurs in thinking is in fact a more internally established dialogically structured relationship between the one thinking and what is being thought.
6. See, for example, James Fowler, *Stages of Faith: The Psychology of Human Development and the Quest for Meaning* (San Francisco: Harper, 1981). For a helpful discussion of Fowler, see John W. Crossin, *What Are They Saying About Virtue?* (New York: Paulist, 1985) 91–101.
7. Here, and with regard as well to the question of content, outlook and comportment, I have, in a more philosophical context, profited from Avery Dulles's schematization of three overall forms of interpretation of faith as conviction, trust and commitment in "The Meaning of Faith Considered in Relation to Justice," in John C. Haughey, ed., *The Faith That Does Justice* (New York: Paulist, 1977) 10–46. This article is helpfully summarized by Richard P. McBrien in *Catholicism*, vol. 2 (Minneapolis, MN: Winston, 1980) 967–969.
8. Tad Dunne speaks, from within the perspective of Bernard Lonergan's thought, of hope more in terms of emotion and affection and as being "about felt expectations." See his *Lonergan and Spirituality. Towards a Spiritual Integration* (Chicago: Loyola University Press, 1985) 123–126. I have in a general way profited from his presentations on faith, hope and love, esp. 118–126.
9. I have taken this idea in its very general formulation from the work of Walter Brueggemann. See, for example, *Hope within History* (Atlanta: Knox, 1987) 84–87.
10. Of present concern is love especially on the human level. From a more cosmological perspective, others have seen love as a characteristic of the relationship between various entities on any level. See, for example, Pierre Teilhard de Chardin, who speaks of love as "l'affinité de l'être pour l'être"/"the affinity of being with being," in *Le phénomène humain* (Paris: Éditions du Seuil, 1955) 293/*The Phenomenon of Man* (London: Collins, 1959) 264. George Tavard writes of love in very broad terms as a "unity, at varying degrees and with many forms, between beings (...) Love exists wherever one may detect unity among diverse realities." *A Way of Love* (New York: Orbis, 1977) 65–66. Out of a Whiteheadian context, John B. Cobb, Jr., "affirms 'self-love' and 'other-love' of every entity whatsoever." *The Structure of Christian Existence* (Philadelphia: Westminster, 1967) 125. This study by John Cobb and his

other work out of a Whiteheadian perspective have proven very helpful.

For a reminder of the difficulties involved in the notion of love as self-giving, see Gene Outka, *Agape. An Ethical Analysis* (New Haven: Yale University Press, 1972) 8–9.

11. In this line, see Cobb, *The Structure of Christian Existence* 125–136.
12. Cobb, *The Structure of Christian Existence* 134–135.
13. On the relation between justice and love, see, for example, Paul Tillich, *The New Being* (New York: Scribner's, 1955) 32, quoted in Tavard, *A Way of Love* 71.
14. Of course, the other in the relationship between self and other can itself be considered from the perspective of the self and in that case our phenomenological reading of its development, from that perspective, would follow what has already been presented concerning the structured movement of the self in relationship with the other.
15. In fact, not only all forms of experience indicated in Chapter Five above, but all forms of such experience wherever they may occur. In this sense, what we are saying here will apply not only in our daily lives here on earth but anywhere in the universe that we may be fortunate enough to visit or inhabit in the future. This is, then, another sense in which the categories and structured movement of experience here worked out will be universally available wherever otherness is acknowledged by the self in that otherness's obstinate perdurance and potential for enrichment.
16. In regard to Kierkegaard's somewhat Hegelian understanding of repetition, see Dale M. Schlitt, *Theology and the Experience of God* (New York: Peter Lang, 2001) 230–231 n. 18.

PART III

Experience and Spirit

7

EXPERIENCE OF GOD

In Part One above, we journeyed along with Hegel as we explored his philosophy of religion, there more precisely redescribed as a philosophical theology. Then in Part Two, as part of our effort to go beyond Hegel, we conjugated various forms of experiences and established an understanding of experience, in particular of human experience, as a dialogically structured relationship between self and other that developed, to put it succinctly, through parallel dialectical movements, respectively, from initial selfhood through to resultant selfhood and from appearance to revelation. There, with reference to the overall, structured movement of experience, we were dealing essentially with ways in which self and other comport themselves in relation to one another in human or, in principle and more generally speaking, finite experience as such. This experience consists in a tetradically structured movement from initial selfhood and otherness in relationship to enriched or impoverished selfhood renewedly in relationship with otherness and otherness with it.

Now in Part Three, but especially in the present chapter, we will look principally and more directly at enriching experience, namely, the movement of spirit's essentially triadic structure: initial selfhood and otherness in relationship, giving rise to enriched selfhood. This focus on the essentially triadic structure of the movement of spirit as enriching experience will in fact, to recall and use terminology worked out in Chapter Four above, be a form of second experience that proceeds as a series of phenomenological and philosophical analyses of the trinitarian experience of God. More exactly, we will work with the overall Christian communal and individual experience of God as Trinity, including various affirmations of that experience as, to use terminology established in Chapter Five, a sort of first experience to which we will refer and upon which we will further reflect.

The reasons for this choice of the overall Christian experience of God as point of reference in working out the here proposed philosophical theology are varied and numerous. Among them, one might especially note that this is a way to acknowledge in serious fashion the resurgent overall interest in spirituality so characteristic of our time. Then, in addition to or, rather, aside from possible questions of personal conviction and familiarity with various Christian religious and theological traditions, from a theological perspective Christianity seems to have developed a notion of Trinity more central to its self-understanding and more elaborately worked out than have most other religious traditions.

From a more philosophical perspective, I would, among various reasons, note that Hegel himself had chosen to work at great depth with the Christian affirmation of God as Trinity. In addition to this reason that is important especially due to its deep rootage in the history of philosophy, there are further considerations based in the notion itself of God as Trinity. For example, this notion and understanding of God is a particularly complex one that allows for considerable further elaboration even by those who would in principle affirm that God is beyond the reach of human discourse. It also incorporates the idea of difference into the "absolute" itself, a move surely of great interest in the present day and age where the phenomenon of globalization seems to be juxtaposing ever more accurately differences in world view, culture, religion, language and history. Furthermore, the structure of God considered as Trinity seems to provide elements that would be of help in working out a philosophical theology in which ontological and epistemological questions remain at the heart of any constructive project in that area of reflection. Indeed, as a further consideration, complexity, difference, epistemology and so many other notions related to a trinitarian understanding of God, taken together, indicate rather cogently reasons why this understanding serves as a particularly propitious point of departure for, and opening to, a philosophically formulated interreligious dialogue with philosophical theologians who themselves might have chosen to refer to and reflect upon communal and individual forms and affirmations of other religious experiences of God, whether those be rooted in Jewish, Islamic, Hindu, Indigenous or other religious traditions.

As we move more directly into our reflection on the trinitarian experience of God and its affirmation, it will be helpful to recall that a second experience is, in one way or another, a further step in and prolongation of a first experience. With specific reference to an experience of God as first experience, a second experience intentionally carried out as a faithful prolongation, into the realm of reflexive thought, of such a first experience is an exercise in what is usually called confessional theology. However, as an exercise in philosophical theology, such a second reflection wishes of course to remain faithful to the first reflection, but proposes, primarily at least, to maintain and develop further only elements of that first experience which can be presented, described narratively, or argued, as the case may be, on the basis of reasoned reflection. In the present instance, that reasoned reflection will occur and proceed according to generally accepted canons of logic and, more particularly, on the basis of and within the context of the understanding of experience worked out in Part Two above. This understanding of experience, with its various possible forms of relationship between self and other, allows us to work out a proposal in the public realm since it is available for self-reflexive review, critique and modification. Of special note, working with this understanding of experience allows us to refer to God in a way that does not subordinate God to a pre-established pattern of thought that would in effect amount to submitting God to a limiting principle.

In Part Two above we were effectively working with the notion of *experientia quaerens intellectum*, experience seeking understanding. Now in Part Three we will be working in a more explicitly philosophical theology mode, which we could to some extent at least call *experientia Dei quaerens intellectum*, the experience of God seeking understanding.

In the present chapter, I would like in a more explicit way to make a contribution to ongoing efforts to develop a contemporary philosophical theology and, more specifically here, a contribution that, in a certain continuity with Hegel, itself is elaborated in the form of a movement of inclusive divine subjectivity. While here prolonging various aspects of the reflections carried out in previous chapters, my more specific intention is to offer several reflections that will permit us to reformulate and reappropriate Hegel's notion of the true infinite. This recuperation of that infinite will take the form of a renewed trinitarian philosophical theology for the twenty-first century. The first part of the present chapter will, then, proceed in two steps. The first of these steps consists in a phenomenological look at, analysis of and reflection on the experience of God as Trinity and the second one in a further philosophical reflection in favor of an understanding of God as Trinity. We will need to carry out these two reflections, namely, the first as a phenomenological look at and analysis of the first experience and the second more in the form of a further philosophical reflection, if we wish to give more adequate, reasoned expression to the rich and complex content of the first experience. One of the two, widely speaking, philosophical reflections alone would not be enough. These two considerations will constitute the above-mentioned second experience in relation to the experience of God to which they refer. After this doubled reflection, namely, phenomenological and more formally philosophical, we will suggest a sort of third experience, namely, a further phenomenological look and analysis and reflection constituting an enriched return to the first experience of God and its affirmation.

In these various moves and this overall effort to work out a post-Hegelian philosophical theology, I would underscore that we are in fact not abandoning notions of subjectivity and of selfhood so dear to Hegel. Rather, as subjects and as selves we ourselves are trying to refocus more appropriately on otherness as possible source of enrichment. The challenge, then, will be to speak of God in critical correlation with our own age and our own cultures, which are characterized by this ongoing concern for appropriate understandings of the relationship between self and other.

Second Experience: Phenomenological and Philosophical Reflections

It is not easy to speak meaningfully in philosophical, and here first more specifically phenomenological, fashion of God as such and of Trinity in particular. Indeed, philosophical theology has taken many different forms over the last two centuries or so, generally along either Kantian lines, where one hesitates to say very much about God, or Hegelian lines, where one tends to say too much. Philosophical theology may well continue to follow one or the other of these two overall approaches well into the third millennium. However, here I propose what I hope will be a helpful middle-of-the-road approach to Trinity at the present moment in the history and development of philosophical theology. Building upon remarks made so far, I would suggest that we now first elaborate a modestly developed theory of Trinity on the basis of, in a general sense of the word, a phenomenology of the trinitarian experience of God.[1] As mentioned above, this phenomenological presentation will then be followed by a further philosophical reflection on, or perhaps more specifically, logical argument as a reconstruction of, certain essential elements of that experience.

A Phenomenological Presentation

Recapitulative Remarks on Experience. As was mentioned at the beginning of Chapter Four above, in the English language, "experience" is a particularly useful and yet terribly diffuse term. In some ways, of course, it is the English language's most basic notion.[2] It functions in English almost as "language" (*langage*) does in French, or "thinking" (*Denken*) in German, or "being" (*esse, ens*) did in medieval Latin philosophy. Indeed, in English usage the fuller sense or meaning of experience includes thinking and language as constitutive elements within it and, in particular, language as a special conditioning factor in experience. Thus experience, even when conditioned by language, is considered the wider and more inclusive of these notions. In addition, we can also see thinking and language, in their own right, as two particular forms of experience. Due in part at least to the heavy influence of North American pragmatist philosophies, experience often comes to mean an objective or real event that is a relationship between self and other. In a sense, then, within the movement of experience we can distinguish subjective and objective moments or poles. But experience as such both precedes and goes beyond this distinction between subjective and objective. If one will pardon the expression, experience is really real.

At the end of this study's overall Part Two above, we concluded that finite experience, and here more specifically human experience, is both a process and the result of the process. It is the multidimensional mutual, dynamically (appropriately dialectically and dialogically) developing relationship between self and other that results in an enriched or impoverished self. In developing through any experience, this enriched or impoverished self has, from the perspective of the negative side to the experience, left something behind and, from the perspective of the positive side to the experience, found itself at a new vantage point. And this self finds itself immediately and ever renewedly in relationship with an other. Experience is, consequently, both constitutive revelatory encounter and resultant impoverishment or enrichment.[3]

Experience of God. In Chapter Six above, we spoke of the four senses in which there was a "given" in a phenomenological analysis of experience: the initial, underlying relationship between self and whatever other is involved; the experiencing self; the other with which the self finds itself in relation; the result of the relationship between self and other. We spoke as well of the conditioned character of this quadruple "given" and of the structured movement that a phenomenological analysis reveals.

These same considerations concerning a conditioned quadruple "given" and an underlying structured movement apply as well when we wish, as is the case here, to propose a phenomenological analysis of the experience of God since, at least in the first instance, we are speaking of human experience of God. Concerning the underlying structured movement, we will need to note that development occurs due to and in line with the various ways in which God as other is present to the experiencing self and due to the differing ways in which the experiencing self responds to this pluriform presence. More specifically concerning structure, we should in the analysis take note of any order possibly characteristic of this pluriform divine presence.

With regard to the question of a conditioned quadruple "given," we will have to keep in mind the qualifying character of this conditioning. If, for example, the experience of God is always conditioned and constitutively affected, even at times perhaps in some way initiated, by such human constructions such as language, thought, interest, tradition, culture and, to some extent at least, by gender and genetic substrate, we might easily conclude that all experiences of God are then relativized and rendered fundamentally unreliable. However, rather than take this route we might also propose, and that is the position espoused here as it was with regard to experience in general in the previous chapter, that such particularity does not in itself necessarily relativize. Instead, it provides the inevitably concrete point of departure for any more universalizing analysis. Varying, and differently conditioned, concrete points of departure do not necessarily force the conclusion either that human experience is inevitably atomized or that human experiences are merely to be maintained in simple juxtaposition. These necessarily conditioned concrete points of departure provide the essential basis for the type of analysis that we envisage here. They are, in fact, that which is taken up into a more universalizing, self-reflexively carried out phenomenological analysis. As so analyzed, they are that which the philosophical theologian then offers for consideration either by those who identify with one or more Christian traditions or, indeed, by those who do not.

In a sense, the reference we just made to a phenomenological analysis of the experience of God involved, so to speak, jumping the phenomenological gun. As part of these initial considerations, we should really first have turned to the rather more general question of religious experience. However, since we have already underscored the variously conditioned character of any phenomenological "given," we can now speak more briefly of what we might find as the generalizable phenomenological "given" in a religious experience. In fact, due to the varieties of such religious experience reported by personal witnesses or in the literature concerned, it is best here, where we are still speaking of a series of experiences bearing a specific structure and sharing a certain common dynamic, to speak of religious experiences in the plural. Under various influences, including those of differing cultures and social settings, instances of what is commonly referred to as religious experience have occurred in numerous shapes and forms down through history and around the world. They have usually not done so as isolated events. Rather, they take place, more rarely, as founding moments of a religious tradition or, more commonly, as moments within the ongoing history of the many and varied already existing religious traditions. However, while continuing to refer to religious experiences in the plural, we can still indicate a characteristic, admittedly variously realized, that both those who speak of their religious experiences and those who study such experiences seem to acknowledge as common to a wide variety of such experiences. Indeed, most if not all of these variously conditioned religious experiences would seem to share a characteristic essential to and constitutive of an overall religious experience as such. This characteristic would seem to be that form of enrichment realized and recognized as the overwhelming[4] sense of an at least momentary wholeness, integration, well-being and balance or harmony with others and the ambient world that the community, couples or friends and individuals come to sense and that they then affirm. For them, life in its many aspects seems to hang together and to have some meaning.[5]

Perhaps the greatest contemporary argument against the validity of such a sense of wholeness, integration, well-being and balance could be made by appealing to the twentieth-century experience of massive, humanly inflicted evil and suffering. And yet, it is precisely in fully admitting this horrid reality of massive evil that people, differently in the various religious traditions, still sense and affirm a sort of wholeness, integration, well-being and balance. These affirmations go at least so far as to give expression to the conviction that there must be some explanation for this sense and felt awareness, an explanation lying beyond both the self more immediately involved and what can be seen here and now.

We can now say more precisely in what the previously mentioned conditioned quadruple "given" in religious experience consists. Here we take our point of departure in the result of the religious experience and follow in order from result to presence to relation, which is the reverse of the underlying phenomenological structure of relation, presence and result indicated in Chapter Six above. In this reverse order, the conditioned quadruple "given" consists, first, in a sense of wholeness, integration, well-being and balance on the emotive, affective and mental levels. It includes, second, a realization that we cannot fully explain the multi-leveled sense of wholeness, integration, well-being and balance simply by reference to ourselves. Third, it points to a self that experiences this multi-leveled sense. Fourth, it refers as well to an awareness that this has its origin in some form of underlying relationship or even identity between self and other. Thus, reference is generally made to some form of "beyond," whether that "beyond" would take the shape of a divine personal reality or simply a "beyond the self."

We should now note that, within more specifically Christian streams of thought, the conditioned character of the quadruple phenomenological "given" takes on particular importance. Indeed, such conditioning had already occurred in previous normative interpretations as, for example, in those conditioned interpretations we find in Scripture. These conditioned scriptural interpretations both of the sense of wholeness, integration, well-being and balance and of the sources of that sense then, in turn, continue themselves to condition present experiences of wholeness, integration, well-being and balance. Along with these scriptural interpretations, past or especially present cultural conditioning is considered crucial to, and a constitutive element in, a community's, a couple's or friends' or an individual's interpretation of religious experiences. Such multiple conditioning is at the very crux of the varied Christian understandings of reality. This particular characteristic of Christianity, namely, its clear acceptance of the conditioned character of religious experiences, reflects its sense of incarnation. We find a witness to the existence of this particular characteristic in the fact that members of Christian communities have, over the long haul, historically emphasized the role of the preached word and the need to adapt preaching to local circumstances. Again, they have more recently stressed the importance of the evangelization of a whole culture.

A further preliminary remark concerning religious experiences is in order. When we look at the notion of religious experience more specifically in terms of what Christians have said, we find that they usually speak more precisely of an experience of God. Here we return to the notion of an experience of God that we touched on earlier in these initial considerations. Referring to an experience of God, for present purposes considered a specification of the wider notion of a religious experience, indicates that we are not presently treating explicitly of an experience of God taken in the most general sense to mean any and every moment of truly human experience insofar as such a moment involves God.[6] Rather, we are now thinking of those moments in which we become aware, at least vaguely, of either a very calm and tender or even perhaps a more upsetting and explosive way of being in relationship with God and, consequently, with all that is around us.

In reflecting on these more explicitly religious experiences of God, we need to proceed with a great deal of sensitivity to individuals, couples, friends, groups and to the variety of Christian traditions as well as to the various formulations of the notion of God to which these traditions or groups, couples, friends and individuals within these traditions have given rise. Our attempt at what might be called a fundamental phenomenology of the experience of God will surface a number of aspects to or elements in the religious experience of God that we are considering here. A specific Christian tradition may not always stress one or another of these aspects or elements and all such traditions may not give them equal importance.[7] Working with an affirmation of the experience of God should provide the various and often quite divergent religious traditions an occasion for discussion concerning the shape, structure and movement of a more explicitly trinitarian formulation of the community's, couples', friends' and individuals' experiences of God. The various religious traditions, groups and even individuals may, with regard to the experiences of God that they affirm, have more in common than the various notions of God that they have so far formulated would lead them to believe. Furthermore, certain groups and individuals may not be fully aware of many of these aspects arising out of this at least intendedly more inclusive phenomenological presentation. They may find that they notice certain elements more than others, and this in different ways at different times in their histories or their lives. Again, the phrase "experience of God" can, as indicated, refer both to ongoing living and to specific experiences of a more explicitly religious nature. We are of course presently making more direct reference to these latter experiences without intending to exclude all reference to ongoing living as such. In principle, it would be necessary on another occasion to consider in more detail, from a philosophical perspective concerned with what can be affirmed on the basis of a reasoned argument, various presentations of the overall structure of human and, more specifically, Christian existence. We would also need to take into consideration, again from a philosophical perspective, more communal witnessings to the experience of God, namely, witnessings that take the form of sacred Scriptures and of classic creedal and liturgical texts. We would, finally, want to consider in some detail the more personal or theological reflections of couples, friends and individuals to be found throughout history and in the contemporary world. We would indeed, through various forms of philosophical reflection in the area of interreligious dialogue, want to bring these more communal, as well as more personal shared and individual, experiences into respectful, comparative and enriching relationship with experiences that are affirmed by communities and members of other religious traditions such as, for example, Islam.

Trinitarian Experience of God. In the present reflection, then, we work with the idea that one of the essential characteristics of any fully realized form of religious experience is an, at least momentary, overwhelming resultant sense of wholeness, integration and well-being as well as balance with the world around us.[8] We will take this to apply especially to any experience of God in which Christians in particular, as our point of reference, become more aware of the experience. Furthermore, we will focus on aspects of the experience of God more specifically germane to our concern to work toward a renewed philosophical theology in the form of a movement of inclusive divine subjectivity.

In our present reflection on and consideration of what Christians have affirmed concerning an experience of God, we will now proceed in two overall steps. The first step, what I have called a second experience, is a doubled one and consists, as mentioned, in an overall phenomenological look at, analysis of and reflection on the Christian experience of God and the affirmation of that experience as well as in a more formally philosophical argument in favor of the affirmation of a true infinite. The second step, which will take the form, in part at least, of a third experience, will involve a further phenomenological look at, analysis of and reflection on the trinitarian experience of God.

The first of our two phenomenological analyses, namely, the first part of what we are referring to as a second experience, will itself proceed in two phases or moments. In the first phase, we will take a more abstractly expressed, phenomenological look at the recurrent structure and dynamic both of Christian living in general but especially of more explicitly religious experiences of God. This more abstractly expressed phenomenological look constitutes a sort of first, underlying phase or moment in the phenomenological analysis that sets the stage for further reflection. Then, in a second phase or moment in that phenomenological analysis, we will turn to the more emotive language Christians use to capture and express the rich affective tenor of their lives and of such experiences. In comparison with the phenomenological look at and analysis of experience as such in Chapter Six above, the present phenomenological look and analysis refers in more direct fashion to a more specific experience, namely, the experience of God. It is equally, then, a reflection on that experience. It will often proceed in a more descriptive and narrative fashion than did the phenomenological analysis of experience, in Chapter Six above, whose purpose was to identify the structure and movement of experience as such.

The basic identity both of structure and of movement that we will find here in these two phases or moments in our first phenomenological analysis shows that the experience of God and its expression in words are not two water-tight compartments. Rather, they are identifiable moments in a continuum whose two moments, when taken together, constitute what is properly meant by "experience of God." In them, factors such as language, thought, interest, gender, tradition, culture, genetic substrate and influences function somewhat differently to condition the experience as relationship, process and result.

These two phases or moments in our present phenomenological analysis of the trinitarian experience of God will open the way to a more philosophically formulated and logically argued reconstruction of the movement from finite to true or inclusive infinite. By way of recall of what was mentioned above and of look ahead, we can already now note that our phenomenological presentation and philosophical argument will be followed by a further phenomenological analysis as a sort of third experience in which we will draw out further the structure and movement of Trinity revealed in our phenomenological look at and philosophical argument concerning the communal, shared and individual trinitarian experience of God.

Now in our first, two-phased phenomenological look or analysis we will focus more on the "subjective" side to the relation between self and other. Later, in our second phenomenological look, we will concentrate more on the divine "other" present to the self in the experience of God. But of course it is never a question of isolating one or the other pole in the relation constituting that experience.

In the first phase of our phenomenological look at the trinitarian experience of God and the affirmation of that experience, we can, first of all and with special focus on recurrent structure and dynamic, from a more general phenomenological and structural perspective reiterate that, in Christian traditions,[9] the sense of wholeness, integration, well-being and balance characteristic of a religious experience is gained through the ongoing process of human experience. Building upon what we concluded earlier on in Part Two of this volume above, we can, in something of a shorthand formulation, recall that the ongoing process of human experience consists in a series of ever-renewed tetradically structured finite experiences.

These finite experiences are relationships, processes and results that, in one way or another, as movements of experience not only follow upon, but also go beyond and supersede, previous experiences. Each moment of human or finite experience is, then, one of becoming in which initial selfhood and otherness in relationship results in the new standpoint of an enriched or impoverished selfhood, a standpoint that necessarily involves, in some sense, the negation of the previous one. This enriched or impoverished selfhood is itself in turn immediately and renewedly initial selfhood in relationship with otherness. In comparison with several forms of, for example, Buddhism and Hinduism, Christians generally do not (except perhaps for one or the other somewhat more "marginal" mystical traditions) try to go beyond, but rather affirm, the ongoing significance of the perduring distinction between self and other. These moments of experience, constituted by and as the relationship between selfhood and otherness, or, more concretely, between the communal, shared or individual self and other, can, for example, be exchanges with other persons, moments of awareness of the beauty of nature, moments of communal, shared or individual prayer, of the awareness of the interplay of good and evil or, again, moments of suffering and joy. In some ways, the community's experiences are surely foundational for other shared or more individual experiences. In any case, in and through these experiences Christians, whether communities, couples, friends or individuals, see that the sense of wholeness, integration, well-being and balance they experience has a doubled present focus and location.

There is, first of all, from the perspective of the self a more immediate feeling of integration within oneself and of oneness with all that is around one. Christians experience in communal, shared or individual "corporeal" self-presence an at least momentary feeling of wholeness, integration and well-being as well as balance that arises from deep within the self but that is not explicable only on the basis of what they know themselves to be. This is an experience variously expressed as one of newness of life, of joy and peace, available as emotional reverberation within, and consequent intellectual conviction on the part of, the self.

There arises, secondly but equally importantly, within the initial, more abstractly analyzed structure of what is affirmed as an experience of God a felt conviction that this wholeness, integration, well-being and balance within themselves and of themselves with all that is around them is rooted in and originates from beyond either the communal or the shared or, again, the individual self. This "beyond" is felt from, and reference to the other as origin of the sense of wholeness, integration, well-being and balance is made in, two directions. First of all, as we just mentioned, from within, as a sort of mediation coming from within. The communal, shared or individual self comes to appreciate an urging or welling up within itself and orienting the self in a generous mode to the other or others in and with whom it finds itself in relationship and, at least momentarily, at one. Secondly, from without, as a sort of mediation coming from without. The self perceives the manifold of others with which it is in relationship and toward which it finds itself oriented as a series of revelatory indications of a greater personal reality manifesting, and thus generously offering, itself to the self in and through these finite realities or others. This other, experienced as coming through the many others to the self from without, is in turn experienced as other in two senses: first, as more immediate source of all human enrichment and thus, in a way, as a call and invitation to that enrichment as well as, in a wider sense, ethical demand upon the self; second, as the goal toward which the self lives.

This more structurally oriented reading of the Christian experience of God reveals a triple affirmation of self-manifesting otherness: otherness within; otherness from without as more immediate external source of, and consequently a call or invitation to, and demand concerning, enriching growth or qualitative increment resulting in, and thus experienced as, a sense of wholeness, integration, well-being and balance; and, otherness from without as goal and purpose for which one lives. What we had earlier spoken of as the tetradic structure of ongoing human experience has here given rise, when we take into consideration the double mediation to which reference was previously made, to this triply affirmed experience of otherness. For Christians in particular the sense of wholeness, integration, well-being and balance (that is experienced) is explained by and rooted in the experience of living, acting and having one's being within the context of a triply structured dynamic personal embrace.

So far we have expressed the religious experience of wholeness, integration, well-being and balance more in terms of overall structure and with an effort to reflect the awareness of some form of ongoing distinction between self and other, a distinction generally considered essential to and a constitutive element in a Christian experience of God.[10] This more abstractly expressed structural analysis of that experience already constitutes an initial critical phenomenological reading of the Christian experience of God and reconstruction of the affirmation of that experience. It is, so to speak, the first phase or moment in the phenomenological analysis of that experience. Since this more abstract analysis has been carried out with a terminology more readily available across the board at least in contemporary Western intellectual traditions, it helps make available or, so to speak, puts on the table for public discussion what Christians wish to assert in affirming an experience of God.

Before exploring the nature of this previously mentioned triply structured dynamic personal embrace, effectively God's experience of us, which we will do toward the end of the present chapter and which will take on the form of a further overall step in our, in a more general sense, philosophical consideration of the experience of God, we can now, on the basis of the so-far affirmed triply structured experience of God as other, pursue a second phase in our present phenomenological analysis and say something concerning each of the three moments in this trinitarian experience of divine otherness in its triply realized movement of manifestation as appearance, presence and revelation. These observations will help us understand somewhat better the three moments themselves of divine otherness in their self-manifesting relationships to humans and, ultimately, to the world in general. Therefore, setting them out now amounts to taking another step toward the development of a renewed philosophical theology, and this not only by helping us to understand further the trinitarian experience of God but also by preparing the way for a brief, more logically argued reflection, on that experience of God and, toward the end of the present chapter, a further, more integrative phenomenological reflection on the Christian experience of God and especially on God's experience of us.

In the first phase or moment in our first phenomenological analysis, we expressed the movement of the experience of wholeness, integration, well-being and balance more in terms of overall structure, and this with an effort to reflect the awareness of some form of ongoing distinction between self and other. Christians and many others have, as was mentioned, generally considered the affirmation of this distinction essential to, and a constitutive element in, their experience of God.

Now, we need to flesh out what was revealed in that first phase, namely, the initial and more abstract structural analysis of the trinitarian experience of God, in a second phase or moment, perhaps better, a second look at that experience by combining further observations on the self-manifestation of the three moments of the inclusive divine embrace with more explicit reference to the present lived experience of the Christian community, of couples, of friends and of individuals. We will make these further observations with full awareness of the varied phenomenological ways, as we saw in Chapter Six above, in which selfhood and otherness as such are related to one another in the movement of enriching experience or spirit. It should, indeed, not be surprising that these basic phenomenological stances of self and other underlie and structure the relationship between self and other even in the experience of God. In working out this more explicit reference to present Christian experience we will also take into consideration the fact that, though these are always new experiences, Christians immediately perceive experiences of God affirmed by them to be a continuation of and in conformity with earlier experiences of God going back 2,000 years to and originating in the life, death and resurrection of Jesus of Nazareth. From the beginning, the experiences of God affirmed by them have been totally interwoven with, and inseparable from, liturgical acts as well as liturgical and scriptural language. Such acts and language often both provide the occasion for an experience of God and quite naturally, and from within the experience, give the means by which to express that experience.

Living within the context of a triply structured dynamic divine other experienced as personal embrace means, more immediately, that those who have participated in this experience discover themselves to be situated within a given, dialogically structured relationship between the Spirit of God and the Risen One. As the communal, shared or individual self considers itself in its relation to God experienced as divine inclusive other or personal embrace, it immediately senses, and at least in moments of greater awareness can refer to, a unique and personal, even individualized, presence within. There occurs an awareness of a certain initial unity between finite self and divine other. Finite spirit's awareness of this presence of the divine other, which awareness take this form of a certain initial unity, is of course always mediated through feeling, emotion, thought, language or action. However, the presence of the divine other, related more immediately to the self in its concrete though analogous individuality depending on whether the self is communal, shared or individual, is neither merely mediated nor fully expressible. This divine other, through its appearance, presence and revelation to the self, is more immediately and interiorly present as necessary initial source, within the self, of the sense of wholeness, integration, well-being and balance felt as welling up within the finite self and for which the finite self realizes it cannot take full credit. Indeed, ideally the self responds to this appearance, presence and revelation on the part of the other by stances of faith, hope and love appropriately realized in relation to an other whose manifestation is normally only partially thematized. But the finite self cannot take credit for the sense of wholeness it feels welling up within it. The self, in turn, finds itself overflowing, so to speak, or turned outward to the other or others in and with whom it discovers itself to be in relationship. This turn outward is the extension of the self's gift of itself to this initial other whose manifestation and presence is usually only partially thematized. The internally experienced, outwardly directing divine personal other, this movement of generosity, is at times addressed directly, and is traditionally named the Holy Spirit. So, Christians in particular are aware of living in the Spirit of God, whom they experience as a partially thematizable appearance, presence and revelation urging them outward toward others, and particularly toward the Risen One, in generous self-giving love. To the extent, then, that they can make explicit who the Spirit is, they refer to the Spirit as the divine, individualized self-gift necessary for them if they are to be enabled to live for others. The Holy Spirit shows itself to be the necessary moment of initial divine selfhood.

From earliest times members of the Christian community have named this moment of initial divine selfhood, the divine other as experienced within them, the Spirit of God. In line with and in the light of their experience of Jesus as Risen One, they have likewise called this Spirit the Spirit of Jesus. It is as if with and in this naming they have spontaneously recognized a murmuring welling up within them and giving rise to impulses of love and goodness and generosity beyond that for which they themselves could take credit.[11] They see in this murmuring and giving rise to impulses of love a moment of liberation from self-enslavement, an orientation toward charismatic service, a cause for consolation, a way of being reminded of Jesus and a necessary condition both for novelty in the world and for the gathering of people in community. So they speak as well of the Spirit of freedom, the Giver of charisms, the Consoler, the Counsellor and the Creator Spirit.

When the communal, shared or individual self finds itself opened to the active manifestation, as appearance, presence and revelation, of this other whom they name Spirit and, consequently, oriented outward within the previously mentioned relationship between the Holy Spirit and the Risen One, that self focuses on a particularized divine other recognized as having been an historically identifiable individual, Jesus of Nazareth. This encounter is of course mediated through a community of believers and through that community's oral and written traditions including, in a special way, the prophetic Isaiah suffering servant traditions. However, there occurs in this encounter both a reflexively available awareness of being in immediate relationship with this particular divine other, whose epiphanic manifestation takes the form of appearance, presence and revelation to the self, and the feeling that through this immediate relationship one is likewise encountering all of nature and all of history. One finds oneself in a certain unity and balance with reality as a whole. It is as if all of finite reality has become divine in and through this particular individual. The finite self has perceived the manifold of others with which it is in relationship, and toward which it finds itself oriented, as a series of revelatory indications of a greater personal reality likewise offering itself to the self in and through these finite realities or others. In the present analysis, this perception of finite others as revelatory indications of a greater personal reality is mediated by the relationship with this particular divine other. This other is present explicitly as and in the form of an other whom one addresses in attitudes of faith, hope and love directly and is traditionally named Christ and Risen One. The Risen One is acknowledged as more immediately identifiable source of human enrichment, as "means" or "way" to wholeness, integration, well-being and balance. The Risen One is recognized as this source existentially manifest to finite consciousness from without and explicitly in the form of an other whose very appearance to the self is a call and invitation to a richer and fuller life as well as a demand to live the requirements of that life, whose presence or, in the case of "absence as presence," is a further manifestation, to the self, of who this particular divine other is, and whose self-revelation to the self is an ever fuller revelation of what it means to be human and divine.

So Christians live and act according to the enriching salvific example of Jesus, now the Risen One. He it is who, especially according to the Synoptic interpretations of his earthly life, had recognized the reign of Yahweh making itself manifest in his healings and exorcisms, and who looked forward to the fullness of that reign in a realm of peace and justice and love. He it is whose life, death and resurrection are themselves, for those who believe in him, a manifestation of God's reign in this world. The result especially of his resurrection is that Christians recognize in him that clearly thematizable divine other whose presence and self-revelation in so many ways gives them courage and brings meaning to their communal, shared and individual lives. He is the One who through the actual acceptance of death has provided for them the perfect living example, the incarnation one should say, of divine generosity and self-giving love. All of this the One who is now risen does, while in historical context having addressed Yahweh God in various ways, including especially using the word *Abba*, loving Father. The Risen One's very being is love incarnate, a generous self-offering to God, to friends and even to enemies.

The Holy Spirit has urged the finite self outward to the Risen One who, in turn, had promised the Spirit and directs attention to, and by his very appearance calls one to, that further otherness manifest from without as goal and purpose for which one lives. The Risen One, this exteriorly experienced divine personal other, is thus the actual moment of divine otherness that is, in its particularity, nevertheless inclusive of finite otherness as such.

Christians find themselves opened to Jesus manifest as the one who rose from the dead. They recognize that he is the more immediate, generous source of all truth, love and goodness and they turn to him. They acknowledge the Risen One as more immediate source of all human enrichment, including the sense of wholeness, integration, well-being and balance accompanying this experience of God. Under the impulse of the Spirit, they turn to the Risen One as more immediate source existentially present to their consciousness from without and explicitly in the form of an other. The Risen One is the other to whose appearance they are opened, whom they recognize, to whose call and invitation they respond, the demands of whose discipleship they accept, to whom they turn, for whose presence they long and to whom in his self-revelation they, urged by the Spirit, spontaneously and generously wish to give themselves in love.[12] In line with and in the light of their experience of Jesus as risen, they have called this Spirit the Spirit of Jesus. The Spirit enables Christians to see in Jesus' life, death and resurrection a pattern of suffering and renewal or newness of life. They experience the suffering

Jesus who is now the Risen One as open to them, recognizing them as friend, turning to them, longing for them and giving himself to them in love. The pattern of generous self-sacrifice and unexpected enrichment that they experience in their lives has found its immediate source and become real for them in the archetypal life, death and resurrection of Jesus of Nazareth now the Risen One. They are, then, those who have answered the call of Jesus, the Risen One, whom they name the Christ. They have responded to his invitation to become disciples and accepted the demands that such discipleship entails. As his followers, they bear the name "Christian." They find themselves oriented by the Spirit immediately to Jesus the Risen One and, with and through the Risen One, to the one whom Jesus of Nazareth had addressed as "*Abba*, loving Father."

When the communal, shared or individual self considers its focusing outward on a particular divine personal other, it finds itself pointed forward, as an extension of its love for this particular divine personal other, toward a form of universally present divine other. The reign of the Holy Spirit within and of the Risen One without direct finite spirit's hope toward a realm of peace and justice and love where divinely given human potential is fully to be realized. The manifestation, as appearance, presence and revelation, of this divine other as universal goal is of course mediated by and partially realized in ongoing moments of human enrichment and liberation. Following the example of Jesus of Nazareth, Christians address this divine other, which manifests itself in such appearance, presence and revelation as goal of finite development in general and human development in particular, among other ways traditionally and personally as *Abba*, "Father, loving Parent." This notion of God as goal gives expression, at least in a partial way, to the bringing of Jesus' previously mentioned awareness of the manifestation of the reign and realm of God together with his addressing God, in prayer, as *Abba*. It picks up on the fundamental insight that the relationship of child to parent, and here of Jesus to *Abba*, is always phenomenologically or in terms of consciousness first a relationship in which one looks up to and toward one's parent or parents. Subsequent to this looking up to or towards, there develops a more explicit sense of origination in or coming from. This looking by Jesus toward, and his speaking to, *Abba* expresses a sense of intimacy and appropriate dependence that comes as well to characterize, in various ways, Christians' own orientation to God. Urged outward by the Spirit and guided by the example of Jesus, the Risen One, they experience themselves called to live sacrificially, truthfully, generously and lovingly for the world around them, for one another and to the glory of God in whom they and the world find their final fulfilment[13] and whom they address intimately as Father or Parent or Friend, hopefully Father or Parent become Friend. This exteriorly experienced divine personal other, who is the universal goal of all reality, of all life and of all activity, is thus the resultant enriched divine selfhood or potential toward which finite spirit lives.

God is experienced as that divine other to whom the Risen One's friends and followers look in trust, longing and love. God is that goal toward whom the Spirit urges and to and of whom the Risen One speaks so intimately that these friends and followers too look forward with confidence and without fear. One is tempted, here, not to say too much before and of this ultimate mystery of God as goal of Christians' lives. But in the Spirit and through Jesus, now the Risen One, one can say that Christians recognize they have the final realization and fullness of their potential only in God who, especially according to divine appearance, presence and self-revelation in the Spirit through the Risen One, is the truth of pure, generous self-giving love that is a movement of enriching experience or spirit.

A Philosophical Reflection: From Finite to Inclusive Infinite

One may indeed be tempted not to say much more before the mystery of God, and especially before the understanding of God as ultimate goal of one's life. Nevertheless, the dynamic of human development from a first experience to what has been treated so far in the present chapter, namely, a second experience giving expression to what can be affirmed by reason in reflection on the experience of God and its affirmation, can work itself out on still other levels and in still other ways in addition to the two-phased phenomenological analysis of the experience of God just presented. In addition to that analysis, we can, and in order to be more complete in our working out of this second experience need to, go further in reflection on the experience of God and its affirmation. This further move will take the form of a somewhat more formally philosophical reflection and rather more reasoned argument carried out with an awareness of Hegel's own philosophical argument.[14]

In light of what we have already noted above in Part One, "Thought and Spirit," of the present essay, we can now recall in somewhat short-hand form that Hegel had proposed to establish his trinitarian claim by means of a progression from God to world. More exactly, for Hegel the divine was necessarily to have othered itself as world in the dualism of nature and finite spirit and to have returned enriched to itself through finite spirit's sublation in absolute spirit as movement of philosophic thought. Within the overall movement of spirit, the world was to have been the finite other of God. Hegel's mature dialectic was, from the perspective of his system, to have been a movement beginning from infinity (*Unendlichkeit, das Unendliche*), understood as what he called *an sich* or, we could say, abstract totality, to its necessary self-othering as finitude (*Endlichkeit, das Endliche*) again, dialectically speaking, taken as momentary totality, and then enriching return as inclusive infinite. When infinite and finite are not maintained in abstraction from one another. For Hegel

> there is this to be said about the coming or going forth of the finite from the infinite: the infinite goes forth *out* of itself into finitude because, being grasped as an abstract unity, it has no truth, no enduring being within it; and conversely the finite goes *into* the infinite for the same reason, namely that it is a nullity.[15]

However, it is my contention that any proposal to argue in the public realm in favor of a post-Hegelian philosophical theology, whether as here on the basis of experience understood for present purposes as enriching growth, or on any other basis, will have to begin systematically in and with finitude if the claim is to be argued in the public realm of thought and discourse. An end-run distinction between epistemologically or noetically necessary starting point in finitude and an ontologically necessary beginning in any type of initial, positing infinite would throw the whole discussion onto the level of preference or opinion.[16] Such a proposed logically prior ontological starting point in infinity would remain merely a premise or ungrounded presupposition. Even the conclusion from finitude to needed grounding infinite could not then justify the indication of an infinite as logically or ontologically prior starting point. The argumentation for Hegel's claim could not, even with various qualifications, move from infinite to finite. The in fact prior movement from finitude to infinite remains, as presupposition verifiable in the public realm of thought and discourse, always logically prior to any movement from infinite to finite. Otherwise, for instance, it would be hard to see how one could argue from that infinite to the specific form of finitude we are and know.

Hegel himself, admittedly in the context of his attempt to justify the logical starting point of the absolute science or logic in pure being, insisted that a true beginning must be without presuppositions. However, only a beginning in and with finitude can claim that givenness or *Dasein* which as finitude is initially premised only upon its own reality and limitation. Any deductively argued position from infinite to finite would necessarily presuppose a logically prior movement from finite to infinite, and this ultimately because logic itself is finite.[17]

The here proposed reconstruction of Hegel's argument to the true infinite is a form of further logical and philosophical reflection on the Christian experience of God and the affirmation of that experience. It is now to be made on the basis of a movement from finite to infinite in that it begins from that finite becoming which is enriching growth or qualitative increment. This becoming itself in turn begins in the finitude of an initial self and other in relationship, and bears an in principle triadic formal structure of initial selfhood in relationship with otherness giving rise to enriched selfhood. However, though the ever-present recurrence of otherness ensures, on the level of the finite, the fundamental pluralistic basis for enriching growth, it equally establishes a de facto tetradic movement of finite or non-inclusive becoming. This tension between triadic and tetradic now urges and leads us on to sketch a reconstruction of a post-Hegelian philosophical argument for the transition from finite to infinite and, then, after this philosophical reflection on to a further, more integrating move, namely, a sort of third phase in our phenomenological analysis of the trinitarian experience of God that will take on some of the characteristics of what we have earlier on, in Chapter Five above, referred to as a third experience.[18] .

The intention now with this positing of the transition from finitude to triadically structured inclusive infinite is not to develop here, in great detail, either the characteristics of finitude as self-contradiction or the structured movement of the true or inclusive infinite. Rather, at this point we will refer to these characteristics and this movement only in as such a reference will be necessary to argue to the transition from finitude to inclusive infinite as an appropriate philosophical expression of what has already occurred in an experience of God, has been asserted in the affirmation of that experience and has been the object of a so far two-phased phenomenological analysis. In the present consideration, the focus is on arguing to this needed transition, a transition now no longer to be conceived in a primordial and paradigmatic formulation as the having gone over of one thought determination into another, as Hegel proposes in the first book of his *Logic*, namely, "The Logic of Being." Of course, this transition from finitude to inclusive infinite does retain his particular concern that it be made as an argument in the public realm. It consists, indeed, in arguing, within the limitations of thought and of consciousness as available to thought and within the context of our so-far developed understanding of experience, to the need to affirm the existence of a triadically structured inclusive infinite. Without this inclusive infinite, finitude, as available to reflective review, would remain finally incapable of explaining the wholeness that humans experience from time-to-time and, more profoundly, would itself remain ungrounded self-contradiction.

It will be helpful to recall that, very generally stated, there can be discerned in Hegel's thought the correct identification of the elements of any positive mediation or becoming as selfhood, otherness and progression as enrichment. Though finite becoming is the formal or, here, general expression for any finite enriching growth or finite qualitative increment, its indisputable reality as such growth and increment is witnessed to, for example, by the sheer inability of thought to remain in its own givenness without further self-reflection. Any finite becoming's formal structure necessarily consists of four variously related elements: initial selfhood; otherness; enriched selfhood (or impoverished selfhood, with which we are not directly concerned here); and recurrent otherness. As we mentioned toward the end of Chapter Six above, initial selfhood is a beginning without which there would be no finite becoming. Otherness as co-constitutively negative and positive is, on the finite level and along with the creative decision on the part of the initial self, a primary source of newness or novelty. Enriched selfhood is that resultant qualitative "more" without which there could be no speaking of progression, enriching growth or qualitative increment and, in relation more specifically to religious experience, a pronounced sense of wholeness, integration, well-being and oneness or balance with the world around one. Recurrent otherness is that which renewedly stands over against and is related to resultant enriched selfhood and thus by its appearance constitutes enriched selfhood as renewed initial selfhood. Renewedly initial selfhood is, again, that which is related to a coconstitutively positive and negative otherness. This finite becoming is the existent, ongoing but formally speaking non- temporal dynamic development from initial selfhood and otherness in relationship giving rise to enriched (or, then of course, impoverished) selfhood ever-renewedly to be enriched (or impoverished) in its relationship with recurrent otherness.

Though this finite becoming is and is real, it is equally problematic. Stated in an initial and more general way, if it is to stand alone, finite experience must be able to explain the at least momentary sense of wholeness and completion expected at the realization of any moment and movement of experience and especially of moments of religious experience, or remain incapable of explaining its own results. Yet its tetradic structure points out that the otherness involved is never finally inclusively or totally related to selfhood and vice versa. The structured movement of finite experience, especially that of religious experience, never reflects and grounds adequately the experienced result of a sense of wholeness, integration, well-being and balance. Furthermore, the collapse of otherness into the multiplicity of others and the recurrence of otherness make manifest the non-unified character of the otherness in question. The resultant relationship of initial selfhood and this recurrent otherness is a never exhaustively realized and ever renewedly one-sided (non-inclusive) relationship. This inadequacy on the part of finite experience to ground and explain certain results of that very experience leads us to examine that finite experience more carefully. Not only, as we shall continue to propose, is this resultant enriched selfhood a self-contradiction in that its very realization is by definition its limit, but the entire process as finite becoming takes on, in light of what it is and in view of its result, the character of a self-contradiction.

In learning from Hegel's presentation on finitude and on limit in particular, which he works out especially well within the context of his overall presentation on finite and true infinite,[19] we can say that the crucial question concerning the self-contradictory character of enriched selfhood as result of finite becoming in particular is the establishment of this enriched selfhood as constitutively both inclusive and one-sided. A first reading of the question might tempt us to say that the one-sidedness of renewedly initial selfhood is simply logically consequent to inclusiveness taking the form of enriched selfhood, a position then analogous to Hegel's positing of a becoming that sinks into *Dasein*.[20] However, though the language "enriched selfhood and recurrent otherness" might in one sense lend itself to this reading, a second look at the enriched selfhood and recurrent otherness in question will show a much closer tie between the two.

The tetradic formal structure of finite becoming is a development from initial selfhood not dialectically through, but in dialogically interactive relationship with, otherness, with this otherness considered as co-constitutively negative and positive, on to the result that is enriched selfhood renewedly initial selfhood standing in relationship with recurrent otherness. Of present particular interest is the way in which enriched selfhood as inclusive of otherness stands in relation to recurrent otherness.[21] Initial selfhood is enriched primarily through the respectful inclusion of otherness, an inclusion achieved, paradoxically, by a generous act of self-gift to otherness. That is, then, the very definition of enriched selfhood, without which there would be no becoming or growth, no sense of wholeness. As we saw in the previous chapter, enrichment is the respectful inclusion of otherness through the paradox of the gift of the self to the other. Yet, equally, enriched selfhood is not the inclusion of otherness. It is not here a question of a logically subsequent incomplete inclusion of otherness, but, by definition in finite becoming, a one-sidedness or incompleteness in the very moment of respectful inclusion that even self-gift in love cannot overcome. In finite becoming, enriched selfhood, as the result of its own dialectical development from initial selfhood, is itself renewedly initial selfhood and is not merely from different points of view to be considered inclusive as regards otherness and one-sided as regards recurrent otherness. The very moment of inclusion or enrichment is the moment of non-inclusion as well since the limit identifying recurrent otherness as not being enriched selfhood is common to enriched selfhood as well. This fact that the limit defining otherness as that which is related to initial selfhood is common to enriched selfhood constitutes enriched selfhood itself as initial selfhood. At the level of human experience in particular, enriched selfhood, and selfhood in general, is never alone. This limit or defining boundary is immanent to enriched selfhood itself so that enriched selfhood is self-contradictorily inclusive and one-sided in its very moment of enrichment. It is and is not inclusive. This has been indirectly indicated in our various analyses by reference to otherness's collapsing, when considered on its own, into a multiplicity of others and more directly by reference to the recurrence of otherness at the very moment of resultant enrichment.

Not only is enriched selfhood self-contradictorily inclusive and one-sided in its dialogically structured relationship with recurrent otherness, but finite becoming's tetradic formal structure as such involves self-contradiction.[22] Initial selfhood in relationship with otherness giving rise to enriched selfhood that is equally initial selfhood in relationship with recurrent otherness constitutes a process itself involving self-contradiction not only because the result is equally inclusion and non-inclusion, but because the process itself in its formal structure occurs equally as inclusion and non-inclusion. It is enrichment and yet at the same time and from the same perspective limitation. Tetradically structured finite becoming bears within it the doubled limit first verified in the definitional relationship between initial selfhood and otherness and then verified anew in the recurrence of otherness as that which is related to enriched selfhood. Otherness is both potential source of enrichment for the self and not the self. Finite becoming is a process that equally establishes itself as real but limited becoming and as that which ought always to have become more and other than what it is. The tetradic formal structure of finite becoming thematizes what finite becoming is in itself, as we are considering it here, namely, that it is an enriching grow th and qualitative increment. It tries to do this, however, as an in principle endless progression of recurrent relationships between selfhood and otherness where, as we have seen in Chapter Six above, there is always a sense both of loss and of gain. Despite this attempt, the sequential process taken as a whole is self-contradictorily equally inclusion and non-inclusion rather than the enriching inclusion of otherness as such.[23] In its enrichment it remains one-sided. As this self-contradiction, tetradically structured finite becoming *qua* finite is restless, unstable, one-sided and incomplete. Neither in its result nor in its process can it resolve its own contradiction as equally and from the same perspective, namely, that of its reality as a finite movement of experience, inclusion and non-inclusion.

Neither the process of tetradically structured finite becoming as a whole nor any of its four constitutive elements, nor again the various ways in which they are related, can resolve the self-contradiction that finite becoming is. As enriching growth, finite becoming should, in principle, simply be triadically structured as initial selfhood in dialogical relationship with otherness giving rise to enriched selfhood. But it is not simply enrichment as such. Rather, equally as enrichment and limitation, inclusion and non-inclusion, tetradically structured finite becoming indicates what it should have been and yet is not. By giving rise to the conception of becoming *qua* becoming in principle exhaustively structurable as triadically structured inclusiveness, tetradically structured finite becoming indicates the only possible context within which its self-contradiction could be maintained and in that sense overcome, namely, a triadically structured inclusive whole containing limit within it but not itself finitized by recurrent limit.

Against the background of Hegel's elaboration of the true infinite and as an alternative to his approach, it is now possible to argue to the existence of that inclusive whole as the essential context without which there could be no respectful resolution of self-contradictorily inclusive and non-inclusive tetradically structured finite becoming. This tetradic structure not only indicates, but, in its own way as reflecting in discursive philosophical language what the trinitarian experience of God reveals, calls for and points beyond itself to that triadically structured inclusive whole wherein the tension of its own self-contradictory inclusion and non-inclusion finds respectful resolution. The crucial question concerning the respectful resolution of this self-contradiction constitutive of finite becoming is the resolution of recurrent limit rooted in the recurrence of otherness. Though otherness as such is not in any sense necessarily recurrent, in finite becoming it both is recurrent and collapses into a multiplicity of "others." In finite becoming this recurrent and ever-unstable otherness is a primary source of enrichment as well as a primary source or cause of limitation. Taken together with the self-contradiction of enriched selfhood ever renewedly equally initial selfhood and together with the equally inclusive and non-inclusive character of the process of finite becoming, this assertion that otherness in finite becoming is self-contradictorily a primary source, on the finite level, both of enrichment and limitation again verifies that tetradically structured finite becoming cannot be conceived of as an immanently self-grounding development. Of particular present concern, unstable and recurrent otherness either taken on its own or in relationship with initial selfhood cannot, on the level of real but finite becoming, fully justify the "more" which is enriched selfhood. This it cannot finally do since it cannot even ground itself. Finite otherness, as that which is related to initial and to enriched-renewedly initial selfhood, remains itself self-contradictory as source equally of enrichment and limitation.

Recurrent and multiple otherness, within the context of the tetradic formal structure of finite becoming, remains ever on the finite level a primary but self-contradictory source both of enrichment and limitation. Thinking this self-contradiction through leads inevitably, given the distinguishing but especially unifying tendency of thought itself, to a consideration of the possibility of the resolution of this contradiction. Though it is tautological, it is nevertheless here significant and true to say that to remain with the self-contradictory is simply to maintain that contradiction unresolved. It has already been argued that there can be no resolution to this contradiction on the finite level, despite the fact that finite becoming's tetradic structure itself does indicate the direction in which a resolution of its self-contradiction lies. Recurrent and multiple otherness, taken in the context of tetradically structured finite becoming, can be a source equally of enrichment and limitation only if otherness as such can be considered within the context of a becoming in which it is neither recurrent nor multiple. Recurrent and multiple otherness functioning as source of enrichment and equally of limitation on the level of finite becoming requires an otherness that functions simply as source of enrichment. If otherness were to function, on the finite level, merely as source of limitation, there would be no need to argue to anything beyond itself. There would in fact be no positive becoming. However, for recurrent and multiple otherness to function in real but finite becoming understood as enrichment, it is necessary to affirm the existence of an infinite becoming, that is, a becoming which includes otherness *qua* otherness. This infinite becoming is the other to and of finite becoming, that other which provides the context within which finite becoming can be maintained as real but self-contradictory enriching growth or qualitative increment.

Without an infinite becoming containing otherness *qua* otherness within it, there would be no final justification for speaking formally of otherness as that unified actuality which is related to a necessary beginning in initial selfhood. This infinite becoming is the totality respectfully inclusive of tetradically structured finite becoming. Were it not so inclusive, it would not be an infinite movement of becoming and could not be argued to as the necessary condition for the possibility of resolving the contradiction inherent in finite becoming. This contradiction has been verified in enriched selfhood's being equally anew initial selfhood, the entire tetradically structured movement of finite becoming's being equally enrichment and limitation, and recurrent and multiple otherness's being equally a source both of enrichment and limitation.

Infinite becoming is that becoming in which otherness *qua* otherness and without recurrence or collapse into multiplicity is fully yet respectfully contained in the possibility of a truly enriched selfhood. This non-recurrent and non-multiple otherness is, therefore, by definition inclusive of tetradically structured finite becoming. This inclusion occurs not as the mere inosculation or unification by juxtaposition or apposition. Rather, it occurs, from various perspectives, dialogically and dialectically, in the sense that infinite becoming is a movement whose necessary beginning lies in initial selfhood, which is of course in relationship with otherness *qua* otherness. From the perspective of infinite becoming, this otherness is an actual unity that, as otherness respectfully inclusive of the multiplicity of "others," is dialogically related to initial selfhood. The dialectically developing resultant selfhood arising out of this actual dialogical relationship between self and other is the possibility of an enriched selfhood, an infinite enrichment without recurrent limit since there is no recurrence of otherness. This infinite becoming is the dialectically argued to, and dialogically functioning, respectfully inclusive other of tetradically structured or finite becoming. Finite becoming and infinite becoming are each, on their own level and in their own way, totality: finite becoming self-contradictorily so as totality and non-totality and infinite becoming as that experienced and argued to, but not fully conceptually grasped finite becoming's needed inclusive and integrating context. Infinite becoming is the context, namely, that other to self-contradictory enriching growth or qualitative increment which ensures that the latter has an adequate framework allowing it to perdure in its real but equally immediately limited enrichment. To be this respectfully inclusive context, infinite becoming must necessarily be triadic in structure.

Infinite becoming must, as the inclusive other of finite becoming, be triadic in structure both in order to be enrichment and to provide the totality finite becoming requires to perdure as real but then self-contradictory enrichment. The need to argue to the existence of a triadically structured infinite becoming lies finally not, as Hegel had thought, in infinity's, when finally considered, erotic[24] need to other itself in order to come to itself, but in finitude's own erotic need to have its self-contradiction mediated or resolved. Then, not only was there latent, and indeed more than latent, in Hegel's thought the valid insight of enriching becoming but, when this insight concerning enriching becoming is coupled with Hegel's strong insistence on the self-contradictory character of finitude, that insight gives rise to the argument for the existence of an infinite becoming as needed context for finite becoming. With the dialectical argument to the need for a triadically structured inclusive infinite, a most fundamental step has been taken in the move to reconstruct Hegel's trinitarian argument. Such questions as the further determination of the three elements constituting the formal structure of infinite becoming as inclusive other will be dealt with further in the following section of the present chapter. In that section we will treat as well both of the further specification of the relationship between otherness in infinite becoming and the recurrent, multiple otherness constituting finite becoming and of the further development of the point of "contact" between infinite becoming, considered for the moment as initial selfhood, and finite becoming as process of enrichment. In a sense, "tetradic" and "triadic" have served here as a sort of metaphilosophical shorthand in this elaboration of the argument in favor of a needed dialectical transition from finitude to triadically structured inclusive infinite.[25] The fact that the existence of such an infinite needs to be argued to in order to explain finite becoming is the final reason why one could never begin, as Hegel tried to do, with certainty and in the public realm from infinite to finite but must always move from a necessary beginning in the finite and the actuality of otherness to a triadically structured inclusive infinite and a new way, with but also beyond Hegel, to express philosophically what Christians affirm when they speak of an experience of God. Their experience of wholeness, integration, well-being and balance or being at one with all around them finds more adequate post-Hegelian expression in a renewed understanding of the "whole of wholes"[26] respectfully inclusive of otherness.

Third Experience: A Further Phenomenological Look

Our initial, two-phased phenomenological analysis of the Christian experience of God and our further philosophical reflection on that experience as a movement from finite to inclusive infinite constitute a second experience, namely, a thoughtful reflection on the more immediate first experience of God and the initial affirmation of that experience. Seen then as a critical, creative and constructive reflection on that first experience, this second experience becomes, if one has participated directly in that first experience, a prolongation, appropriate to a more reflexive level of human functioning, of that first experience. If such a prolongation is carried out in fidelity to the overall first experience and in more systematic fashion, it becomes a form of confessional theology. If that prolongation occurs as a reflection whose intention is to do a "reason-based" and especially conceptually rigorous presentation, it can become a form of philosophical theology. If, however, one has not oneself participated in that first experience, one focuses more on and reflects on the basis of the affirmation of that first experience. In this case, of course, the "second" experience is as such a prolongation of the first experience only in a more attenuated sense. However, in either case, in a philosophical theology mode, phenomenologists and philosophers try to carry out their analyses and reflections, as mentioned, on the basis of reasoned argument. In the present case, that presentation is rooted in the various ways in which self and other relate to one another in the moment and movement that is experience.

The relationship between first, second and third experiences is itself rooted in the very structure of experience. Given the previously presented idea that in any movement of finite experience the resultant self is equally renewedly initial self, whether the development involved be from one movement of experience to another or through a series of experiences, there is indeed continuity through development from the non-substantialist human self, if that self is participant in and finally constituted by the first experience, to the human self that participates in and is constituted by the second experience.[27]

The self resulting from the second experience is of course, then, capable of being the initial self in a third experience, where an effort is made to bring together in a further, creative way the first experience and its possible prolongation in the second, more reflective experience.

As noted in Chapter Five above, this further, creative bringing together of first experience and second experience as third experience is a form or phase of experience that leads to a deeper understanding and appreciation of first experience understood and lived now in a fuller way. This third experience is a return in a new way to first experience that will further validate and consummate the second experience. If the self concerned has participated in the first experience, this third experience is, indeed, a prolongation of the first and second types of experience of God. If not, it is a prolongation, in a somewhat modified sense of that word, of the affirmation of that experience. In either case, as is appropriate in a project in philosophical theology, our intention here is to proceed on the basis of reasoned phenomenological presentation.

In this move to consider a third experience, we wish to recapture something of the emotional vigor that characterized more intensely the first experience of God and remained characteristic of a large part of the phenomenological analysis making up a major element in what we have called the second experience, namely, in our previous phenomenological look at the Christian experience of God.

Our sketching of this third experience will appropriately take the form of a two-phased phenomenological look at that experience. As we begin describing this third experience, we in a first phase or moment can take a cue from Hegel himself who chose to work closely with a particularly interesting religious metaphor that was central to the teaching of Jesus of Nazareth. That metaphor was the "reign and realm of God."[28] It is this religious representation (*Vorstellung*), as he would call it, that provided him with a way to give a more religious formulation both to his conception of identity as identity *of* difference and to his way of relating the one and the many. His philosophical interpretation of the kingdom of God (*Reich Gottes*) enabled him to integrate, on the level of religion, his response to the questions of identity and difference and of the one and the many, a response that took the form of a movement of spirit as inclusive divine subjectivity.

We too can profitably work with this phrase, namely, that of the reign and realm of God, which continues to evoke great emotional reaction and seems to leave very few people indifferent, even those who live in highly secularized areas of the world. Over the last century or so this metaphor and teaching of Jesus has been the subject of major efforts at interpretation. Indeed, many aspects of these interpretations show parallels in terminology, structure, and even content with Hegel's own efforts. Some twentieth-century interpreters, in either direct or perhaps more indirect response to the eschatological challenge posed in fact, if not in intention, by Johannes Weiss and Albert Schweitzer at the turn of the twentieth century, focus on explaining the meaning and significance of the metaphor either for Jesus or in the various biblical traditions. There are, again, interpreters who attempt to give a more constructive sociological, philosophical, or theological interpretation of "kingdom of God." These range from Gustavo Gutierrez to Walter Rauschenbusch, Karl Barth, Paul Tillich, Ernst Bloch, Jürgen Moltmann and Wolfhart Pannenberg, Marjorie Suchocki and so many others. Again, among these we could identify those who tend to speak, in a more particular and almost Kantian way, of the kingdom of God in relation to the good and the moral community. Others take what could very generally be called a somewhat more Hegelian route and tend to speak of the very being of God when they speak of the kingdom of God.[29] Among those who would follow this more inclusive Hegelian route we could name Karl Barth, who, in a general way followed by Pannenberg, has identified God's rule or kingdom with God's being. And, given Barth's trinitarian interpretation of revelation, would we not need to say Barth has brought together Trinity, revelation, divine being, and kingdom? Moltmann in turn speaks particularly of Joachim of Fiori, but Moltmann's own kingdom of freedom certainly finds at least linguistic parallels in Hegel as well. Without wanting to read Pannenberg in an overly Hegelian direction, we still find it hard not to think of Hegel when Pannenberg speaks of history and the God of the kingdom. It is this overall, twentieth-century Hegelian trajectory, in which the reign and realm of God are identified with the very presence and being of God, that we will follow in an effort to spell out, by means of a first moment in our present phenomenological look or analysis, a form of third experience of God as the very recognition of, and rejoicing in, the coming of the reign of God that introduces us into the realm of God.

The Reign and Realm of God

Now to focus more explicitly on the theme "Reign and Realm of God" that is by nature a particularly integrative metaphor. Ongoing reference to this metaphor will help us bring together, in this final overall two-part section of the present chapter, reference to first experience of God, along with its affirmation by the experiencing self, and the more reflective phenomenological and philosophical review that is second experience. For the theme of the reign and realm of God is a particularly dynamic and inclusive one whose value has been demonstrated, as mentioned above, time and again especially over the course of the twentieth century. It is as well perhaps the most ancient of Christian theological notions, dating back to Jesus himself. Surely it was his own intimate experience of God that led him to proclaim this inbreaking of the reign and establishment of the realm of God, with "reign" and "realm" indicating two sides to the biblical metaphor, *basileia tou theou*. "Reign of God" focuses our attention on the divine intervention to which the term points and "realm of God" challenges us to long for the integrating and inclusive reality that God is.

With these brief remarks on the reign and realm of God in mind, we can now proceed, in a more general way and then in more of a step-by-step approach, with our phenomenological look at and analysis of the here presented third experience, namely, one that leads to further understanding and to action. We can even say that this look, proceeding in two phases or moments, presents, in a certain sense and following our earlier phenomenological analysis, a sort of third and fourth phases or moments in our overall phenomenological analysis of the Christian experience of God.

Over the course of our reflections, used here in a wide sense of the word, we have noted that experience of the Spirit of God leads to a recognition of the Spirit as the One who initiates the reign of God among and within Christians by urging them outward in a generous way toward others.

The Spirit's initiating of the reign of God among and within Christians complements, and is complemented by, both the Risen One's enriching call and invitation to form a more inclusive Christian community that will better serve as sacrament of the reign and realm of God, and the ethical demands that discipleship places on the followers of the Risen One. Christians live in and through the relationship between Spirit and Risen One.

In rereading their lives, Christians are able, with the help of the Holy Spirit and in light of the example of the Risen One, to remind the Christian community and its members that the reign of God is breaking in upon them. They are in a position to remember God as the One for whom they are to live, the One who is the goal of their lives. They are able to recall that they are called to live and move and have their being in the realm of God.

We considered the experience of God from the perspective of an open and enriching movement from self to other. We named the moments in this turn from self to other "faith," "hope" and "love." We can now recognize a more clearly systematic structure to the movement of the human communal, shared or individual self toward the Risen One as divine other, toward others in general and toward God as goal of Christians' lives. The lesson learned, namely, that enrichment comes paradoxically through generous self-gift, witnesses in its own way to the fact that God's reign breaks in mysteriously and is not "of this world."

Earlier on, in Chapter Six above, we recognized as well that there can be an unsuccessful or negative relationship between self and other, namely, a refusal blocking a more positive and enriching relationship between self and other, a refusal for which the self could in some way be responsible before God and which, in the moment of that refusal, the self is that refusal while still not being reduced only to it.. Again, in this relationship between self and other, the presence of the other is not a source of enrichment because the self refuses to enter into a possibly enriching relationship with the other, because the other withdraws from or threatens the self, or because of both. The relationship becomes then one of impoverishment for which the self, the other, or both are in some way responsible. Already now we can say that, where such impoverishment occurs, the inbreaking of the reign of God is, at least for the moment, thwarted.

Now, we want to complement our previous reflections by putting into words something of the basic structure and movement of the Christian experience of the Trinity as itself experiencing finitude, including the Trinity's varied experience, in some mysterious way, both of what is good and of what is evil. Each of these movements, namely, that of the Christian experience of the Trinity itself and the Christian experience of the Trinity as experiencing finitude and what is good and evil is, in its own way, finally a movement of enriching experience or spirit. Indeed, God's experience, as movement of inclusive divine subjectivity and spirit, and the reign and realm of God are, with appropriate nuance to respect the ongoing difference between finite and infinite, ultimately one and the same.

It is of course true that the tetradically structured finite movement of human experience, namely, initial selfhood and otherness in relationship giving rise to enriched or impoverished selfhood renewedly in relationship with otherness could not, as such, be identified with the inbreaking of the reign of God. Such a tetradically structured immanent movement of experience can explain impoverishment. The ways in which the finite self or other act in or contribute to a movement of experience suffice, on their own level, to provide an explanation for such impoverishment. However, this tetradically structured movement of experience does not in itself adequately ground the enrichment occurring in a movement of enriching experience or spirit and, more specifically, in an experience of God. This tetradically structured movement of experience does not, either as a whole or in its various moments and without further reference beyond itself, account for that at least momentary sense of wholeness, integration, well-being and balance of which one becomes aware as a result of an experience of God. This ongoing, tetradically structured movement of finite experience does not itself account for the irreducible givenness of the divine embrace, namely, that triply manifest divine other experienced as, to use the words in a wide sense, context and cause of such wholeness, integration, well-being and balance.

Rather, the inbreaking of the reign of God is the triply occurring divine movement as manifestation and, more precisely, appearance, presence and revelation, of Spirit, Risen One, and God as goal enabling all three to be active in and through the tetradically structured movement of experience that, as a movement of enrichment respectfully including otherness and the other, is a generous divine movement of self-giving love. In this movement the infinite other is itself a movement of enriching experience and, thus, a movement of spirit. The reign of God is the triple inbreaking of the Spirit, the Risen One and God, respectively as divine urge, call and goal, into the tetradically structured movement of enriching experience.

This threefold inbreaking reign of God in and through experience has, then, various effects throughout the universe. To the extent that all of reality is, in some way, a series of relationships between "self" and "other," there is a cosmological effect, which cannot be further developed here. More specifically with regard to interaction among humans and to human interaction with the world in which humankind lives and of which it is a part, we can say that there are at least two special effects of the inbreaking of the reign of God into the tetradically structured finite movement of experience. The first of these is a certain slow, almost imperceptible, enrichment of life within a tragically wounded world. We could think, for example, of the moments of faith, hope and love recognized, or gone unrecognized, in so many billions of human lives. We could note as well the existence of countless gestures of communal, shared and individual concern for others and the struggles for social justice, mutual respect and ecological balance. In all of these, the reign of God remains of course the Spirit, Risen One and God active in and through finite selves and their world.

We can highlight the second effect by referring to the fact that all this enrichment or qualitative more one experiences as coming ultimately from the Trinity is taken up into the Trinity. Christians experience the Spirit, the Risen One and God as experiencing them. The Spirit, Risen One and God are themselves respectively, according to Christians' experience of God, divine self and divine other in dialogical relationship giving rise to the divine enriched self, a movement of inclusive divine subjectivity and spirit. The Spirit urges all that is good and enriching. In the Risen One's humanity, the Risen One experiences all that is good and enriching as well as all that is evil and impoverishing. With the Spirit, the Risen One offers all to *Abba*, God who has, in the Spirit and through the Risen One, received and thus experienced all. The second result of the threefold inbreaking of the reign of God in finite experience is, from the perspective of finitude, the slow and imperceptible introduction of finitude into God, who is the context and goal of life and finite reality, and thus into the whole realm of the triune God.

We have briefly reviewed our varied, more generally speaking philosophical reflections on the experience of God considered as prolongations of that experience if the phenomenologist and philosopher participate in the first communal, shared or individual experience or as reflections on the affirmation of that experience, and thus prolongation in a more attenuated sense, if the phenomenologist and philosopher do not participate in that experience. We have also reviewed this third type of experience, namely, an enriched return to first experience of God or to the affirmation of that experience. After these reviews, we can now note that Christians experience God as the threefold inbreaking of the reign of the triune God in their lives, an inbreaking that liberates them from self-enslavement. And, in turn, the triune God in a certain sense experiences them. They are, in fact, taken up into the experience or life of the Trinity, which is a threefold dialectically developing, but between the Spirit and Risen One dialogically structured twofold movement of enriching experience and of spirit. While ever maintaining the essential distinction between God and them, we can note that the divine experience of them and of the world brings them, to use another biblical expression, to the banquet in the Kingdom. Or, to speak in terms we have been using, the reign of God introduces them into the realm of the triune God in which God will be all in all.

The Trinitarian Movement of Divine Self-giving Love

So far, here in Chapter Seven, in our working out of a second experience as reflection on the Christian experience of God and its affirmation we have taken a phenomenological look at the first experience, namely, that of the communal, shared and individual self in its experience of God. In that look or analysis we spoke of the general structure and dynamic of that experience and then took a second look at that experience in order to focus on the three forms of divine otherness the experience reveals. In this second look we likewise employed more personalizing emotive language Christians use to describe their sense of the triply present divine enriching other. This was followed by a more philosophically formulated reflection and argument concerning the movement from finite to inclusive infinite.

Now, in what we can even consider a continuation especially of the previous, two-phased phenomenological analysis but also of the further philosophical reflection concerning the movement from finite to infinite, we have in the first phase of the present phenomenological analysis considered the reign and realm of God a movement of enriching experience and spirit and presented it in the form of a movement of inclusive divine subjectivity. Now in a second phase of that analysis, and by a sort of recapitulation of the previous phenomological looks at the Christian experience of God, we can speak more directly of the trinitarian God in whom Christians live, and move and have their being.

On the basis of their human experience of God, Christian communities, couples, friends and individuals around the world celebrate the truth and goodness of God whom they experience as a divine embrace, a triple movement of generous, divine self-giving love. This experience and resultant understanding of God as movement of love or enriching experience provides the means by which they can speak of God more directly, but of course quite modestly and with some restraint. Given the very nature of experience as the dialogical relationship between selfhood and otherness giving rise, through dialectical development of self and other, to enriched or impoverished selfhood, this finite human experience of God justifies and provides the point of departure for a reflection on God as movement of inclusive or infinite divine subjectivity, the true infinite, to use phrases that harken back to Hegel's philosophy. However, in line with and agreement with Hegel, we are making no effort here to return to a sort of *theologia naturalis* in which one would propose to speak of God in abstraction from either the world or the experiencing human self, whether communal, shared or individual. Rather, we here speak of God as the one who, in being experienced by finite selves, is revealed as one who in turn experiences, that is, is in relationship with, the world and finite selves.

The human experience of God as movement from the Spirit through the Risen One to God as One whom Christians dare address in intimate relationship reveals the divine personal embrace, the framework or context within which and on the basis of which they can speak, in a certain way, of God's active and passive experience of the world and of human history. If the triune God is experienced as the movement of initial divine selfhood (Spirit) and the divine other (the Risen One) in relationship which latter, namely the Risen One, upon further reflection, is in principle seen to include all others, then the resultant enriched divine selfhood (God as the One Christians address in intimacy and appropriate dependence) is of course all in all. The active presence of the Spirit and the incarnation of the One who is now risen establishes a series of three real relations not only between world and God but also between God and world. This approach to God as movement from the Spirit through the One now risen to God traditionally addressed as Father enables one in the twenty-first century to speak of God as the true infinite, a triadically structured movement of inclusive or infinite divine enriching experience, a movement of divine subjectivity and of spirit in the form of divine self-giving love.

This structured divine context to human and Christian living is a movement of love both in its own dynamic development and in that each moment in the movement is a moment of divine self-gift to finite selves. It is one all-embracing and unrepeated, finally non-temporal triadically structured infinite or inclusive movement of initial selfhood (the Spirit) and otherness (the Risen One) in relationship resulting in enriched selfhood (God as loving Father, Parent or Friend). These three moments taken more generally now are not reducible one to the other, for without any one of them there would not be any movement of enriching experience, either human or divine. The one, overall divine movement of enriching experience or self-giving love is itself, to use more classical trinitarian language reminiscent of Gregory of Nyssa,[30] one concrete divine essence realized in three distinct and different instantiations of divine self-giving love to finite selves and, by generalization, to all of created reality. Thus, while the whole movement of divine enriching experience itself is one of self-giving love as epiphanic self-manifestation, namely, a movement of appearance, presence and revelation, each moment or instantiation is itself a particular moment, itself developing in its own dialectical way as a movement of appearance, presence and revelation, and thus a moment of self-giving love offered to finite selves and all of created reality.

In order to help recall what we said in some of our previous analyses, we can refer to the fact that in prayer Christians address each personal divine other directly, though according to the mode of thematization appropriate to each divine other. Their relationship to the Spirit is one of self and other more immediately present to one another. Their relationship to the Risen One is characterized by intentional identification with a clearly defined other immersed in the flow of history. The stance they take in their relationship to God as the goal of their lives is one of longing for and self-gift toward. In the experience of God, each personal or self-giving divine other is in its own way a unique source of true human enrichment and, more particularly, of the resultant religious sense of wholeness, integration, well-being and balance. The three personal divine others are, as mentioned, not reducible one to the other. And yet, because Christians find themselves within one overall loving divine embrace, they are quite comfortable in focusing now on one manifestation, then on another. They experience God as a movement of true love respectfully embracing and empowering them in community, as couples or friends and individually, though of course not always successfully, toward justice and peace and love. They experience the triune God in whom they live and move and have their being as a movement of love, a triply structured movement of inclusive divine subjectivity and enriching experience that is a movement of spirit.

This movement of love is one of ordered relationality. Christians find themselves within the initially given dialogical relationship between Spirit and Risen One. Within this relationship, the Spirit is experienced as the necessary initial moment in their phenomenologically based analysis of the triply structured movement of enriching experience that God is. The Spirit is that divine other manifest through appearance, presence and revelation intimately within the finite self. As initial divine self-gift, the Spirit is so intimately present, to use the word in a more general sense, that its own selfhood is hardily thematized. Yet its presence as free self-gift hints at that selfhood and at its own personal character. The Spirit is experienced as free self-gift in two senses. First, in that the Spirit is present to the finite self in such a way as to ground, from within, the sense of wholeness, integration, well-being and balance that the finite self experiences as given to it. Second, in that the Spirit is experienced equally as force making demands upon the finite self by orienting it outward beyond itself. As self-gift in this twofold sense, the Spirit is experienced as actively empowering the finite self, and along with the finite self the entire realm of nature, to take a chance and to go beyond itself in various potentially enriching experiences. We can thus say that the Spirit itself enters the world of human experience, addressing itself through a subtle dialectical movement of appearance, presence and revelation, in individualized fashion, to each finite self as necessary source of all that is true and good and self-giving. In this way, the Spirit actively experiences the world. The Spirit is that divine other who enters into primordial,[31] intimate, direct relationship with the finite self. In this relationship, the Spirit, who urges and thus empowers in a way reminiscent of what is traditionally called efficient causality, presents itself as self-giving love in the form of initial divine selfhood.

Within the relationship between the Spirit as initial divine selfhood and the Risen One, the latter is experienced by the finite self as that permanently present actual other whose historical existence and risen presence is, for the Christian, the more immediate, explicit source of human enrichment. The Risen One is the divine other on whom one focuses one's attention and through whom one encounters all of nature and history. This particular One upon whom one focuses provides, in that Risen One's life and death and resurrection, the paradigm of all human enrichment. For human enrichment and, in the present discussion in particular, the sense of wholeness, integration, well-being and balance that one experiences comes about through the paradox of generous sacrificial loss of oneself. True wholeness, integration, well-being and balance come ultimately from the appropriately offered gift of oneself to another. The Risen One has, in historical existence, repeatedly and continually lived in relationship with others and with Yahweh. The Risen One has literally experienced life and death and newness of life. In historical existence, Jesus of Nazareth experienced, and in resurrectional presence the Risen One experiences, the whole range of human and natural phenomena. Jesus of Nazareth, now the Risen One, is the divine self who has intentionally identified with humankind and with the world in general. This identification has occurred through a definite, historically identifiable epiphanic movement of appearance as call and invitation to discipleship, with that discipleship's demands, then supportive presence and generous self-revelation. In this intentional identification, the divine self experiences, both actively and passively, the ebb and flow of history and the ongoing experiences that constitute it. Indeed, this incarnate divine self lives a life of faith, hope and love in relation to humans and to their world. The Risen One is experienced by the finite self as that particular, clearly identifiable actual divine other who ever offers to humankind the example, taken more or less in the traditional sense of formal causality, of new life through suffering and death and who receives from humankind all that can then be offered to God.

The God to whom Jesus referred so intimately is the fullness of the divine potential toward whom the Spirit urges, to whom the Risen One constantly points and, consequently, for whom Christians are called to live. God is seen as that final moment of wholeness and integration glimpsed from time-to-time by the finite self especially in a moment of religious experience. As realized fullness working in a way akin to what we have traditionally called final causality, God is the overall potential for wholeness and integration, namely, that which constitutes human selves as full persons. It is this realized fullness that, in the Spirit and through the Risen One, reigns already now in Christians' lives and promises to be a realm of peace and justice and love. This God toward whom the Spirit urges and to whom Jesus referred so intimately is revealed as self-giving fullness and thus as personal in character. As effective goal, God is consequent[32] or resultant enriched divine selfhood inclusive of all that has been urged by the Spirit and either offered or received by the Risen One.

The Christian experience of God is, then, one rooted immediately in the experience of the Spirit of God and ultimately in the triadically structured embrace or divine supportive context of the Spirit and the Risen One leading Christians to God as loving Father, Parent or Friend and goal of their lives. This divine embrace is an infinite movement of self-giving experience or love. It is an all-embracing and unrepeated, finally non-temporal triadically structured movement of initial selfhood (the Spirit) and otherness (the Risen One) in dialogical relationship resulting in enriched selfhood (*Abba*). This movement of enriching divine experience or spirit itself includes, in three different ways, the divine experience of the universe and of humankind. The Spirit is experienced by finite selves as experiencing finitude as the field in which it actively moves them outward to others and to the Risen One. The Risen One, in turn, is experienced as experiencing finitude both as that to which the Risen One makes an intentional self-offer and as that from which all that the Spirit has successfully urged is received. Given this unlimited intentional self-offer, truly incarnation, the Risen One is equally open to and experiences that which has not been successfully urged by the Spirit, all that one would call evil and suffering because it is at least immediately impoverishing rather than enriching. God as goal and fulfilment of all human striving for wholeness, integration, well-being and balance is experienced as experiencing finitude as that through which all Spirit-urged human endeavor patterned on the life, death and resurrection of the Risen One arises. Equally, God experiences all that has not been successfully urged by the Spirit and patterned on the life, death and resurrection of the Risen One. This evil and suffering is, in line with Christian hope, to be transformed in the light of the life, death and resurrection of the Risen One. Thus, in this proposal to develop a post-Hegelian philosophical theology God is the true infinite, a movement of enriching experience, divine subjectivity and spirit respectfully inclusive of all finite otherness, a movement of love.[33] The triune God is, finally, not simply the instantiation of a general theory or schema but, rather, the triadically structured movement of inclusive divine subjectivity whose epiphanic manifestation becomes point of reference for working out and validating any philosophy of generosity and, more particularly, any theory concerning the tetradically structured movement of finite subjectivity.[34]

Further Remarks

By way of anticipation of what we will say in the next chapter, we can now note that for us to say more about the triune God experienced by Christians and that God's experience of them and their world will require that we explore the possibilities of a trinitarian analogy based on the irreducible distinction between finite becoming that is tetradic in structure and divine, finally non-temporal becoming that is triadic in structure. This form of analogy will ground similarity and difference between human and divine predication in real distinctions within the divine. Whereas, for instance, the various forms of Thomistic analogy between human and divine tended to be based in the distinction of reason between divine essence and divine existence, here in a trinitarian analogy, divine predication will be grounded in the real distinctions among the divine "Persons."

We can, however, already now note that an incipient trinitarian metaphysics elaborated on the basis of a phenomenology of and a further philosophical reflection on the Christian experience of God and its affirmation shows, in the present, somewhat provisional following proposal, the character of a movement from necessity through actuality to potentiality. In such a metaphysics, with reference to the infinite movement of enriching experience, within the dialogical relationship between Spirit and Risen One the initial necessary moment is that of Spirit. The actuality to which one makes reference is the Risen One. The potentiality toward which this necessary beginning in the Spirit and actual realization in the Risen One move is God as our goal. With reference to a finite movement of experience, within the dialogical relationship between initial selfhood and otherness, the necessary moment is that of initial selfhood. The actuality to which one makes reference is otherness. The potentiality toward which this necessary beginning in initial selfhood and otherness as actuality move is resultant enriched or impoverished selfhood that, again as necessary moment is that of initial selfhood renewedly in relationship with otherness as actuality. This essentially trinitarian metaphysics of experience is a movement from initial selfhood and otherness in relationship ideally giving rise to enriched selfhood. Thus it is a movement of spirit.

Though the notions of necessity, actuality and potentiality take on quite different coloring in various philosophical systems, we can very briefly contextualize our remarks by recalling metaphysical alternatives, offered more explicitly by Hegel and perhaps more implicitly by Kierkegaard. Putting it very crudely, I would suggest that Hegel's overall systematic and speculative thought proceeds as a movement from potentiality to actuality to necessity. This is simply a way of referring to his movement of thought from its first moment as, generally stated, "in itself" or implicit (*an sich*) to "for itself" or the explicitation of what was implicit in the first moment (and so *für sich*) to "in and for itself" or the advancing resultant integration (*an und für sich*) of what was previously merely implicit and explicit.[35] Kierkegaard in turn suggested we reject Hegel's move toward necessity. So he worked out a dynamic movement from potentiality to necessity to actuality. For him actuality is then a unity of potentiality and necessity. In this dynamic, actuality arises in a free moment of decision.[36] In contrast to these two approaches, the trinitarian metaphysics, perhaps more implied than worked out in our phenomenological look at the Christian communal, shared and individual experience of God and its affirmation as well as our subsequent philosophical reflection and further phenomenological regard, would, as mentioned, be one in which the movement goes from necessity through actuality to potentiality.[37]

In its present form, this proposal of a phenomenology revealing the trinitarian structure of Christians' experience of God and of God's experience of finite selves and the world around them perhaps raises more questions than it answers. We might ask, for example, whether we could appropriately speak of the triune God experiencing a "sense" of wholeness, integration, well-being and balance as a result of the divine experience of finitude. Another question might be the advantages and disadvantages of using the classical forms of efficient, exemplary and final causality to describe, respectively, the roles of the Spirit, Risen One and God as goal in relation to finite selves. A third question might be how best to describe the relationship between a finally non-temporal divine movement of spirit and the de facto temporally conditioned movement of tetradically structured finite experience. These and other such basic questions will surely require further reflection.

For now, I would hope that my proposal toward a post-Hegelian philosophical theology as a movement of infinite divine subjectivity respectfully inclusive of finitude as otherness, indeed a movement of enriching and generous divine self-giving love or spirit, does offer real potential for responding to some of the hesitations arising time and again concerning various philosophical theologies. For example, this phenomenological analysis, philosophical reflection, and further phenomenological regard provide, we could say, a more horizontal structuring of reality that is less liable to be interpreted in a quasi-Neoplatonic hierarchical fashion. It also helps us to continue moving beyond the tension that supposedly exists between universally formulatable and positively revealed religion. Furthermore, it attempts to go beyond the mere juxtaposition of social and monosubjectival expressions of Trinity. It retains certain aspects of the social or societal formulation of Trinity in that each phenomenologically distinguished divine personal other is addressed as "You." And yet the overall movement of divine self-giving experience or love is clearly one. Furthermore, in this proposal the formulation of Trinity arises, at least in principle, in critical dialogue with contemporary cultures and ways of thinking. It maintains the importance of the notion of subjectivity in line with the direction of thought taken by the "moderns." And yet, along with the "post-moderns," it gives otherness a certain prominence and renewed emphasis. It helps us to move to a more open and dialogical relationship with religions other than Christianity, thus enabling us to be more at ease with our growing sense of religious pluralism. Stressing otherness and the threefold divine presence as other reinforces and enlarges the "space" Basil and others had created for the playing out of the relationship between divine and human freedom. With the "anti-moderns," it retains the notion of a communal and a shared as well as an individual "self." Furthermore, the proposed under-standing of the triune God as self-giving love both provides a basis for affirm-ing our liberation from self-enslavement and opens out to a renewed under-standing of the spiritual as well as to prophetic concerns for engaged ethical action.

Experience, subjectivity, relationship, otherness, the communal, shared and individual "self," liberation from self-enslavement, engaged ethical action —these are some of the themes with which we must continue to deal if we wish to go on working toward a post-Hegelian philosophical theology for the twenty-first century by speaking of the reign and realm of God as a movement of inclusive divine subjectivity and spirit.

NOTES

1. Note that from a theological perspective Jürgen Moltmann, *Trinität und Reich Gottes. Zur Gotteslehre* (Munich: Chr. Kaiser, 1980) 18–21/*Trinity and the Kingdom of God* (New York: Harper and Row, 1981) 2–5, for example, has made some preliminary remarks on the relation between Trinity and experience of God. It may be helpful to recall that the present phenomenological reflection approaches, from a more philosophical perspective, the same experience of God and affirmation of that experience that was treated from a more fundamental and systematic theology perspective in my study, *Theology and the Experience of God* (New York: Peter Lang, 2001) Chapters One and Seven.

2. It would be interesting to explore the uses of the word "experience" in other major languages. In French, for example, *expérience* tends to bear with it connotations, especially in the verbal form (*expérimenter*), of a controlled scientific experiment. So in French one often speaks rather, in circumlocutionary form, of "making an experience of" (*faire l'expérience de*) and of "the lived" (*le vécu*). Nevertheless, there is a tradition in French-language circles of speaking of the "experience of God" (*expérience de Dieu*), as witnessed to by the writings of Jean Mouroux and of Maurice Zundel. On Mouroux, see Jean Mouroux, *L'expérience chrétienne. Introduction à une théologie* (Paris: Aubier, 1952)/*The Christian Experience. An Introduction to a Theology*, trans. George Lamb (London: Sheed and Ward, 1955) and Gilles Bourdeau, "La théologie de l'expérience chrétienne chez Jean Mouroux," doctoral dissertation, University of Montreal, 1975. On Zundel, see Ramón Martinez de Pisón L, O.M.I., *La liberté humaine et l'expérience de Dieu chez Maurice Zundel* (Montréal: Bellarmin/Desclée, 1990). In German, the question of the notion of experience becomes quite complex. This is partly so because in German there are two words, *Erlebnis* and *Erfahrung*, that are both generally translated in English by "experience." See the helpful remarks in the "Translators' Preface," by Joel Weinsheimer and Donald G. Marshall, in Hans-Georg Gadamer, *Truth and Method*, 2nd, rev. ed. (New York: Crossroad, 1989) xiii–xiv. More specifically regarding the notion of "experience of God" in German-language discussion, on one hand we might simply recall that Martin Buber speaks of a person being in relation with God but not of experiencing (*Erfahrung, erfahren*) God. See his *Werke*, Erster Band, *Schriften zur Philosophie, Ich und Du* (Munich: Kösel, 1962) 77–170/*I and Thou* (New York: C. Scribners [Sons], 1970). To experience God would for Buber, from his more existentialist perspective, be to reduce the I-Thou relation to an I-It relation (see, e.g., p. 81 in the German text and p. 56 in the English translation). It would be to objectify God. Nicholas Lash, *Easter in Ordinary. Reflections on Human Experience and the Knowledge of God* (Charlottesville: University Press of Virginia, 1988) 178–218 esp. 185–186 with n. 25, refuses to speak of an experience of God and will go no further than at times to use the phrase "to experience the mystery of God." He follows Buber in this regard. On the other hand, Karl Rahner, in "The Experience of God Today" ("Gotteserfahrung Heute"), *Theological Investigations*, vol. 11 (New York: Seabury, 1974) 149–165 esp. 152–160, does not hesitate to speak of the experience of God.

   There are as well in English a number of subtle nuances hard to capture succinctly, but which can be alluded to by citing several English phrases. The direct phrase, "I experience God," sounds harsh, as if the "I" dominates. But when the phrase is further qualified as, for example, "I experience God in my life," there is a delicate shift of emphasis to an "I" functioning in a more receptive fashion. The simple phrase, "experience of God," seems quite acceptable since it again bears with it the suggestion that God is the more active one in the relationship. This phrase can of course also have another meaning, that of the subjective genitive. Then one would be speaking of God's experience.

3. For an interpretation of experience in terms of language, see Hans-George Gadamer, *Wahrheit und Methode*, 2nd ed. (Tübingen: J. C. B. Mohr, 1965) 329–344/*Truth and Method*, 2nd revised ed., trans. and revised by Joel Weinsheimer and Donald G. Marshall (New York: Crossroad, 1990) 346–362, and brief remarks on Gadamer in Chapter Four above. On John E. Smith's more realist understanding of experience and his use of "revelatory encounter," see Dale M. Schlitt, "John E. Smith on Experience," *Philosophy and Theology* 2 (1987) 105–123, but, again, concerning the difficulty raised with regard to the reading of the earlier writings of Smith, see Schlitt, *Theology and the Experience of God* 62–63 n. 16.

4. As our earlier reflection in Part Two above on experience would lead us to conclude, some at least minimal sense of a form of wholeness, integration, well-being and balance would seem to characterize any experience resulting in an enriched selfhood.

5. Given that we are beginning our phenomenological reflection from a specific experience or, as will be mentioned, more specifically the result of an experience, perhaps we should note the proposition by Bernhard Welte, cited by Raymond Lemieux, that where the experience of God has disappeared there we find introduced the experience of nothing (*l'expérience du rien*). Lemieux asks, with Welte, if this has not become the fundamental religious experience of humanity today? Lemieux and Welte raise an important question but, so it would seem to me, go too far in suggesting that this experience of nothing is perhaps *the* fundamental religious experience today. Setting aside for the moment the question of Buddhism with its very special notion of nothing, and depending on how one might define a religious experience, I would think, rather, that for large numbers of people this experience of nothing serves as a point of departure for, and an important element in, their possibly having a religious experience properly speaking and, more specifically, an experience of God in their lives. See Raymond Lemieux, "Préface," in François Nault, *Derrida et la théologie. Dire Dieu après la déconstruction* (Montréal: Médiaspaul, 2000) 14, where he cites Bernhard Welte, *La lumière du rien. La possibilité d'une nouvelle expérience religieuse*, trans. Jean-Claude Petit (Montréal: Fides, 1988) 54.

6. Karl Rahner is one who has reflected at great length on this important notion of the experience of God in every moment of human experience. In his own way, Alfred North Whitehead has also proposed the involvement of God in every moment of experience. For present purposes, however, in this chapter I am referring to experiences of God of which people are more explicitly aware. Evidently, what is said about experiences of God in which one is more explicitly aware of such experiences would apply as well, *mutatis mutandis*, to any experience of God.

7. For example, in a report, "Congregational Studies from the Perspective of Empirical Theology," in Marc Pelchat, ed., *Les approches empiriques en théologie/Empirical Approaches in Theology* (Québec: Faculté de théologie, Université Laval, 1992) 101–130 but especially 110–127, Johannes A. van der Ven reports on an empirical study of five Roman Catholic parishes in Ottawa, Ontario, Canada, where the members

participating in a survey manifested a religious consciousness clearly theocentric in character. It would be easy to imagine that such a survey carried out among, for example, selected Protestant parishes might exhibit a more Christocentric focus. A survey of Pentecostal and charismatic groupings might show a more pneumato- logically oriented awareness.

8. The phrase, "wholeness, integration, well-being and balance," provides in brief form a certain summary of feelings, sensations and awareness that accompany to a greater or lesser extent a religious experience in general and, more specifically, an experi- ence of God, and that at least in part define such an experience. This summary phrase and the reality to which it refers arise in various ways out of experience. First of all, it is rooted in the nature and development of experience as they have been presented in the present essay. Second, it serves to capture and express what I have come to observe in numerous discussions with others and in various forms of spiri- tual direction in which I have participated either as director or directee. Third, it draws at least indirectly upon the writings of diverse authors known for their holi- ness or for their erudition such as, for example, Augustine, Theresa of Avila, Marie of the Incarnation, Thérèse de Lisieux, Pope John XXIII, Thomas Merton, Dag Hammerskjöld, William James and Rudolf Otto.

I have recently run across an item of anecdotal evidence that helps exemplify what is expressed in this phrase "wholeness, integration, well-being and balance." In a documentary aired on VisionTV, channel 61 Rogers Cable in Ottawa, Ontario, on 12 October 2006 at 10:00 p.m., Margaret Visser, during a program entitled "The Geometry of Love," a program on the Roman church called Sant'Agnese fuori le Mura, explains how she found God in a fitness class at the University of Toronto on 22 July 1982. In the documentary, she takes the viewer back to the fitness class where this occurred and identifies the exact spot where, when she was lying on the floor, she rolled over and looked up at a florescent light and had an experience of God. In the documentary she refers to her experience of oneness and the whole. In a related newspaper article by Vanessa Farquharson entitled "Finding God in a Fitness Class" and published in the *National Post*, 12 October 2006, p. B4, Margaret Visser describes the experience as follows: "I can't really describe it (...) It was everything coming together, seeing everything all at once. It's amazing that this happens to people. You just see it and then you've got to get your mind around it. There's a moment when everything's clear and then you have to unpack it, look at it, figure it out. [That moment] has informed everything I've done ever since, it's always there. I think it's very very important. (...) I suppose psychologists would call it an integration or some other abstract term, but it's not abstract at all."

9. And seemingly in the Jewish and Islamic traditions as well, though I need to leave this for others more expert than I to discuss.

10. In comparison with several forms of Buddhism and Hinduism, for example, main- stream Christian, Jewish, Islamic and indigenous religious traditions do not generally try to go beyond but, rather, affirm the ongoing importance and meaning of the perduring distinction between self and other, and especially between self and God.

11. There is no intention here with such phrases as "murmuring," "welling up," "urge" and "impulses of love and goodness" to describe exhaustively the variously recog- nized and identified results attributed in the Christian community or in other reli- gious communities to the active presence of the Holy Spirit. Rather, these phrases more modestly attempt to capture something of that multifaceted work of the Holy

Spirit indicated, for example, in Paul's first-century letter to the Galatians, with special reference to Ga 4:6, in the patristic theological reflections of Basil of Caesarea on the functions of the Holy Spirit as developed in his "The Treatise *De Spiritu Sancto*," chs. 9 and 16, in the succinctly presented medieval theological argumentation of Thomas Aquinas regarding the differentiation between the trinitarian processions of the Son and of the Spirit in his *Summa theologiae* I q. 27, a. 4, c, where he speaks of will, and consequently of the Holy Spirit, in terms of an "urge and motion towards" (*"secundum rationem impellentis et moventis in aliquid"*) and in the twentieth-century exegetical approach of James D. G. Dunn, *Jesus and the Spirit* (London: SCM, 1975). The reference to Basil Caesarea is according to *Traité du Saint-Esprit, Basile de Césarée*, trad. Benoît Pruche (Paris: Éditions du Cerf, 1947)/*On the Holy Spirit. St. Basil the Great*, trans. David Anderson (Crestwood, NY: St. Vladimir's Seminary Press, 1997). The reference to Aquinas is according to the Leonine text and follows the standard form identifying part, question, article and body of the article. For practical purposes, see Sancti Thomae Aquinatis, Doctoris Angelici Ordinis Praedicatorum, *Summa Theologiae*, cura Fratrum ejusdem Ordinis, vol. one (Matriti: Biblioteca de Autores Cristianos, 1961)/ *Summa theologiae* (Cambridge?, England: Blackfriars in conjunction with Eyre and Spottlswoode, 1964).

12. The expressions "opened to," "recognize," "turn to" and so forth are used to capture something of the effects of grace envisaged by several major Christian theologians. Stated very generally here and merely by way of example, "opened to" attempts to include something of the insights of Martin Luther, who spoke of human receptivity before God, of Friedrich Schleiermacher, who spoke of a sense of absolute dependance ,and of Karl Rahner, who writes of God present as divine mystery and horizon gifting people with the capacity to receive God. "Recognize" tries to pick up on Gregory of Nyssa's understanding of grace primarily as a second divine offer, through the incarnation, to the innate human drive for God. "Turn to" proposes to express something of Augustine's notion of grace as the divine creative reorienting of bad human willing (*male velle*) to good human willing (*bene velle*).

13. It should be noted that these affirmations concerning the Spirit of God, the Risen One and God as goal rest upon three underlying phenomenological "givens" with "givens" referring in this case to certain basic human experiences and attitudes. The reflection on the Spirit of God rests upon the inner experience of an urge outwards on the part of the self. The reflection on the Risen One rests upon the experience of otherness in general and others in particular as source of enrichment. The reflection on God as goal rests upon the fundamental human attitude of looking toward and longing for. Working with these underlying phenomenological "givens" constitutes a basis upon which the philosophical theologian can carry out her or his reflection in dialogue both with Christians and with others. These phenomenological "givens" are available to all for further examination. In a sense, they encapsulate the moments in a movement of enriching experience, a movement of spirit.

14. Hegel gave his self-mediating movement of absolute spirit, a movement ultimately of thought, essentially logical, phenomenological, philosophy of religion and philosophical formulations.

Now, after giving the movement of spirit a phenomenological formulation, I am presently proposing a more formally philosophical reflection and reasoned argument that was preceded by a two-phased phenomenological analysis and will be followed toward the end of the present chapter by a more integrative phemenological review as a sort of third experience.

15. "So ist über das Herausgehen des Endlichen aus dem Unendlichen zu sagen, das Unendliche gehe zur Englichkeit *heraus*, darum weil es keine Wahrheit, kein Bestehen an im, wie es als abstrakte Einheit gefaßt est, hat; so umgekehrt geht das Endliche aus demselben Grunde seiner Nichtigkeit in das Unendliche *hinein*." Georg Wilhelm Friedrich Hegel, *Gesammelte Werke*, vol. 21: *Wissenschaft der Logik*. Erster Teil: *Die objektive Logik*. Erster Band: *Die Lehre von Sein (1832)*, ed. Friedrich Hogemann and Walter Jaeschke (Hamburg: Meiner, 1985) 141 lines 22–26/*Hegel's Science of Logic*, trans. A. V. Miller (New York: Humanities, 1969) 154. Hegel says this in a Remark concerning his formulation of finitude and infinity as thought categories in the movement of pure thought. In the context of his discussion on the true infinite, he insists that it does not matter whether one begins with the finite or the infinite. However, there he is not speaking of the beginning of his system as such, which beginning can for him only be made in pure being, inclusive momentary totality constituting the absolute beginning of the movement of pure thought.

16. See Dale M. Schlitt, *Hegel's Trinitarian Claim* (Leiden: Brill, 1980) 250–251.

17. For detailed argumentation, see Schlitt, *Hegel's Trinitarian Claim*.

18. For a description of the contours of Hegel's own presentation of finite "and" infinite, see Schlitt, *Hegel's Trinitarian Claim* 252–267, reproduced below in the Appendix to the present study.

19. Again, note Schlitt, *Hegel's Trinitarian Claim* 252–267 and the Appendix at the end of the present volume.

20. See, by way of example, Schlitt, *Hegel's Trinitarian Claim* 64–65, 84–85, 178–184.

21. Here we could note that Alfred North Whitehead posited a temporal transition in which the resultant self ceased to exist and was, then, past in relation to the beginning of the subsequent concrescing self. Though this arrangement satisfied a number of requirements of physics and Whitehead does account in several ways for the human sense of being with others, it still seems to me to have resulted in the argument to a lonely world in which each concrescing subject is fully alone. I am here, at least on the human level, trying to argue to a resultant self that is equally initial self so that, in a sense, the self is never alone. This more paradoxical and dialectical view seems to me to represent in a fuller fashion the complex reality of the human self.

22. If we refer to the experience of God itself as first experience, we will in a phenomenological analysis of that experience speak not of self-contradiction but of tension. However, here where we are speaking of that experience as being examined in a more directly conceptual and reflexive fashion, we can speak more properly of "contradiction" and "self-contradiction."

23. This is witnessed to, for example, by the simple fact that there are movements of enrichment that occur experientially and chronologically parallel to one another.

24. The term "erotic" is gratefully borrowed from William Desmond, *Hegel's God. A Counterfeit Double? Ashgate Studies in the History of Philosophical Theology* (Aldershot, Hants, England: Ashgate, 2003), where it is used here and there throughout the book.

25. Though the relationship between finitude and true infinite is, from various perspectives, dialogical, the philosophically expressed argument to the need for that relationship can be termed dialectical in that the argument is based on the thinking through of a self-contradiction. In this way, the "dialectical" reflects, at the level of conceptu-

ally reflexive discussion and argument, namely, in a form of second experience, what occurs "dialogically" in a first experience.

26. The expression is that of William Desmond in *Hegel's God*, though the positive attitude expressed here toward a possible "whole of wholes" does not characterize his use of the phrase.

27. The continuity is more direct if the self concerned has itself participated in the first experience and less direct, namely, through an affirmation concerning the first experience, if the self concerned has itself not participated in the first experience.

   The terms "first experience" and "second experience," as well as the here soon to be introduced term "third experience," refer of course not to any simply sequential ordering of experiences, but to the three types or phases of experience previously described in Chapter Five above, where we spoke of overall types and phases of experience.

28. For an overview of Hegel on the Kingdom of God, see Dale M. Schlitt, *Divine Subjectivity. Understanding Hegel's Philosophy of Religion* (Scranton, PA: University of Scranton Press, Toronto: Associated University Presses, 1990) 271–318.

29. For several references, see Schlitt, *Divine Subjectivity* 318.

30. See, for example, letter n. 38 attributed to Basil of Caesarea but surely written by his brother, Gregory of Nyssa. For the Greek and French texts, see *Saint Basile. Lettres*, vol. 1 (Paris: Les Belles Lettres, 1957) 81–92. For the English text, see *Letters I*. In *The Fathers of the Church*, vol. 13 (New York: Fathers of the Church, Inc., 1951) 84–96.

31. "Primordial" here makes allusion to Alfred North Whitehead's proposed primordial nature of God. However, whereas for Whitehead God's initial involvement with the world takes the form of an offer of interrelated conceptual possibilities presented to an actual occasion as initial aim, here God's primordial involvement with the world occurs in more action-oriented fashion as an "urging outward." God's initial involvement with the world in the conceptual realm would take place more through the manifestation of divine otherness, often traditionally referred to as the *logos*.

32. "Consequent" here alludes to a number of aspects of Whitehead's notion of the consequent or receptive nature of God.

33. While God as this inclusive infinite is a rather more circular or even triangular movement, the movement of God through history can best be understood, so to speak, as a spiral movement. Such is the way that the infinite relates respectfully to finitude.

   Though God remains the triadically structured movement of enriching experience or spirit, this triadically structured movement appears in history as such a spiral movement in the sense that the dynamic divine embrace or context as movement from initial selfhood (1) and otherness (2) in relationship giving rise to enriched resultant selfhood (3) is, from a historical perspective, recurrently embrace or context of each consecutive movement of finite experience from initial selfhood (1) and otherness (2) in relationship giving rise to enriched resultant selfhood (3) renewedly initial selfhood and recurrent otherness (4) in relationship. The one moment of divine initial selfhood is every renewedly present to the initial moment of selfhood and throughout that initial moment of selfhood's dialectical development in the tetradically structured movement of finite experience. The one moment of divine otherness is ever renewedly present to the moment of otherness and throughout that moment of otherness's dialectical development in the tetradically structured movement of finite experience. The one moment of resultant divine selfhood is ever renewedly present to the moment of enriched resultant selfhood in that tetradically structured movement.

34. The intention here, as mentioned, is not to subordinate God to a pre-established schema, but simply to recognize that an infinite God must accept to work with the human in its condition if that God wishes to relate with humans, or finitude, while remaining infinite and not changing those humans or that finitude into what they or it are not.

35. On Hegel, see Schlitt, *Hegel's Trinitarian Claim* e.g. 11–49.

36. On Søren Kierkegaard see, for example, Frederick Sontag, *A Kierkegaard Handbook* (Atlanta: John Knox, 1979) 97–103, 109–116.

37. From the perspective of the finite, this potentiality is something ever to be realized. From the perspective of the infinite, it would rather more appropriately be considered realized potentiality.

8

SPEAKING OF GOD

Throughout the present study we have been working toward a post-Hegelian philosophical theology. Our project has slowly come to take the form primarily of what we have termed a second experience, namely, a phenomenological analysis of the trinitarian experience of God and a philosophically and logically argued reflection on that experience. This analysis and reflection constituted a form of prolongation of that experience into the realm of reflexive self-awareness. There followed a further phenomenological analysis of or look at the first experience, an analysis taking the form of a third type or stage of that experience, what we have called a third experience. We have spoken of the communal, shared or individual finite self's experience of the triune God. Especially toward the end of the previous chapter, we came to speak more tentatively as well of our experience of the triune God's experience of us and of our world. In the present chapter we now need to account as best we can in the public realm for how we have, over the course of two millennia, spoken of God.

To speak responsibly of God today means of course more than discussing linguistic modes of predication, referring to "gilded" dogmas and liturgical formulations, or merely respecting authoritative ecclesiastical pronouncements, important in its own way as each of these is. It means as well more than merely bending and shuffling borrowed philosophical concepts to make them fit into the received tradition of a triadically structured divine puzzle. Again, it means neither abandoning rigorous formulation in favor of a more loosely expressed flow of history painted in three colors nor of course casually setting the notion of a triune God aside as fundamentally incoherent or at least irrelevant. Rather, speaking responsibly of God today in an increasingly globalized yet diverse and in a sense secular world requires quite concerted reflection in the public realm, that is, reflection responsible to canons of consciousness, thought and language. In view of the contemporary awareness of pluralism, one could say reflection responsible to diverse ways of being aware of reality and of oneself, of thinking and of giving expression to thought. In the overall Christian context, this concerted reflection in the public realm involves searching for ways to come to terms with Protestant theological traditions' generally feeling more at home with dialectical modes of thought, with Catholic traditions' sense of comfort with analogy and, consequently, dialogical modes of thought, and with Orthodoxy's contemporary insistence on what Protestant and Catholic theologies also have traditionally stressed to some extent, namely, the final ineffability of the divine. But whether the attempt to speak of Trinity be made in such a more focused and specifically Christian frame of reference or within the wider context of a dialogue with various religions of the world and spiritual traditions and, especially in the context of a concern for Trinity, with Islam as well as with diverse forms of agnosticism or atheism, this speaking cannot merely presuppose the existence of the reality to which it refers or that reality's already given threeness in oneness. To speak responsibly of the triune God in the public realm, one must somehow include in and as a part of this very speaking an argument[1] toward the affirmation of the reality of that triadically structured divine reality.

Referring to a triadically structured divine reality in turn involves critical reflection on possible values at stake in affirming a triune God, concerns similar to those especially evident in the Greek patristic theology down to Basil of Caesarea and in Hegel's thought.[2] In this chapter I intend to continue to address these concerns, though in a very general way and without explicitly naming them, by means of a critical and constructive reflection first of all on analogy and then, somewhat more indirectly, on the dialectically developing trajectories of self and other with self and other considered, as worked out so far, in dialogically structured relationship with one another.

Already now it will be helpful to recall that analogical predication and dialectical assertion have both been the subject of a similar criticism. Despite analogy's insistence on a similarity against the background of real difference and despite dialectic's assertion of the total otherness of the infinite, both have, at least in their respective, generalized Thomistic and Hegelian formulations, found themselves open to the accusation that they do not effectively avoid ending up, presuming one retains an understanding of God as infinite, in a philosophically and theologically unacceptable univocity. Moreover, both analogy and dialectic, as attempts to refer to and speak of the infinite and at least in their more generalized Thomistic and Hegelian formulations, exhibit an astonishingly similar dynamic structure: positing; negating; reaffirming on a higher level. Hegel's dialectical thinking has already at least indirectly been subjected to extensive critique elsewhere.[3] Reviewing Thomas Aquinas and his formulations of analogical predication is one of the tasks of the present chapter. Here, we will focus more on the strengths of his approach as well as certain hesitations concerning his formulations of analogy in order to set the stage, then, for a somewhat more programmatic proposal toward an integration of analogy, dialectic, and dialogical thinking in the form of a renewed reformulation of a dialectically and dialogically based analogical divine predication.

Previously in the present study, especially from Part Two, Chapter Four above on, we have stressed that experience is the wider category including, yet also conditioned by, thought and language, which are themselves forms of experience that occur when one is thinking or speaking. We can now, then, by way of anticipation indicate that the justification of and for our speaking about God will directly involve the notion of experience, since speaking is, from different perspectives, itself a way of structuring experience, a prolongation of experience and, indeed, a form of experience. Our efforts to give a reasoned explanation of how Christians can speak of God will then constitute a further effort toward the formulation of a philosophical theology that takes the form of a trinitarian metaphysics of experience, a movement of inclusive divine subjectivity and spirit, that was briefly mentioned at the end of the previous chapter and that had arisen slowly over the course of the development of the various reflections carried out so far throughout the present study.

In this eighth chapter we will, stated in preliminary and very general fashion, first review and reflect upon certain aspects of Aquinas's carefully nuanced explanations of how Christians can truly speak of God. Then we will proceed with Aquinas but also propose to go beyond him on analogy. He rooted speech about God in a distinction that, though it is real in finite reality, is only a distinction of reason in God. We will say more about this below, but for now we can simply indicate that our speech about God should be based in real distinctions constitutive of dialectically developing and dialogically related finite and infinite, human and divine.

It should come as no surprise that we choose to carry out the present philosophical reflection by referring specifically to, and wanting to profit from, Aquinas and his thought. He occupies a preeminent place in the long history of the discussion about how to speak responsibly of God and constitutes a natural choice as point of departure for us as we try to give an accounting of such speech. His efforts to speak of an infinite God constitute, in many ways, the paradigm for western attempts to refer from world to God by means of analogical predication. His preeminent and paradigmatic role justifies our present exploratory,[4] but critical, review of his struggling with the problematic question of analogy and, more specifically, of analogical divine predication. His wrestling with various theories of analogy will open the way for us to the immense question of finding an appropriate contemporary way to speak responsibly of God and, more particularly, of the triune God. A critical review of his struggling with a way to ground and explain a justifiable and acceptable form of analogical divine predication can itself also further contribute to our development of a philosophical theology understood as a trinitarian movement of inclusive divine subjectivity and forming a trinitarian metaphysics of experience based on systematic phenomenological and philosophical reflections on the experience of God.

In this present turn to Aquinas there will, however, be few direct references to his explicit thought on Trinity. We will focus our critical attention, rather, on that fundament[5] which he thought would justify his speaking of God and elaborating a theory of Trinity. That fundament is analogy as the way in which he is able as a philosopher, but primarily as a theologian, to refer to and speak, in the public realm, of God and, more specifically, of Trinity. Of particular present interest are his explanations of those forms of analogy which he at one time or another considered philosophically and theologically legitimate ways of referring to the divine essence and, given revelation, to the trinitarian divine Persons.[6]

With Aquinas

The intention in this chapter, as has already been mentioned, is to work toward an explanation of how we can speak of God responsibly in the public realm while at the same time respecting overall divine transcendence. The idea of formulating my intention in this way comes from, and itself parallels, Aquinas's own desire to develop a viable theory of analogous divine predication and the approaches Aquinas takes to elaborate such a theory. He set for himself a goal that was at once modest and yet profoundly challenging. He recognized that we do speak of God and he was committed to the position that such religious and theological language functioned legitimately. He wanted, then, to show how this language worked.

Later on in this chapter, after having learned from Aquinas, I would like to propose a significantly modified way of grounding and justifying such analogical divine predication. However, first we need to learn from him, which we will do by reviewing in some detail what he has said about such predication. Though I have found myself embroiled in several heated discussions with others who did not share my reading of Aquinas on analogy and, more specifically, on analogical divine predication, I remain convinced that his overarching solution was, stated very briefly, to work with the idea that any effect represented in some way its cause. In the question at hand, then, all that is not God, namely, the effect, in some way represents God, who is the cause. I would argue Aquinas claimed that speaking of God was justified ultimately on the basis of this representation.[7] As preliminary justification of my understanding, I would note, among others, that in his *Summa theologiae* Aquinas regular enough speaks of our being able to know through effects that God exists,[8] and constantly uses the language of causality when he speaks of God as creator and of humans as creatures. Indeed, for Aquinas we speak of God on the basis of divine causality and, more so, on the basis of the fact that what we do predicate of God preexists eminently in God.

> When we say God is good or wise we do not simply mean that he causes wisdom or goodness, but that these perfections preexist in him in an eminent way.[9]

> And so whatever is said both of God and of creatures is said in virtue of the order that creatures have to God as their source and cause in which all the perfections of things preexist in a more excellent way.[10]

Again very generally stated, Aquinas was convinced that when we speak of God we not only point in the direction of God but that we really do speak of God. Though for Aquinas God's essence could not as such be known,[11] perfections or those things said of God not just metaphorically are predicated essentially and intrinsically in the various theories of analogy that Aquinas developed.[12]

Indeed, though in Aquinas's thought the formal function of analogy with regard to speaking of God does not change through the years, there is a development of content marked by shifts and fresh starts.[13] Of the many types of analogy Aquinas discusses through the years, namely, of attempts to establish some similarity within a context of real diversity between creature and Creator, finite and infinite, two stand out for him at one time or another as legitimate: proportionality and intrinsic attribution. We will briefly present each of these explanations and justifications of analogical divine predication and then note various hesitations concerning their viability. After having thus learned from Aquinas, I propose we go beyond him by explaining analogical divine predication on the basis of, and grounding it in, a theory more directly rooted in the trinitarian distinctions in God, an approach that Aquinas himself did not use but which I would suggest respects his overall intention and allows us to reiterate, or in a Kierkegaardian sense to repeat, much of what he wanted to say.

Now, with an overall idea of Aquinas's intention regarding his explanation of analogical divine predication in mind, we turn to a review of his two main approaches to, and explanations of, what he considered legitimate explanations of that predication and how it functions.

Analogy of Proper Proportionality

Presentation. First of all, a few more general remarks concerning Aquinas's theory of proper proportionality. It is in the gathered disputed questions, *De Veritate*, written 1256–1259, that Aquinas treats of the analogy of proportionality and generalizes the analogy by applying it to the whole God-creature relationship.[14] For Aquinas, proportionality is metaphysically expressed most fundamentally as follows: the divine *esse* or act of "to be" is to the divine essence as the finite *esse* is to the finite essence. In *De Veritate*, this establishes a similarity not of proportion but of proportionality, in which infinite is compared to infinite and finite to finite. Such proportionality involves for Aquinas no comparison of infinite to finite or vice versa.[15] Several authors claim the analogy of proportionality has its historical roots in a geometrical relationship exemplifiable as 6:3::4:2.[16] They also note that this form of analogy, as found in *De Veritate,* is a further specification of overall cause-based analogy, namely, of what has come to be called intrinsic attribution.[17]

Now, however, to turn to a more detailed reading of Aquinas's theory of the analogy of proper proportionality. The principal pertinent *De Veritate* text is question two, article eleven, with clarifying supplementation from question two, article three, particular response four and question twenty-three, article seven, particular response nine.

Question two, article eleven's heading reads: "Is Knowledge Predicated Equivocally of God and Us?"[18] The initial objections in this article serve to raise the difficulty of speaking of God in view of the fact that an infinite distance between God and creature apparently eliminates any commonality of predication. It is this infinite distance and yet perceived need for some commonality with which Aquinas struggles in this article eleven. Already in the preliminary consideration of a negative response to the article's opening question, Aquinas refers to Aristotle and to Genesis 1:26. In the longer response, he insists that univocity between God and creature is out of the question. When an intelligible principle or characteristic (*ratio*) is in two subjects, it is so according to the way in which they exist. In God the divine essence is identified with the divine act of "to be" (*esse*). This unique divine act of existence is not communicable, so creatures could never attain possession of something in the way God does. There can be no intelligible principle or characteristic (*ratio*) common to God and creature. Still, Aquinas will not accept a merely equivocal predication of knowledge to God and creature. Otherwise, all-importantly, God could not know creatures and, as well, creatures could never come to a knowledge of God in which they could distinguish appropriate terms from inappropriate ones. However, at this point Aquinas presumes that God and creatures do in fact know one another. Therefore, there must be some predication of God and us which is neither univocal nor equivocal but analogous. Here he makes a concrete distinction between proportion and proportionality. Two things can be proportionate to each other on the basis of a determinate distance or some other relation. The example given is 2:1, a form of proportion in which two is the double of one. But Aquinas then proposes another, second way of being proportionate, namely, proportionality, a similarity of two proportions. For example, 6:3::4:2. He then moves quite unselfconsciously from these mathematical examples to other, more philosophical ones. He insists that the first type of agreement, namely, that of a proportion based on some definite relationship, is not applicable to the question of God and creature. Interestingly, he will also reject as inappropriate a determinate relationship of one to another in which one intelligible principle or characteristic (*ratio*) becomes part of the definition of another or one thing becomes part of the definition of two others.[19] But the second type, that of proportionality, is for Aquinas not predicated upon any determinate distance between infinite and finite. So, in this way one can speak legitimately of God and creature. Aquinas ends the longer response by making a distinction in which he notes that there are perfections which cannot be predicated of God because they include defect or dependence on matter.

The particular responses to the initial, specific difficulties or objections contain for the most part applications of or appeals to the distinction between proportion and proportionality. The specific response to objection number four is particularly illuminating. From the beginning, Aquinas's concern had been with preserving the infinite distance between God and creature while attempting to establish some acceptable form of commonality or, as he writes, community of analogy. In this response to the fourth objection, Aquinas recalls that 2:1::6:3::100:50, and so forth. The distance between the pairs of proportioned members makes no difference. The similarity remains constant.

To this summary of the argument as it is developed in question two, article eleven, we need to add two further points. In the context of his concern with how God knows finite creatures through the medium of the divine essence, Aquinas in question two, article three, particular response four clarifies the similarity involved in the analogy of proportionality. There is no proportion of God to creature or vice versa. Rather, there is a proportion of infinite to infinite and finite to finite, most fundamentally of divine *esse* to divine essence (a distinction of reason) and of finite *esse* to finite essence (a real distinction).[20]

The second point to be added is indicated in question twenty-three, article seven, particular response nine. Aquinas insists that there can be no objection to speaking of such a proportionality of a human being to God, since the human being is made by (*effectus*) and subject to God. Not only this statement but his preferred terms of God and creature as well as his explicit statements recall that the analogy of proportionality is finally grounded in and cannot be held extrinsic to his overall conception of creation and conservation in being in terms of a causal relationship between God and world. In this response nine of article seven we can already note that he is making a transition from the analogy of proper proportionality to the analogy of attribution.[21]

Critical Reflections. The viability of Aquinas's ultimately cause-based analogy of proportionality has of course been challenged at various times. Wolfhart Pannenberg represents a helpful example of such challenges. In his habilitation writing,[22] he proceeds by means of a closer examination of the type of agreement Aquinas posits between the two proportions constituting the proposed proportionality between infinitely distant God and creature. As mentioned, Aquinas speaks of a *similarity* of proportions that Pannenberg says was worked out of the four-membered geometrical expression, 6:3::4:2. But then Pannenberg argues that only an *equality* of relationship guarantees an agreement between the two proportions, and here that equality is 2:1 on each side of the expression. Some have tried to distinguish between the *equality* of relationship required for mathematical proportionality and only a *similarity* of relationship required for metaphysical proportionality. But Pannenberg responds that similarity means, in common scholastic parlance, "partial equality." To say, however, that the basis for proportionality, namely, for similarity, lies not in an equality but in another similarity leads to an infinite regress. Never to arrive at an element of equality finally either denies similarity of proportions or reduces analogy to equivocation or, again, leaves a proposed analogical predication unfounded and unexplained. Interestingly enough, again according to Pannenberg, not only did Aquinas himself not make this distinction between mathematical and metaphysical analogy, but he used mathematical analogy as the prime example for the metaphysical analogy of proportionality. Though Aquinas had spoken of a "similarity" of proportions rather than of an equality of proportions, according to Pannenberg little can be made of this since an equality of proportions in the strict sense of qualitative likeness would be a mere tautology anyway. For Pannenberg, whether mathematical or metaphysical, the proportionality Aquinas argued to either rests on a equality of proportions or there is no similarity at all. That there is such an exact proportion underlying and common to each pair of members in the analogy of proportionality is verified in the very predictability of the fourth member, given the other three. According to Pannenberg, when proportionality is finally constituted by and reducible to an univocal element, in this case an equality, Aquinas's attempt to establish a third alternative to univocity and equivocation appears to collapse.

Pannenberg's critique of proportionality needs to be taken into serious consideration to the extent that Aquinas's theory is based on the establishment of a specific proportion not only in the creature but in God as well. In a footnote,[23] Pannenberg briefly remarks further about, but does not develop, another point of entry in examining Aquinas's analogy of proportionality, namely, the positing of the relation between divine *esse* and divine essence as a distinction of reason alone. Aquinas's fundamental stance is that the divine essence is absolutely simple. Real divine distinctions can only be spoken of with reference to the trinitarian divine Persons which, in turn, are only distinct from the divine essence by a distinction of reason.[24] For now, and for present purposes, it is best not to enter into a detailed discussion of these knotty issues but, rather, to remain with Aquinas's brilliant move beyond Aristotle in the application of the principle of act and potency to the relationship between existence (*esse*) and essence.[25] Aquinas characterized the relationship between existence and essence as one respectively of act to potency. This move allowed him to apply the distinction even to God insofar as it was possible for the human mind to make a distinction of reason between the divine *esse* and the divine essence, though in reality God's essence was God's "to be." The two were identical. For Aquinas, God was pure act without potency or potentiality.[26] This stroke of genius, namely, Aquinas's affirmation of a distinction of reason between act and potency as existence and essence in God, seemed to allow Aquinas to work with a metaphysical tissue, namely, act and potency, common to and characteristic of the totality of reality while at the same time not subordinating God to a principle common to finite and infinite. When seen in conjunction with his analogy of proper proportionality, it becomes clear that he wished, to put it colloquially, to have his metaphysical cake and eat it too. On the one hand, to justify speaking of proportionality he had to stress the distinction of reason between divine *esse* and divine essence. On the other hand, to affirm the infinite distance between God and creature he had to stress the real identity between divine *esse* and divine essence. The way in which he tried to balance both aspects of analogy, namely similarity and difference, in one theory of act and potency is a major tribute to his extraordinary metaphysical insight.

Nevertheless, Aquinas's position allowing only for a distinction of reason in the divine, relative to *esse*/essence, would seem to constitute as well the very Achilles heel of his theory of the analogy of proper proportionality. This distinction would appear to be the systematic, internal difficulty more basic even than Pannenberg's, and so many others', argument that Aquinas's theory of an analogy of proportionality requires an univocal element. Aquinas needed to affirm intrinsic attributes or perfections of the divine itself and not merely of God as cause of such perfections in creatures. The only basis he found appropriate was a distinction of reason, a distinction existing not as such in God but only in the mind, and specifically in the finite mind. Aquinas would seem to be caught. If he stressed a distinction of reason as basis for a proportion in the divine, his theory of analogy over against univocity and equivocation would seem more susceptible to the critique that it may presuppose a necessary univocal fundament. If he stressed the otherness of the divine, namely, the real identity of divine *esse* and divine essence, the only basis for the analogy rests in the finite mind and its making a distinction of reason between the two. Such cannot ground essential, intrinsic divine predication. Finally, to say that such a distinction of reason exists also in the divine mind and therefore establishes the needed proportion in the divine would mean the analogy of proportionality rests on what would be either an indefinite series of distinctions of reason or a, for Aquinas, unacceptable distinction between divine mind and divine essence.[27]

This dilemma, into which the theory of an analogy of proper proportionality proposed by Aquinas would seem to settle, is rooted first of all in his emphasis on the relationship between divine *esse* and divine essence, where he could only establish a relation of reason. Later on I will suggest that he should perhaps have concentrated on the level on which he could speak of real, trinitarian distinctions in the divine.

His emphasis on the relationship between *esse* and divine essence has several rootages in his system, including his predilection for or prejudice in favor of simple identity against the background of or, perhaps better, within the context of a western, as well as overall Neoplatonic, stress on the oneness of God. It could be argued that the most fundamental problematic basis for Aquinas's concentration on the relationship between *esse* and divine essence lies, to put it irreverently if not even crudely, in his overly distinguished, at times almost quantitative, conception of the relationship between philosophy and theology, reason and revelation, nature and grace. Without entering into the intricate details of his envisioned "grace presupposing nature,"[28] and while acknowledging that Aquinas is fundamentally a theologian working on the finite level with the idea of inclusive wholes, namely, with given unified but composite entities, one can still suspect that in his system reason and revelation remain less integrated, though this would have to be the subject of a separate study. He worked with the idea that revelation brought new content to reason and at times corrected reason's inadequate conclusions. However, revelation did not for him change the structures of reason. It built upon them.[29] Even this cursory sketching illustrates the possibility of an apparent de facto extrinsecism involved in an affirmation that "grace presupposes nature," important as this phrase has been in preserving an essential role for reason in theology. What is called for is an understanding of revelation that will allow for a clearer integration of reason as essential moment in, and not primarily presupposition for, revelation. It could perhaps better be said that revelation takes the form of a movement of experience with reasoning as included element.

Analogy of Intrinsic Attribution

Presentation. After *De Veritate*, Aquinas never again explicitly used the analogy of proportionality vis-à-vis God, despite Cajetan's influential interpretation to the contrary.[30] Perhaps he sensed that he had not focused sufficiently on what underlay even the idea of proportionality to which he had appealed in his efforts to explain how we speak of God while respecting God's transcendence. Though he did not as such explicitly repudiate the theory of proper proportionality as a way of explaining analogical divine predication, his last efforts at clarifying analogy did in fact center on another approach, namely, the analogy of intrinsic attribution, as a way of explaining essential predication rooted in a similarity of cause in its effect so that a name or term can be applied in an essential way to the cause on the basis of a perfection observed in the effect.[31]

His clearest elaboration of the analogy of intrinsic attribution is found in his mature work, the *Summa Theologiae*, written about 1266–1273, and more specifically for present purposes in the first part of that work, question thirteen, article five with supplementation from article six and also from articles two, three and four.

In question thirteen, article five, Aquinas asks, "Whether those things said of God and of creatures are said univocally of both?"[32] The three initial objections or observations speak for univocal predication, but the two contraries or preliminary responses suggest equivocal predication. In the body of the article, Aquinas first argues insistently and directly against both univocal and equivocal predication of God and creatures (the terms "univocal" and "equivocal," as used here, should become clearer as we proceed with the review of Aquinas on analogy of intrinsic attribution). Such predication cannot be univocal, first of all, because an effect receives the similarity to its cause or agent, though admittedly always defectively. In the cause, all perfections exist as one and in the same way. In effects, they exist divided and multiple. Such divided and multiple perfections pre-exist as one in God. Univocal predication is not possible, secondly, because perfections exist differently in the simple divine essence and in the composite which the creature is. Perfections exist as delimiting qualities in the rational creature, but as nothing more than the divine essence, power and act of being in the divine.

At this point Aquinas makes what is for him the crucial distinction between the name which would be predicated commonly of God and creatures and the *ratio*, which he in the previous article four had defined as the intellect's conception of the thing signified by the name.[33] So for Aquinas the name signifies both that which is known (*res*) and the concept (*ratio*) of the thing known. In the following article six, Aquinas will further designate the *ratio* as definition (*definitio*). On the basis of a deficient similarity of cause in effect and of a distinction of conception or *ratio,* no name can be spoken univocally of God and creature. But equivocation is equally unacceptable for Aquinas, since the fallacy of equivocation would obviate anything's being known or demonstrated of God from creatures. This would run counter to what philosophers have done over the centuries and Paul has claimed in Romans 1:20.

With the rejection of both univocal and equivocal predication, it becomes clear that this whole article five has been set up to lead to a third alternative, namely, analogical predication. In the body of the article, Aquinas continues briefly to distinguish the type of proportion or relation that cannot be applied to the God-world relationship. The unacceptable relation Aquinas describes is one in which two (or many) have a relation effectively to a third (or another).[34] He distinguishes a second type of relation in which one thing is related or proportioned to another. This is a relationship in which creatures are ordered to God as effect to cause or principle, the one in whom all the perfections of created things pre-exist in an eminent way. The body of this article five reaches a climax with Aquinas's famous claim that analogy forms the mean between univocity and equivocation. Most importantly for Aquinas, though the same name may be used of God and creatures, there is in analogical predication no common *ratio* or conception as in univocity, nor is there a total diversity of *ratio* as in equivocation.

For a fuller picture of Aquinas's mature elaboration of analogy as intrinsic or inner attribution it is necessary to highlight several points made in the following article six, and more indirectly presented in the prior articles two and three, all in this question thirteen. In article six, Aquinas, somewhat surprisingly after his earlier denial that God is involved in the definition of creatures,[35] now, in view of the understanding of attribution as an ordered relationship of one to another, sees the original and originating one as placed in the definition of all. God becomes, as cause, part of the definition of all else.[36] On this level, then, any name predicated of God and creatures is predicated first of God, i.e., of the one placed in the definition of all others. Aquinas continues with several distinctions. First, in his understanding of "metaphorical" usage, the first or primary referent is the creature. Second, as was the case with "metaphor," again if one were to try to speak of God only causally, the *ratio* would remain the same and the primary referent would be the creature. But he reminds the reader that in article two of this question it had been established that some names are properly spoken of God not only causally but essentially. God is designated not only cause of goodness, for example, but is the one in whom goodness preexists in an eminent way. He closes the body of article six with an application of the distinction that he made earlier in article three between the orders of being and of knowing. In analogical predication, with reference to that (*res*) which is signified by the name, the primary reference is to God. In regard, however, to how one uses the name, it is applied first to creatures since they are known first.

Aquinas has integrated Neoplatonic and Aristotelian elements into his theory of the analogy of inner attribution. The distinction he made between the order of being and the order of knowing belongs to the Neoplatonic in his thought.[37] When integrated with his Aristotelian stance that all knowledge is the result of abstraction from sense experience, this distinguishing of two orders clearly establishes the inadequacy of all human knowledge of God. Apparently Aquinas was the first to link difference of order with the Averroist analogy of one to another so that the question of "prime analogate" depends, in a sense, on point of view. With this distinction of orders, he no longer seemed to need an analogy of proper proportionality to preserve the infinite distance between finite and infinite.

Aquinas has as well brought together in his theory of analogy of intrinsic attribution various forms of Platonic and Aristotelian causality.[38] He works with the Platonic exemplary cause and with Aristotelian efficient and final causes. He has significantly modified the Neoplatonic causal schema by giving priority to the final cause, the "cause of causes,"[39] while retaining, and thereby regrounding, the Platonic notion of participation. An effect's finality is to become, as far as possible, like its cause. It is for this that the effect is brought into existence. Still, even with his reference to multiple causality, when it comes to the God-world relationship as such, Aquinas speaks of cause in the singular. From the perspective of the divine there is only one cause and one causality. The distinction into types of causes is rooted in finite ways of knowing and not in the simple divine essence itself. This causal relationship between God and creature remains for Aquinas within the overall Neoplatonic causal and even *existus/reditus* schema despite a shifted emphasis from efficient to final causality and a consequent stress on divine and human freedom.[40] There is, indeed, a real relation of dependence of effect upon cause and, thus, of creature upon God.[41] Given this relationship, on the one hand the cause is not available to the effect in such a way that the cause could be adequately known from the effect. On the other hand, there must exist some similarity of cause in effect, whether cause be considered, from the perspective of the divine or infinite, in terms of simplicity or, from the perspective of the finite, in terms of multiplicity.[42] Were there no similarity of cause in its effect there would in fact be no existent effect, no patterning after a first cause and no intrinsic tending towards a goal. This cause-based similarity is the grounding for Aquinas's analogy of inner attribution.[43]

Critical Reflections. Again, now with regard to the analogy of inner attribution, Pannenberg can serve as a convenient point of reference and representative of those who do not accept the viability of Aquinas's theory of intrinsic attribution. As Pannenberg did in regard to the analogy of proper proportionality, so here concerning the analogy of inner attribution he argues that, from the perspective of Aquinas's modified Neoplatonic causal schema, to proceed in knowledge from known to unknown necessarily presupposes some element of identity between the two.[44] He claims that this would be all the more true if there were the presupposition of an ontologically prior movement from the unknown grounding the knowability of the known. For Pannenberg, there must be some identical *logos* between effect and cause if one is to be able to know the cause from its effect. This holds true, he would claim, for the entire Platonic tradition, and all the more so when that tradition is coupled with an Aristotelian abstractive theory of knowledge as opposed to remaining simply with a Platonic illuminationist epistemological theory.

Perhaps it would be helpful to make more precise Pannenberg's insistence on the necessity of such an univocal element by recalling again that Aquinas[45] has, in connection with this Aristotelian abstraction theory of knowledge, elaborated a complex interrelationship among name of the thing or perfection signified and *ratio* or intellectual conception of the thing or perfection signified. For Aquinas the name or external word signifies first the mental concept and through the mental concept the thing or perfection signified. Thus he is able to move back and forth between ontological and epistemological. There is, he would admit, one name used in predicating a perfection of God and of creature. But the question of univocal, equivocal or analogical predication arises only in terms of whether and how the concept or *ratio* is common to God and creature. In univocal predication the concept is exactly (*omnino*) the same. In equivocal predication the concept is totally (*omnino*) different. In analogical predication the concept, for example, the concept of the perfection "wisdom," is held by Aquinas to be different in its doubled predication, on the one hand, of God, since in God the perfection is identified with the simple divine essence, and, on the other hand, of the creature, since wisdom is not identified with the creaturely essence but only qualifies it. He claims that this difference in the divine and creaturely ways of existing enters into the *ratio* in such a way that there is no *ratio* or conceptually expressible element common to Creator and creature but only a similarity. However, helpful as this whole series of distinctions may be, for Pannenberg as far as I can see it has merely shifted and further focused the level on which the question of similarity and of identical or univocal element is to be raised. For Pannenberg, Aquinas's implicit distinction of *whatness* from way of existing and subsequent integration of the two in the *ratio* involved would either still leave an identifiable univocal element on the level of the distinguishable *whatness*, or there would result equivocation.

There have been several attempts to protect Aquinas's analogy of attribution from a reduction to univocity. For instance, some have spoken of an analogous causality.[46] One could argue, however, that this would seem to be stating the obvious and appear merely to be shifting somewhat the way in which Pannenberg's critique, or other critiques similar to his, would have to be made. The question of Aquinas's concern, and our own, with predicated, identifiable and intellectually expressible perfections would seem to remain.[47]

A much more significant attempt to protect the theoretical explanation Aquinas developed concerning analogy of attribution from the accusation of a final univocity appeals to and revolves around the strong negative element in his theology.[48] More specifically, this attempt is often characterized by a stress on the fact that the fundament for any attribution in Aquinas's cause-based analogy is the first result of any divine creational causation's being the very "to be" or *esse* of the effect.[49] Thus the critique of an identical *logos* is not supposed really to touch Aquinas's position. A first response to this defense would amount to pointing out that it does not adequately take into account Aquinas's own intentions and the context of his discussions of analogy. Though the first effect of divine causation is indeed existence, Aquinas is, in his explanations of analogy, truly concerned with how to refer specific perfections such as "wisdom" or "knowledge" to God essentially.[50]

However, now in going beyond this first response, we need to point out that this approach, which stresses more the negative[51] in Aquinas's theology,

often tries to avoid the admittance of an univocal element in Aquinas's analogy of attribution by asserting that the affirmation of existence is the result
not of concept-forming intellection but of judgement, and that often as a
judgement in the form of intellectual intuition.[52]

So a further triple response to this general appeal to the negative in Aquinas's theology would need to be made by referring to ways in which an appeal
is made to judgement. Such a response might take the following form. First,
this appeal to judgement has, despite an insistence on existence, as such in
effect at least implicitly amounted to unacceptably bracketing out, from the
immediate analysis, a consideration of Aquinas's Neoplatonically structured
order of causality. This appeal to judgement has, then, tried in its analysis of
the analogy of attribution effectively to concentrate solely on the order of
knowing.[53] Second, in view of this at least implicitly restricted concentration
on the order of knowing, there tends to arise an interpretation of analogy
such that one speaks of God as being referred to, for example, apparently not
as good in God self, but as lying in the direction or perspective opened by the
finite concept of goodness.[54] As has been mentioned in the initial response
above, such "analogous" predication does not seem to take adequately into
consideration or fully express Aquinas's insistence on an essential predication
in regard to God. Thirdly, within this order of knowing, it is important to
distinguish between the act of judgement involved in the affirmation of the
existence of a finite entity known on the basis of "abstraction" from sense
immediacy and the judgement involved in the affirmation of the existence of
God, a considerably more complex affirmation arrived at by reasoning in
demonstration.[55] To speak of a dynamic intellectual intuitional judgement
affirming God's existence would, without significant further distinction, seem
to amount to confusing these two distinguishable forms of judgement.

Aquinas himself speaks of judgement as that reflexive intellectual activity
establishing truth as the conformity of thing known to the form which the
intellect apprehends of the thing known. This judgement establishing truth is
a bringing together and a dividing[56] which, in regard to finite entities, has
available an immediate perceivable referent whereas, in demonstration that
"God is," there is the linkage of subject and predicate as the result of a process
of reasoning.[57] Such a distinction of referent or object calls for a distinction

of act or of type of judging. The specific judgement that affirms the existence of God is further conditioned by the more complex process of reasoning leading to the affirmation, by the affirmation made ("God is"),[58] and by the character of the referent itself. It would seem that such a reasoned and apparently analogous judgement, which completes the demonstration that God is, either remains only with the truth claim of that specific statement, and is therefore not of help in regard to analogous predication, or goes on to assert specific predications of God. In this latter case, it then again becomes subject to the challenge of a possible reduction to univocity.

Aquinas could accept an univocal element neither on the level of concept, nor of causality, nor again of judgement. Apparently he feared such would, in an unacceptable sense, divinize the creature. From another perspective, one could also say that it would place God within the reach of the creature. He claimed to have been able to avoid the need for such an univocal element in his explanation of the analogy of intrinsic attribution. In his specific argumentation, he justified this claim by referring to what was, for his system, the essential and radical distinction between uncaused and caused being. To preserve the transcendence of God, Aquinas had to stress the simplicity, i.e., the otherness and non-composite character of divine being or existence. Yet to speak of God he had to underscore the creature's causal dependence as participated being. The more an appeal was made to the simplicity of the divine essence (*esse subsistens*) as the final reason for not acknowledging an univocal element, whether that univocal element be located in terms of being or of specific perfections, the less could the divine essence be referred to in terms either of being or of specific, essential perfections. Given the cause-effect basis for Aquinas's analogy, it would seem to many that Aquinas would be obliged either to acknowledge an univocal element regarding specific perfections or, as Pannenberg[59] has proposed to conclude at least regarding existence between God and creature, in effect to eliminate the grounding for any such cause-based dependence. For Pannenberg and for others fearful of the presence of an unacceptable univocal element underlying Aquinas's theory of analogy of inner attribution, that theory, with its denial of an univocal element, would in effect then finally be left, one might dare say, "hanging in the air."

Further Remarks

In closing these presentations of, and critical reflections on, Aquinas's theories of the analogy of proper proportionality and of the analogy of inner attribution, we should note that in both of these forms of analogy the prime analogate is God, though less explicitly and directly so stated regarding the analogy of proper proportionality. In the case of either of these two forms of analogy, terms used to describe creaturely perfections are affirmed of God not in the way they are realized in the creature but in a higher, more eminent and, indeed, perfect realization. God is source and cause of all creaturely perfections.[60] That which underlies Aquinas's varying formulations of what he considers viable analogical divine predication is his own interpretation of the Old Testament notion of the dependence of creature upon Creator in terms of effect and cause. It is a dependence interpreted by Aquinas most fundamentally as creation and preservation in existence,[61] a creation and preservation expressed as participation rooted in causality.[62] Though Aquinas spoke of analogy primarily in regards to the logic of predication, whether that analogy be one of proper proportionality or of intrinsic attribution it remained for him fundamentally a cause-based analogy of being. The order of being or the ontological was the necessary ground for the order of knowing or the noetic and the linguistic. By the writing of the *Summa Theologiae*, cause-based analogy was for Aquinas explicitly a middle way between unacceptable univocal and equivocal ways of speaking of God. It produced no "meaning" or concept or *ratio* common to creature and Creator.[63]

Aquinas's Lasting Contributions

Aquinas's analyses of the ways in which we may responsibly speak of God surely constitute one of, if not the, most important treatments of the subject by a Christian thinker. Aquinas elaborated his explanation of how we so speak of God in line with, and on the basis of, his own extremely creative theological and philosophical synthesis. In working out his explanation, he drew upon a rich variety of sources, including the history of overall human, and more specifically Christian, speaking about God, the Scriptures, previous theological reflection and Platonic and Neoplatonic as well as Aristotelian philosophies. Examining his theories of analogy has involved touching in one way, or another, on many fundamental aspects of his thought.

Highlighting several aspects of the contribution Aquinas made to the discussion on analogical divine predication will help us appreciate his lasting importance in the history of the effort to explain how we can speak responsibly of God.

First of all, then, Aquinas has laid out the framework for any viable theory of analogical divine predication. Such a theory must respect the very otherness of God, the difference between the infinite and the finite. The use of the same term to refer to God and to us must not be carried out either in any simply univocal or equivocal way.

Second, his wrestling especially with the analogy of proportionality has revealed the essential role that the affirmation of distinction must play in any attempt at divine predication. His focusing on a distinction of reason in God was surely the minimum necessary to ground speaking of the divine. The result of affirming no distinction at all in the divine would seem to be the falling away of all predication, as would be witnessed to, for example, in the case of the non-dualist understanding of the ultimate self in several strands of Hindu thought. Distinction in the divine, and I will say later on real distinction in the divine, will constitute a necessary element in any attempt to reconstruct a theory of divine analogical predication and, more specifically, of course in any attempt to speak responsibly of the trinitarian God in the public realm.

The third aspect of the overall contribution made by Aquinas comes to light in the course especially of his presentation of his theory of the analogy of inner attribution. Here his insistence on a specific form of attribution, that of an ordered relation of one to another, has provided a general framework[64] in which one can avoid subordinating God and creature to a third, or some principle, over against the two. However, the mere discussion of an ordered relation of one to another, which he sees as beginning in God in the order of being but in us in the order of knowing, opens the way to an attempt at an explanation of analogical divine predication that goes beyond this distinction between orders of being and of knowing. Raising this question of an ordered relationship also, and most importantly, allows us to ask if there are not other alternatives to rooting the relationship between the two here in question, namely the infinite and the finite, in causality. Such alternatives might prove less problematic and better suited to contemporary reflection. Not only does the idea of a causally based relationship between infinite and finite seem to draw accusations of an underlying univocal element between the infinite and the finite, but the very question of causality has, at least in its classic Platonic and Aristotelian formulations, become quite problematic. This is especially true with regard to a more straightforward understanding of efficient causality.[65] Furthermore, to avoid reducing the infinite to another finite over against the finite, Aquinas stressed that the effect did not enjoy any finally independent being of its own, but participated, as finite, in the being of the infinite. Aquinas's stress on participation reminds us that any theory elaborating a relationship between infinite and finite must assure that the infinite is not reduced to another finite over against the finite.

When all is said and done, we must admit what Aquinas has correctly noted, namely, that humans in general and Christians in particular do speak about God. Given this fact, he wished to explain, in a modest yet ingenious and creative way, how this is possible. He wanted to sketch out an explanation of how we can really speak about God and say something that actually expresses both the conviction that God is and, indeed, what are God's perfections.[66] His efforts have met with great admiration, yet mixed reviews. Generally speaking, due to their different overall attitudes and orientations, on the one hand Roman Catholic thinkers have been more appreciative of Aquinas's theories of essential analogical divine predication. On the other hand, Protestant thinkers have tended to challenge those theories and their viability. In this chapter I myself have so far tried to indicate my profound appreciation for Aquinas's efforts to work out a viable theory of analogical divine predication while noting the serious challenges proposed to such a theory by various thinkers, especially Protestants, who have been represented here, in exemplary fashion, especially by Wolfhart Pannenberg.

I suspect that Aquinas could learn to live with various theories of analogical divine predication to the extent that they explain how we can speak responsibly about God, namely, how we are able to affirm in the public realm that God is and how we can legitimately predicate various perfections of God while maintaining the distinction between infinite and finite. We now need to go with Aquinas beyond Aquinas as we take another look at analogical divine predication within the context of our own concerns for a post-Hegelian philosophical theology that will take more directly into consideration both Roman Catholic and Protestant interests. As well, but perhaps more indirectly, we need to be sensitive to the directions taken by Eastern Christian thinkers who tend to stress more the apophatic nature of God while, ironically, speaking constantly and in great detail about God.

With Aquinas Beyond Aquinas

Setting the Stage

Aquinas's own magnificent efforts to propose a viable theoretical explanation of analogical divine predication stand as a permanent challenge to us today to find ways to continue his project of trying to explain how we can speak responsibly of God, and, more particularly, of the triune God. Indeed, with regard to the development of such a theory, Aquinas has left us a legacy upon which we can build and that can be boiled down to two basic points, namely, his recognition of the importance of some form of distinction as characteristic, even constitutive, of both finite and infinite and the need to establish an appropriate, ordered relationship between them.

In the coming section of the present chapter, we will pick up again on and need to repeat a number of remarks made in Chapters Six and Seven above concerning the structured movement of experience. This forward moving recapitulative review, carried out now in light of our presentation on Aquinas, will serve as an essential step in our effort to work with him while going beyond him concerning distinction and ordered relationship. By way of initial remark and to put it rather bluntly, I propose, first, that we replace his working in terms of a dyadic distinction between essence and existence with our analysis of a tetradic distinction of elements constitutive of a movement of finite experience. Second, we will work with a dialectically argued dialogical relationship between finite and infinite, the philosophical form and prolongation, in various forms, of trinitarian experiences of God and, at a minimum, their affirmation, rather than with his interpretation of the relationship between finite and infinite conceived in terms of effect and cause.

A Dialectically Argued Dialogical Relationship

A comment made by one of Aquinas's critiques and cited earlier in the present chapter, namely, to the effect that Aquinas's cause-based theory of analogical divine predication would be left hanging in the air were no univocal element between finite and infinite, opens the way to a remark or two on the problematic underlying any systematic beginning with an ontologically prior infinite cause or even infinite in general. Such an infinite cause, as infinite, would never be directly accessible to consciousness, thought or speech in the public realm. It is always mediated. Philosophical insistences, dogmas, liturgical formulations, authoritative ecclesiastical statements or so-called private intuitions and experiences cannot serve as the reason for accepting an ontologically prior movement from infinite to finite as the basis for a systematic beginning with the infinite. They themselves always inevitably rest upon a prior interpreting movement from finite to infinite.[67] In the public realm it is not easy, and probably neither desirable nor necessary, to work with such a distinction between the orders of being and knowing, especially if one is working with the notion of experience as fundamental phenomenological and philosophical category. Given the finitude of consciousness, thought and speech, there would seem to be no alternative to beginning with the finite as ever-present, conditioned and conditioning, point of departure for making appropriate reference to an infinite God. Even Aquinas's admittedly most impressive demonstrations of the existence of God that, as demonstrations, move from finite to infinite would not, then, ground a subsequent, fully viable distinction of the orders of being and knowing capable of serving as a basis for a systematic beginning with the infinite. Among various considerations, such demonstrations are, I would say, inevitably conditioned by their dependence on a particular logic and must continually come to terms with that fact. Indeed, the underlying reason for many of the difficulties various thinkers have found with Aquinas's efforts to establish a viable theory of analogical divine predication would seem to lie in his trying to work with an ontologically prior movement from infinite to finite, a movement he expressed in terms of cause and effect. Working with the category and notion of experience will permit us to take as our epistemological and ontological point of departure the givenness of the relationship between self and other at the beginning of the tetradically structured finite movement of experience. Of course, in the finite self's more specific experience of an infinite God, this relationship between self and other is, as we have seen in the previous chapter, one between a finite self and a triadically structured divine other.

Returning, however, for the moment to a consideration of Aquinas, I would note that, despite the existence of disagreements with some of Aquinas's more basic positions and assumptions that emanate from various quarters, I myself still find that his efforts to elucidate analogy as proportionality and as attribution have, in addition to being convincing to many thinkers, yielded insights valid and valuable for those who would strike out in other directions. First of all, in this ordered relationship a beginning (in the order of knowing for Aquinas) must always be made not in the infinite but in and with the finite, without which there would be no need even to refer to a possible infinite. In fact, any proposed beginning in the infinite would inevitably always presuppose and be dependent upon a beginning in the finite. Second, the danger that the very denial of an unacceptable univocal element required of a cause- based relationship between finite and infinite would seem to leave Aquinas's analogy of intrinsic attribution, to use the previously cited more colorful phrase, "hanging in the air" and, in fact would seem to leave all cause-based analogy between finite and infinite ungrounded, indicates the need to explore some other way of grounding and elucidating the relationship between finite and infinite. Third, any transition from finite to infinite would have to be made on the basis of an analysis of real distinctions constitutive of finitude leading to an argument in favor of the affirmation of the existence of real distinctions in and constitutive of the infinite. Fourth, with the here proposed focus upon experience and the consequent relativisation, one could even say effective elimination, of the distinction between two orders there remains only one option: a transition from finite to infinite.

If the only option open after a critique of the theories of analogy that Aquinas worked out is a possible transition from finite to infinite, this transition will occur as a reintegration of his concerns for linguistic predication, ontological affirmation and conceptual formulation. Any such transition must then begin in and with the givenness of finitude. Aquinas himself had been concerned with explaining change in the sense that the finite was that which existed but could equally cease to exist. "To be" and essence were for him related as really distinct act and potency in the finite. When, however, concern now shifts from this explanation of change to the givenness of finitude as structured movement of experience, the analysis of its composite character shifts as well. The most immediately available, directly given expression of finitude is surely one's own reflexive thought.[68] In it there is encountered the sheer inability of thought to remain in its own givenness without further self-reflection. Self-reflexive thought is not like the water in a faucet that can normally be shut off at will or even, with some effort, frozen in mid-air. It is, however, but the most immediate witness to that into which one runs in any sphere of human life—whether studied in sociology, political science, theology, psychology, history, philosophy, the sciences and so forth. That fundamental given is the real but finite process of becoming as enriching growth and qualitative increment or, in principle as well, of impoverishing and qualitative decrease, with which we are less directly concerned here. Aquinas's fundamental explanation of finitude, based on an analysis of change, was dyadic. In comparison, our analysis of the givenness of finite becoming yields not a dyadic but a tetradic structure.

Toward the end of Chapter Six above, and again in Chapter Seven, we spoke of the structured movement of experience. We need to come back again at some length to those remarks, now from the specific perspective of our concern for the affirmation of real difference in both finite and infinite and for the dialogical relationship between them, a concern and interest that is grounded, from a philosophical perspective and in philosophical formulation, in a dialectical argument concerning the move from finite to infinite. This dialectically argued dialogical relationship will provide the basis for a viable theory of analogical divine predication that is rooted in the rich notion of experience and is not left "hanging in the air."

In Chapters Six and especially Seven, we had argued that any finite becoming's formal[69] structure, while starting from the given relationship between initial selfhood and otherness, must consist of the following four elements: initial selfhood; otherness; enriched selfhood or impoverished selfhood; recurrent otherness. Here, however, we will not be directly concerned with impoverished selfhood since we are in fact working with a notion of spirit as movement of enriching experience.

By way of longer recall, initial selfhood is a beginning[70] without which there would be no finite becoming. Otherness as co-constitutively negative and positive is, on the finite level and along with the creative decision on the part of the initial self, a primary source of newness or novelty. Enriched selfhood is that resultant qualitative "more" without which there could be no speaking of progression, enriching growth or qualitative increment and, in relation more specifically to religious experience, a sense of wholeness, integration, well-being and balance or oneness with the world around one. Recurrent otherness is that which renewedly stands over against and is related to resultant enriched selfhood and thus constitutes enriched selfhood as renewed initial selfhood. Renewedly initial selfhood is, again, that which is related to a co-constitutively positive and negative otherness. This finite becoming is the existent, on-going but formally speaking non-temporal dynamic development from initial selfhood and otherness in relationship giving rise to enriched selfhood ever-renewedly to be enriched, or of course impoverished, in its relationship with recurrent otherness.

Given our transition from Aquinas's system with its distinction of two orders, namely, of being and knowing, to a systematic beginning in and with the finite understood as moment or movement of experience, there is no longer a need to make such a distinction. Now, however, the finite as finite seems to exhibit a greater and more explicit internal tension. Not only is finite, real but limited becoming composite and characterized by contingency, but it bears a more clearly expressed negative tone, an essentially real but, to speak in a more logical way justified by the fact that we are presently *thinking* about finite experience, self-contradictory finite becoming. Its tetradic structure verifies that the otherness involved is never finally inclusively or totally related to selfhood and vice versa. The resultant relationship of initial selfhood and otherness, with the latter as de facto collapse into the multiplicity of others and as recurrent otherness, is a never exhaustively realized and ever renewedly one-sided relationship. Not only is this resultant enriched selfhood a self-contradiction in that its very realization is by definition its limit, but the entire process as finite becoming takes on the character of self-contradiction.

The crucial question concerning, more specifically, the self-contradictory character of enriched selfhood as result of finite becoming is the establishment of this enriched selfhood as constitutively both inclusive and one-sided. A first reading of the question might tempt one to say that the one-sidedness of renewedly initial selfhood is simply logically consequent upon its inclusiveness as enriched selfhood. However, though the terms "enriched selfhood" and "recurrent otherness" might in one sense lend themselves to this reading, a second look at enriched selfhood and recurrent otherness will show a much closer tie between the two.

Of present particular interest is the way in which enriched selfhood as inclusive of otherness stands in relation to recurrent otherness. Initial self-hood, is, on the finite level, enriched primarily through the respectful inclusion of otherness, an inclusion achieved, paradoxically, by a generous act of self-gift to otherness. That is the very definition of enriched selfhood without which there would be no becoming or growth, no sense of wholeness and integration. Indeed, as was just mentioned, true enrichment is the respectful inclusion of otherness through the paradox of the gift of the self to the other. Yet, equally, enriched selfhood is not the inclusion of otherness. It is not here a question of a logically subsequent incomplete inclusion of otherness but, by definition in finite becoming, a one-sidedness or incompleteness in the very moment of respectful inclusion. In finite becoming, enriched selfhood, as the result of its own dialectical development from initial selfhood in relationship with otherness, is itself renewedly initial selfhood and is not merely from different points of view to be considered inclusive as regards otherness and one-sided as regards recurrent otherness. In the finite moment or movement of experience, no matter how generous is the self's gift of itself to the other in love, the very moment of inclusion or enrichment is still the moment of exclusion as well since the limit identifying recurrent otherness is common to enriched selfhood. The limit defining otherness as that which is related to but not identified with initial selfhood is common to enriched selfhood, thus constituting enriched selfhood itself as renewedly initial selfhood. This limit or defining boundary is immanent to enriched selfhood itself so that enriched selfhood is self- contradictorily inclusive and one-sided in its very moment of enrichment. Whereas for Aquinas finitude was that which is but could not be or could cease to be, here finitude is and is not inclusive under the same aspect of limit, and at the same time. It is and is not inclusive. This has been indirectly indicated in our various analyses by reference to otherness's collapsing, when considered on its own, into a multiplicity of others and more directly by reference to the recurrence of otherness at the very moment of resultant enrichment.

Not only is enriched selfhood self-contradictorily inclusive and one-sided in its dialogically structured relationship with recurrent otherness, but finite becoming's tetradic formal structure as such involves self-contradiction. Initial selfhood in relationship with otherness giving rise to enriched selfhood that is equally initial selfhood in relationship with recurrent otherness constitutes a process itself involving such self-contradiction not only because the result is equally inclusion and non-inclusion, but because the process itself in its formal structure occurs equally as inclusion and non-inclusion. It is enrichment and yet at the same time and from the same perspective limitation. Tetradically structured finite becoming bears within it the doubled limit first verified in the definitional relationship between initial selfhood and otherness and then verified anew in the recurrence of otherness as that which is related to enriched selfhood. It is a process that equally establishes itself as real but limited becoming and as that which ought always to have become more and other than what it is. The tetradic formal structure of finite becoming thematizes what finite becoming is in itself, as we are considering it here, namely, that it is an enriching growth and qualitative increment or, of course, impoverishment and qualitative decrease. It tries to do this, however, as an in principle endless progression of recurrent relationships between selfhood and otherness. Despite this attempt, the doubled process of dialectically advancing self and other along parallel trajectories constituting their dialogical relationship taken as a whole is self-contradictorily equally inclusion and non-inclusion rather than the enriching inclusion of otherness as such. It is indeed characterized by this very tension of being self-contradictorily equally inclusion and non-inclusion rather than the enriching inclusion of otherness as such. In its very enrichment it remains one-sided. As this self-contradiction, tetradically structured finite becoming *qua* finite is restless, unstable, and one-sided as well as incomplete. Neither in its result nor in its process can it resolve its own contradiction or even ground its perduring self-contradictory character.

Neither the process of tetradically structured finite becoming as a whole nor any of its four constitutive elements can resolve the self-contradiction that finite becoming is. As enriching growth, finite becoming should, in principle, simply be triadically structured as initial selfhood in dialogical relationship with otherness giving rise to enriched selfhood. But it is not simply enrichment as such. Rather, a thoughtful analysis of tetradically structured finite becoming equally as enrichment and limitation, inclusion and non-inclusion, shows us what it should have been and yet is not. The phenomenological and philosophical analyses of it carried out in Chapter Seven above, and partially repeated here in our forward moving recapitulative review carried out from our present perspective of a concern to focus more on the dialectically argued dialogically structured relationship between finite and infinite, concomitantly give rise to a conception of becoming *qua* becoming in principle exhaustively envisioned as triadically structured inclusiveness: initial selfhood and other ness in relationship giving rise to enriched selfhood. Thus a careful thinking through of tetradically structured finite becoming leads to an awareness of the only possible integrating context within which its self-contradiction could be maintained and, in that sense, overcome. That context is a triadically struc- tured inclusive whole containing limit within it but not itself finitized by recurrent limit. Aquinas's understanding of the infinite as subsistent being, simple pure form characterized only by a distinction of reason between "to be" and essence is transformed in and through this shift in focus to a dialecti- cal analysis of finitude leading to the affirmation of an infinite becoming as triadically structured inclusive totality. Indeed, whereas Aquinas worked with a dyadic metaphysical structure and a revealed triadic divine structure, we here are working with a phenomenologically analyzed tetradically structured finite movement of experience and a triadically structured infinite movement of divine experience that can be argued to in a demonstration which takes on the form of second experience.

When it is subject to further analysis, the tetradic structure of finite be- coming not only indicates but, in reflecting in discursive philosophical lan- guage what the trinitarian experience of God reveals, then calls for and points beyond itself in dialectical fashion to that triadically structured inclusive whole wherein the tension of its own self-contradictory inclusion and non- inclusion finds respectful resolution. The crucial question concerning the respectful resolution of this self-contradiction constitutive of finite becoming is the resolution of recurrent limit rooted in the recurrence of otherness. Though otherness as such is not in any sense necessarily recurrent, in finite becoming it both is recurrent and collapses into a multiplicity of "others." In finite becoming this recurrent and ever-unstable otherness is a primary source of enrichment as well as a primary source or cause of limitation. Taken to- gether with the self-contradiction of enriched selfhood ever renewedly equally initial selfhood and with the equally inclusive and non-inclusive character of the process of finite becoming, this assertion that otherness in finite becoming is self-contradictorily a primary source on the finite level both of enrichment and limitation again verifies that tetradically structured finite becoming cannot be conceived of as an immanently self-grounding development. Of particular present concern, unstable and recurrent otherness, taken either in an abstract sense on its own or, more concretely, in relationship with initial selfhood, cannot on the level of real but finite becoming justify the "more" which is enriched selfhood. This it cannot finally do since it cannot even ground itself. Finite otherness, as that which is related to initial and enriched-renewedly initial selfhood, remains itself self-contradictory as source equally of enrichment and limitation.

Within the context of the tetradic formal structure of finite becoming, recurrent and multiple otherness remains ever, on the finite level, a primary but self-contradictory source both of enrichment and limitation.[71] Thinking this self-contradiction through leads inevitably to a consideration of the possibility of the resolution of this self-contradiction. Though it is tautological, it is nevertheless here significant and true to say that to remain with the self-contradictory is simply to maintain that contradiction unresolved, ungrounded and unexplained. We have already argued that there can be no resolution to this contradiction on the finite level, despite the fact that finite becoming's tetradic structure does indicate the direction in which a resolution of its self-contradiction lies and, when subject to further reflective review, leads by dialectical argument to the affirmation of the existence of a triadically structured context sustaining this self-contradictory tretadically structured movement of experience. Indeed, recurrent and multiple otherness, taken in the overall context of tetradically structured finite becoming, can be a source equally of enrichment and limitation only if otherness as such can be dialectically argued to in the context of a becoming in which it is neither recurrent nor multiple. Recurrent and multiple otherness functioning as source of enrichment and equally of limitation on the level of finite becoming, dialectically considered, requires an otherness that functions simply as source of enrichment. If otherness were to function on the finite level merely as source of limitation, there would be no need to argue to anything beyond itself. There would in fact be no becoming. However, for recurrent and multiple otherness to function in real but finite becoming understood as enrichment, it is necessary to recognize, on the basis of dialectical argumentation, an infinite becoming, namely, a becoming that includes and thereby grounds otherness *qua* otherness. This infinite becoming is the other to and of finite becoming, that other which provides the integrating context within which finite becoming can be respectfully maintained as real but self-contradictory enriching growth or qualitative increment.

Without an infinite becoming containing otherness *qua* otherness within it, there would be no final justification for speaking formally of otherness as that unified actuality which is related to a necessary beginning with initial selfhood. This infinite becoming is the totality respectfully inclusive of tetradically structured finite becoming. That is to say, this infinite includes finite becoming paradoxically by giving itself to that finite becoming. Were it not so inclusive, it would not be an infinite movement of becoming and could not be argued to as the necessary condition for the possibility of resolving the contradiction inherent in finite becoming. This contradiction has been verified in enriched selfhood's being equally anew initial selfhood, in the entire tetradically structured movement of finite becoming's being equally enrichment and limitation, and in recurrent and multiple otherness's being equally a source both of enrichment and limitation.

Infinite becoming is that becoming in which otherness *qua* otherness and without recurrence or collapse into multiplicity is fully, and yet respectfully, contained in the possibility of a truly enriched selfhood. The non-recurrent and non-multiple otherness indicated here is itself by definition respectfully inclusive of, but not destructive of, tetradically structured finite becoming. This inclusion occurs not by mere inosculation or by unification through juxtaposition or apposition. Rather, it occurs, from various perspectives, dialogically and dialectically in the sense that infinite becoming is a movement whose necessary beginning lies in initial selfhood in relationship with otherness *qua* otherness. In infinite becoming otherness is an actual unity that, as otherness respectfully inclusive of the multiplicity of "others," is dialogically related to initial selfhood. The dialectically developing resultant selfhood arising out of this actual dialogical relationship between self and other is an enriched selfhood, an infinite enrichment without recurrent limit since there is no recurrence of otherness. This infinite becoming is the dialectically argued to, dialogically functioning respectfully inclusive other of tetradically structured or finite becoming. As the respectful inclusion of otherness, it is indeed the realized structure of pluralism. This infinite becoming is the context or, dialectically speaking, inclusive other of tetradically structured or finite becoming. Finite becoming and infinite becoming are each, on their own level and in their own way, totality: the finite self- contradictorily so as totality and non-totality, and the infinite as that dialectically argued to but not conceptually fully grasped finite becoming's needed inclusive and integrating context. Infinite becoming is the context, namely, the other to self-contradictory finite enriching growth or qualitative increment, which ensures that the latter has an adequate framework allowing it to perdure in its real but equally immediately limited enrichment. Context as such does not crush and, to be this inclusive context, infinite becoming must necessarily be triadic in structure. Furthermore, to be respectfully inclusive, this triadically structured infinite must be a triple movement of self-gift to finitude, if of course there is finitude.

Analogical Divine Predication

Following upon our phenomenological analyses, first, of the movement of experience as such in Chapter Six above and, then, of the trinitarian experience of God, as well of course as our more critical and constructive phenomenological, philosophical and logical reflections on that experience of God in Chapter Seven, reflections that have been further developed here in Chapter Eight, we are now in a position to explain how one can speak responsibly of an infinite God in the public realm without reducing that God to another finite reality alongside of existent finitude and without inappropriately and falsely transforming finitude into the infinite.

Indeed, people do speak of an infinite God. They do it on the basis of an experience of God and a subsequent understanding of the relationship between finite and infinite that is variously dialogically structured and dialectically argued to. On the level of the initial or first experience of God, this relationship bears a clearly dialogical[72] structure, as is exemplified in the whole notion of prayer. On the level of a second experience, that is, first of all in a phenomenological look at, analysis of and reflection on this initial experience, this relationship develops, within the parallel movements of self and other, according to a dialectical[73] structure from one momentary totality to another. The developing relationship between self and other, in turn, is dialogically structured. Again on the level of a second experience, this varyingly dialogically structured and dialectically developing relationship takes the form of a philosophically and logically argued reflection on and, depending on the case, variously realized prolongation on the philosophical level of, what the Christian community and individuals together or separately have experienced and affirm concerning that experience.

More precisely, now, in this philosophically and logically argued reflection, the existence of the relationship between finitude and the infinite is argued to dialectically.[74] The initial moment, that which is given, is finitude. However, finitude cannot be thought through coherently, that is, in non-self-contradictory fashion and without self-contradiction, without reference to an inclusive infinite serving as finitude's wider, supportive context.

Thus, on the basis of this, from various perspectives, dialogical and dialectical relationship, the infinite becomes part of the definition of finitude or, more concretely, the finite that, in dialogical and dialectical ways, gives itself to the infinite. And, given finitude's existence, the infinite must contain finitude within it, that is, experience it dialogically so to speak in its self-gift to finitude, otherwise the infinite either "crushes" the finite or simply becomes one form of finitude over against another form of finitude. Finitude exists within the true infinite as respectfully included otherness. It is, then, that ongoing movement of ever-renewed enrichment (or impoverishment) that occurs within the wider, dialogically experienced and dialectically argued to, infinite context of enriching experience. In this ordered relationship, finitude remains the point of departure and the infinite that finitude's wider, inclusive context.

Finitude and the infinite are each characterized by real distinctions. Finitude is, by definition, the movement of initial selfhood and otherness in relationship resulting in enriched or impoverished selfhood equally renewedly initial selfhood and otherness in relationship. Finitude is tetradic in structure. That structure is characterized by three real distinctions, namely, those between initial selfhood and otherness, between initial selfhood/otherness and resultant selfhood, which is equally renewedly initial selfhood, and between this renewedly initial selfhood and renewed otherness. The infinite is, by definition, triadic in structure and is the movement of initial selfhood and otherness in relationship resulting in enriched selfhood. Its structure is characterized by two real distinctions, namely, those between initial selfhood and otherness and between initial selfhood/otherness and resultant selfhood. Though all of reality as movement of experience, but here more specifically human and divine experience, is characterized by a dynamic development of really distinct moments or elements, finitude and the infinite are not reducible one to the other, nor do they exhibit, in their concrete reality, any common element that is realized in a univocal way in each of them. There are no proportions as such established in finite and in infinite, which proportions could then be compared in a univocal way one to another. Human or finite and divine or infinite do manifest a similarity, namely, a likeness in certain aspects, of structured movement based neither on such parallel proportions nor on a distinction that is real in the finite but only on a distinction of reason in the infinite. Rather, predication is now grounded in real distinctions in both finite and infinite. The similarity of structured movement here argued to consists, for example, in a relationship between initial selfhood and otherness, the role of otherness as source of enrichment, and a resultant selfhood. There is indeed this similarity, but the structured movement occurs, in fact, in fundamentally different ways in finite and infinite. So without needing to affirm parallel proportions, we can now speak of a similarity of structured movement based on real distinctions in both finite and infinite. Whatever is predicated of the human or finite is predicated in a way fundamentally different from the way in which it is predicated of the divine or infinite.[75] In regard to the human or finite, predication is provisional, transitional, temporary and incomplete since the human or finite is as such itself, as tetradic movement, provisional, transitional, temporary and incomplete. In regard to the divine or infinite, predication is definitive, permanent and complete since the divine or infinite is as such itself, as triadic movement, definitive, permanent and complete.

Furthermore, working with real distinctions constitutive of finitude and the infinite allows us to understand better not only how one can responsibly speak of the triune God as a movement of infinite love but also of each of the three Persons in God. With this emphasis and focus on real distinctions in the divine and within the dialectically argued dialogically structured relationship between finitude and the infinite, it is easier to free oneself from a formerly predominant idea that, when a specific word or phrase is predicated of a specific divine Person, it is done only by "appropriation." Often theologians so stressed the unity of God that they insisted specific divine action, and hence predication, was attributable only to God as a whole. The Latin phrase commonly enough used was *ad extra omnes unum* ("outside, all as one"). Thus, we can now more easily explain how one can really speak directly of one or the other divine Person without needing to appeal to a theory of appropriation. Certain words and phrases can refer properly to one divine Person in particular without threatening the overall divine unity as an inclusive movement of enriching experience or love.[76]

As we have seen above, there arise major hesitations especially, but not necessarily only, from Protestant thinkers concerning a theory of analogical divine predication based in one or another form of causality, namely, that such a cause-based theory seemingly requires an univocal element predicated in an univocal way or it is, to use the colorful phrase, "left hanging in the air." It is less evident, however, that a theory of analogical divine predication rooted in a variously dialectically argued and dialogically structured relationship between finite and infinite, would require, or could be accused of presupposing, a univocal element univocally applied. Rather, I would argue, in a sense with Aquinas, that working with finitude and the infinite dialogically related on the basis of dialectical argument does not imply either what Aquinas calls a univocal characteristic or intellectual conception or *ratio* or what various Protestant thinkers have been greatly concerned about. This is so since the way of realization of such a characteristic is an essential aspect of the characteristic itself. Since we are speaking of specific, concrete realities, the approach here proposed does not require applying such a predicate, indicating a perfection, univocally as a condition for one being able to use the same word to speak of one and then of the other since the *ratio* is different due to the mode of realization. The way in which a characteristic is realized enters into its very definition. One could think, for example, of the notion of love. As used in the present study, love is understood essentially as "self-gift to the other." Evidently, there is no way that God's love for humankind and, in turn, its love for God can be considered as one, univocally applied and qualitatively equivalent predicate. There is similarity or likeness in certain aspects, but not in the full definition. In the case of God's love, there is a question of one, unique and total self-gift that is creative of the finite other receiving this divine self-gift. In the case of human love, there is a question of repeated, ever different and partial self-gift that only in a very attenuated sense could bring the other with which it is in relationship into existence. In each case, love means self-gift, but there is a qualitative difference between the two forms that such a self-gift takes. In this case, total self-gift and partial, or better, incomplete self-gift are surely qualitatively different and not merely quantitatively so. Thus, Christians speak legitimately of God's love for them and of their love for God or one another without reducing God's love to their love or inappropriately elevating their love to God's love and without reducing the infinite to some form of finite or trying to transform the finite into the infinite.

In fact, it should be no surprise to us that there would be no identical or univocal element in analogical divine predication, for to a certain extent at least there is no such univocal predication, in the strictest sense of the word, even within our admittedly somewhat more nominalist formulation of finitude, namely, ourselves and the world around us. In this somewhat more nominalist understanding, we stress a certain individuality. Consequently, in this understanding it is the very nature of a dialogically structured relationship to recognize the otherness of the other. So the predication of a quality to one member or element, namely, to the self, in an appropriate, dialogically structured relationship is necessarily different from the predication of that same characteristic or quality to another member or element, namely, the other, in that relationship. And yet the predication is valid in both cases. If there is, then, no simply univocal predication even between self and other in a finite or tetradically structured relationship between finite self and finite other, *a fortiori* there would be no such simply univocal predication between finite self and infinite other. In either case, that is, in a relationship between finite self and finite other or in a relationship between finite and infinite, if the application of a predicate to self and other would not in some way be different, by definition the relationship would be other than dialogical. For the application would not be respectful of the otherness of the other.

Perhaps we can elaborate somewhat more on this point. With regard to the very nature of a truly dialogically structured relationship, it is necessary to recognize and respect the otherness of the other. So the application or predication of a quality to a particular movement or to one specific moment[77] in that movement, within an appropriately dialectically developing and dialogically structured relationship, is necessarily different from the way in which the application or predication of that same characteristic or quality occurs in relationship to another moment in that movement. For, in a dialectically developing trajectory of self or other, each moment in that movement is, insofar as it is thought through in a philosophical and logical fashion, a non-temporal momentary totality. In regard more particularly to the dialectically argued relationship between finitude and the infinite as such, with "dialectical" here used in a somewhat different, but related, sense to the way in which it was just used, the former is self-contradictorily momentary totality and the latter is inclusive totality. The necessarily positive and negative character of finitude and the necessarily positive character of the infinite insure that what is predicated of finitude cannot be predicated in the same way of the infinite. Indeed, the positive characteristic of finitude makes it possible for us, in a transfer to the infinite, to recognize that one is truly speaking of the infinite. And the negative characteristic of finitude makes it impossible for us to make such a transfer without recognizing that one can never fully express the divine or the infinite in words or concepts.

The here presented theory of analogical divine predication, based in a specific understanding of the variously dialectically argued and dialogically structured relationship between finitude and the infinite and, ultimately, in the trinitarian experience of God, takes up and proposes to account for a number of philosophical interests as well as concerns on the part of various Christian communities who struggle to explain how they can speak legitimately of the triune God. For example, among their various concerns, Roman Catholics seek ardently to affirm the fact that what they say about God has a basis in the divine reality. Especially those in the more classical Protestant communities, in turn, focus heavily, though not exclusively, on their felt need to protect the transcendence of God from any effort to reduce the divine to the human. And Eastern Christians often stress the apophatic nature of our knowledge of God, all the while speaking profusely of God and of each of the divine Persons. Continuing to try to explain from a philosophical theology perspective how Christians can, in all their diversity, speak responsibly of God will surely remain an ongoing, important challenge, especially in an increasingly secular world where certain distinctions among Christians may not seem as crucial in such a secularized future as they may have been in the past. Though such distinctions may indeed seem less important, the issues and concerns these various Christian traditions raise remain important and need to be considered in any elaboration of a theory attempting to explain how one can speak responsibly of God in the public realm.

Concluding Observations

In the course of this chapter, we have reviewed two ways in which Aquinas proposed to explain how Christians, and perhaps humans in general, speak legitimately of God, namely, by analogy of proper proportionality and analogy of inner attribution. We then proposed another approach that attempted to learn from Aquinas's working with each of these approaches to and ways of explaining analogical divine predication while looking to some basis other than a form of causality and a distinction of reason in the divine to ground the relationship between finitude and the infinite, the human and the divine. Rather than rooting the relationship between the two in causality, even a theory of causality justified by reference to the biblical notion of creation, here we proposed to turn to, and base our theory in, what one might perhaps call an even more spiritual rootage, namely, the trinitarian experience of God and reflection on that experience.

As part of this reflection on the experience of God, we sketched a dialectical argument in favor of an infinite becoming as triadically structured totality respectfully inclusive of a tetradically structured real but self-contradictory enriching becoming. I would suggest that this approach serves as a way to clarify how one can speak responsibly of God and attribute to God various qualities in a more eminent and perfect way than they are attributed to finite reality without reducing God to that finite reality and without transforming the finite into the infinite. Furthermore, it constitutes an important step toward a renewed trinitarianism. It is an attempt to free philosophical theology from an ontologically prior transition from infinite to finite so that it might pursue a dialectically argued transition from finite to inclusive triadic infinite. This alternative to Aquinas's cause-based analogy, and incidentally also an alternative to Hegel's dialectically self-othering infinite thought, will hopefully prove more congenial to post-modern and, more widely speaking, contemporary consciousness.

The present proposal has been argued out of an intendedly appreciative though critical review of two theories of analogical divine predication that Aquinas presents. In this critical review we noted a significant accusation make by a good number of thinkers, namely, that his theories seem to require or at least build upon some form of univocal predication, which Aquinas of course tried constantly to avoid. Behind these philosophical and theological critiques of Aquinas there often stands a concern to avoid a compromise that those who make such critiques fear will be found lurking under any universalizing theory of analogy. They are convinced that any such generalizable theory, except, for instance, something like analogy as doxology proposed by Pannenberg,[78] compromises the uniqueness of particular saving acts of God in history. Though it would be too far afield presently to respond here to such concerns in detail beyond what has been said briefly above, we could note that what is here proposed may not be as far from "analogy as doxology" as one might think. Indeed, we could here note, first, that the saving acts of God in history must always be considered within a wider context of interpretation. Second, a sufficiently modified theory of analogical divine predication that starts from finitude and is rooted in dialectical argumentation reflecting the affirmation of an experience of God, and especially a doxological affirmation, should provide that experience or interpretative context within which such acts could be seen and recognized as divine. This experience as inclusive and interpretative context, as context having been given a certain ontological density, opens the way to an integration of universal and historical, as well as of subjective and objective. It could indeed be identifiable as revelation.

The theory here proposed, namely, a transition from finite to infinite, transforms cause-based analogy into a more unified approach to, and interpretation of, the question of how one can responsibly speak of the trinitarian God in the public realm. In working with a widely conceived notion of experience, we see that linguistic predication, ontological affirmation and conceptual formulation coalesce at least in principle into one overall dialectically argued dialogically structured movement from finite to infinite. Dialectical argumentation from finite becoming as real but self-contradictory totality to

an infinite becoming as triadically structured inclusive totality, the true infinite, replaces dependence of effect upon cause. This dialectically argued
transition allows for speaking of God as initial selfhood, otherness and enriched selfhood on the basis of a reflective analysis of finite tetradically structured becoming, but without positing either a conceptually expressible or a
judgement-based affirmation of an element simply common to finite and
infinite. Initial selfhood, otherness and enriched selfhood indicate as such not
a conceptually expressible triply realized divine essence, but functional positions to be acknowledged as constitutive of the divine if God is to be the One
who grounds and maintains as other a finite becoming that is itself self-contradictorily such becoming. These functional positionings are: initial selfhood;
otherness; resultant selfhood. Any human terms to be applied to the divine in
a more eminent, indeed perfect, way would be applied in view of their appli-
cability, not as appropriation but as real predication, to these functional positionings. As triadically related, these positionings simply do not exist in
finite becoming, though they can be concluded to by dialectical argumentation. On the basis of this dialectic, the terms or predicates used to indicate
functional positionings in the divine do remain finite. Yet in reflecting and
prolonging that which occurs in the experience of God in which they are
rooted or to which at least they refer, they truly reach the divine in argument
and say what it is while never fully grasping it in thought. That which links
finite and infinite is not a triadic realized in both, but an argumentation from
the tetradic to a needed triadic, the reality for which an argument can be
made by finite consciousness, thought and language but which is not reducible to any of these. For want of a better name, this approach to analogical
divine predication could be referred to as a dialectically argued analogy of
functional positioning.

Developing a refined understanding of analogical divine predication as
cause-based knowledge was the approach Aquinas took to explain how we
speak of God in a publicly responsible way. In the present proposal, his overall
emphasis on knowing and being has been refocused on experience in which
real distinctions are discerned in the finite, dialogically discovered in the
infinite through experience of God, and then dialectically argued to as being
constitutive of the infinite. The present integration of various aspects of the
thought of Aquinas and Hegel, including various considerations of dialectical

argument, dialogical relationship, real distinction and analogical predication, constitutes in fact an effort to recognize and come to terms with the richness of the wider notion of enriching experience or spirit. Taken together, and considered as essential elements in the affirmation of, and making of, the transition from tetradically structured finite movement of becoming to a triadically structured infinite becoming, these considerations give more adequate expression, than would any single approach, to the very structure and dynamic of the trinitarian experience of God. They help give expression to the affirmation of that experience, to an understanding of God as movement of inclusive divine subjectivity and to an understanding of how one can speak responsibly of the triune God in the public realm of discourse.

NOTES

1. In fact, an argument has already been presented in Chapter Seven above, as a second experience prolongation of a first experience of God or at least as a philosophical reconstruction of the Christian affirmation of an experience of God. In the present chapter, the same argument will need to be developed with a somewhat different focus in mind, namely, from the perspective of a concern to identify the basis or bases upon which analogical divine predication is possible and justifiable.

2. To some extent, we will take up these concerns more explicitly in the next chapter where we will treat of evil, freedom, and mystery.

3. In regard to Hegelian dialectic, this accusation of a final univocity is implicit in the thesis argued in Dale M. Schlitt, *Hegel's Trinitarian Claim. A Critical Reflection* (Leiden: Brill, 1984). Throughout the present study reference to Hegel and his critiques or commentators has often been made in a more general way, presupposing previous studies by myself on these topics. However, reference to specific texts in Aquinas and to his critiques will be made in a more explicit and detailed way since he has not been the subject of prior studies on my part.

4. Necessarily always exploratory in the sense that most of Aquinas's complex, wide-ranging thought, his biblically inspired critical reworking of Plato and Aristotle and his awareness of Jewish and Islamic religious and philosophical reflection come together in what is an exceedingly complex philosophical effort (ultimately in his case at the service of theology) at comprehension, namely, his various formulations of what analogy, and more specifically analogical divine predication, is and how it functions.

5. In speaking of "fundament," we should recall that as grace for Aquinas does not supplant nature but builds upon it, so too for him revelation does not replace but presumes, builds upon, corrects, adds the knowledge of specific truths to and yet thus is conditioned by the structures of human intellection. See the helpful interpretation by Per Erik Persson, *Sacra Doctrina: Reason and Revelation in Aquinas* (Oxford: Blackwell, 1970) esp. 227–297 with reference on p. 230 to Thomas Aquinas, *Summa Theologiae* I, q. 2, a. 2, ad 1 and *De Veritate* q. 14, a. 10, ad 9. The *Summa Theologiae* is hereafter abbreviated *S.Th.* and the *De Veritate* as *De Ver.* References to and citations from Aquinas's works are according to the Leonine text and follow the standard form identifying, for the *S.Th.*, "part" (I, I-II, etc.) and, for the *S.Th.* and the *De Ver.*, "question" (q.), "article" (a.), " location in the body of the article" (c.), and "particular response to the introductory objections" (ad 1, ad 2, etc.). The Latin Leonine text of the *S.Th.* with which I have, for convenience' sake, worked is Sancti Thomae Aquinatis, Doctoris Angelici Ordinis Praedicatorum, *Summa Theologiae*, cura Fratrum ejusdem Ordinis, 5 vols. (Matriti: Biblioteca de Autores Cristianos, 1961–1965, 3rd ed.). Translations of texts from the *S.Th.* are taken from *Summa theologiae* (Cambridge?, England: Blackfriars in conjunction with Eyre and Spottlswoode, 1964–1981). The Latin Leonine text of the *De Ver.* with which I have worked is found in Sancti Thomae de Aquino, *Opera Omnia*, iussu Leonis XIII P.M. edita, Tomus XXII, 3 vols, ed. Antoine Dondaine, *Questiones Disputatae de Veritate*, cura et studio fratrum praedicatorum (Romae: Ad Sanctae Sabinae, 1970–1976). Translations of texts from the *De Ver.* are taken from Thomas Aquinas, *Truth*, 3 vols., trans. Robert W. Mulligan, (Chicago: Henry Regnery, 1952–1954).

6. In the context of a discussion of the three types of knowing in the human mind, i.e., knowing temporal things, knowing oneself and knowing God, Thomas orders these three as successively more adequate representations of Trinity, and remarks concerning self-knowledge, "Sed in cognitione qua mens nostra cognoscit *seipsam*, est repraesentatio Trinitatis increatae secundum analogiam"/"But in the knowledge by which our mind knows itself there is a representation of the uncreated Trinity according to analogy." *De Ver.* q. 10, a. 7, c. See further in M. T.-L. Penido, *Le role de l'analogie en théologie dogmatique* (Paris: J. Vrin, 1931) 257–345, esp. 258–267, cited by Persson, *Sacra Doctrina* 152 n. 263.

    It is important to acknowledge a certain distinction with reference to analogy when one speaks of the divine essence which is the divine "to be," and to analogous speaking of Trinity. Speaking of the divine essence is in principle based in the mind's functioning in the light of natural reason and speaking of Trinity is in principle dependent for Aquinas on the revelation that there are three Persons in one God. Note for example *De Ver.* q. 10, a. 13, c. That these two usages of analogy are not to be totally distinguished from one another is rooted in Aquinas's position that person and essence are distinguished in the divine only by a distinction of reason. *S. Th.* I, q. 39, a. 1, c. In the present critical study we are concerned with the structure of analogical predication in Aquinas, and will thus concentrate on his explicit statements in conjunction with what I will describe ultimately as his theory of cause-based analogical divine predication.

7. My presentation of Aquinas on analogy has profited from remarks graciously offered by a number of anonymous readers of a previous version of this chapter.

8. For example, *S.Th.* I, q. 2, a. 2, c.

9. "Cum enim dicitur *Deus est bonus*, vel *sapiens*, non solum significatur quod ipse sit causa sapientiae vel bonitatis, sed quod haec in eo eminentius praeexistunt." *S.Th.* I, q. 13, a. 6, c. (English translation amended).

10. "Et sic, quidquid dicitur de Deo et creaturis, dicitur secundum quod est aliquis ordo creaturae ad Deum, ut ad principium et causam, in qua praeexistunt excellenter omnes rerum perfectiones." *S.Th.* I, q. 13, a. 5, c. (English translation amended).

11. It is possible to know that God is (*S. Th.* I, q. 2, a. 3) but not what God is (*S. Th.* I, q. 3, introduction).

12. On proportionality this is implied in: "Quidquid autem est in Deo, hoc est suum proprium esse; sicut enim essentia in eo est idem quod esse, ita scientia idem est quod scientem esse in eo."/"But whatever is in God is His own act of being; and just as His essence is the same as His act of being, so is His knowledge the same as His act of being a knower." *De Ver.* q. 2, a. 11, c. On intrinsic attribution, explicitly stated with reference to what is not said of God merely metaphorically, in *S. Th.* I, q. 13, a. 6, c: "Sed supra (a.2) ostensum est quod huiusmodi nomina non solum dicuntur de Deo causaliter, sed etiam essentialiter"/"But we have already shown that words of this sort are not only said of God causally, but also essentially" (English translation amended).

13. Elizabeth Ann Johnson, "Analogy/Doxology and Their Connection with Christology in the Thought of Wolfhart Pannenberg," Ph.D. dissertation, The Catholic University of America, 1981, 48.

    In addition to, and among, the many well-known expositions and interpretations of Aquinas's theory of analogy, the following have proven particularly helpful: Edward Schillebeeckx, "Het Niet-Begrippelik kenmoment in onze Godskennis volgens

S. Thomas," *Tidschrift voor philosophie*, 14 (1952) 411–453, republished in his *Openbaring en theologie* (Bilthover, H. Nelissen, 1966, 2nd ed.) 201–232, cited according to the English translation: *Revelation and Theology*, vol. 2 (London: Sheed and Ward, 1967) 155–206; Hampus Lyttkens, *The Analogy between God and the World. An Investigation of Its Background and Interpretation of Its Use by Thomas of Aquino* (Uppsala: Almquist, 1952); Wolfhart Ulrich Pannenberg, "Analogie und Offenbarung. Eine kritische Untersuchung der Geschichte des Analogiebegriffs in der Gotteserkenntnis," Habilitation Writing, Theologische Fakultät der Rupprecht-Karls Universität zu Heidelberg, 1955, 105–131; Laurencino Bruno Puntel, *Analogie und Geschichtlichkeit* (Freiburg: Herder, 1969) 175–302; William J. Hill, *Knowing the Unknown God* (New York: Philosophical Library, 1971) 1–29, 111–144, and the discussion in 163–217; Johnson, "Analogy/Doxology," 47–55; Elizabeth Ann Johnson, "The Right Way to Speak about God? Pannenberg on Analogy," *Theological Studies* 43 (1982) 673–692.

14. Pannenberg, "Analogie und Offenbarung" 113.
15. *De Ver*. q. 2, a. 3, ad 4; q. 2, a. 11, ad 4; q. 23, a. 7, ad 9.
16. Among Protestant authors, one might note, for example, Lyttkens, *Analogy between God and the World* 16 with 323; Pannenberg, "Analogie und Offenbarung" 21, 115, 118–120.
17. In a general way stated by Lyttkens, *Analogy between God and the World* 449–451, 464–465 and specifically noted by Pannenberg, "Analogie und Offenbarung" 116–117. See also the general discussion by the Roman Catholic author, Schillebeeckx, in *Revelation and Theology*, vol. 2, 189–192.
18. "Utrum Scientia aequivoce praedicetur de Deo et nobis" (English translation in text amended).
19. *De Ver*. q. 2, a. 11, ad 6. Pannenberg, "Analogie und Offenbarung" 129, points out that later on, in the discussion on inner attribution, Aquinas insists that the cause does become part of the definition of the effect. See *S. Th.* I, q. 13, a. 6, c.
20. As can be inferred from, "Quidquid autem est in Deo, hoc est suum proprium esse; sicut enim essentia in eo est idem quod esse, ita scientia idem est quod scientem esse in eo."/"But whatever is in God is His own act of being; and just as His essence is the same as His act of being, so is His knowledge the same as His act of being a knower." *De Ver*. q. 2, a. 11, c. See, further, in Aquinas's *De Ente et Essentia*, chs. 4 and 5, here referred to according to *"Le 'De Ente et Essentia' de S. Thomas d'Aquin. Texte etabli d'après les manuscrits parisiens. Introduction, Notes et Études historiques. Par M.-D. Roland-Gosselin, (Paris: J. Vrin, 1948) p. 34 line 30 to p. 35 line 2; p. 35 lines 16–19; p. 37 lines 13–16; and p. 38 line 12 to p. 39, line 3/St. Thomas Aquinas, *On Being and Essence*, trans. Armand Mauer (Toronto: The Pontifical Institute of Mediaeval Studies, 1965, 2nd ed.) 56, 57, 60, 61–62. Also, *S. Th.* I, q. 3, a. 3, c. and ad 1; I, q. 3, a. 4, c.
21. Schillebeeckx, *Revelation and Theology*, vol. 2, 192–193. It is of interest to note that Schillebeeckx had published this research on analogy in Aquinas already in 1952 (see n. 13 above).
22. The critical remarks in this paragraph are taken from "Analogie und Offenbarung" 117–122. For Pannenberg's most important other writings on analogy, see Johnson, "The Right Way to Speak about God" 673–674 n. 4. Prof. Johnson most kindly provided this writer with access to a copy of Pannenberg's habilitation writing.
23. "Analogie und Offenbarung" 121 n. 48.

24. *S. Th.* I, q. 39, a. 1, c. with *De Ver.* q. 10, a. 13, c.
25. E.g., more indirectly in *Le 'De Ente et Essentia'* ch. 4 p. 35 lines 19–25/*On Being and Essence* 57; *S. Th.* I, q. 3, a. 4, c. Apparently knowledge of God by analogous divine predication was the invention of the neoplatonists. See Lyttkens, *The Analogy between God and the World* 101–102.
26. *De Ver.* q. 2, a. 11, c. with *S. Th.* I, q. 3, a. 1. c.; I, q. 3, a. 2, c.; I, q. 3, a. 4, c. On the distinction between real relation and relation of reason, see *S. Th.* I, q. 28, a. 1, c.
27. At first glance, an appeal might be made to the distinction made by Aquinas between the orders of being and knowing, a distinction he later linked with analogy in the *Summa Theologiae*. However, claiming that the difficulties here indicated can be overcome by assigning the distinction of reason to the order of knowing and the real identity to the order of being is, first of all, an application Aquinas himself did not make. Second, such an application would in fact seem to do nothing to resolve the difficulties involved, since it would only in an apparent fashion provide the differing perspectives needed to resolve the dilemmas. So assigning the distinction of reason and the real identity to different orders would seem to be a misuse of that distinction, which functions for Aquinas to indicate on which level or order God and creature are indicated as primary referent. Third, such an application would imply a separation between the two orders that would result in rendering equivocal any divine predication it was used to explain.
28. "Gratia [praesupponit] naturam." See, e.g., *S.Th.* I, q. 2, a. 2, ad 1.
29. See n. 5 above.
30. Schillebeeckx, *Revelation and Theology* vol. 2, pp. 189 and 192; Lyttkens, *Analogy between God and the World* 304, 329, 475; Pannenberg, "Analogie und Offenbarung" 122.
31. *S. Th.* I, q. 13, a. 6, c.
32. "Utrum ea quae de Deo dicuntur et creaturis, univoce dicantur de ipsis?" (English translation in text amended).
33. "Ratio enim quam significat nomen, est conceptio intellectus de re significata per nomen"/"What we mean by a word is the concept we form of what the word signifies." *S.Th.* I, q. 13, a. 4, c. See also Puntel, *Analogie und Geschichtlichkeit* 291–293.
34. One might profitably see Pannenberg's remarks in "Analogie und Offenbarung" 126.
35. *De Ver.* q. 2, a. 11, ad 6.
36. *S.Th.* I, q. 13, a. 6, c.
37. On remarks made in this present paragraph, see Pannenberg, "Analogie und Offenbarung" 128–129.
38. By way of entry into the question of Thomistic causality theory, see: Cornelio Fabro, *Partecipazione e causalità secondo S. Tommaso d'Aquino* (Turin: Società editrice internazionale, 1960) 241–246; Persson, *Sacra Doctrina* 93–158, esp. 93–112.
39. E.g., *S. Th.* I, q. 5, a. 2, ad 1.
40. Pannenberg, "Analogie und Offenbarung" 131. Pannenberg discusses the *Summa Theologiae* presentation of the analogy of attribution especially on pp. 125–129.
41. *S. Th.* I, q. 13, a. 7, c.
42. *S.Th.* I, q. 3, a. 5, c.
43. Aquinas himself insists on grounding analogical predication in divine causality: "Et sic, quidquid dicitur de Deo et creaturis, dicitur secundum quod est aliquis ordo creaturae ad Deum, ut ad principium et causam, in qua praeexistunt excellenter

omnes rerum perfectiones"/"And so whatever is said both of God and of creatures is said in virtue of the order that creatures have to God as to their source and cause in which all the perfections of things preexist in a more excellent way." *S. Th.* I, q. 13, a. 5, c. See Lyttkens, *The Analogy between God and the World* e.g., 244, 301, 330–360, and Perssons, *Sacra Doctrina* 96 n. 14.

44. On this paragraph see Pannenberg, "Analogie und Offenbarung" 125–131, esp. 131, with his discussion of Neoplatonism on pp. 43–58.

45. See *S. Th.* I, q. 13, a. 4, c.; I, q. 13, a. 5, c.; I, q. 13, a. 6, c., with Puntel, *Analogie und Geschichtlichkeit* 291–293.

46. See Aquinas himself, e.g., *S. Th.* I, q. 13, a. 6, ad 1.

47. Note again, e.g., *S. Th.* I, q. 13, a. 5, c.

48. From early on in the *Summa Theologiae*, Aquinas insists one can only know that God is, not what God is. See, for example, *S. Th.* I, q. 1, a. 7, ad 1; I, q. 2, a. 1, c.; I, q. 2, a. 2, c. and ad 3; and so forth.

49. This position can be seen for example as represented and argued at length by William J. Hill, *Knowing the Unknown God* (New York: Philosophical Library, 1971) esp. 1–29, 111–144 with further discussion from 163 on.

50. Note for example *De Ver.* q. 2, a. 11, and *S. Th.* I, q. 13, a. 5, c. concerning perfections (*perfectio*) and *S. Th.* I, q. 13, a. 6, c. concerning names (*nomen*) such as good (*bonum*) and wise (*sapiens*).

51. Negative first of all in the sense of a negative theology and secondly, but rather more implicitly, concerning the more specific negation constituting the second moment in the structure of analogous predication, which structure is, in a fashion strikingly similar to certain forms of dialectical thinking, a triple movement of affirmation, negation and reaffirmation in a new way.

52. Arguably Hill's position is such. See n. 49 above. See also William J. Hill, *The Three-Personed God* (Washington, D.C.: The Catholic University of America Press, 1982) 248–249 and 259–260. Johnson presents this appeal to judgement as a possible response to Pannenberg's critique, in "Analogy/Doxology" 279–281; _____, "The Right Way to Speak about God" 690. In this last article, Johnson (p. 690) also lists further possible responses to Pannenberg: being as not properly conceptualizable; a transcendent interpretation of analogy not as a mean between univocity and equivocation but as "prior to and ground of the distinction between univocity and equivocity"; giving more attention to the role of negation in analogy.

53. Note as a possible example of this tendency, despite disclaimers and complex treatment, the explicit statement in Hill, *Knowing the Unknown God* 127–128 with 225 n. 39, and the distinction "3. Analogy as Participation" 131–136 and "4. Analogical Knowledge of God" 136–144.

54. See Hill, *Knowing the Unknown God* e.g., 142, 143, 183–184; _____, *The Three-Personed God* 249, 260.

55. On judgement in Aquinas, see e.g., J. Peghaire, *Intellectus et Ratio selon S. Thomas d'Aquin* (Paris: J. Vrin, 1936); Peter Hoenen, *Reality and Judgement according to St. Thomas* (Chicago: Henry Regnery Company, 1952), esp. 162–163; Robert W. Schmidt, *The Domain of Logic according to Saint Thomas Aquinas* (The Hague: Martinus Nijhoff, 1966), esp. 215–221; Benoît Garceau, O.M.I., *Judicium: vocabulaire, sources, doctrine de saint Thomas d'Aquin* (Montréal: Institut d'études médiévales, 1968), whose subtle and, in the Conclusion (251–255) in the best sense of the

words, "philosophically poetic" presentation of judgement in Aquinas as act and expression of human spontaneity in its tendency toward truth make most other presentations including the present brief remarks seem rather wooden; Hill, *Knowing the Unknown God*, 1–29, esp. 14–17. All with abundant references to Aquinas. I am particularly grateful to Prof. Robert Warner for initial reference to Schmidt, to Prof. Michael Vertin for various background references, and to Prof. Benoît Garceau for longer discussion.

56. On judgement, see briefly, *S. Th.* I, q. 16, a. 2, c. and further as indicated in the preceding note.
57. As occurs in *S. Th.* I, q. 2, a. 3 against the background of I, q. 2, a. 2.
58. According to Aquinas, one does not know God's act of being (*actus essendi*) but only the existence stated in the affirmation "God is" (*Deus est*). *S. Th.* I, q. 3, a. 4, ad 2.
59. Pannenberg, "Analogie und Offenbarung" 131.
60. *S. Th.* q. 13, a. 5, c. Note, however, that in *S. Th.* I, q. 13, a. 6, c., Aquinas recalls God is spoken of as good, for example, not only because God is the cause of goodness in creatures but because such a perfection preexists in God eminently.
61. *S. Th.* I, q. 8, a. 1, c. and ad 1.
62. On participation and causality in Aquinas, see the classic study by Fabro, *Partecipazione e causalità*, and especially the helpful critical discussion in L.-B. Geiger, *La participation dans la philosophie de S. Thomas d'Aquin*, 1953, 2nd ed.) 49–55. For a very succinct and helpful presentation, see Paul-Bernard Grenet, *Le thomisme* (Paris: Presses universitaires de France, 1953) 90–101 and esp. on participation 90–94. Prof. Jacques Croteau, O.M.I., kindly brought these references to my attention.
63. *S. Th.* I, q. 13, a. 5, c.
64. Not of course necessarily in terms of cause and effect.
65. Whitehead's revision and reworking of efficient causality in terms of what he called "causal efficacy" does, however, open the door to new ways to understand and "rehabilitate" the philosophical notion of efficient causality. See his discussions in *Process and Reality* (New York: Free Press, 1978).
66. As has been alluded to here and there in the present chapter, Aquinas seems to want to maintain that we can know God exists but not what God is. Yet, he also wants to explain how we can speak of real divine perfections.
67. For a fuller argument of this position with specific reference to Hegel's philosophy, see Schlitt, *Hegel's Trinitarian Claim*.
68. To some extent, then, this is an implicit reference to Descartes and his *cogito ergo sum* ("I think, therefore I am"), although the reflexive thought referred to in the text is not considered in relative isolation but as a more monosubjectively functioning form of the wider, and more inclusive notion of experience.
69. Formal in the sense of bracketing out such questions as the specific nature of the self, similarities and dissimilarities with various philosophical systems, the technical question of internal relations, and the question of the priority of individual and/or community. But not formal in the sense of abstracting from concrete finite becomings, whose very structure is indicated here. Note too this analysis is not to be understood in a merely psychologizing vein, but after the fashion of a phenomenology with its own ontological density, i.e., in the direction of a concrete metaphysics whose point of departure is finite becoming.
70. While of course recognizing that the relationship between initial self and otherness is *the* beginning.

71. Though the other can variously serve as source of enrichment or limitation, indeed impoverishment, as we have seen in Chapter Six above, here we are speaking of the formal role of otherness as, at the same time, source of enrichment and of limitation, indeed, possibly impoverishment as well.

72. "Dialogical" is being used here and elsewhere to refer to a relationship between self and other in which the two interact with one another rather than one going over into, appearing as, or developing into the other, as was the case in the dialectically structured relationships Hegel set up among succeeding thought categories in his elaboration of the movement of logical thought and among various phenomenological forms or figures in his *Phenomenology of Spirit* or, again, among various aspects of reality as thought through in his numerous lecture series.

73. "Dialectical" is used more specifically here to refer to the movements of self and of other in which, in and as each of these movements, the self and the other each move from one momentary totality to another. That is to say, in a movement of enriching experience or spirit, the self is, stated in abbreviated fashion, first of all a stance of faith, then, second, a stance of hope and, third, a stance of love, all three of which have been described in Chapter Six above. In this movement, the other is first of all a moment of appearance, then one of presence and, third, one of revelation, again as described in Chapter Six above. Here, then, I am using "dialectical" to cover or mean one major aspect of what Hegel had used the term to indicate. See further in the note immediately below.

74. "Dialectical" is used here to refer to the movement of thought that occurs when one attempts to think through a specific reality and finds that its self-contradictory character effectively forces one to arrive at and think of another reality the thinking through of which provides some form of resolution to the self-contradictory character of the previously thought reality. This usage of "dialectical" covers or expresses another major aspect of what Hegel had used the term to mean. See further in the note immediately above. Our shift from a more monosubjectively structured dialectical relationship between two realities to a more dialogically structured relationship between them makes it possible for us now to distinguish various aspects of Hegel's understanding of "dialectic" and to work with these various aspects in differing contexts and in a way somewhat different from that of Hegel.

75. It may be helpful to recall that Aquinas rightly noted we apply predicates bearing with them an inherent limitation to God only in a metaphorical way. Predicates that do not bear within them an inherent limitation can be applied to God analogously. *S.Th.* I, q. 13, a. 6, c.

The reason why the way in which a predicate indicating a perfection enters into the definition of the predicate is the fact that we are in each case of predication speaking of a specific, concrete reality with its proper mode of existence and becoming. One might, however, ask why one should not simply stay with Aquinas's theory of the analogy of inner attribution if one is willing to assert that the way in which a predicate indicating a perfection is realized in God or in a finite reality enters into the very definition of the *ratio* that is being predicated of God and a finite reality. The response would be that causality, as link between finite and infinite, has become quite problematic in contemporary philosophical discourse. Furthermore, working with real distinctions rather than with a distinction of reason provides a surer basis for predication, which of course requires determination and complexity. We might helpfully recall Hegel's classic remark that in the night all cows are black.

76. It might indeed be possible, at some point, to classify certain types of predicates responsibly applicable to an infinite God on the basis of the functioning of each of the divine Persons as, respectively, initial selfhood, otherness, and resultant selfhood. More widely speaking, we might be able to work out a theory of types of language more properly applicable to the other manifesting itself within or without, with the latter in turn considered as present, using the word in a wide sense, or in the future. On the complex question of speaking essentially of God and applying specific predicates to particular divine Persons, see, for example, *S.Th.* I, q. 39, a. 7.

77. It might be helpful to note that "moment" is used in at least two overall senses in the present essay. In the phrase, "moment and movement of experience," it gives expression to the overall event of experience taken as a whole, while "movement" refers to the dynamic and developmental character of that event. In the phrase used here, namely, "specific moment in that movement," it can refer either to an element such as self, other or resultant self in that movement or again to a momentary "stance" on the part of the self or a form of self-manifestation on the part of the other.

78. Pannenberg, "Analogie und Offenbarung" e.g., 51-53, 137-140; see Wolfhart Pannenberg, "Analogy and Doxology," in *Basic Questions in Theology*, vol. 1, trans. George H. Kehm (Philadelphia: Fortress Press, 1970) 212–238. Also, Johnson, "The Right Way to Speak about God?" 678–680.

9

EVIL, FREEDOM, MYSTERY

In this last chapter I would like to return to a number of philosophical but especially religious criticisms of Hegel's philosophy and, more particularly, of his philosophical theology. In Chapter Three above, we noted that, from an explicitly philosophical perspective, critics of his overall philosophical system have put forward various difficulties and expressed a number of hesitations relating more directly to the underlying concept of spirit with which he works.

Among these difficulties, here we can note two. First of all, some critics were not convinced that Hegel could justify the systematic beginning of his philosophy, and thus of the movement of spirit as he conceived it, in a moment of being when that moment is understood as the totally indeterminate beginning of, and equally first moment in, a dialectically developing movement of pure, conceptual thought. I have tried to learn from that criticism and have myself attempted to develop it further elsewhere.[1] Following upon that criticism, I have now proposed in the present study that the true point of departure for philosophical reflection is not pure being but, rather, the initial givenness of selfhood and otherness in relationship that constitutes the beginning of a moment and movement, indeed a dynamic event, of experience. A second critique centered around Hegel's identification of otherness with negation so that for Hegel otherness became essentially the second moment in the movement of dialectical thought and, as such, was defined at least initially as the negation of the dialectically prior, positive moment of affirmation. In contrast to this identification of otherness with negation, for my part I have insisted that in a movement of experience otherness is initially co-constitutively positive and negative. From the beginning otherness is both potential source of enrichment and at the same time not selfhood. To identify otherness, even only initially, with a phenomenological appearance as negation was a brilliant move on Hegel's part, but remains reductionist and does not give otherness its "due."

In addition to these more philosophical critiques of Hegel's thought, various philosophers but especially thinkers in more religious circles have concluded that his interpretations of what members of religious communities have experienced do not adequately reflect, or *a fortiori* express, what they have come to discover in their religious traditions and in their communal, shared and individual lives. So, in the present chapter I would like to make, at slightly greater length, three proposals that take into consideration three such critiques, emanating often enough from more religious circles, of Hegel's thought and especially his philosophical theology. These critiques concern Hegel's understanding and interpretation of evil, freedom, and mystery. According to these critiques, establishing evil as necessary second moment in an overall dialectical movement of thought in fact relativizes evil and does not do justice to either its obstinate and perduring reality or to its finally irrational character. Redefining freedom ultimately as the necessary movement of logically structured thought and as that thought's necessary self-othering into reality does not seem to allow sufficient "space" within which the potential for alternative realization,[2] so basic to the notion of freedom, can be given its due. And understanding mystery as the transparent movement of pure conceptual thought does not seem to capture adequately the essence of what humans wish to express when they speak of mystery that gives rise to wonder.

Indeed, speaking of thought, over the centuries philosophers have generally felt the urge to elaborate, and been more comfortable with the idea of working out, a system of thought or at least a systematic and coherent presentation of their own thought. Going a step further, Hegel recognized that this tendency toward system and coherence was indeed innate to and characteristic of thought as such, and chose to base his philosophical system on it.[3] Whether this tendency be rooted more directly in the nature of thought or in a wider human urge toward systematization, embracing it has borne much fruit and provided some of the greatest reasoned insights to which we as humans have collectively and individually managed to give expression. Consequently, however, with a few notable exceptions such as, for example, Søren Kierkegaard, major philosophers have often enough manifested a certain tendency to respect, or perhaps better to emphasize, somewhat less the concrete and the individual,[4] with the result that their immense efforts at system and coherence tend to lead them to stress less the obstinate and perduring character of individual realities as such and evil actions and situations in particular. In contradistinction to some of these approaches, I would propose that our working with the basic notion and reality of experience will provide us with the means both to work toward a certain systematization or at least wider contextualization of and, at the same time, to maintain a central focus on concrete realities such as evil and on the even more elusive but still very concrete realities of freedom and mystery.

My remarks on these three, namely, on evil, freedom, and mystery will, in a sense, at least indirectly take the form of an ethical reflection, that is, reflection concerned in a very general way with right thinking leading to right action. Given the understanding of experience and, at least ideally, of spirit as movement of enriching experience as relationship between selfhood and otherness giving rise to enriched selfhood[5] with which we are working, we avoid facing the question of the ethical.

Ethics has of course been conceived in many ways and today takes on a variety of shapes as theological ethics, philosophical ethics and, more recently, multidisciplinary, interdisciplinary and transdisciplinary ethics.[6] In these last three ways of carrying out ethical reflection, specialists in various areas of study take up and consider, respectively, from their specific perspectives, from a series of perspectives, or from a more holistic overview the just mentioned questions of right thinking leading to appropriate and, especially in a social context, fair and just action. Unfortunately, however, often especially multidisciplinary and interdisciplinary ethics turn out to be reductive in that they can devolve into a sort of deontology in which one is content merely to decide whether specific activities or approaches respect appropriate rules of professional ethics.

In their more elevated and elevating forms, however, especially theological and philosophical ethics but also more carefully constructed forms of multidisciplinary, interdisciplinary and transdisciplinary ethics tend to develop as areas of somewhat more practical reflection that have as their purpose the accomplishment of one or more of four specific objectives. The first of these objectives is to obtain further insight into what we mean by the ethical as such. It is toward this objective that fundamental theological, philosophical, or multidisciplinary, interdisciplinary and transdisciplinary ethics tend to work. The second is to provide for the intellectual and virtuous, in a word, integral formation of a person or a group capable of and ready "to bring to the fore the ethical dimension and concerns at least implicitly present in a more specific concrete situation."[7] The third is to work toward the development of a capacity for right reflection and just decision-making in more specific areas of human activity. The fourth is to arrive at concrete guidelines to help people make appropriate decisions in particular situations. It is especially on these last objectives that more concrete forms of ethics, less felicitously called applied ethics or, perhaps better, sectoral ethics, tend to focus.

In the following remarks on evil, freedom, and mystery, I would like to work toward achieving all four of these objectives by making a modest contribution to ethical reflection in its various forms, more directly to philosophical ethics given the nature of the present study as one in philosophical theology, and more indirectly to theological, multidisciplinary, interdisciplinary and transdisciplinary ethics. In each of these forms of ethical reflection, philosophers, theologians and other specialists have variously been concerned with right thinking and appropriate, fair and just doing. Some have pushed the consideration of ethics further to include reference to feeling and even to being. I would propose that working now with a notion of experience, which as a reality is ever concrete, will permit us to include all of these foci, namely, being and feeling, thinking and doing in a wider notion of ethics that will at the same time allow for a consideration of the specific and the concrete as well as the more systematic and generalized without inappropriately subordinating the more specific to the more systematic. While having implications for more concrete ethical reflection, then, the following remarks will move in the overall direction of a fundamental philosophical ethics rooted in the dialectically developing movements of self and other as these latter relate dialogically in an overall dynamically developing moment of experience.

Evil

For millennia now there has been an ongoing, somewhat more theoretical, discussion concerning the nature of evil considered in itself, namely, precisely as evil. Various thinkers, and even whole philosophical and religious traditions, have ultimately denied the reality of evil. For some of them evil, including especially suffering, is an illusion to be overcome. For others evil is simply the absence of good. Others, again, have taken a somewhat more Manichaean position in asserting not only that evil is real but that it stands in its own right over against and in opposition to good. Among those who embrace one or the other of these approaches, some have made further distinctions in order better to situate and explain their understanding of evil. Aquinas, for example, maintains that evil and good are contraries. However, in the carefully nuanced first article of his "disputed question" on evil, entitled "Is Evil an Entity,"[8] he first distinguishes between two ways of speaking of evil, namely, with reference to the subject or agent that is evil and with regard to evil in itself. More specifically regarding this latter, namely, evil as such, he argues, on the basis of an understanding of creation as an act of efficient causality bringing something particular into existence, that good exists and evil, as its contrary, is the privation of a particular good. After further argument, Aquinas concludes: "And so I say that evil is not an entity, but the subject that evil befalls is, since evil is only the privation of a particular good."[9]

This somewhat more, in effect, abstract distinction between subject or occurrence and evil as such serves Aquinas well in his efforts to avoid, within the context of his stress on efficient causality, affirming that God is the creator of evil. However, such a distinction also easily gives the impression that it does not, insofar as it results in a more abstract definition of evil considered in itself, recognize sufficiently the givenness of real evil. Indeed, several decades ago, a German theologian, Traugott Koch, with great nuance argued that evil is, to paraphrase his thought, that which is but should not be rather than that which is not but should be.[10]

Within his own context and in light of his concerns, Aquinas's understanding of evil as privation seems appropriate. However, for those who have lived through much of the quite violent twentieth century, considering evil as that which is but should not be seems to focus our attention better and more directly on the evil act or occurrence and resulting situation, and so to express more accurately what we have experienced over the course of the twentieth century and, regrettably, given the reality of terrorist acts, what we continue to experience well into the present century. Considering evil in this way, namely, as that which is but should not be, helps us recognize evil and speak of it in a manner that reflects more clearly and adequately the way in which we have experienced it. It directs our attention more specifically to the concrete movements of experience that we are, in which we encounter evil in its many forms and come up against its obdurate character, whether in ourselves, in others or in a given situation.

It may well be that more abstract definitions of evil will always fall short of the terrible reality of evil that conditions all we are and so much of what we do. Perhaps rather than continuing efforts to elaborate such definitions, the best we can aim for at the present time is finding a way to put our experience of evil in some sort of framework or overall context that will allow us, to some extent at least, to come to terms with its reality without trying to "tame" it. For trying to "tame" it is in effect an effort to deny its ultimately unexplainable, even savage, reality, mixed in as well as it usually is with undeniable experiences of goodness and enrichment.

Now, as we come in the present chapter toward the end of our overall study in philosophical theology, we have at our disposal a proposal to understand finite experience as a movement of dialogically related selfhood and otherness each dialectically developing along trajectories of enrichment or impoverishment that then give rise to resultant selfhood ever renewedly dialogically related with otherness. It is this understanding that provides us with an initial framework permitting us in a provisional way to come to grips with evil, for it will help us to "situate" evil in its various forms without, however, trying to "tame" it or giving the impression of ultimately denying its reality.

We can recall more specifically that an experience is a movement of spirit insofar as it is a movement resulting in an enriched communal, shared or individual self, namely, one characterized by qualitative increment that occurs, paradoxically, through self-gift to the other. It is a moment and movement of generosity. However, there are ever so many other experiences that are, in various ways and for so many reasons, not movements of spirit. They result in an impoverished self, namely, one characterized by qualitative decrease. It is to these impoverishing experiences that we refer as we try to some extent at least to explain evil and, more indirectly, then propose ways to cope with it.

In the phenomenology of experience presented in Chapter Six above, we started from the givenness of self and other in relationship, but gave a certain at least implicit priority to the self within that relationship. Evil as such, however, so often at least in first instance appears to us as something happening to us or to someone else and imposed on us or them, even if in fact we have at times brought it upon ourselves or caused it in others. In an effort to reflect this situation and our sensitivity toward evil as something "imposed," we will here in this first part of our overall, broadly speaking, ethical reflections, focus on the other, then on the self and, third, on the resultant finite self ever renewedly in dialogical relationship with an other.

Other

Impoverishing Appearance. As we saw in Chapter Six above, in our phenomenological look at the movement of experience from the perspective of the other, that other manifests itself to the initial self along a dialectically developing trajectory of appearance, presence and absence, and revelation. In the case of an impoverishing movement of experience, ultimately an experience of impoverishment, from the perspective of the other the very appearance of the other can be the cause of such impoverishment. There may be a fundamental incompatibility between the other and the self to which it appears. In the universe we know and, on a much more local or terrestrial level, the organic world in which we live with its accompanying food chain, there necessarily occur certain basic incompatibilities in the internal functioning of an interrelated physical environment. Natural or physical disaster and the need for sustenance witness abundantly to such incompatibilities involving some form or other of impoverishment, including disappearance, in a given communal, shared or individual self. Quantitative decreases result in qualitative decrease, or even radical disappearance, on the part of a given initial self. Already here we can identify what is usually called physical evil, namely, that which afflicts us due to the given, material structure of our universe and whose negative effects can at least be mitigated by careful preparation and planning.[11]

There may, again, be a type of incompatibility between other and initial self caused by an other that is itself volitionally endowed and that in some way or other should be a potential source of enrichment for the self. However, rather than being that potential source of enrichment, that other intentionally falsifies, in a wide sense of the word, its appearance to the self. Such an other can appear to, call upon and invite, as well as make demands upon, the self in an inappropriate way that misleads, demeans or threatens the self to which it appears. Here, then, we have an initial case of what is usually called moral evil. The other, as itself a self, misuses its privileged position as other to bring about a qualitative decrease in the self to which it appears, a decrease that can take many different forms: communal or personal calamity; anxiety, suffering and pain; even death. The other can, then, whether regarding physical or moral evil, appear in such a way as to hinder or even arrest what should have been an initial moment in the epiphanic movement of the other's appropriate, dialectically developing self-manifestation to the initial self as potential source of enrichment in an overall enriching experience. More specifically with regard to moral evil, what in fact occurs, namely, an impoverishing initial moment of self-manifestation by the other, has indeed taken place, but should not have. The other should have made a truer appearance as a potential source of qualitative enrichment.

If the dialogically structured relationship between other and self has not already ended with this initial moment of impoverishing appearance, it continues and the other can either follow or modify the initially established trajectory of its own resultantly impoverishing, either to the self or to the self and the other itself, self-manifestation to the self. What has begun as an impoverishing experience can so continue, or of course change into an enriching experience due to a modification in the way in which the other manifests itself to the self. What has begun as an impoverishing experience can continue and intensify as such or can be transformed, en route so to speak, into a more enriching form of experience. However, the moments in the movement of experience to which we here are turning our attention more directly are those in which the other moves beyond initial appearance to presence and "absence as presence" insofar as these forms of presence are sources of impoverishment or qualitative decrease on the part of the self with which the other is in relationship. Given this relationship, these forms of presence become sources of such decrease even, then, on the part of the other itself and the experience as a whole.

Impoverishing Presence. Considering the other now as presence or "absence as presence" will allow us to prolong our consideration of the previously made distinction between physical and moral evil and to delineate further each of these two types of evil. If the movement of experience continues, after its initial appearance the other is present to the self both more directly and through signs. If the other is not itself an autonomous self endowed with what can be identified as volition, this presence is more characteristically direct and is the cause of what we tend to call physical evil. As has already been mentioned briefly above, it would seem indeed to be impossible to think of an ordered physical universe containing organic creatures in which there would be no possibility of such things as accident and pain. A world of self-producing creatures with a built-in natural balance imposes certain conditions that necessarily make for impoverishment as well as enrichment. The presence of physical beings one to another in our temporal-spatial framework would seem to render certain incompatibilities inevitable, often with resultant great suffering and pain in sentient selves.

When we come to the question of what is usually called moral evil, presence and especially "absence as presence" naturally take on particular significance and importance. In the case of moral evil, the other becomes a morally evil agent in that the other bears at least some responsibility for creating in the self unneeded anxiety, pain, suffering and loss, in a word, impoverishment as qualitative decrease. This self to which the other is in dialogically structured relationship is, then, less integrated and whole than before. The other, whether a communal, shared or individual self, presents itself, usually through various signs, as something which it is not, or at least not fully. This ultimately self-contradictory, false presence of the other occasions an unfounded or at least inadequately founded hope and longing, within the self and which the self is, for the other as potential source of enrichment. If one were to wish to provide a particularly poignant example of such false presence with consequent disastrous results, one might note cases where one or both persons planning to marry are not honest with each other. In this and so many other cases, the presence of the other becomes the occasion and a cause, variously, for the self's indifference, despair or violent response.

If the other's presence can be a cause of impoverishment, namely, a reason why the resultant self is an impoverished self, that other's "absence as presence" can under certain circumstances be even more impoverishing than a more straightforward form of presence would be. We say that "absence makes the heart grow fonder." And it is true that a certain absence can at times be beneficial for all concerned. However, withdrawal after an initially enriching appearance can easily amount to a pulling back on the part of the other in which the other refuses to continue along the trajectory of further transparency and intensified presence to the communal, shared or individual self, with a resultant, usually memory-based, despairing longing for the other on the part of that self. This longing easily leads the self to various forms of depression, sense of loss, and withdrawal from further interaction with the ambient world, in a word, to further disintegration rather than to a sense of wholeness within the self and of harmony with the world around it.

Impoverishing Revelation. The final moment in the other's dialectically developing movement of self-manifestation to the self with which it is in dialogically structured relationship is that of revelation and, in the circumstances of our present concern for evil, impoverishing revelation that can take the form of concealment or even deception.

The relationship between other and self can of course simply be interrupted during or at the end of the moment of impoverishing presence, and before that of revelation. However, if the other continues its self-manifestation to the self, then, in a case of what we identify as physical evil, the already well begun quantitative and, consequently, qualitative decrease brought about in the self, and perhaps even in the other itself, continues and climaxes either in such a decrease or in the total disappearance of the self concerned.

In the case of physical evil there hardily arises any significant question of exposing what the other is not only externally but also internally, even though of course all otherness is characterized at least by a minimal form of interiority. The question of self-revelation of what one is "within," through signs and gestures as well as words, as the case may be, arises more particularly in relation to moral evil, namely, that evil which is brought about by a communal, shared or individual self as other characterized by self-awareness and volition. In the case of the other that is a communal, shared or individual human self, the other renders itself vulnerable to potential abuse by the self in revealing itself to the self. In fact, a common enough tendency on the part of the other will be to protect itself even by going beyond a certain legitimate prudence on to false self-revelation, that is, through concealment or deception. Whether for self-protection or for other reasons, the other can, and would often seem to, manipulate the quality and quantity of its self-revelation for its own self-seeking and domineering purposes. In so hiding, so to speak, from the self or even deceiving the self, the other contributes not only to the impoverishment of the self but, especially in the case of deception, through its own internal incoherence and discontinuity renders itself qualitatively less than it was before. Evil gestures, acting, words and the like should not, but really do, occur and, in this very occurrence, damage or even destroy the at least potentially enriching relationship between other and self.

When the other inappropriately and even falsely conceals, or exteriorizes and misrepresents, what it is to the self, the other manipulates and deceives the self, usually as a power play of one sort or another. It is hard to put adequately into words the depths of horror and perversion to which these evil acts, and of course the others as selves that perpetuate them, can sink. The violence involved varies so much from the petty forms often unfortunately characteristic of human interaction to the horrendous, massive violence against individuals and whole peoples so widespread throughout the twentieth century. Such massive moral evil, often justified by arguments rooted in myopic world visions, ultimately seems to defy comprehension. As something that is but should not be, it cries out for recognition as such and for the taking of appropriate measures to prevent it in the future.

These remarks, from the perspective of the other, should help us at least to situate somewhat better the reality of physical and moral evil within the wider context of the structured movement of human experience. We now focus in more detail on moral evil, considered from the perspective of the self in the overall dialogically structured relationship between self and other, as self-impoverishing refusal to follow a path of paradoxically enriching conversion to the other. As we will note, this self-impoverishing refusal amounts to a self-enslavement taking various, progressively more serious forms.

Self

As we saw in our phenomenological look, in Chapter Six above, at the movement of experience from the perspective of the self, that initial self moves through and evolves as a series of contextually conditioned volitional or "decisional" acts vis-a-vis a self-manifesting other along a dialectically developing trajectory of faith or indifference, hope or despair, and love or violence or, again, some combination of these shapes or attitudes of the self. In the case of an impoverishing movement of experience, the balanced combination of fascination and fear characteristic of the initial self in relation to the self-manifesting other in a potentially enriching experience, or at least what should be such a balanced combination, is disturbed and fear predominates.

Impoverishing Indifference. We have previously noted three moments and subforms, so to speak, of impoverishing and disintegrating indifference attributable to the initial self, namely, the self's triply possible refusal generously to embark upon a path of conversion to the other by allowing itself to be opened to the initial appearance of the other, to recognize the other, and to turn in trust toward the other. In this basic, rhythmically structured and dialectically developing movement, the self loses courage either initially or after an initial "openedness" to the other. It is indifferent here not in the banal sense in which conscious selves, as a sort of coping mechanism, necessarily and legitimately filter out less important information in order better to focus on specific realities and events of more importance or urgency. Rather, it is indifferent in the sense of being a refusal, on the occasion of the appearance of an other rightly expecting to be acknowledged or manifesting a real need to be acknowledged, to do so. We are here speaking of a self that is, but should not be, indifferent. If the self is inappropriately indifferent to the other, the potentially enriching dialogically structured relationship can be "still born" in the sense that the initial self refuses to be opened to, and by, the initial appearance of the other.

As such a "decisional" moment often rooted in a form of primordial fear or distrust of otherness as such, or at least of a given other in particular, the self is a refusal to acknowledge the initial appearance of the other and, thus, the self is, in its very stance, the elimination of a potentially enriching content. Its outlook is one of fear that overcomes any potential reception of and fascination with the other. An initial refusal to be opened to the other terminates the potentially enriching, dialogically structured relationship between self and other, to the detriment of both. If the self is opened to the other, it can still refuse to take the next step, namely, to move dialectically forward in recognizing the other as making a legitimate, even ethical, call and demand upon the self and in its overall appearance as a potential source of enrichment.

Again, the self can subsequently take on an outlook in which it refuses to show an initial trust toward the other. Then, even if the self were to be opened to the other and recognize that other with an attitude of initial trust, it could still refuse, in its comportment, to turn more actively toward the other as potential source of enrichment. It can, indeed, turn away from the other even though it may initially have been opened to that other and have trustingly recognized its appearance. It can refuse to respond to the initial call, invitation and then demand on the part of the other.

With this notion of the self, and here we are of course referring to the communal, shared or individual human self, as indifference toward an other rightly expecting to be acknowledged by it, we have identified the first of three overall stances or attitudes that the self can develop into a movement of impoverishing experience. This stance or attitude of the self, indeed that the self is, thus constitutes the first form that what we traditionally call "moral" evil can and does take.

Indifference is, then, this first form of moral evil that the self can become along its dialectically developing trajectory of conversion to the other or its refusal to be converted to the other or, again, some combination of these two possibilities. It is characteristically a stance or attitude in which the self refuses to get involved, even perhaps initially. This form of moral evil is thus further characterized by, and as, an attitude of initial neglect of the other and coldness toward that other. As a form of moral evil, indifference is rather subtle and devious. By remaining indifferent, refusing to be opened to the other by the other, to recognize and turn toward the other in her or his or its needs, and so initially neglecting the other, the self remains to a great extent oblivious of that other and that other's initial appearance. The harm that is caused, for example, by walking past a truly needy homeless person on the street without even noticing that person or, again, by remaining unjustifiably satisfied with what one is and the way one lives, such harm goes largely unnoticed especially by the self itself. This insensitivity to the other, whether an other internal or external to the self, results in a missed opportunity to be with that other and, more importantly, it ends in one form or another of initial self-enslavement on the part of the self concerned. The self remains inappropriately within itself and misses an opportunity to be generous as it participates in a potentially enriching experience.

The self, then, is impoverished in, through and as its identification with indifference as first form of moral evil, but is not reducible completely to that form of evil. The self is, of course, this very stance of indifference toward the other in its initial appearance to the self. It is cold, oblivious, calloused, and hardened in its *status quo* rather than being welcoming, aware and sensitive to the other. The self is, indeed, identified with this first form and moment of evil that is, in a sense, the momentary totality of the self. However, as mentioned, the self is not totally reducible to this totalizing moment. The self here concerned is also subject to various present and previously experienced influences arising from the wider context in which it moves dialectically along its trajectory of conversion or non-conversion to the other. Indeed, in its self-enslavement the self remains conditioned by its wider context, whether finite or, as indicated in Chapter Seven above, infinite. This conditioning can, when due to a finite context, reinforce the self's present, potential trajectory or, when due again to a finite but especially to an infinite context, simply influence or even seem to determine a possible shift in that trajectory. The self as initial moment of indifference on a potentially dialectically developing trajectory can be transformed by influences from its wider context and through its own decisional activity, in response to an appearance or reappearance of an other, into a new movement of faith as openedness to, recognition of and turning toward the other. Thus it can dialectically develop into a moment of hope or, unfortunately, also of despair.

Impoverishing Despair. If the initial self is opened to, recognizes and turns toward the potentially enriching other, it can then continue in and as a phenomenologically and dialectically sequent stance or attitude of hope or despair in relation to the other as possible source of enrichment. When the self appropriately desires and longs for the possibly enriching other that is present to it or whose absence becomes a form of presence, then of course the self continues its overall dialectically developing trajectory of conversion to the other. If, however, the self's stance vis-a-vis the other either degenerates into a form of escapism or takes on the semblance of a naively positive, polyanna reading of the world in which we live, the self falls into a form of presumption that ultimately descends into despair due to the thwarting of the self's repeated, unfounded and unreasonable longing that so often ends in failure. The presumptive self effectively blocks its own longing for the other, and gives up on its hope to reach the other. Finally, in not recognizing appropriately the reality of evil, presumption in its various forms leads to despair, a second overall form of moral evil.

Whether the self follows the tragic path of presumptive escapism or functions with a seriously flawed polyanna world view that leads paradoxically to its giving up on any expectation of attaining the possibly enriching other, or whether out of fear and for various other reasons it so gives up on any expectation of reaching the potentially enriching other, the self becomes this totalizing refusal to desire and long for the other. In its anguish and sorrow, inner turmoil and external agitation, it cannot perdure in its dialogically structured relationship with the other manifesting itself as a presence or even an "absence as presence." The self gives up on the other and descends ever further into despair through a self-perpetuating, disintegrative and false turn inward that becomes an ever stronger form of self-enslavement.

In despair, the self no longer desires and longs for phenomenologically or temporally realized transparency in the relationship between itself and the potentially enriching other. Indeed it goes so far as no longer to hope for a future final fulfillment in which evil will be overcome. Massive evil in the world, terrorism, inter-ethnic and interreligious conflict, ethical failure, societal and individual selfishness reflect, in human history, what is going on in the innermost depths of the despairing self.

Despair, then, is the perspective or outlook and comportment of the previously believing communal, shared or individual self insofar as that self gives up on any expectation of attaining the possibly enriching other. It is, furthermore, the abandonment of any hope for the final overcoming of evil in a full realization of final enrichment of human life beyond all possible impoverishment. Despair is indeed a Dantesque form of hell.

The self, then, is impoverished in its self-realization as this second form of moral evil. The previously described form of that evil, namely, indifference, is itself a form of selfishness arising out of fear. It is evil as indifference toward the possibly enriching other and as potential cause of suffering and hurt in the other. Now, this second form of moral evil, namely, despair, is a form whose regrettable effects occur in a particularly harsh and devastating way within the self itself. Despair becomes a hopeless spiral inward that contrasts so sharply with that type of enriching turn inward concerning which Augustine and Kierkegaard, for example, have so eloquently written. This despairing stance of the self inevitably also seriously affects, in a negative way, the other that manifests itself as presence to the self concerned. The self's inappropriate, ultimately despairing and false turn inward is a refusal to long for the possibly enriching other. It is, ironically, the rejection of the potentially enriching other, or better here otherness, for which the self, or again better selfhood, is destined by the very nature of experience to long. Despair is the very denial of spirit.

As was the case with the first form of moral evil, so here the despairing self is identified with the abandonment of all longing for the other. Of course this is stated here in more absolute terms to cover the extreme case of this form of moral evil, but all forms of despair do share to a greater or lesser degree in the description of despair here presented and, thus, are in their own way and to varying degrees forms of moral evil. In any case, the despairing self is, at least momentarily, this totalizing stance or attitude toward the potentially enriching presence of the other. However, as was also the case with regard to indifference, so too here the self is not reduced solely to this form of moral evil. Due to wider contextual conditioning and a possibly renewed openness to the other, the newly initial self can recommence an overall trajectory of generous conversion to the other. It can become a stance of faith and of hope and take on such attitudes so that it can give itself in love to the other or, tragically, attempt to dominate the other through violence.

Impoverishing Violence. If the initial self, whether communal, shared or individual, participates in a dialogically structured relationship of hope or despair with the other who is present to it, that self can then continue to develop as a phenomenologically and dialectically sequent stance either of love or of violence or, again, strangely enough of a sad combination of both, in relation to the other who reveals itself as possible source of enrichment. Hope can and should lead to the self's appropriately expressed, loving gift of itself to the other. In this way, the self continues, and indeed reaches the climax of, its overall dialectically developing trajectory of conversion to the other. However, despair can lead to a violent reaction on the part of the self to the self-revelation of the other and hope can degenerate into a violent desire to keep, take and dominate rather than give of oneself to the other. Violence, then, is the stance or attitude and, more precisely, the perspective or outlook and comportment of the previously hoping or despairing communal, shared or individual self as one who now, in fear, keeps, takes or dominates. It develops as the third, culminating and most severe form of moral evil, whether as violence against oneself or against another reality or, worst of all, another person or persons.

Violence as evil can take three forms of refusal on the part of the self. The first of these is the refusal to give appropriately of oneself to the other. Instead of so giving oneself, the self keeps and takes. It keeps what it is to itself and takes in an inappropriate or disrespectful way what belongs to or, better, is the other. The second of these is the refusal to give oneself over to and to become, by letting go of one's old self, that self which others' love has called one to be. One hangs on rather than letting go, a form of self-violence. The third form of refusal is that of blocking a movement of mutual love, a refusal to accept love from others and, thus, to give oneself in this way to the other. These three forms of refusal can further degenerate into the determination to relate oneself inappropriately to the other by dominating the other, by forcing one's will on the other. Ultimately, the self does not relate to the other in such a way as to respect the otherness of the other, which can finally only be done by a gift of oneself to the other. Selfishness overrules generosity and the desire for dominance paradoxically enslaves ever more the one trying to become the master. This desire for dominance creates a self-contradictory situation within the self that as self is destined, rather, to give itself generously to the other if it wishes truly to reach the other as other. The result is impoverishment of both self and other.

The self as a moment of impoverishing violence is, to paraphrase Saint Paul, never patient or kind. It is envious and boastful, arrogant and rude. It insists on its own way, is irritable and resentful, rejoices in wrongdoing and hates the truth. It puts up with nothing, believes ultimately in nothing but itself, and despairs of all things. Sadly, with violence the movement that should have been an enriching conversion to the other dissolves into an effort at possession and domination of the other by the self. In the case of mutually inflicted violence that can occur when both self and other are selves, what should have been mutual love ends up as parallel efforts at possession and domination. Self and other are at war with one another.

From the perspective of the self, we have now identified a third, culminating form of moral evil. Though the self is, in fact, this attitude of violence toward the other, as was the case with regard to the self as indifference and as despair, the self can, within a wider context and on the basis of a renewed appearance of the other, be opened to, recognize and turn toward an other in response to the call and invitation launched by the appearance of that other.

Seen from the perspective of selfhood in its dialogically structured relationship with otherness, the stances of indifference, despair and violence constitute, then, three progressively more serious forms of moral evil that the initial self can become as it moves along a dialectically developing trajectory of what should have been an appropriate conversion of that self to the other. That self should have participated in and been the result of a movement of enriching experience in which selfhood and otherness in relationship give rise to enriched selfhood, a movement of spirit. However, the relationship between self and other can be transformed or, more accurately, deformed into a movement of impoverishing experience and, from the perspective of the self or selves involved, a movement of self-enslavement rather than one of being freed from such self-enslavement through conversion to the other.

Resultant Self

Our review of the dialogically structured relationship between communal, shared or individual other and self resulting in an impoverished self (and other) has provided us with a way of contextualizing, though certainly not fully comprehending, evil. We began with a look at the roles of the other in this relationship, which helped us further situate the more traditional distinction between physical evil and moral evil. Essentially, physical evil occurs when that which is but should not be is a result of the universe as we know it and not as such caused by an other as self characterized by self-awareness and volitional activity. Moral evil occurs when that which is but should not be is in some way a result of volitional activity on the part of a self. We then reviewed the roles that a self plays in an impoverishing relationship between self and other. We have grouped these roles, stances or perspectives and ways of comporting oneself on the part of the self into three forms of moral evil, namely, indifference, despair, and violence. Among these forms of evil, the self as indifferent is more passive and here evil takes on a more neutral coloring, neither hot nor cold. As despair, the self is more actively involved and gives up. Here evil takes on a particularly agonizing coloration and characterizes especially the self concerned. As violence, the self is quite active, indeed, in a sense too active in an inappropriate way, and that is the fundamental problem with regard to violence. In an act of violence, the self keeps, takes and dominates. It contradicts its own vocation and mission of respectfully relating itself to the other through the gift of itself to the other. Here evil is in the truest sense that which is but should not be. It is the impoverishing and thoroughly unethical domination of the other that does not respect the otherness of the other.

The impoverished resultant self arises out of an inappropriately developed dialogically structured relationship between other and self, self and other. This result of either physical or moral evil, or some combination of the two, is itself something that is but should not be. Along with physical evil and moral evil, we can then here identify a third form of evil, namely, resultant evil, which can refer to a communal, shared or individual self, an other, and even a situation or series of societal or institutional structures.

In our earlier phenomenological analysis of the movement of experience, in Chapter Six above, we identified the self as a series of dialectically developing stances or perspectives and comportments of faith or indifference, hope or despair and love or violence in dialogically structured relationship with an other that manifests itself to the self through a dialectically developing series of moments as appearance or non-appearance, presence or absence, and revelation or concealment. In the present chapter we have made an effort to contextualize and situate physical, moral and resultant evil within this overall phenomenological analysis without, however, "taming" evil or trying to fit it within a system. In the present review, evil remains a form of self-enslavement, as well as enslavement of others, that are intractable and ultimately inexplicable. As evil, they make no real sense. They are but should not be.

In the final analysis, perhaps the best we can do is recognize that relationships between self and other ultimately involve some at least minimal ethical reflection concerning right thinking leading to right action. Fundamental philosophical ethics becomes a study of the appropriate relationship between self and other in which one proposes ways that the self can fulfill its mission of conversion to the other and the other can manifest itself as a source of potential enrichment for the self. In ethics so understood, criteria of personal integrity on the part of the self and the need to respect the otherness of the other, as well as generosity on the part of both self and other become fundamental points of reference. When right thinking and right action by the self take on and, better, occur as the various forms that we have identified, namely, faith and hope and love, and when the other participates in the relationship between self and other as dialectically developing movement of honest self-manifestation, then we have a moment of enriching experience, something which, in contradistinction to self-enslavement and the enslavement of others, is and should be. We have an ethics of generosity rooted in a moment and movement of enriching experience, a free and freeing movement of subjectivity and spirit.

Freedom

In turning to a consideration of the free and freeing movement of spirit, we need to recall that any movement of experience is a movement of subjectivity, with subjectivity understood in a very wide sense to cover and refer to any relationship between initial selfhood and otherness giving rise to resultant selfhood. While any movement of experience is then a movement of subjectivity so understood, spirit is a movement of experience or subjectivity whose result is, at least ultimately, one of enriched selfhood. Reference to experience more specifically as a movement of subjectivity helps us now to focus on the role and functioning of the self as pole and participant in that wider reality which is the moment and movement of experience. It is, then, more especially to the self, or also the other if it is itself a self-aware self, within that wider movement that we will focus now in our reflection on the free and freeing movement of spirit as we move through a series of considerations concerning regret, options, self-determination, and "freedom, ethics, self and other."

Regret

The experience of regret is a telling moment in human communal, shared or individual life. The human self can and often does regret that it was not harsher and more violent in relation to someone or something else, or even to itself. So often we unfortunately hear phrases like, "I should have crushed him while I had the chance." In a much more elevating vein, the self can regret it or another's not having been more available to and supportive of someone or something else, of not having properly followed the path of conversion to the other. Regret is, then, in either case an emotionally charged review of something past that one wishes had been different.[12] This experience of regret can, though, also take on new and more positive meaning as the regretting self looks to the future and resolves to act differently. When this resolve involves the intention of turning from evil as participation in an impoverishing experience to good as participation in a basically enriching experience, then regret becomes contrition. Within the context of our concern to work out a philosophical theology, this contrition takes on its highest form when the self admits that it has failed God and others in what it has done and in what it has left undone and, with help, resolves to do better in the future.

Options

The experience of regret is indeed very telling. In its character as reflection on the past, it brings into particular relief the subtle awareness of options and, consequently, choice that normally accompanies moments of experience characterized by a heightened sense of awareness on the part of the self concerned.

This subtle awareness of choice, as well as the whole experience itself as such, is of course conditioned, and even constitutively affected or even at times perhaps in some way initiated by various factors or human constructions such as language, thought, interest, tradition, culture and, to some extent at least, gender and genetic substrate. That sense of choice perdures through these various forms of conditioning. Furthermore, something of that "sense of choice" would seem to pervade all of reality, at least to the extent that there is a certain minimal randomness which seems to qualify all activity as we know it.

In the transition from Hegel's working with conceptual thought to our thinking in terms of what I would dare to call, *pace* Hegel, the wider and more inclusive category of experience, there has arisen, perhaps initially only somewhat more implicitly, the recognition that experience, especially what we have in Chapter Five above called first and third experiences, is less determined and logically necessary in its structured movement than is conceptual thought. The self and other in relationship or, more precisely here, the self participating in the experience, retains the option of entering further into the relationship, and this in various ways, or of withdrawing at some point from the relationship.

Once this overall transition from thought to experience was carried through from Chapters Three through Six, we then in Chapter Seven turned more directly to a consideration of an infinite movement of experience, a movement of inclusive divine subjectivity and spirit that we identified with the triune God of Christian traditions. Here again the human self regularly affirms a certain at least subtle sense of option and choice as to whether it will turn to, long for and give itself to the triple divine Other or, usually accompanied by all sorts of obfuscation, block such a relationship.

In describing the triune God as a movement of love in which divine self-hood or Spirit and divine otherness or Risen One are in relationship leading to resultant (from the perspective of a relationship to finite reality) divine selfhood or God, we have presented an understanding of the triune God that affirms option and choice even and especially for God as the unique and paradigmatic, infinite or fully inclusive moment and movement of enriching experience or spirit. With this understanding of God, we can continue to maintain, with Hegel, the affirmation that God is a movement of inclusive divine subjectivity in as that subjectivity is a movement of enriching experience. In summary fashion, Christians could say that God so loved the world as to send the Spirit and the Son to hold the world in a divine embrace. The generalized understanding of tetradically structured experience with which we are working permits us to speak of God as a movement of triadically structured experience without subordinating God to some overall cosmic scheme that would restrain God's freedom. In fact, in this presentation God remains free to enter in a personal way into human history or not. God could indeed have maintained a relationship, as true or inclusive infinite, with finitude without personally entering into human history. For example, the structure of initial divine selfhood, otherness and resultant enriched selfhood could be maintained in divine covenants with Noah, Abraham, and the Jewish people through Moses that are spoken of in Jewish and Christian traditions. In these three cases, otherness would be, respectively, divine promise and rainbow, promised land, and Torah. Furthermore, God could bring into being a variety of parallel universes in which God's involvement might well exceed any human expectation, as indeed Christian traditions affirm it does even in the human history we know. In this scenario, and given the understanding of experience with which we are working, it makes sense, without falling into an exaggerated or even arbitrary voluntarism, to speak of options available to God, namely, to create finitude or not to do so, to give rise to one universe or a multiplicity of parallel or consecutively existing universes, and to give of God self or be present in any number of ways to one or more such universes. If God relates to finite otherness, the act of so relating, and the consequent divine turning to the other, is so radical that it constitutes the very bringing into existence of that finite otherness to which God relates.

Self-Determination

Regret, contrition, options—in various ways these at least imply a sense of responsibility for what we have decided, done and become in the past, what we decide, do and become in the present and will decide, do and become in the future. In its diverse forms, regret leads us to acknowledge that we could have acted differently than we did. Contrition involves the resolve to act differently in the future, and the existence of options creates the space, so to speak, within which we can act differently. This possibility of acting differently brings with it the opportunity, indeed often the necessity, to choose one option rather than another. Such choosing bears with it, then, a certain responsibility for the choice or choices made.

Understood in a very wide sense, this responsibility is always present in and characteristic of any moment and movement of experience. It accompanies the self in its conversion to the other as well as the other in its epiphanic manifestation to the self. It likewise characterizes the resultant self that is, so to speak, responsible, again in a very wide sense of the word, for what it has become.

Indeed, with all of reality being in some way characterized by a certain indeterminacy and randomness, a notion of responsibility accompanies and qualifies any moment and movement of experience. However, such a notion of responsibility for deciding, doing and becoming takes on a particular, ethical cast when considered in relation to self-aware selves and others capable of reflexively reviewing their options before deciding, doing and becoming, thus moving in one direction rather than another. Such selves and others, who are themselves self-aware and consequently volitionally endowed selves, not only decide on one course of action rather than another but, given their capacity for reflection, at least in more important situations are faced with a great variety of considerations to be studied, weighed and evaluated before acting. Especially when this review of various factors in the, so to speak, experiential equation, is carried out in a more self-reflexive way, it further strengthens and reinforces the sense of responsibility accompanying selves in their deciding, acting and becoming. In the resultant self this sense of responsibility develops into, as mentioned earlier, a sense of regret if another option or other options not chosen now appear better. One would hope, however, that it flowers in a sense of satisfaction confirmed, as the case may be, in one's own self-awareness and by others around one or even the wider community at having thought and acted rightly.

Human deciding, doing and becoming are, however, always, as elements in or aspects of a moment and movement of experience, conditioned by language, established thought patterns, cultural and social influences, gender, temperament, genetic predispositions and the like. This conditioning is in fact essential to any such human action. It constitutes and creates the possibility for such action. Deciding, doing and becoming, indeed a moment and movement of adult human experience in general, would remain quite mute without language, unreflected without recourse to various already established and perhaps now modified thought patterns, lacking in context and interpretational point of reference without cultural and social influences, and so forth. Evidently, the self is further conditioned by being limited in its choice of options due to the range of options theoretically and concretely, mentally, physically, psychologically and spiritually available to it. Yet in and through all this conditioning and even limitation, there usually perdures in the self concerned a certain stronger or weaker sense of responsibility for what one has decided, done and become. Satisfaction, regret and contrition are indeed phenomena that tell us of our communal, shared and individual responsibility for decisions, actions, even "destiny." Others, in turn contribute to this sense of responsibility by confirming or qualifying their evaluation of the appropriateness or inappropriateness, rightness or wrongness of such decisions, actions and, consequently, development of the self concerned. These telling reflections and the existence of options remind us that the conditioned and limited but real role of the human self in the determination of the direction of its becoming or development through decision and action, in a word through appropriate conversion to the other, is ultimately rooted in the very nature of experience as selfhood and otherness in relationship giving rise to enriched or impoverished selfhood. The conversion of self to other and the self-manifestation of the other to the self, especially if the other is itself a self-reflexive self, proceed dialectically as a series of stances taken by the self in dialogical relationship with the self-manifesting other. Though conditioned by various factors and confronted by a limited number of options, each stance is in principle and by the very nature of experience as relationship between self and other open to a specific orientation taken in that relationship by the self concerned.

It may well be that certain factors so determine a self in a given moment of experience that the self acts without a sense of options, indeed without options. This situation could of course arise due to factors internal to the self such as psychological compulsion or to external factors such as being physically forced to follow a certain course of action. The number of forms of such internal distress or external violence would seem almost endless, but experience as such, in principle and certainly regularly in practice, is a moment and movement in which the self develops in relationship to an other through a series of decisions and actions that involve choices among options. Some of these choices lead to the self's appropriately giving itself to the other in light of the other's initial appearance and subsequent developing manifestation to the self, thus constituting a freeing moment and movement of enriching experience, a movement of spirit. Conversely, the self can block any such conversion in a moment of impoverishing experience and self-enslavement.

Self-enslavement can only be overcome through the self's being opened anew by the reappearance of otherness and consequent gift of self to the other. And in the context of our reflection as a study in philosophical theology, we need to consider in a special way the all-important more particular question of the self's being opened by the reappearance of divine otherness and the more general question of human freedom as conditioned and limited self-determination in relation to divine self-manifestation. In its experience of God, that is, in its relationship with the true infinite, the communal, shared or individual finite human self, as we have seen in Chapter Seven above, variously experiences the infinite as the divine Spirit within, the Risen One as divine Other in history, and God as goal of life. These three relationships between the finite self and the infinite divine Other are created by the true infinite's free self-gift to the finite self. As inner urge, exterior model and ultimate goal, they establish a context or, perhaps better, divine embrace of the finite self that provides a "space" within which the finite self can itself comfortably and trustingly embrace finite others, even to the point of loving its enemies. In a sense, this is implied already in the ages old reference to the Spirit and the Risen One as the two "hands" of God.

If, on the one hand, the infinite were simply to stand over against the finite rather than respectfully relate to the finite in a creative embrace, either the finite would be destroyed by a subsequent violent divine grasping of it, so to speak, or the infinite itself would be reduced to a further finite reality over against created finitude. If, on the other hand, among the various options open to God, the relationship between infinite and finite occurs as inner urge, transforming an efficient causal relationship into one of profound and often efficacious divine persuasion, as model in history incarnating divine formal causality in a particular human, and as goal, namely, final divine causality, then these three forms of creative and salvific divine causality generously establish that "space" in which the finite self can decide, act and thus become its best self through conditional and limited but real self-determination exercised through and as ethical choices of appropriate options constituting steps in an overall conversion to finite others and to the triply experienced divine Other.

Freedom, Ethics, Self and Other

Freedom is the self's, and the other's if the other is also a self, capacity, in a moment and movement of experience, to give itself appropriately to the other with which the self is in relationship. It is equally the exercise of this capacity, an exercise that is, on the part of a finite self, always conditioned by various factors and limited by the realistic options available in a given situation. At times the conditioning or the limitation of options is such that the self, always in principle free, is unable to determine for itself how it will relate or not relate with and to the other that has manifest itself to the self. While recognizing this possibility of the absence of the ability to exercise the freedom that one is in a specific situation, we can still describe freedom then as the self in its conditioned and limited but real capacity, and especially the exercise of that capacity, to follow the path of conversion to the other by and through a series of stances of the self, which is itself indeed these stances, vis-à-vis the other. Widely stated, then, freedom is the self as movement of faith or indifference, hope or despair, and love or violence in relation to the other as this latter appears or does not appear, is present or absent, and reveals itself to, or conceals itself from, the self. Freedom is the conditioned and limited but real self-determining self (and of course the other if the other is itself also a self-aware and volitional self). Far too often the exercise of this freedom results in one or another form of self-enslavement as the finite self closes itself in upon itself in a moment of impoverishing experience. But in its best form, that is, as a movement of enriching experience, the exercise of this freedom culminates in a moment of conversion to the other through a generous gift of itself on the part of the self to the other. This latter exercise of freedom gives rise to an enriched resultant self renewedly in relationship with an other or others. It is a movement of subjectivity, of finite experience as spirit.

Self-determination on the part of the infinite, God, is, due to the very nature of the infinite, which is likewise conditioned and limited, but in a way quite different from that of a finite movement of spirit. The exercise of freedom on the part of God as inclusive divine subjectivity, namely, the Spirit as initial divine selfhood urging finite selves outward, the One recognized as risen divine Other manifesting itself in creation and in human history, and God as goal of life, is creative and salvific. Self-gift on the part of the Spirit, the Risen One and God as goal of life bring into existence or create, and through a new relationship bring into renewed existence or save, the other to whom this triple divine self-gift, generous in the truest send of the word as altruistic, self-disinterested and other-oriented activity, is made. Creative and salvific divine self-determination is, then, *post factum* conditioned by the nature of the other or others brought into existence and indeed limited by the options that the existence of this other or these others allows for. The divine exercise of freedom gives rise to an enriched resultant self, God as goal of life. This divine exercise of freedom is a movement of enriching experience, a movement of inclusive divine subjectivity, an infinite movement of spirit.

If freedom, then, is identified at the finite level with the self's variously conditioned and limited but real capacity, and especially the realization of that capacity, to determine for itself whether or not it will follow the road of conversion to the other, then freedom becomes the condition for the possibility of any ethics or concern for right thinking leading to right action and for any attribution of responsibility with regard to such thinking and such action. In a very wide sense, of course, all of reality is "responsible" for its action or inaction and any self, whether self-reflective or not, bears "responsibility" for what it becomes. However, here we are concerned more properly with self-aware and self-reflexive selves who must, by the very nature of what they are, choose among various options available to them in their relationships with others. For it is in and as these very choices that such selves determine who they are and what they are to become.

Ethics in general, then, and fundamental philosophical ethics and sectoral ethics, as the case may be, in particular become the study of, but, more basically, the reflection by, a self-aware communal, shared or individual self concerning options before it in its dialogically structured relationship with a self-manifesting other or others. Ethics is, though, most fundamentally the practice of informed and responsible decision-making on the part of the self working with criteria of personal integrity, the need to respect the otherness of the other, and overall generosity. It is equally the practice of such decision-making on the part of an other who, as a self-aware self, ideally in generous fashion manifests itself to the self in a way coherent with what the other is in itself, and in respectful relationship to the self. Thus the more formally stated phrase "right thinking leading to right action" takes on further determination as dialectically developing movements of what is ideally enriching manifestation of the other to the self and respectful conversion on the part of the self to the self-manifesting other. The criteria for ethical decision-making become in the truest sense, as characteristics of self and other in a moment and movement of enriching experience, internal criteria. Our ethics of generosity and our overall philosophy of generosity are reflections on and prolongations of the dialectical development especially of self-reflexive self and other through and as a series of volitional choices, among options available, when these choices are indeed conditioned and limited but, even in that conditioning and limitation, real and self-determined. Where there is a movement of subjectivity or experience as spirit, there has been an appropriate exercise of freedom.

Mystery

Evil, freedom, self, other, subjectivity, ethics, finite, infinite—these and so many other notions we have worked with refer in one way or another to experience, in its many forms and types, as moment and movement of initial selfhood in dialogically structured relationship with otherness giving rise through dialectically advancing development on the part of each to resultant selfhood. Evil describes a movement of experience in which either other or self, or both, act in such a way as to make of the experience an impoverishing one, namely, one characterized by qualitative and often also quantitative loss. The resultant self is qualitatively less than it was before, something which is but should not be. Conversely, though we have not treated so explicitly of it here, good refers to a movement of experience resulting in qualitatively enriched selfhood, with "qualitative" here understood to refer to an enhanced sense of wholeness and well-being in relationship with oneself and with the ambient world, something which is and should be. With reference to that which is good, we have more regularly spoken of a moment of enriching experience as a movement of spirit.

Freedom as used here with reference to self-aware selves is the capacity and especially the realization of that capacity on the part of a self to participate in a movement of appropriate conversion to the other or refusal to so participate. This participation, or refusal to do so, occurs through and as one or more dialectically developing sequentially taken decisions. Freedom is likewise the capacity and especially the realization of that capacity on the part of an other to manifest itself or not, and in this way or that, to a self with which it is in relationship. The communal, shared or individual self is a decision, or a series of decisions, that are taken in a dialectically progressing movement of conversion to the other or a refusal to carry through with that conversion. The other is a decision, or a series of decisions, taken in a dialectically progressing movement of epiphanic self-manifestation to the self with which it is in relationship. Subjectivity is essentially the movement of experience itself, with a particular focus on the self. Ethics is then fundamentally the responsible exercise by self and other of their freedom. Ethics refers as well, and here it takes on the character of what we earlier on in chapter Five above called "second experience," to the study of various aspects of the self's and the other's responsible exercise of freedom. Finite of course refers to that form of experience, whether enriching or impoverishing, in which resultant selfhood is renewedly in relationship with recurrent otherness, a tetradically structured movement of experience. And infinite describes the triadically structured form of experience as a movement of inclusive subjectivity when there is no recurrent otherness and thus, no external limitation. Without such limitation, the infinite is by its very structure a movement of enriching experience, a movement of spirit.

Each and any of these finite moments and movements of experience carries with it some element of the unexpected, even if that element be in many or even most cases quite minimal. There is something about the very nature of experience that never ceases to surprise, whether that something be what was left behind from previous experiences, what has newly come to be and was not there before or, again, the very way in which the experience occurs. Transparent, honest and communicative as we all may wish to be, there is something existential and particular, especially about each human experience including the more fully reflexive ones, that is ultimately untransmitable to others much as we may try to express it to them in words and gestures, by allusion and even Kierkegaardian indirection of description. Even in the form of a second experience, which is a more reflexive reflection on and conceptually expressed prolongation of a first experience, there remains something incommunicable. We see this so often when we use language to convey our thoughts to others. No matter how many times we may try to reformulate and represent that conceptual prolongation of a first experience, or even a conceptually expressed movement of thought as itself a first experience, we can always say more about what is supposed to be a clear thought, idea, judgement, syllogistic argument or other conclusion. There remains something incommunicable, even to ourselves, about any first, second or third experience. This at least minimal incommunicability, both to others and to the self itself concerned, is surely rooted in the very notion of experience as, to put it in summary fashion, unique though to some extent recurrent, decisional, new, characterized by a sense of immediacy as well as by both a sense of loss and of gain, and bearing a particular emotional tone.

When we refer to an experience of evil, especially moral evil, the experience itself, while able to be situated in a wider context, ultimately remains inexplicable and incomprehensible. It is, but it should not be. We look at it practically in despair. When we refer to an experience of good, however, we stand in awe and wonder at something that is, should be and yet still surprises us to the point of drawing us out beyond what we have been, seen and known until then. This awe and wonder are our natural reaction to an experience of good both because it is such an experience and because there always remains something attractive and yet unexpressed, unexpressible and consequently mysterious to us about the experience.

It is not surprising, then, that one would stand in awe and wonder before an experience, whether communal, shared or individual, that one may have of God. Such an experience of God bears all the characteristics of an experience that have just been noted. As so many saints and mystics have insisted, there remains something of their experience of God that they could not communicate to others. More profoundly, there remains something they cannot even communicate to themselves. And beyond the question of communicability, in the case of a movement of infinite experience there is a depth of reality in the triune Other that seems inexhaustible. From the perspective of the finite self, experience of that inexhaustible, triply realized selfhood is never ending. Indeed Saint Gregory of Nyssa has gone so far as to affirm that even in heaven one will enter ever more deeply into the mysterious depths of the infinite God.[13]

With delicate reference here to the creative and saving experience God has of finitude and in light of the understanding of experience we have worked out, we need not be surprised that God remains ever a mystery. That the triune God has decided to bring into existence a finite other to God self and, according to Christian tradition, has entered that finite reality in a new and more personal way in order to save that finite reality by bringing it under the effective reign of God and ultimately into the realm of God equally remains a mystery. In line with our overall understanding of the development of the self in a movement of experience, an understanding slightly modified in view of the creative nature of conversion of divine self to finite self, such decisions are the expression of the very being of God who, in triune fashion and with creative effect, turns toward, longs for and generously gives God self in triple self-gift to created finitude. From the perspective of finitude and, more specifically here, of the human self-aware and reflexive self, that self experiences the triple divine self-manifestation as one of appearance, presence and indeed often "absence as presence," and revelation. In this, from various perspectives, doubled creative and salvific move, namely, in the movement of conversion to the finite other, a movement that is equally epiphanic self-manifestation to the other, God is God self this doubled movement or development. While each and every moment and movement of experience remains to some extent a mystery, that is, something never finally fully comprehensible to the finite self, divine self-gift in creation and in salvation remain, due to its special character, forever beyond the complete comprehension of any finite self. The movement of experience that God is remains forever unique and bears the character of decisional event so mysteriously ever new, without leaving anything behind. Such is, according to the Christian traditions that serve as our point of reference and in line with our understanding of experience, the mysterious, namely, wonderful and yet forever beyond final full comprehension, generous and loving gift of God self as movement of inclusive divine subjectivity and spirit.

* * * * *

From the beginning of this chapter on, we have noted that our reflection on the very concrete but still elusive notions of evil, freedom, and mystery would, in part at least, take the form of a fundamental philosophical ethics. At the end of our remarks on evil, we drew out several very general criteria for establishing right thinking leading to right action. Then, at the end of our reflection on freedom we recognized that these are truly internal criteria since they are the characteristics of the self itself, and the other if it is likewise an aware and self-reflexive self. While ethics is of course an area of study, it is more fundamentally the appropriately established, decision-based move of conversion on the part of the self to the other with which it is in relationship. Ethics is equally the appropriately carried out, decision-based move of self-manifestation on the part of the other, if that other is itself an aware and self-reflexive self, to the self with which it is in relationship. Now at the end of our reflection on mystery we recognize that, in regard to evil, our sense of mystery expresses itself as horror and incompehension and, in regard to good, as wonder accompanied by the recognition that one can never finally and fully comprehend the experience concerned. With this understanding of the ultimately mysterious character of experience as such, ethics, as most fundamentally the appropriate and respectful development of self and other in a moment and movement of experience, itself takes on something of that mysterious character of experience as such. Much as one needs rules and guidelines, clarity and balance in our communal, shared and individual efforts at right decision-making, one needs much more a paradoxical attitude akin to that of the Gospel beatitudes expressing itself as generosity of spirit in such decision-making. In the final analysis, perhaps ethics is more gift than guideline.[14]

NOTES

1. See *Hegel's Trinitarian Claim. A Critical Reflection* (Leiden: Brill, 1984).
2. This notion of "alternative realization" finds expression, for example, among other ways in contemporary themes of potential multiple parallel universes.
3. Hegel of course saw that thought distinguished and united. Here we are stressing the aspect of uniting or bringing together.
4. We should recall that the word "individual" here is not to be taken in any excessively nominalist sense since it can refer to a self that is communal, shared or individual.
5. And, in the case of a finite movement of experience, an enriched selfhood renewedly in relationship with recurrent otherness.
6. In a very general way, "multidisciplinary" of course identifies an approach to ethics in which one or more persons carry out their ethical reflection from the perspectives of different intellectual disciplines. "Interdisciplinary" describes a multidisciplinary approach to ethics in which a further effort is made to interrelate and bring into closer relationship the various disciplines to which appeal is made. "Transdisciplinary" tends to refer to multidisciplinary approaches to ethics that approach ethical reflection not only through an effort to relate the various disciplines employed to one another, thus tending toward interdisciplinary ethics, but, more fundamentally, to try to work with a more holistic view of persons and situations that can better ground multidisciplinary and interdisciplinary approaches to ethical reflection. Each of these, namely, multidisciplinary ethics, interdisciplinary ethics and transdisciplinary ethics as well as philosophical ethics and theological ethics can pursue either more fundamental or more applied reflection in ethics, hence fundamental or applied, some would say sectoral, ethics.
7. I am indebted to Prof. Chantal Beauvais for this expression.
8. The Latin text reads, "Questio est de malo. Et prima questio an malum sit aliquid." Sancti Thomae de Aquino, *Opera Omnia* issu Leonis XIII P.M. edita, Tomus xxiii, *Quaestiones disputatae de malo*, cura et studio Fratrum praedicatorum (Roma: Commissio Leonina, 1982) Question 1, First Article, in the body of the answer, pp. 5–6/Thomas Aquinas, *On Evil*, trans. Richard Regan, ed. with an Introduction and Notes by Brian Davies (Oxford: Oxford University Press, 2003) Question 1, First Article, in the body of the answer, pp. 58–59.
9. "Unde dico quod id quod est malum non est aliquid, sed id cui accidit esse malum est aliquid, in quantum malum privat nonnisi aliquod particulare bonum." *Quaestiones disputatae de malo* Question 1, First Article, in the body of the answer, p. 6/*On Evil* Question 1, First Article, in the body of the answer, p. 59.
10. "Das Böse as theologisches Problem," *Kerygma und Dogma* 24 (1978) 285–320. On p. 309 Koch speaks of evil as "das kategorisch Nicht-sein-Sollende." His overall formulation applies especially to what will be referred to later on in the present chapter as "moral evil." Regarding "physical evil," perhaps, following Koch's general approach, we could say physical evil is that which, given our known universe, is but which should be foreseen and then avoided or whose bad effects should at least be mitigated as much as possible. In this article, Koch very helpfully discusses the ways in which one can consider evil in relation to God, something I have not considered explicitly or at any length in the present study. He also provides helpful bibliographic information on various presentations of Hegel on evil (see p. 309 n. 108).

11. On this and what follows concerning evil, I am particularly grateful to Fr. William P. Clark, O.M.I., who graciously and generously provided me with a copy of notes he had made on the questions of evil and suffering.

12. In a somewhat different vein, Søren Kierkegaard affirms that sin is the misuse of freedom that posits freedom. See Dale M. Schlitt, *Theology and the Experience of God* (New York: Peter Lang, 2001) 201. In a sense, Kierkegaard is moving from the experience of sin, or we could with further nuance say evil, as point of departure to an argument in favor of freedom, perhaps under the influence of Schelling. On Schelling, see Koch, "Das Böse als theologisces Problem" 305–309. I am grateful to Dr. Philippe Constantine for recalling the importance of Schelling's taking evil as a point of departure for his consideration on freedom.

13. For helpful remarks concerning Gregory of Nyssa on unending human progression into the divine, see, for example, Peter C. Phan, *Grace and the Human Condition* (Wilmington, DE: Michael Glazier, 1988) 176–193, esp. 189–193. Phan includes with his remarks helpful longer quotations from Gregory's works. For a fuller study of Gregory of Nyssa on the infinity of God, see Ekkehard Mühlenberg, *Die Unendlichkeit Gottes bei Gregor von Nyssa: Gregors Kritik am Gottesbegriff der klassischen Metaphysik* (Göttingen: Vandenhoeck & Ruprecht, 1966).

14. This may be something of what Gabriel Marcel meant when he spoke of ethics as gift. In this regard, see the helpful study by François Poitras, "Transcendence et technique chez Gabriel Marcel. Une contribution à l'éthique théologique," Ph.D./D.Th. dissertation, Saint Paul University, Ottawa, 2006.

CONCLUSION

The overall thrust of the present essay has been toward the development of a renewed, post-Hegelian philosophical theology that continues, with Hegel, to take the form of a movement of inclusive divine subjectivity. Yet we have dared to use the phrase "going beyond Hegel" to indicate, among several other points, that such a movement is now to be understood as one of experience rather than, according to Hegel, as one of conceptual thought. To help make our point, we spelled out in greater detail what the noun and verb "experience" mean and indicated more precisely the realities to which they refer. Developing further this understanding of experience then provided us with the means to reinterpret "spirit," a word and concept so dear to Hegel, as a movement of enriching experience. In a sense, the purpose of the present study was to develop a philosophical theology by uncovering the deeper meaning of the word "and" hidden in its use as a rather innocent looking conjunction bringing together, in one phrase, the words "experience and spirit."

In the first step in this overall philosophical endeavor we reviewed certain aspects of Hegel's brilliant but, in the view of many, problematic philosophical position in general and his philosophy of religion in particular, which latter he in effect elaborated as a philosophical theology, namely, a movement of conceptual thought constituting a movement of inclusive divine subjectivity. In this first step and throughout the rest of the study, Hegel and his philosophical system have served as a source of enrichment, an "other" with which we entered into ongoing dialogue and from whom we learned so much.

Our overall philosophical project progressed beyond this initial review of Hegel in a second step, in which we entered into dialogue with several philosophers who themselves had carried out prolonged reflection on the nature and role of experience. We then sketched out a longer, constructive description of the nature, role, types, phases, forms and structured movement of experience.

This elaboration on, perhaps we could even say celebration of, experience

resulted in a richer and fuller notion of experience with which we then proceeded, in a third step in our overall philosophical project, to carry out a
longer phenomenological and philosophical reflection, using "reflection" in a
wide sense of the word, on several topics in philosophical theology. We
examined the Christian experience of God and its affirmation, argued to a
way of grounding efforts to speak of God, and explored an understanding of
fundamental philosophical ethics arising out of our effort to situate the notions of evil, freedom, and mystery within the context of our previously
established understanding of experience.

Over the course of this reflection on experience, and on enriching experience in particular, we have endeavored, then, not only to discover the deeper
meaning implied in the conjunction "and" relating "experience and spirit" in
that phrase but also to replace that conjunction with the word "as." Thus we
can speak of a movement of enriching experience as a movement of spirit and
of a movement of spirit as one of enriching experience.

In conceiving spirit as a movement of enriching experience we have
attempted to recognize a certain element common to so many different uses
of that word "spirit." That element, I would now suggest, is the stress, in so
many cases, on some form of openness to the other and to reality beyond
ourselves, whether that openness be to reality in its ordinariness or in some
form of that reality's appearance beyond what we might loosely call "the
ordinary." Though this word "spirit" conjures up many varied, even contradictory meanings, we can at least vaguely sense an idea of openness expressed
subtly or not so subtly in the following uses of the word, that are here cited
simply by way of example. We might, first of all, think of the biblical understanding of spirit as animating "breath" coming from without us but existing
within us. Again, in more common parlance, "spirit" often bears with it at
least a hint at characteristics such as "energetic," "playful," "enthusiastic,"
"whimsical," and "self-involving" that qualify self and other in a given experience. We might, for example, note the experience described by a phrase like
"a spirited debate." In more religious and philosophical circles "spirit" often
comes to describe that which is not material, or which surpasses the material
and is invisible. Thus, it can often, particularly in philosophical theology, be
used in a special way to speak of God. In recent years, in academic as well as
everyday discourse, we regularly enough refer, in a rather minimalist way, to

something as spiritual, meaning that it is in one way or another beyond the everyday and the mundane. More specifically in academic circles, the study of "spirituality" seems often to mean the study of any aspect of reality that, as the subject of that study, involves some notion of the experience of, and commitment to, something beyond the immediate and the empirical. We can see this in the establishment of programs in spirituality or courses in spirituality in which one is open to a consideration of various forms of the "beyond," including anything from traditional Christian mysticism to Yogic practices on to new-age self-awareness and westernized techniques for self-improvement. In all of these uses of "spirit," and so many more that could be cited, we can see common to them some at least implicit reference to a "beyond" and, thus, to a form of transcendence. It is this reference to and sense of the "beyond" that, along of course with reference to many other elements, we have tried to capture in the affirmations that a movement of enriching experience is a movement of spirit and a movement of spirit is one of enriching experience.

With regard again more directly to Hegel's concept of spirit, we should note that he has often been accused of not developing an open enough understanding of spirit. His understanding of spirit ultimately as true infinite, inclusive of finitude and what he called the "bad infinite," namely, the infinite over against finitude and the infinite as infinite progression, seems to many to have remained too closed and, thus, for them totalitarian. Though serious arguments could be made to the contrary with regard to Hegel's concept of the true infinite, I also do not think that his understanding of the true or inclusive infinite occurring as a movement of conceptual thought is sufficiently flexible in itself and fully capable of expressing that to which it is meant to refer. While brilliantly conceived, its dialectical structure as enriched return of conceptual thought to its initial moment seems to remain, to so many of us, insufficient in the light of further reflection and of subsequent developments in so many fields of human endeavor that have occurred since his time. In response to this generalized malaise vis-à-vis his conception of spirit, over the course of the present study I have worked toward the formulation of a notion of spirit that would be more open and flexible while remaining a true infinite respectfully inclusive of finitude. To do this, I have proposed that we no longer envision the true infinite as a dialectically developing movement of conceptual thought but, rather, as a movement of enriching experience that itself needs to be understood in terms both of the dialectical and the dialogical if it is to be comprehended more fully and adequately though, mysteriously, never completely.

In this Conclusion, which is a sort of *apologia pro exercitione mea*, I would underscore that we have in this essay considered "enrichment," understood especially as qualitative increment and thus complexification internal to the self accompanied by a sense of wholeness, integration, well-being and balance, as something desirable. This consideration of enrichment as desirable has been a self-evident one rooted in the very nature of what enrichment is as well as in the structured movement that constitutes experience. It is the very vocation and mission of the self to relate itself respectfully to the other though the gift of itself to the other and, thus, paradoxically, to become an enriched self. This consideration is based as well in a careful reading of what has been valued in the overall history of the development of humankind and its various cultures, world views and philosophies.

With regard to the self-evident character of the desirability of enrichment, it will be good to recall, further, that a moment and movement of experience consists, in principle and in what we can now call its paradigmatic formulation, in initial selfhood and otherness in relationship giving rise to resultant selfhood. In this movement, resultant selfhood is an enriched selfhood. As verified in the structured movement of inclusive divine subjectivity, such a movement is, given the dialogical nature of the relationship between selfhood and otherness, both open to otherness in its seemingly unending variety and inclusive of that otherness in that the movement respectfully, indeed paradoxically, includes that otherness through selfhood's gift of itself to that otherness.

This, then, is the way in which I would propose we understand and describe spirit, namely, as a movement of enriching experience, whether finite or, paradigmatically, infinite. This movement of enriching experience is a movement of generous self-giving to the other that assures the openness we desire to find realized in, and I would say especially in, the true infinite as movement of inclusive divine subjectivity.

Given this interpretation of spirit as well as our variously developed understanding of experience, we can then consider our philosophical theology an elaboration of a second, and to some extent even third, experience in relation to a first, communal, shared and individual experience of God. A philosophical theology so developed provides us with a privileged point of departure for further reflection to be carried out in the form of an interreligious dialogue elaborated, among various helpful ways, on a philosophical level that could result in what one might call comparative philosophical theology. The philosophical theology that we have proposed can, then, serve as a privileged point of departure in the elaboration of such a comparative philosophical theology especially in view of, first, the dialogical structure of reality upon which the philosophical theology here developed has been constructed and, second, the form that philosophical theology has taken as a movement of inclusive yet open divine subjectivity. The very nature of the absolute here presented is such that finite selves, whether communal, shared or individual, whether the world-wide Christian community, a particular Church, couples and friends, or individuals, will want to remain open, in stances of faith, hope and love, to other religious traditions as possible sources of enrichment. They will likewise long for such enrichment and discover that really to appreciate these other religious traditions they must, in appropriate ways respectful of their own religious traditions, give themselves over to these other religious traditions. A particular task and challenge for the philosophical theologian will be to enter this interreligious dialogue at a philosophical level, ready to dialogue on the basis of reasoned presentation and argumentation, even when the dialogue may end up focusing on differences concerning the very notion of reason itself, its nature and its functions.

In closing, I would hope that the philosophical theology developed here will help us come to grips with the perduring importance of what is often referred to as revealed or positive religion, with religious pluralism and with the massive reality of evil, as well as allowing us to speak more clearly to the large numbers of people who show a renewed interest today in spirituality. I would like to consider this philosophical theology, in principle at least, a philosophy of freedom and generosity, I hope that in some small way it will, from a philosophical perspective, help people interested in various faith-traditions to understand Christianity better, enable Christians to appreciate ever more the richness of their communal, shared and individual experience of God, and encourage philosophers, theologians and others to continue their enriching dialogue with various religious traditions. We can wish that this deeper understanding of Christianity, greater appreciation for the Christian experience of God, and the here encouraged interreligious dialogue be marked by a sense of inner freedom, for where the spirit is there is freedom. And may this understanding, appreciation and dialogue all occur as the result of generous self-gift. For, indeed we are told that God loves a cheerful giver.

APPENDIX

HEGEL'S FINITE AND INFINITE

In Hegel's *Science of Logic, Etwas* or "something" without emphasis on "thing" is Hegel's axial category or thought determination that can provide one with easy access to the overall movement of logic or pure thought in its preceding, primordial elementary movement and instantiation as being/nothing/becoming. *Etwas* considered as first more concrete negation of negation and "only the beginning of the subject"[1] can equally provide one with a particularly useful point of departure in an effort to obtain an overview of Hegel's understanding of finite and infinite in his *Science of Logic* as momentary totalities of pure thought. In the first edition of the "Logic of Being" (1812), which is the first part of his *Logic*, Hegel had proposed to establish a transition to "other" (*Anderes*) out of *Dasein*, and only then spoke of *Etwas*. However, by the second edition of the "Logic of Being" (1831) he had proposed a transition from *Dasein* to quality to *Etwas*, and then from *Etwas* and other on eventually to his various formulations of finitude and infinity. Though Hegel did not change his basic understanding of finite and infinite from the first to the second editions of the "Logic of Being," he did elaborate, make more consistent and thereby sharpen his presentation of the movement from *Dasein* to the true infinite. This sharpness and greater internal consistency as well as his fuller elaboration were the result of his many years of reflection on the relationship between finite and infinite. The present summary of the contours of Hegel's finite and infinite will therefore profit by concentrating on Hegel's presentation of finite and infinite in the second edition of the "Logic of Being."

Hegel's positioning of *Etwas* in the "Logic of Being's" second edition as result in the triad *Dasein*/quality/*Etwas* had allowed him to set the stage more exactly for his discussion of finite and infinite by explicitly introducing the elements with which he would work to accomplish his transition from finite to true infinite. Principal among these elements are the notions of negation and negation of negation, with negation of negation being the structure of inclusive self-mediating subjectivity. "The negative of the negative is, as

Etwas, only the beginning of the subject" (115, trans. amended). Already here Hegel has clearly introduced the distinction between a first negation or negation as such and a second negation, the negation of negation; "the latter is concrete, *absolute* negativity, just as the former on the contrary is only *abstract* negativity" (116). By recalling that this negation of negation, *Etwas*, is and is *Daseiendes*, a concrete becoming which has as its moments "now determinate being, and, further, *a* determinate being" (116) Hegel moves rather too quickly to announce the transition to "a *determinate* being, but determined as a negative of something—an *other*" (116) Since the moments of *Etwas* are themselves *Etwas*, Hegel proposes *Etwas* and other merely over against one another. With negation of negation and initially independent otherness Hegel had established the basic parameters of his discussion of finite and infinite and laid the groundwork for his brilliant resolution of the opposition between finite and infinite.

It is by means of a subtly developed and progressively more explicit series of negations of negation that Hegel moves from *Etwas* to infinite. This logically sequenced series of ever more concrete categories was for him to have been the movement of pure thought as the sphere of *Dasein*. As we provide a resume of Hegel's presentation leading to finitude and then through it to infinity, what will be of concern is an overview of Hegel's understanding of the thought determinations "finite" and "infinite" in themselves, to the extent that this is possible given Hegel's conception of them. This overview will equally be concerned with them in their mutual transition to one another in order to provide access to the overall contours of Hegel's conception of finite "and" infinite.

The overall elaboration of finite as a subtle progression of negations of negation occurs in the *Logic* by a recurrent analytic and synthetic treatment of otherness, otherness always at least implicitly and quite soon explicitly established within the movement of pure thought. Under the first subheading, "*Etwas* and an other" (117, trans. amended). Hegel proceeds in three steps. First, in an initial way he in several moves indicates that *Etwas* and other are the same, each is other to the other, so that in change *Etwas* remains identical with itself. In a second step he typically progresses, that is, follows the movement of conceptual thought forward by presenting two opposing categories, "being-for-other" (*Sein-für-Anderes*) and "being-in-itself" (*Ansichsein*). It is important to underscore that Hegel presents otherness as both contained in *Etwas* and separated from *Etwas*. However, thinking the category being-for-other immediately gives rise to or better has already immediately given rise to the thought determination being-in itself. *Etwas* and other indicated independence; now being-for-other and being-in-itself are relational determinations. In a third step Hegel stresses that being-for-other and being-in-itself are moments of one and the same *Etwas*. The dialectically developed resultant identity of being-for-other and being-in-itself allows him to assert being-for-other's being in *Etwas,* and then, as simple being, "determination" (*Bestimmung*).

From "*Etwas* and an other" Hegel progresses through the second subsection, "Determination, Condition and Limit," to the thought determination, "the finite." Determination is at hand as the "determinateness which is in itself" (123). In the first of three moves Hegel distinguishes determination from determinateness (*Bestimmtheit*) in such a fashion as to establish determination as that which *Etwas* remains in itself in the face of its own being-for-other. In a second move, he again gives expression to the arising of otherness, but this time determinateness is present as that into which determination has separated itself, constitution (*Beschaffenheit*). Constitution at first expresses the externally relational and changeable. But constitution is related to *Etwas* as the quality of *Etwas* so that for Hegel change now is transition that is internal to *Etwas* itself. Though determination and constitution are to be distinguished from one another, they are as well both mediated as the determinateness of *Etwas*. Constitution is otherness now explicitly considered with determination as co-constitutive of *Etwas*. "The *Etwas* itself is further determined and the negation is posited as immanent in it, as its developed being-within-self." (125, trans. amended). This "being-within-self" (*Insichsein*) is the non-being (*Nichtsein*) of an otherness contained in that being-within-self and equally distinguished from it. Determination and constitution are movements of negation of negation which mutually limit *Etwas* so that *Etwas* is its limit (*Grenze*). In a third move, Hegel returns to this enriched and more unified positing of *Etwas* as limit. As thought determination in the movement of pure thought, limit is developed by Hegel first as that which establishes what *Etwas* as such is not. Since limit is equally the non-being of the other, "*Etwas* at the same time *is* through its limit" (126, trans. amended). Hegel recalls therefore that limit is now the first negation and other the negation of negation, *Etwas'* being-within itself. "Limit is the mediation through which *Etwas* and other each as well *is* as *is not*" (127, trans. amended). Hegel secondly observes that the negative determinate being (*das Nicht-dasein*) and the *Dasein* of *Etwas* fall outside one another. The *Dasein* of *Etwas* lies without *Etwas* and the negative determinate being as limit lies within *Etwas*. Third, Hegel slowly reintegrates the negative determinate being of *Etwas* and the *Dasein* of *Etwas* by concluding that *Etwas* and other share a common limit so that *Etwas* has its *Dasein* only in limit. But *Etwas* equally separates itself from itself and "points beyond itself to its non-being, declaring this to be its being" (127). *Etwas* equally then has as determination its own restlessness, which pushes it out beyond itself. "*Etwas* with its immanent limit, posited as the contradiction of itself, through which it is directed and forced out of and beyond itself, is the *finite*" (129, trans. amended).

Hegel posited the transitions from *Dasein* to the finite as a specific sequence within the overall movement of self-positing and self-determining pure thought or logic as series of ever more concrete thought determinations. In the *Logic* any specific presentation of thought determinations must be considered as taking place simultaneously on various levels. Since the series of logical transitions from *Dasein* to the finite occur within the overall logic of being, their fluidity consisted in the transition already having taken place in their being thought. From a methodological perspective, these categories amounted for Hegel to an ever more explicit thinking of otherness, especially from the presentation of "*Etwas* and an other" on. Hegel had observed that the categories *Dasein*, quality (reality, negation) and *Etwas* were developed in an affirmative determination, while " *Etwas* and an other," being-for-other and being-in-itself, determination, constitution, being-within-self and limit developed the negative determination, a negation of negation with *Dasein* then as a first negation. By means of a growing opposition and a sense of internal contradiction contained ever more explicitly within an increasingly determinate *Etwas*, Hegel progressed to the finite and would continue through the finite to the bad infinite, infinite progression and the true infinite.

With the coming into being of the category "limit" Hegel has thematized the contradiction for him constitutive of finitude and has given initial expression to the fluidity characteristic of finitude. It is this fluidity as finitude's drive beyond itself that will allow Hegel to make the transition to a discussion of infinity. Limit is the mutual boundary between *Etwas* and other, but a boundary equally immanent to *Etwas* itself. So on the basis of limit Hegel concludes that the being or here the *Dasein* of *Etwas* lies outside itself. Yet with limit immanent to *Etwas* the being (*Sein*) of *Etwas* is equally its non-being (*Nichtsein*). With the thinking through of limit there arises for Hegel the thought determination "the finite." With the coming into being of the finite Hegel has sublated into one category the crescendo of progressively more explicit internal contradiction now seen to have been characterizing the categories in the movement of pure thought from *Dasein* on. In the finite, otherness is now for Hegel not only limit as such but limitation (*Schranke*). However, while making thematic the being-in-itself of the finite, limitation is also inevitably taken as limit distinguishable from being-in-itself, so that limitation is ought (*Sollen*). The contradiction progressively more explicitly characteristic of the categories of pure thought from *Dasein* on forms a climax in the identification of limitation and ought as moments of the finite, and therefore themselves respectively explicitly and implicitly finite. "What ought to be *is* and at the same time *is not*" (132). Hegel dialectically identifies limitation and ought. As ought *Etwas* has gone beyond its limitation, and yet only in as *Etwas* is ought does it have its limitation. For Hegel ought contains limitation and limitation contains ought. They are opposed as negation over against one another. "The finite is thus inwardly self-contradictory" (136). This negation or going over into one another results first not in the ceasing to be of the finite but only in another finite in an infinite progression. On closer examination, for Hegel each of the moments of ceasing to be, namely, limitation and ought, go over into an other which is really itself. "This *identity with itself,* the negation of negation, is affirmative being and thus the other of the finite, of the finite which is supposed to have the first negation for its determinateness; this other is the infinite" (137).

Before more clearly establishing the infinite as a becoming (*Werden*) which is an inclusive whole (*Ganze*), Hegel pursues a further elaboration of the movement of pure thought so as to heighten the contradiction between finite and infinite. After recalling that it is the very nature of the finite itself to become the infinite, the affirmative being or negation of negation which the finite truly is *an sich*, Hegel asserts that "what *is*, is only the infinite" (138). On the basis of the fact that the infinite is, Hegel proceeds to conclude that the infinite is "at the same time the *negation* of an *other*, of the finite" (136, translation slightly amended). As equally the being and the non-being of an other the infinite has however fallen back into the finitude of an *Etwas* with a limit. The thought of the finite has gone over into the infinite and vice versa. But the two equally stand over against one another "in a qualitative relation, each *remaining* external to the other" (138). However, again not only are finite and infinite other to one another. Rather, finitude is posited limitation and infinity is what the finite ought to be. The infinite as ought is again burdened with an opposition to the determinate finite as its other. The infinite is thus determined as "indeterminate void, the beyond of the finite" (139). The infinite in these ways set over against the finite in a qualitative relationship of otherness is Hegel's well-known "bad infinite" (*das Schlecht-Unendliche*). It is the infinite of understanding, which is supposed to be the absolute truth but in fact is absolute contradiction: the infinite standing over against the finite, two worlds with the infinite as limit of the finite and so itself a finite infinite. Hegel then works out this contradiction in ever more explicit fashion as the alternation of finite and infinite. As separated as the finite and the infinite of understanding remain from one another, they are equally related by the very negation that separates them, the mutual limit each has against the other. Finite and infinite are then equally inseparable. "But this their unity is *concealed* in their qualitative otherness" (141). Out of this inseparability of finite and infinite there again arises limit so that the finite recurs in thought. Yet this new limit and therefore the finite it engenders is in turn to be gone beyond so that the infinite reappears as indeterminate void, "and so on to infinity" (141). This infinite progression is itself the bad or finite infinite pushed to its extreme self-contradiction. "The infinity of the infinite progress remains burdened with the finite as such, is therefore limited and is itself *finite*" (142). The truth or mediation of finite and infinite is for Hegel already present in this infinite progression, but remains so far obscured by understanding's insistence on a strict separation of finite and infinite to avoid contradiction rather than embrace it.

It now becomes clear why Hegel proceeds not directly from finite to true infinite but, rather, from finite to infinite renewedly finitized as bad infinite and most importantly infinite progression. True to form, Hegel intends to establish the true infinite by making explicit the truth for him already implicit or at hand in the back and forth between finite and infinite. He needs the infinite progression as momentary totality in the movement of pure thought since in it "[the] truth [of the infinite progression] is already implicitly *present,* and all that is required is to take up what is before us" (143, trans. amended).

Hegel begins to make this truth explicit by recalling that finite and infinite are each a movement. He wants to make explicit the type of unity present in and between each of these movements or moments simply by comparing them as they have come to be seen so far. Hegel examines and compares the two movements twice, each time in as they appear related and separated. In the first comparison, on the one hand when considered from the aspect of their relatedness, the infinite and the finite are defined in terms of movement beyond self (*Hinausgehen*). The infinite *is* only as movement beyond the finite; it is the negation of the finite. The finite *is* only as that which must be gone beyond; it is "the negation of itself in its own self, which is infinity" (143). In each, in the finite and in the infinite, there lies the determination of the other. Though in the infinite progression finite and infinite are held apart and presented alternately, neither can be conceived without the other. On the other hand, again in this first consideration or comparison, when the two movements are considered as separated, the infinite is not seen as a whole. This infinite contains a limit over against the finite and is therefore itself finite. The finite in turn becomes, as separated, a relationship to itself, gaining an independence "which the infinite is supposed to be" (144). This doubled movement gives one result: each contains the other in itself as moment. For Hegel this one result provides a new type of unity or infinite, a unity of finite and infinite and which includes infinite and finite. He now makes a second comparison of finite and infinite. In as the two must be related, each moment is itself the unity of finite and infinite. Each of these two unities has then in common that it posits the negation of the two determinations so that they lose their qualitative difference. In as the two movements are distinct, there is in each a different determination of the unity of the infinite. The infinite determined as such is only an "in itself" (*an sich*); finitude remains mere determinateness and limit. So here the infinite is merely a finitized infinite. In the same way, since the finite as such is only the negation of the in-itself (*das Nichtansichsein*), it contains the infinite within its determination and is the infinitized finite.

So far now Hegel has come to assert that both finite and infinite each contain the other in their determinations. The understanding has continually failed to acknowledge this by ignoring the negation in this doubled unity of infinite and finite. The unnegated infinite remains for understanding a mere *an sich* without determinateness and limitation. The unnegated finite remains merely perduring infinitized determination. According to Hegel understanding forgets what is the very concept of these moments, their unity. Each is in itself this unity as the sublation of itself. The finite sublates itself in the infinite, which is the negation of finitude. And finitude has long since been established as non-being. So the infinite is negation of negation. But as negation of determinateness as such, "the sublating of itself in the finite is a return from an empty flight, a *negation* of the beyond which is in its own self a *negative*" (146). There is present in each the same negation of negation, affirmation as return to itself, namely, mediation. In infinite progression both finite and infinite are in fact negated but still only as following upon one another and not in their last truth.

Whereas Hegel had so far considered infinite progression primarily from the perspective of finite and infinite in their separation, now in order to arrive at their last truth he takes a second look at that infinite progression especially in as it gives expression to the connection (*Zusammenhang*) between finite and infinite. By an examination parallel to but more briefly developed than in his look at finite and infinite and then infinite progression as such, Hegel now looks at the negation of finite and infinite as the negation is posited in infinite progression. Beginning with the finite, one sees that it is negated in the transition to an empty infinite, which is then itself negated in the return to the finite. In one sense this is merely a series of external acts, but in a deeper sense this is "the complete, self-closing movement which has arrived at that which constituted the beginning" (147). By a similar observation Hegel posits a movement beginning from the infinite, negating that infinite and then returning to that infinite as to itself. So finite and infinite are this movement of mediation, negation of negation, result. The finite is no longer merely a hardened existence over against an empty infinite and vice versa. Understanding has continued to fail to see that both finite and infinite are negated, "that they occur therein only as moments of a whole" (147). The objection that two different points of departure dictate two results does not stand since according to Hegel the difference in points of departure is here without significance. Hegel illustrates his position with reference to infinite progression as a line wherein each moment occurs as the transition to the other. Together as moments finite and infinite are the finite. Equally together negated in the result they are, as this result, "as negation of the finitude of both (...) with truth the infinite" (148).

For Hegel the true infinite (*wahrhaft Unendlisches*) is the process of mediation in which the infinite, having become finite, sublates its difference or finitude into its own self-affirmation. The true infinite is not to be thought of as an abstract unity of static moments, but as a more determinate becoming whose moments themselves, finite and infinite, are in the process of becoming. This true infinite is for Hegel "the consummated return into self, the relation of itself to itself" (148). From the perspective of the true infinite, the unattainable (*unerreichbar*) bad infinite is only a first negation, and infinite progression appears as if it were a straight line with the infinite appearing only at both limits. The true infinite is to be pictured as a determinate circle, a line bent back upon itself without beginning or end. The true infinite is for Hegel the true reality. It is negation of negation, affirmation inclusive of the finite, a finite now seen as "*das Ideele*," namely, not as independent but as posited moment of the infinite. The true infinite is for Hegel inclusive totality.

The thought determinations from *Dasein* on to true infinite constituted for Hegel a series of logical transitions in which each category was to have been momentary totality in the movement of pure thought. These specific thought determinations formed a particular segment in the movement of pure thought, which thought was to have begun in pure being and would for Hegel have continued through the transition from the true infinite to "being-for-self" (*das Fürsichsein*) on through the "Logic of Essence" and the "Logic of the Concept" to the final logical totality, the absolute Idea. Since the absolute idea was itself to have been an enriched return to the immediacy of pure being, Hegel's logic itself, as he intended it, can be described as a circle so to speak without beginning and end, an infinite or inclusive totality which was necessarily but freely to have othered itself as the immediate finitude which is nature.

Hegel has argued that when finitude is adequately evaluated it is seen by definition to be a contradiction, even self-contradiction. He has stated this contradiction in its most abstract formulation as *Etwas* which both is and is not. More determinately expressed, this contradiction arises in the fact that finitude is a limitation which ought to be gone beyond. Still more determinately expressed, finitude is the contradiction that appears to be resolvable only in an oscillation between a finite and an infinite. Hegel's finite, the bad infinite and infinite progression are all finite in that they bear within themselves their own real and recurrent limit. Hegel's definition of the finite as the self-contradiction of *Etwas* with limit immanent in it, and thus forced to go beyond itself, thematizes limit as that which had finitized *Dasein* from the beginning. Whether *Dasein* now be taken as first moment of a finite movement of thought or as the *Dasein* or givenness of any becoming as finite qualitative increment, it is always limited being. *Dasein*, as made explicit in *Etwas* defined by its immanent limit, both is and is not in and through that very limit in so far as *Dasein*, as *Etwas*, is determinate in and through its limit always over against an other. As this self-contradiction, finitude is therefore *qua* finitude restless, unstable, one-sided and incomplete. It cannot resolve its own self-contradiction. It is not self-explanatory but continually points beyond itself to the possibility of an inclusive whole as the context wherein the self-contradiction inherent in recurrent limit might find resolution. To remain merely with the self-contradictory finite would ultimately imply abandoning the public realm of discourse.

According to Hegel, the finite as itself self-contradictory was to have gone over into the true or inclusive infinite. As logical category this true infinite was the negation of finite and infinite taken as mutually independent. It was posited negation of negation. The true infinite found expression for Hegel as progressively more explicitly inclusive in the logic of self-determining inclusive subjectivity, the appearance of absolute divine subjectivity in the sphere of religion, and absolute spirit in philosophy as concept or enriched return to the immediacy of the absolute idea and thus to pure being. Hegel's encyclopedic system as a whole was meant to present the infinite in its truth.

NOTES

1. *Hegel's Science of Logic,* trans. A. V. Miller (New York: Humanities, 1969) 115 (hereafter cited by page in the text).

    The contents of this Appendix on the contours of Hegel's finite and infinite are taken from Dale M. Schlitt, *Hegel's Trinitarian Claim. A Critical Reflection* (Leiden: Brill, 1984) 252–265 and are now provided here for convenient reference. The sources of direct English quotations of longer phrases or sentences from Hegel's *Science of Logic* in English translation will be indicated here. The German citations as well as further notes and remarks can be found on the above-mentioned pages in *Hegel's Trinitarian Claim.*

INDEX